lonely planet

Kyoto

"All you've got to do is decide to go and the hardest part is over.

So go!"

TONY WHEELER, COFOUNDER – LONELY PLANET

THIS EDITION WRITTEN AND RESEARCHED BY

Chris Rowthorn

Contents

Plan Your Trip 4

Explore Kyoto 44

Understand Kyoto 149

Survival Guide 183

Kyoto Maps 214

Left: Nishiki Market (p56)

Above: Kiyomizu-dera (p81)

Right: Tōfuku-ji (p76)

Welcome to Kyoto

Kyoto is old Japan writ large: quiet temples, sublime gardens, colourful shrines and geisha scurrying to secret liaisons.

Temples, Shrines & Gardens

There are said to be over 1000 Buddhist temples in Kyoto. You'll find true masterpieces of religious architecture, such as the retina-burning splendour of Kinkaku-ji (the famed Golden Pavilion) and the cavernous expanse of Higashi Hongan-ji. Within the temple precincts are some of the world's most sublime gardens, from the Zen masterpiece at Ryōan-ji to the riotous paradise of moss and blossoms at Saihō-ji. And then there are the Shintō shrines, monuments to Japan's indigenous faith. The mother of all shrines, Fushimi-Inari-Taisha, has mesmerising arcades of vermillion *torii* (shrine gates) spread across a mountainside.

Cuisine

Few cities of this size offer such a range of excellent restaurants. Work your way through the entire spectrum of Japanese food, from impossibly refined cuisine known as *kaiseki* to hearty plebeian fare like *rāmen*. There's also a wide range of French, Italian and Chinese restaurants, where the famed Japanese attention to detail is paired with local ingredients to yield fantastic results. Best of all, many of Kyoto's restaurants are in traditional wooden buildings, where you can gaze over intimate private gardens while you eat.

The Japanese Way of Life

While the rest of Japan has adopted modernity with abandon, the old ways are hanging on in Kyoto. Take a morning stroll through the textile district of Nishijin and watch the old Kyoto ladies emerge from their *machiya* (traditional townhouses) to ladle water onto their stoops. Visit an old *shōtengai* (shopping street) and admire the ancient speciality shops: tofu sellers, fishmongers, pickle vendors and tea merchants. Then join the locals at a local *sentō* (public bath) to soak away the cares of the day.

The Changing Seasons

No educated Kyotoite would dare send a letter without making a reference to the season. The city's geisha change their hair ornaments 12 times a year to celebrate the natural world. And Kyoto's confectioners create seasonal sweets that reflect whatever is in bloom. Starting in February and lasting through the summer, a series of blossoms burst open like a string of firecrackers: plums, daphnes, cherries, camellias, azaleas and wisteria, among many others. And don't forget the *shinryoku* (the new green of April) and the brilliant autumn foliage of November.

Why I Love Kyoto

By Chris Rowthorn, Author

I love Kyoto because it's rich, deep and incredibly liveable. I've spent almost 20 years in the city and I still make new discoveries every day. If I vary my daily walking route just a bit, I am bound to find something new: a secret temple, an interesting shop or a great place to eat. The city is surrounded by mountains on three sides and the hiking is excellent. It's also one of the most bike-friendly cities on earth. I love the people and the dialect they speak. Finally, it's just the right size: not too big and not too small.

For more about Chris Rowthorn, see p232

Above: Pontochō (p57)

Kyoto's Top 10

JOHN ELK III / LONELY PLANET IMAGES ©

Ginkaku-ji *(p95)*

1 A paradise tucked at the base of the Higashiyama mountains, Kyoto's famed Silver Pavilion is everything a Buddhist temple ought to be. The eponymous pavilion looks over a tranquil pond, and the expansive stroll garden is sublime. Make your way past the unique Ginshadan sand mound (used to reflect moonlight into the main hall for moon-viewing ceremonies), then climb the pathway to a viewpoint that offers panoramic views over the entire city. The autumn foliage here is among the best in the city.

Northern Higashiyama

Gion District *(p87)*

2 Gion, Kyoto's traditional entertainment district, is the best place in the city to catch a glimpse of 'old Japan'. With no fewer than three geisha districts scattered about, you stand a good chance of spotting a geisha scurrying to an appointment. But geisha are only part of the story here: Gion also contains some of the most picturesque lanes in Kyoto, including Shimbashi, which may be the single most attractive street in all of Asia. And don't forget Minami-za, the city's traditional kabuki theatre.

Southern Higashiyama

1

ARIF IQBALL PHOTOGRAPHY / ALAMY ©

2

3

RACHEL LEWIS / LONELY PLANET IMAGES ©

5

JUDY BELLAH / LONELY PLANET IMAGES ©

Arashiyama Bamboo Grove *(p114)*

3 Western Kyoto is home to one of the most magical places in all Japan: the famed bamboo grove in Arashiyama. The visual effect of the seemingly infinite stalks of bamboo is quite different from any forest we've ever encountered – there's a palpable presence to the place that is utterly impossible to capture in pictures, but don't let that stop you from trying. If you've seen *Crouching Tiger, Hidden Dragon,* then you have some idea of what this place is about.

Arashiyama & Sagano

Kyoto Imperial Palace Park *(p71)*

4 Home to the Kyoto Gosho (Imperial Palace), this vast swath of green in the city centre is a true sanctuary. Often overlooked by tourists, who rush to see the city's temples and shrines, the Kyoto Imperial Palace Park is the perfect place to spend a lazy afternoon reading a book, napping, playing with the kids or picnicking. The variety of trees here is amazing, and there's usually something in bloom. In the spring, don't miss the fantastic *shidare-zakura* (weeping cherry trees) at the north end of the park.

Central Kyoto

Kinkaku-ji *(p106)*

5 Talk about eye candy: the gold-plated main hall of this immensely popular temple in northwest Kyoto is probably the most impressive sight in all Kyoto – especially if your tastes run to the grand and gaudy. The main hall rises above its reflecting pond like an apparition. If you are lucky enough to be there on a bright sunny day, you almost need sunglasses to look at it. Go early on a weekday morning to avoid the crush of people that descend on the temple each day.

Northwest Kyoto

Fushimi-Inari-Taisha *(p76)*

6 This sprawling Shintō shrine is arguably Japan's most arresting visual spectacle. Thousands of vermillion *torii* (Shintō shrine gates) line paths that criss-cross this mountain in southeast Kyoto. Visit the main hall and then head up the hill toward the summit. Be prepared to be utterly mesmerised – it's quite unlike anything else on earth. If you have time, do the circular pilgrimage route around the top of the mountain. And don't be afraid to get lost – that's part of the fun at Fushimi.

Central Kyoto

Chion-in *(p82)*

7 Called by some 'the Vatican of Pure Land Buddhism', this temple complex in the Southern Higashiyama district is a thriving hub of religious activity. The main hall is one of the largest temple structures in Japan. Take off your shoes, go inside, take a seat on the floor and allow yourself to be transported to blissful realms by the chanting of the monks. Then head up the hill to admire the enormous 70-ton temple bell. This is truly the best place in Kyoto to see how the Japanese practise Buddhism.

Southern Higashiyama

6

JTB PHOTO / PHOTOLIBRARY ©

FRANK CARTER / LONELY PLANET IMAGES ©

Blossoms & Foliage *(p71)*

8 Real Kyotoites don't use calendars to tell the season. Rather, they just look out their windows to see what's blooming. Starting with daphnes and plums in February and ending with crimson maple leaves in December, the year in Kyoto is a delightful progression of colourful blossoms and foliage (which is perhaps why the old calendar was divided into no fewer than 24 seasons). Sure, everyone wants to see the cherries of early April, but don't despair if you can't make it then: even in winter there are blossoms of some sort to be found. For the widest variety of blossoms and foliage in the city, head to the Kyoto Imperial Palace Park.

AUTUMN FOLIAGE, KYOTO

Central Kyoto

Nishiki Market *(p56)*

9 There's something strangely enjoyable about touring a food market where over half of the goods on display are utterly baffling (is it a food, a spice or some sort of Christmas tree decoration?). Even after years in Japan, we're not sure about some of the things on sale here, but we love wandering Kyoto's Nishiki Market. The place positively oozes 'old Japan' atmosphere and you can imagine what it was like here before someone decided to attach the word 'super' to the word 'market'.

◉ ***Downtown Kyoto***

GREG ELMS / LONELY PLANET IMAGES ©

10

GREG ELMS / LONELY PLANET IMAGES ©

Kurama-dera *(p122)*

10 This mountain temple in the hills north of the city (a mere 30 minutes away by direct train) is easily the most pleasant half-day trip out of the city. New-Agey Kyotoites claim that UFOs regularly land here. We're not sure about that, but we can certainly understand why visitors from near and far love this place: the walk through the soaring cedar trees to the main hall near the summit is pure magic. If you have the time, hike over the top to the village of Kibune.

◉ ***Kitayama Area & Greater Kyoto***

What's New

New Kyoto Tourist Information Center

The new Kyoto Tourist Information Center, very near both the *shinkansen* (bullet train) and regular train platforms, sure beats the old TIC, which was hidden up on the 9th floor of the station building (p196).

New Downtown Tourist Information Center

There is also a new tourist information centre right in Downtown Kyoto (p196).

Kyoto Night Cruise Bus Tour

Tour the ancient capital by bus and watch the sights light up as you pass. This is a great option for those who don't enjoy bar hopping (p187).

Kyoto-Navi System

Kyoto City has just introduced a new online English-language transport and timetable search system that makes finding transport routes and departure times a snap (p189).

Machiya Boom

Kyoto's traditional townhouses, known as *machiya,* are being given a new lease of life as restaurants, shops, bars and even accommodation for travellers.

Expanded No-Smoking Areas

Kyoto has banned outdoor smoking Downtown, around Kyoto Station and in the Kiyomizu/Sannen-zaka/Ninen-zaka sightseeing areas. Enforcement is still spotty.

Giant New Shopping Outlets

Kyoto has been undergoing a retail renaissance in the past few years. New offerings include Yodobashi Camera (cameras, electronics and just about everything else; p52) and Kyoto Marui (a fashion-oriented department store; p66).

Everything Old Is New Again

Young Japanese are discovering the beauty of traditional Japanese fashions and you'll see more *yukatas* (light cotton robes), kimono and *hakama* (men's kimono) than ever before on the streets of Kyoto.

Kyoto Is Cheaper than Ever

Since the March 2011 earthquake and tsunami that devastated northern Honshu, prices in Kyoto – which was unaffected by the disaster – have been slashed across the board (see p150). It's possible to find first-class hotel rooms for as little as ¥10,000 online.

For more recommendations and reviews, see **lonelyplanet.com/kyoto**

Need to Know

Currency
Yen (¥). ¥100 = US$1.30, £0.81, A$1.24.

Language
Japanese

Visas
Visas are issued on arrival for most nationalities for stays of up to 90 days.

Money
ATMs that accept foreign cards are available in post offices and some convenience stores. Credit cards are accepted in most hotels and department stores, but only some restaurants and ryokan.

Mobile Phones
Only 3G phones work in Japan. SIM cards are very hard to find. Mobile phone rental is common and easy.

Time
Japan Standard Time (GMT/UTC plus nine hours)

Tourist Information
Kyoto City Tourist Information Center (Map p220; ☎343-6655; ⏲8.30am-7pm) Located in the main concourse on the 2nd floor of the Kyoto Station building that runs between the *shinkansen* (bullet train) station and the front of the station.

Your Daily Budget
The following are average costs per day:

Budget under ¥8000
- Guesthouse accommodation ¥2800
- Two simple restaurant meals ¥2000
- Train/bus transport ¥1500
- One temple/museum admission ¥500
- Snacks, drinks, sundries ¥1000

Midrange ¥15,000–¥20,000
- Business hotel accommodation ¥9000
- Two midrange restaurant meals ¥4000
- Train/bus transport ¥1500
- Two temple/museum admissions ¥1000
- Snacks, drinks, sundries ¥2000

Top end over ¥20,000
- First-class hotel accommodation ¥20,000
- Two good restaurant meals ¥6000
- Train/bus transport ¥1500
- Two taxi rides ¥3000
- Two average temple/museum admissions ¥1000

Advance Planning
Several months Make accommodation reservations several months in advance if you are travelling in cherry-blossom season (March and April) and the autumn-foliage season (October and November).

One month Buy a Japan Rail Pass. This pass (p186) can save you a lot of money if you are planning to travel extensively by rail within Japan after visiting Kyoto.

A few days Buy a pair of comfortable slip-on walking shoes (you'll be taking your shoes off a lot in Kyoto).

Websites
- **Lonely Planet** (www.lonelyplanet.com/kyoto)
- **Kyoto Visitor's Guide** (www.kyotoguide.com)
- **Kansai Scene** (www.kansaiscene.com)
- **Deep Kyoto** (www.deepkyoto.com)
- **Inside Kyoto** (www.insidekyoto.com)
- **Kyoto-Navi System** (www.kyoto-navi.org/indexE.html)

WHEN TO GO

Kyoto is crowded in the cherry-blossom (late March to early April) and autumn foliage (November) seasons; be sure to advance book your accommodation.

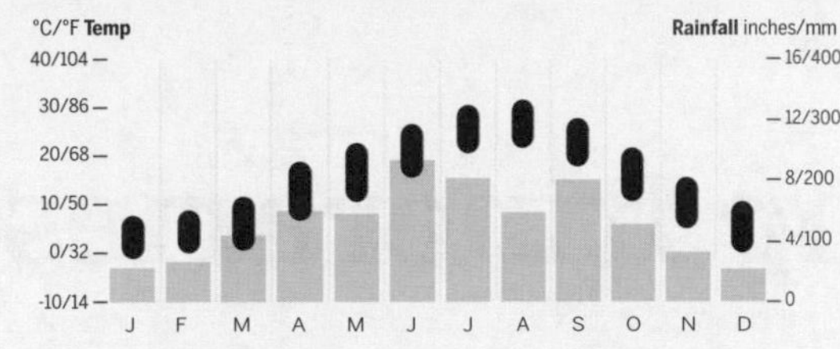

Arriving in Kyoto

Kansai International Airport *Haruka* airport express trains run direct to Kyoto in 75 minutes for ¥2980; limousine buses run direct to Kyoto in 90 minutes for ¥2500; shared taxis run to Kyoto in about 90 minutes for ¥3500.

Osaka Itami Airport Limousine buses run to Kyoto Station and various hotels in Kyoto in about 55 minutes and cost ¥1280. Shared taxis cost ¥2300.

Shinkansen from Tokyo *Shinkansen* run from Tokyo to Kyoto in two hours and 43 minutes for ¥13,220.

For much more on **arrival**, see p184.

Getting Around

Kyoto is a compact city with an excellent public transport system.

➡ **Taxi** The best way to get from Kyoto Station to your hotel or ryokan unless you're on a tight budget (in which case the bus or subway is a good choice).

➡ **Subway** Gets you quickly between north and south (the Karasuma subway line stops at Kyoto Station) or east and west (the Tōzai subway line runs between Higashiyama and the west side of the city).

➡ **Bus** For destinations not well served by the subway lines (including sights in the northwest of the city like Kinkaku-ji).

➡ **Bicycle** A brilliant way to explore Kyoto (the city is mostly flat).

➡ **Walking** Kyoto is a walker's paradise.

For much more on **getting around**, see p185.

Sleeping

Kyoto has a wide range of foreigner-friendly accommodation, with some of the best **ryokan** (traditional Japanese inns) in Japan. **First-class hotels** are also well represented, along with cheaper **business hotels** and even a few **capsule hotels**. You'll also find plenty of **guesthouses** and the odd **youth hostel** scattered about.

Websites

➡ **Welcome Inn Reservation Center** (www.itcj.jp) A free service that represents hundreds of affordable hotels, *minshuku* (Japanese-style B&B), ryokan, capsule hotels and hostels in Japan. You can make reservations online through the website.

➡ **Japanese Inn Group** (www.jpinn.com) A collection of foreigner-friendly ryokan and guesthouses. You can book member inns via its website or phone/fax.

For much more on **sleeping**, see p139.

Top Itineraries

Day One

Southern Higashiyama (p79)

Start your Kyoto experience by heading to the city's most important (and popular) sightseeing district: Southern Higashiyama. This area contains the thickest concentration of worthwhile sights in Kyoto. See p85 for a description of the main sightseeing route here.

Lunch Eat at a restaurant on Sanen-zaka/Ninen-zaka or on Sanjō-dōri.

Northern Higashiyama (p92)

If you have the energy after lunch, continue heading north along the base of the Higashiyama mountains. Start at **Nanzen-ji** and follow the **Path of Philosophy (Tetsugaku-no-Michi)** all the way to **Ginkaku-ji**, stopping at **Hōnen-in** along the way. See p98 for a description of the main sightseeing route here.

Dinner Omen (p100), a fabulous noodle restaurant, is close to Ginkaku-ji.

Downtown Kyoto (p54)

After dinner, head back to your lodgings (which may very well be located in Downtown Kyoto). You'll probably be pretty walked out if you've done both Southern and Northern Higashiyama in one day, so a short amble around the streets of Downtown Kyoto will probably be sufficient to round out this day.

Day Two

Arashiyama & Sagano (p112)

After exploring the Higashiyama on Day One, you'll want to head west to the Arashiyama & Sagano district, which has a dense concentration of first-rate sights. The typical route involves starting at **Tenryū-ji** and working your way north to **Giō-ji** or **Adashino Nembutsu-ji**. See p115 for a description of the main sightseeing route here.

Lunch Eat near Keifuku Arashiyama Station or along the route at Komichi.

Northwest Kyoto (p104)

It makes sense to stay on the west side of town in the afternoon of this day. Take a taxi from the end of the morning's route or lunch stop to **Kinkaku-ji** and/or **Ryōan-ji**. If you still have energy to burn, you can check out **Myōshin-ji** late in the afternoon.

Dinner Head back downtown (p58) to eat near your lodgings.

Downtown Kyoto (p54)

Like Day One, this is a pretty big day, with a fair bit of transport, so you probably won't feel like doing too much walking on this evening. Again, we recommend some strolling around Downtown Kyoto. The atmospheric lane of **Pontochō** is a great place to wander, as is **Kiyamachi-dōri**, particularly the stretch between Shijō-dōri and Gojō-dōri.

Day Three

Southeast Kyoto (p124)

You'll probably be feeling like a break from the crowds about now. For this reason we suggest heading to Southeast Kyoto. Here, you'll find two absolutely ripping attractions: **Tōfuku-ji** (don't forget to enter the Hōjō Garden) and **Fushimi-Inari-Taisha**, Kyoto's mind-blowing Shintō sanctuary.

Lunch There's not much to eat near the above, so head downtown (p58).

Downtown Kyoto (p54)

After exploring Southeast Kyoto in the morning and eating lunch downtown, it makes sense to spend the afternoon exploring Downtown Kyoto and perhaps doing some shopping. Be sure to take a pass through the wonderful **Nishiki Market**, then visit one of the awesome **'deppa-chika'** (department store basement food floors) at nearby **Daimaru** or **Takashimaya** department stores. Then, walk through the **Teramachi Shopping Arcade**. When the covered section runs out, keep following Teramachi as far as **Marutamachi-dōri** (the last few blocks contain some of Kyoto's best traditional shops).

Dinner Eat dinner downtown (p58) or across the river in Gion.

Gion District (p87)

This day involves less walking than the preceding two, so it's a great day to do our Gion evening walking tour (p86).

Day Four

Kitayama Area (p119)

Today's the day to step off the beaten track and immerse yourself in some greenery. Heading north into the Kitayama (Northern Mountains) is the perfect way to relax after three days of urban sightseeing. Heading to **Kurama** and hiking over the hill and down to **Kibune** is our favourite day trip out of the city. Other options include **Ōhara** or **Takao**.

Lunch Eat in Kurama, Kibune or Ōhara (pack a lunch for Takao).

Central Kyoto (p69)

If you spend the morning in the Kitayama, you will probably return to Kyoto city in the early afternoon. If this is your last day in the city, you might want to spend the remainder of the day shopping for souvenirs in Downtown Kyoto. But, if you still have the energy for sightseeing, you might consider visiting the enclosed Zen world of **Daitoku-ji**. Other options include **Nijō-jō** or a stroll in the **Kyoto Imperial Palace Park**.

Dinner Eat dinner downtown (p58) or across the river in Gion.

Downtown Kyoto (p54) or Gion (p87)

If you haven't done it yet, try the Gion evening walking tour (p86). Otherwise, find a bar downtown and rub shoulders with the locals as you reminisce about your time in the Old Capital.

If You Like...

Temples & Shrines

Nanzen-ji A world of Zen temples and subtemples scattered amid the trees. (p94)

Ginkaku-ji The famed 'Silver Pavilion' boasts one of Kyoto's finest gardens. (p95)

Hōnen-in A secluded retreat a short walk from the perpetually crowded Ginkaku-ji. (p97)

Kinkaku-ji A golden apparition rises above a tranquil reflecting pond – arguably Kyoto's most impressive single sight. (p106)

Tenryū-ji This temple takes *shakkei* (borrowed scenery) to a new level – it borrows the entire sweep of Arashiyama's beautiful mountains. (p114)

Daitoku-ji Each subtemple at this Zen complex has a sublime garden: a must for garden lovers with an aversion to crowds. (p72)

Myōshin-ji Like Daitoku-ji, this is a walled complex containing many fine subtemples and one of Kyoto's most famous gardens, Taizō-in. (p110)

Kurama-dera Climb a path lined with towering cedar trees to this mountain temple in the hills north of the city. (p122)

Chion-in A vast Pure Land Buddhist temple – the Vatican of Japanese Buddhism. (p82)

Shōren-in The crowds usually give this Southern Higashiyama temple a miss – don't make that mistake. (p87)

Museums

Kyoto National Museum The special exhibits here are often spectacular and the permanent

Kabuki poster at Minami-za kabuki theater (p90)

collection is a good introduction to Japanese art. (p83)

Kyoto Municipal Museum of Art Holds two of Kyoto's best yearly art shows: the Kyoten and the Niten. Other special exhibits are often worth a look. (p99)

National Museum of Modern Art The permanent collection here is small but interesting and the special exhibits are usually excellent. (p99)

Kyoto International Manga Museum If you are a fan of Japanese manga (comics), you simply must make a pilgrimage to this fine downtown museum. (p57)

Japanese Theatre

Minami-za (Kabuki) Kabuki is a visual spectacle like none other, and Minami-za, Kyoto's main kabuki theatre, is the place to see it. (p90)

Miyako Odori Held in April, this is the grandest of all Kyoto geisha dances. If you are in town, ensure you *do not miss it*. (p91)

Kamogawa Odori Held in May by the Pontochō geisha district, this is a smaller scale but charming geisha dance. (p65)

Kyō Odori The Miyagawa-chō geisha district holds their dance in April and it's also a must-see affair. (p91)

Kitano Odori Held up north in the Kamishichiken geisha district every April, this is a quaint and touching dance. (p21)

Gion Odori The only major geisha dance held in the autumn (November), this is put on by the Gion Higashi geisha district. (p91)

Food & Drink

Omen Noodles are only the beginning of the offerings at this comfortable and welcoming restaurant in Northern Higashiyama. (p100)

Kane-yo Sit at the tables downstairs or on the tatami mats upstairs at this popular downtown eel specialist with 'Old Japan' atmosphere. (p59)

Yoshikawa We don't know which is more impressive here: the sublime tempura or the perfect Japanese garden. (p58)

Ōzawa This friendly Gion tempura specialist lays claim to one of the most beautiful settings of any restaurant in town. (p87)

Ippūdō Just the thought of the noodles and *gyōza* (Chinese dumplings) makes us want to dash downtown to this bustling *rāmen* joint.(p58)

Nishiki Market Head to this downtown food market to see the wild and wonderful things that go into Kyoto cuisine preparation. (p56)

Yoramu Work your way through a sampling set of the good stuff at this tiny downtown sake specialist. (p64)

Gardens

Ryōan-ji Ponder the meaning of the 15 magical rocks at Japan's most famous Zen garden. Head there early to avoid the crowds. (p109)

Tōfuku-ji This abstract expressionist garden is like none other in Kyoto – it also happens to be one of the city's most beautiful. (p76)

Heian-jingū The stroll gardens behind the main hall of this Shintō shrine are worth the trip when the cherries bloom in April. (p99)

Kyoto Botanical Gardens The cherries in these stunning and expansive gardens are superb and the greenhouse contains some great orchid species. (p73)

Ginkaku-ji The gardens at the 'Silver Pavilion' have it all: luxuriant moss, a bamboo forest, waterfalls, ponds and maples that turn crimson in November. (p95)

Sentō Gosho While Katsura Rikyū garners most of the attention, we've always been fond of the rolling greenery of this walled paradise. (p72)

Katsura Rikyū Imperial Villa The garden at this detached palace is sublime. For fans of Japanese gardens, a pilgrimage here is a must. (p126)

Murin-an Blink and you'll miss this tiny pocket garden. That would be a shame as it's a charming little sanctuary. (p96)

Ōkōchi-sansō Villa Wander the paths and admire the views over the city, the maple leaves and the wonderful hidden contemplative corners of this Arashiyama villa. (p116)

Saihō-ji (Koke-dera) 'Koke-dera' means 'Moss Temple' and this place more than lives up to its name. (p127)

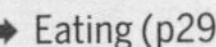
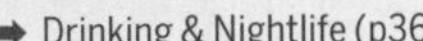

For more top Kyoto spots, see:

- Eating (p29)
- Drinking & Nightlife (p36)
- Entertainment (p38)
- Shopping (p40)
- Temples & Shrines (p42)

Markets

Tenjin-san Held on the 25th of each month at Kitano Tenman-gū, there are always treasures hidden among the bric-a-brac here. (p111)

Kōbō-san Held on the 21st of each month at Tō-ji, this is a good market for used kimono and antiques. (p78)

Nishiki Market Kyoto's main downtown food market is a must-see attraction. There are plenty of souvenir shops scattered among the food shops. (p56)

Chion-ji Tezukuri-ichi *Tezukuri* means 'handmade' and that's what you'll find at this market held on the 15th of every month. (p102)

Scenic Strolls

Daimonji-yama There is no finer walk in the city than the 30-minute climb to the viewpoint above Ginkaku-ji in Northern Higashiyama. (p97)

Kurama The climb to the mountain temple of Kurama-dera is a classic (continue to Kibune if possible). (p122)

Fushimi-Inari-Taisha Paths lined with *torii* (Shintō shrine gates) criss-cross this mountain shrine in Southeast Kyoto. The walking here is great. (p76)

Kyoto Imperial Palace Park If you prefer your strolling on the flat, the broad arcades of Kyoto's Central Park are just the ticket. (p71)

Kamo-gawa Riverbank Make like a local and take your morning or evening constitutional on the banks of Kyoto's main river.

Path of Philosophy (Tetsugaku-no-Michi) We've saved the best for last: the stroll along this canal in Northern Higashiyama is beautiful in any season. (p98)

Traditional Architecture

Katsura Rikyū Imperial Villa Connoisseurs often rank this as the finest example of Japanese traditional architecture. Join a tour and judge for yourself. (p126)

Ōkōchi-sansō Villa Perched on a hillside overlooking Arashiyama and Kyoto, this traditional house is the stuff of dreams. The gardens are spectacular. (p116)

Byōdō-in One of the few extant examples of Heian Era architecture, Byōdō-in will make you wish that a lot more survived. (p125)

Gion District Head to the preserved streets of this entertainment district: Hanami-kōji and Shimbashi. Both are lined with lovely traditional wooden buildings. (p87)

Nishijin District Kyoto's weaving district, Nishijin is home to the thickest concentration of *machiya* (traditional townhouses) in the city. (p108)

Month by Month

TOP EVENTS

Gion Matsuri 17 July

Cherry blossom viewing late March/early April

Daimon-ji Gozan Okuribi 16 August

Kurama Hi Matsuri (Kurama Fire Festival) 22 October

Shōgatsu late December/early January

January

Kyoto comes to life after the lull of the New Year holiday (things open on 3 or 4 January). It's cold, but not too cold for travelling and the city is uncrowded.

Hatsumōde

This raucous festival on 1–3 January marks the first visit of the new year to a Shintō shrine. Kyoto's three most popular shrines at this time are Yasaka-jinja (p84), Heian-jingū (p99) and Fushimi-Inari-Taisha (p76). Transport and accommodation will be crowded.

Tōshiya (Archery Contest)

Held at Sanjūsangen-dō (p83) from 8am to 4pm on 15 January. Hundreds of kimono-clad archers gather for a competition of accuracy and strength.

February

It's still cold in February and snow is possible in the city (but usually melts by noon). The mountains north of the city may be covered in snow all month.

Setsubun Matsuri at Yoshida-jinja

Held on the day of *setsubun* (2, 3 or 4 February; check with the TIC), this festival marks the last day of winter. People climb up to Yoshida-jinja in the northern Higashiyama area to watch a huge bonfire in which old good-luck charms are burned. The action starts at dusk.

March

By March it's starting to warm up. Plums start the annual succession of blossoms in the city. It's a pleasant, uncrowded time.

April

Spring is in full swing by April, although mornings and evenings can still be chilly. The cherry blossoms usually peak in early April, which means thick crowds in the sightseeing districts.

Cherry Blossom Viewing

Hanami (cherry blossom viewing parties) take place all over town when the cherries blossom in early April. Top spots include Maruyama-kōen (p84), Kyoto Imperial Palace Park (p71) and the Kamo-gawa riverbanks. In the evening, join the crowds on Gion's Shimbashi (p87).

Kitano Odori

Held from 15 to 25 April at Kamishichiken Kaburen-jō Theatre, east of Kitano-Tenman-gū at Imadegawa-dōri-Nishihonmatsu nishi iru, this charming geisha dance is put on by the Kamishichiken geisha district.

May

May is one of the best months to visit Kyoto. It's warm and sunny, and the blossoms are out wherever you go. Note the dates of the Golden Week holidays (29 April to 5 May) and book well in advance.

Yabusame at Shimogamo-jinja

The annual *yabusame* (horseback archery) event on 3 May is one of the most exciting spectacles in Kyoto. Held on Tadasu-no-mori, the tree-lined approach to Shimogamo-jinja (p73), the action runs from 1pm to 3.30pm.

Aoi Matsuri (Hollyhock Festival)

One of Kyoto's leading festivals involves a procession of imperial messengers in ox carts and 600 people dressed in traditional costume; hollyhock leaves are carried or used as decoration. The procession leaves around 10am on 15 May from the Kyoto Imperial Palace (p71) and heads for Shimogamo-jinja (p73) where ceremonies take place. It sets out again at 2pm and arrives at Kamigamo-jinja (p128) at 3.30pm.

June

June is generally a lovely time to travel in Kyoto – it's warm but not sweltering and the new green on the trees is beautiful. However, it is also the month of the rainy season, so expect humidity and occasional downpours.

Takigi Nō

Held at Heian-jingū (p99) on 1–2 June, this is a festival of nō drama held by flaming torchlight in the outdoor courtyard.

July

When the rainy season ends in late June or early July, the heat cranks up and it can be very hot and humid. Still, if you don't mind sweating a bit, travel is perfectly possible.

Gion Matsuri

Perhaps the most renowned Japanese festival, this month-long celebration (peaking on 17 July) covers myriad events. Yoi-yama is held on 16 July, when more than 200,000 people throng the Shijō-Karasuma area in Downtown Kyoto, and reaches a climax on the 17th, with a Yamaboko-junkō parade of magnificent floats. On the three evenings preceding the 17th, people gather on Shijō-dōri, many dressed in beautiful summer kimono, to look at the floats and carouse from one street stall to the next.

August

August is hot and humid in Kyoto, but the skies are usually sunny and most tourist sites are uncrowded, except during the O-Bon holiday in mid-August – book ahead.

Daimon-ji Gozan Okuribi

Mistakenly referred to by many as Daimon-ji-yaki (literally, 'burning of Daimon-ji'), this impressive event on 16 August is held to bid farewell to the souls of ancestors. Enormous fires are lit in the form of Chinese characters or other shapes on five mountains. The main fire is the character for *dai*, or 'great', on Daimonji-yama, behind Ginkaku-ji (p95), which is lit at 8pm. The other fires are lit at 10-minute intervals thereafter, working anticlockwise (east to west). Watch this event from the banks of the Kamo-gawa, Yoshida-yama or pay for a rooftop view from a hotel.

Tōki Matsuri

Kyoto's largest ceramics fair, held from 7 to 10 August, is a good place to snap up some bargains, especially late on the last day. The market runs along Gojō-dōri, between Kawabata and Higashiōji. It's a 10-minute walk from Gojō Station om the Keihan line.

September

Sometime in early to mid-September, the heat breaks and temperatures become very pleasant in Kyoto. Skies are generally clear at this time, making it a great time to travel.

Karasu Zumō

Held at Kamigamo-jinja (p128) on 9 September, this festival, which is also called 'crow wrestling', starts at 10am. Young boys compete in bouts of sumō.

October

October is one of the best months to visit Kyoto: the weather can be warm or cool and it's usually sunny. The leaves start turning colour at the end of the month, particularly in the hills.

Jidai Matsuri (Festival of the Ages)

One of Kyoto's big three festivals features more than 2000 people dressed in costumes ranging from the 8th to the 19th centuries parading from the Kyoto Imperial Palace (p71) to Heian-jingū (p99) on 22 October.

Top: Yamaboko-junkō parade, Gion Matsuri festival

Bottom: A participant dresses as Tomoe-Gozen, wife of General Kiso Yoshinaka, at the Jidai Matsuri (Festival of the Ages)

Kurama Hi Matsuri (Kurama Fire Festival)

Mikoshi (portable shrines) are carried through the streets of this mountain hamlet, accompanied by young men in loincloths bearing giant flaming torches. The festival climaxes at 10pm on 22 October at Yuki-jinja in Kurama (p122). Note that trains to and from Kurama will be packed (we suggest going early and returning late).

November

November rivals October and April/May as the best months to visit. Skies are clear and temperatures are pleasantly cool. Foliage usually peaks late in the month.

December

December is cool to cold in Kyoto. The autumn foliage may still be good early in the month. Most sights and restaurants shut down from 29 or 30 December, but transport runs and accommodation is open.

Ōmisoka (New Year's Eve)

People gather in their homes on 31 December to feast then visit local temples to ring temple bells before heading to their local shrine to pray for a lucky year. Bell ringing happens around midnight and shrine visiting happens all evening on New Year's Eve and for the first few days of the New Year. Yasaka-jinja (p84) and Heian-jingū (p99) are great places to enjoy the action.

With Kids

Kyoto is a great place to travel with kids. The usual worries aren't an issue in ultra-safe and spotless Japan. Your biggest challenge will be keeping your children entertained. The very things that many adults come to Japan to see (temples, gardens and shrines) can bore kids silly.

ERIC WHEATER / LONELY PLANET IMAGES ©

A young girl dressed in kimono

Keeping Kids Happy

The best way to keep your kids happy in Kyoto is to mix your diet of traditional Japanese culture with some things the kids are more likely to enjoy.

Fortunately, there is no shortage of child-friendly attractions in Kyoto, ranging from game centres to parks and the Kyoto City Zoo.

If your children are older, you have lots of options: go on a hike in the mountains around the city, rent a bicycle and explore, or take them to the youth-oriented shopping areas downtown such as Shingyōgoku Arcade and the Shijō-Kawaramachi shopping district.

Where Do the Children Play?

On a sunny day in Kyoto, local parents of young children tend to congregate in the Okazaki-kōen area (p99). This region of Northern Higashiyama features a park, several playing fields, a playground, the Kyoto Municipal Zoo and museums (parents of young children can take turns visiting the exhibits while their partner plays with the kids outside). Best of all, the area is completely flat and has wide pavements, making it perfect for those with strollers. In addition, it can be accessed by subway (take the Tōzai subway line to Higashiyama Station and walk north along the Shira-kawa Canal). Tip: the pond behind the Kyoto Municipal Museum of Art is great for picnics.

Getting Around with a Stroller

Kyoto is pretty easy to navigate with a stroller. Most train stations have elevators, as do large departments stores and museums. The major streets downtown have wide pavements, but once you get into the narrower streets, pavements may not exist at all. Fortunately, Kyoto drivers are relatively sane. While taxis do not have child seats, most drivers will leap out and help you get your stroller into the trunk. You can usually get your stroller into restaurants – but you'll find that some fancy places are not willing to accommodate a stroller and/

or fussy children. Go for larger 'family restaurants'. As for sightseeing, most areas of Kyoto are relatively easily negotiated with strollers, but the Southern Higashiyama area has some hills and stairs. Most temples in Kyoto do not have access ramps – you just have to carry your child inside (it's usually safe to leave the stroller outside).

Kid-Friendly Attractions

Arashiyama Monkey Park Iwatayama

Both kids and adults will find the antics of the monkeys here fascinating, and it's easy to combine this with a trip to the sights of Arashiyama (p114).

Kamo-gawa

There's a river running through Kyoto and it's a great place to bring the kids for an afternoon picnic. On hot days they can wade in the river while you relax on the banks. The area around Demachiyanagi is one of the most popular spots for parents and children to play.

Kyoto Imperial Palace Park

The Central Park of Kyoto (p71), this sprawling expanse of fields, trails, ponds and woods is a great place for a picnic, walk or bicycle ride with the kids.

NEED TO KNOW

- **Changing facilities** Department stores, some train stations and public buildings
- **Cots** Available in hotels (book in advance) but not ryokan
- **Health** Diseases not a big problem
- **Highchairs** Available in some restaurants
- **Kids' menus** Usually only in 'family restaurants'
- **Nappies (diapers)** Widely available
- **Strollers** Available, but consider bringing your own
- **Transport** Comfortable and safe; child seats available in rental cars but not taxis

Kyoto City Zoo

This small zoo (p99) is far from world-class, but it is quite convenient to the other sights of Northern Higashiyama so you can easily combine it with a trip to the temples, shrines and museums nearby.

Umekōji Steam Locomotive Museum

With 18 vintage steam locomotives, one of which you can ride, this museum is a must for train-crazy boys and girls (p74).

Shinkyōgoku Shopping Arcade

This is where the Japanese kids from across the country come on their school excursions (after they've seen the obligatory temples). If it's tacky, cheap and gaudy, you'll find it here.

Shijō-Kawaramachi Shopping District

This is the downtown shopping district preening kids go to, to see and be seen and to shop for the latest fashions. There are several new youth-oriented shopping complexes here.

Eating with Kids

Food can be an issue in Japan if your child is a picky eater. Let's face it: even adults can be put off by some of the things found in Japanese cuisine – asking a kid to eat sea urchin might simply be too much.

With this in mind, choose your restaurants carefully. If you're going to a *kaiseki* place, have your lodgings call ahead to see if they can rustle up some kid-friendly dishes. Ditto if you'll be dining at your ryokan.

You'll find quite a few so-called 'family restaurants' in Kyoto and these usually serve something that even finicky kids can stomach (pizza, fried chicken and French fries etc). These places often serve special children's meals.

In addition to family restaurants, you'll find all the usual Western fast-food chains represented in Kyoto. And, needless to say, there are supermarkets and convenience stores everywhere where you can do some self-catering for kids who simply won't eat what's on offer in restaurants.

For Free

A glance through the pages of this book might convince you that sightseeing in Kyoto is going to require taking a second mortgage on your home. Luckily there's plenty you can do for free. Indeed, you could fill at least a week with activities that are absolutely free. Here are just a few.

CHRISTIAN KOBER / ROBERT HARDING WORLD IMAGERY / CORBIS ©

Kamo-gawa riverbank

Temples

The general rule is that you can tour most of the grounds for free, but you pay to enter the gardens and the main hall. There are exceptions to this, so if you see a temple, don't hesitate to march in and check it out. If the main hall is open, remove your shoes and enter. If you have to pay, rest assured that someone will let you know. The following are some temples with spacious grounds that can be toured free of charge.

Nanzen-ji

The sprawling grounds of this superb Northern Higashiyama temple (p94) make it our favourite temple for a stroll.

Chion-in

You can tour the grounds *and* enter the soaring main hall for free here (p82).

Tōfuku-ji

At the south end of the Higashiyama Mountains, this fine Zen temple (p76) has expansive grounds.

Hōnen-in

Not nearly as large as the above three temples, this tiny Pure Land paradise (p97) is a must-see. There is a gallery in one of the halls that often has free art exhibits.

Shrines

Like temples, you can usually tour the grounds of Shintō shrines completely free of charge. Of course, some faithful believers pay a special fee to enter the *haiden* (prayer hall) to be blessed, but this is unlikely to concern the tourist. If there is a treasure hall or garden, you may have to pay to enter, but otherwise, shrines are free.

Fushimi-Inari-Taisha

One of Kyoto's top sights (p76), the only money you're likely to drop here is to buy a drink after climbing the mountain.

Heian-jingū

This vast popular Northern Higashiyama shrine (p99) has a huge gravel-strewn courtyard that you can explore for free. Note that you must pay a fee to enter the gardens.

Shimogamo-jinja

Take a stroll through the magnificent Tadasu-no-Mori (Forest of Truth) that leads to the main hall (p73).

Yasaka-jinja

Overlooking Gion both physically and spiritually, this popular shrine (p84) is highly recommended in both the daytime and evening, when the lanterns make it magical.

Parks

Kyoto is studded with parks, ranging from the huge Imperial Palace Park to tiny pockets in residential neighbourhoods where local kids gather to play. All of Kyoto's parks are free.

Kyoto Imperial Palace Park

Kyoto's Central Park (p71) is a treasure that many visitors to the city overlook. It has everything from baseball diamonds to carp ponds.

Maruyama-kōen

Above Yasaka-jinja and smack on the main Southern Higashiyama sightseeing route, this lovely park (p84) is a great spot for a picnic. It also happens to be Kyoto's most popular *hanami* (cherry blossom viewing) spot.

Imperial Properties

All of Kyoto's imperial properties can be toured for free – Kyoto Imperial Palace (p71), Sentō Gosho (p72), Shūgaku-in Rikyū Imperial Villa and Katsura Rikyū Imperial Villa (p126). Keep in mind, however, that only the main one, the Kyoto Imperial Palace, allows children (as long as they are accompanied by adults). Children below the age of 20 are not permitted at the other three.

Other Attractions

Kamo-gawa

Like the Imperial Palace Park, this is a great place to spend a relaxing afternoon strolling and picnicking. In the summer you'll be treated to free fireworks shows as local youths hold impromptu *hanabi-taikai* (fireworks festivals).

Nishiki Market

It costs nothing to wander through this wonderful market (p56). Of course, you might find something that you just *have* to buy…

Department Stores

Have a look at the fabulous variety of goods for sale in Kyoto's department stores (p65). While you're there, stop by the food floor and snag some free food samples.

Kyoto Station

Kyoto's new station building (p51) is pretty impressive and the view from the rooftop observatory is the best you'll get – short of paying to ascend Kyoto Tower or expending the energy to climb Daimonji-yama.

Festivals

There's nothing like a colourful Kyoto festival (p21), and they're always free. If you're lucky, you might even be asked to participate.

Hikes

It doesn't cost anything to enjoy Kyoto's natural beauty. There are myriad hikes in the mountains that surround the city. The best of these is the Daimonji Yama climb (p97).

Saving Money

Other ways to save money include buying special transport passes (see p188) or by renting a bicycle (see p187).

You can also save money by buying takeaway food and having picnic lunches in parks or by the river. If you prefer to eat in a restaurant, the Downtown area, especially around Sanjo-Kawaramachi, is chock-a-block with restaurants offering meals for less than ¥800 (look for big signs giving the price of their signature dishes or set meals). And, needless to say, due to the decline in tourists numbers caused by the 2011 Great East Japan Earthquake, you can score some incredibly cheap accommodation deals if you look online.

Like a Local

While other Japanese sometimes accuse Kyotoites of being haughty, our experience reveals the opposite. If you approach people with an open mind and a smile on your face, you'll more than likely find them to be extremely welcoming. Here are places where you can meet the various tribes of the city.

Central Kyoto shopping street

Pretty Young Things

Kyoto's fashion-conscious teens and twenty-somethings spend their evenings and weekends seeking others of their kind in the shopping emporiums downtown (the square formed by Shijō and Sanjō streets to the north and south, and Kawaramachi and Karasuma streets to the east and west). While the main streets here have the big-name stores, don't be afraid to head into the narrower backstreets to peruse the many boutiques, galleries, music shops and cafes.

Students

Kyoto is packed with universities, including Kyoto University (or Kyōdai as it's commonly known) in the Northern Higashiyama district, near the intersection of Imadegawa and Higashiōji streets (Hyakumamben Intersection). If you're after cheap eats and drinks, this is the place to go. It's also a good place to meet young Japanese, many of whom speak some English. Kyoto's university students are also fond of drinking in the cheap watering holes along Kiyamachi-dōri, between Sanjō and Shijō streets. On hot summer nights, you'll also find them drinking along the Kamo-gawa, near Sanjō-Ōhashi bridge. They'll often be street performers entertaining the crowds.

The Smart Set

Kyoto's yuppies spend their weekend days shopping in high-end department stores like Takashiyama and Daimarui, which also happen to be loaded with good restaurants and cafes in which to refuel before another bout of shopping. Down on street level, these same types can also be found browsing the boutiques that line Shijōd-ōri. For those whose finances run to imported sports cars, the destination of choice is Kitayama-dōri, where they park their sweet rides long enough to duck into the latest gallery or French bistro. In the evening, these well-heeled Kyotoites do their drinking and dining in such elegant venues as Gion or Pontochō.

Sashimi

Eating

Kyoto is famous the world over for its temples and gardens. What few people outside Japan realise is that Kyoto is also one of the world's great food cities. In fact, when you consider atmosphere, service and quality, it's hard to think of a city where you get more bang for your dining buck.

Kyoto's Restaurant Scene

Kyoto punches way above its weight in the culinary arena. Among the reasons for this is that Kyoto was the centre of the country for most of its history, and its chefs had to please the most demanding palates in the realm: the imperial court, the nobility and the heads of the main religious sects.

Even after losing the imperial court to Tokyo, Kyoto remained a major sightseeing destination for both domestic and international visitors, meaning a continual stream of demanding diners passing through. In addition, Kyoto sits atop excellent groundwater (essential for making good tofu, sake and tea) and has excellent soil for growing vegetables in the city and surrounding areas. In fact, you can still find several distinct subspecies of vegetables in the city's markets known as *kyo-yasai* (Kyoto vegetables). The result is a relatively small city packed with excellent restaurants.

Naturally, Kyoto is packed with restaurants that specialise in local cuisine (see Kyoto Specialities, p30, for details). In addition, you'll find all the other major types of Japanese cuisine and regional specialities represented in Kyoto: sushi, *rāmen*, tempura, *okonomiyaki* (savoury Japanese cabbage pancakes) and a lot of things you may not have heard of.

NEED TO KNOW

See p204 for our Menu Decoder.

Price Ranges

In our listings, we've used the following price codes to represent the cost of a meal for one person, not including a drink:

¥	under ¥1000
¥¥	¥1000 to ¥5000
¥¥¥	over ¥5000

Opening Hours

Most restaurants are open 11am to 2pm for lunch and 6pm to around 11pm for dinner, although some places (especially cafes) stay open all afternoon as well. Most places close one day a week (Tuesday being the most common day for a day off).

Tipping

There is no tipping in restaurants or cafes.

Credit Cards

Credit cards can be used at some mid-range and high-end places, especially those in department stores. Credit cards cannot be used in most small local eateries. To be safe, *never* count on being able to use a credit card at a restaurant in Kyoto.

Reservations

You won't need a reservation at most of the restaurants listed in this chapter. However, at traditional high-end restaurants (*kaiseki* etc), a reservation is a good idea. If you don't speak Japanese, the easiest thing to do is simply ask someone at the place you're staying to call and make the reservation for you.

Dress Code

For casual restaurants, you can wear whatever is comfortable. For nicer places, smart casual is usually fine (note that you'll feel very out of place in shorts at a high-end restaurant in Kyoto).

In addition to Japanese cuisine, Kyoto is packed with good international restaurants, particularly French, Italian, Chinese and Thai, as well as the usual international chains that you'll find elsewhere.

At the time of writing, the yen is very strong, but you shouldn't worry about going broke to eat well in Kyoto. There are scores of restaurants offering full meals in the ¥600 to ¥800 range, especially at lunchtime. Even some of the city's esteemed high-end eateries have been forced to slash their prices and offer various specials in hopes of luring cost-cutting clientele.

Eating by Neighbourhood

- **Kyoto Station Area** (p52) There are eateries scattered all around the station building, ranging from plebeian to posh.
- **Downtown Kyoto** (p58) The centre of Kyoto's dining scene, it has the thickest concentration of restaurants in the city.
- **Southern Higashiyama** (p87) Offerings here fall into two categories: tourist eateries near the temples and refined places in Gion.
- **Northern Higashiyama** (p100) Not a dining centre, but plenty of eateries are scattered about, including cheap places near Kyoto University.
- **Arashiyama & Sagano** (p112) Cheap eateries for tourists cram the main drag, with a few high-end spots further out.

Kyoto Specialities

Kyō-ryōri, or Kyoto cuisine, is a style of cooking that evolved out of Kyoto's landlocked location and age-old customs of the imperial court. The preparation of dishes makes ingenious use of fresh seasonal vegetables and emphasises subtle flavours, revealing the natural taste of the ingredients. *Kyō-ryōri* is selected according to the mood and hues of the ever-changing seasons, and the presentation and atmosphere in which it's enjoyed are as important as the flavour.

KAISEKI

Kaiseki (Japanese *haute cuisine*) is the pinnacle of refined dining, where ingredients, preparation, setting and presentation come together to create a dining experience quite unlike any other. Born as an adjunct to the tea ceremony, *kaiseki* is a largely vegetarian affair (though fish is often served). One usually eats *kaiseki* in the private room of a *ryōtei* (traditional, high-class Japanese restaurant) or ryokan. The meal is served in several small courses, giving one the opportunity to admire the plates and bowls, which are carefully chosen to complement the food and seasons. Rice is eaten last (usually with an assortment of pickles) and the drink of choice is sake or beer. The Kyoto version of *kaiseki* is known as *kyō-kaiseki* and it features a variety of *kyō-yasai,* or Kyoto vegetables.

A good *kaiseki* dinner costs upwards of ¥10,000 per person. A cheaper way to sample the delights of *kaiseki* is to visit a *kaiseki* restaurant for lunch. Most places offer a boxed lunch containing a sampling of their dinner fare for around ¥2500. An easy way to sample *kaiseki* is by booking a night in a first-class Kyoto ryokan and asking for the breakfast/dinner option.

TOFU-RYŌRI

Kyoto is famed for its tofu (soybean curd), a result of the city's excellent water and large population of (theoretically) vegetarian Buddhist monks. There are numerous *tofu-ya-san* (tofu makers) scattered throughout the city and a legion of exquisite *yudōfu* (tofu cooked in an iron pot) restaurants – many are concentrated in Northern Higashiyama along the roads around Nanzen-ji (see p94) and in the Arashiyama area (see p117). One typical Kyoto tofu by-product is called *yuba*, sheets of the chewy, thin film that settles on the surface of vats of simmering soy milk. This turns up in many ryokan meals and *kaiseki* restaurants.

Eating in a Japanese Restaurant

When you enter a restaurant, you'll be greeted with a hearty *irasshaimase* (Welcome!). In all but the most casual places the waiter will next ask you *nan-mei sama* (How many people?). Answer with your fingers, which is what the Japanese do. You will then be led to a table, a place at the counter or a tatami room.

At this point you will be given an *oshibori* (a hot towel), a cup of tea and a menu. The *oshibori* is for wiping your hands and face. When you're done with it, just roll it up and leave it next to your place. Now comes the hard part: ordering. If you don't read Japanese, you can use the romanised translations in this book (p199) to help you, or direct the waiter's attention to the Japanese script. If this doesn't work, there are two phrases that may help: *o-susume wa nan desu ka* (What do you recommend?) and *o-makase shimasu* (Please decide for me).

When you've finished eating, you can signal for the bill by crossing one index finger over the other to form the sign of an 'x'. This is the standard sign for 'bill please'. You can also say *o-kanjō kudasai.* Remember there is no tipping in Japan and tea is free of charge. Usually you will be given a bill to take to the cashier at the front of the restaurant, but some places allow you to pay while seated at your table. Only the bigger and more international places take credit cards, so cash is always the surer option.

When leaving, it is polite to say to the restaurant staff, *gochisō-sama deshita,* which means 'It was a real feast'. Note that if you are invited to dine in a private home, it's also polite to use this expression when finishing the meal and some people repeat the phrase when leaving the house.

EATING ETIQUETTE

When it comes to eating in Japan, there are quite a number of implicit rules, but they're fairly easy to remember. If you're worried about putting your foot in it, relax – the Japanese don't expect you to know what to do, and they are unlikely to be offended as long as you follow the standard rules of politeness from your own country. Here are a few major points to keep in mind:

➡ **Chopsticks in rice** Do not stick your *hashi* (chopsticks) upright in a bowl of rice. This is how rice is offered to the dead in Buddhist rituals. Similarly, do not pass food from your chopsticks to someone else's. This is another funeral ritual.

➡ **Polite expressions** When eating with other people, especially when you're a guest, it is polite to say *itadakimasu* (literally 'I will receive') before digging in. This is as close as the Japanese come to saying grace. Similarly, at the end of the meal, you should thank your host by saying *gochisō-sama deshita* which means, 'It was a real feast'.

➡ **Kampai** It is bad form to fill your own glass. You should fill the glass of the person next to you and wait for them to reciprocate. Raise your glass a little off the table while it is being filled. Once everyone's glass has been filled, the usual starting signal is a chorus of *kampai*, which means 'cheers'.

➡ **Slurp** When you eat noodles in Japan, it's perfectly OK, even expected, to slurp them. In fact, one of the best ways to find *rāmen* (egg noodle) restaurants in Japan is to listen for the loud slurping sound that comes out of them!

Major Cuisine/Restaurant Types

With the exception of *shokudō* (all-round restaurants) and *izakaya* (pub-eateries), most Japanese restaurants concentrate on a speciality cuisine. In this section, we discuss the main types of restaurants you are likely to encounter and we provide sample menus for each type. If you familiarise yourself with the main types of restaurants and what they serve, you'll be able to get the most out of Kyoto's incredible culinary scene.

SHOKUDŌ

A *shokudō* is the most common type of restaurant in Japan, and is found near train stations, tourist spots and just about any other place where people congregate. Easily distinguished by the presence of plastic food displays in the window, these inexpensive places usually serve a variety of *washoku* (Japanese dishes) and *yōshoku* (Western dishes).

At lunch, and sometimes dinner, the easiest meal to order at a *shokudō* is a *teishoku* (set-course meal). This usually includes a main dish of meat or fish, a bowl of rice, *misoshiru* (miso soup), shredded cabbage and some *tsukemono* (Japanese pickles). In addition, most *shokudō* serve a fairly standard selection of *donburi-mono* (rice dishes) and *menrui* (noodle dishes). When you order noodles, you can choose between *soba* (thin brown buckwheat noodles) and *udon* (thick white wheat noodles), both of which are served with a variety of toppings. Expect to spend from ¥600 to ¥1000 for a meal at a *shokudō*.

IZAKAYA

An *izakaya* is the Japanese equivalent of a pub-eatery. It's a good place to visit when you want a casual meal, a wide selection of food, a hearty atmosphere and, of course, plenty of beer and sake. When you enter an *izakaya*, you are given the choice of sitting around the counter, at a table or on a tatami floor. You usually order a bit at a time, choosing from a selection of typical Japanese foods, such as *yakitori* (skewers of grilled chicken and vegetables), sashimi and grilled fish, as well as Japanese interpretations of Western foods like French fries and beef stew.

Izakaya can be identified by their rustic facades and the red lanterns outside their doors bearing the kanji for *izakaya* (居酒屋). Many also stack crates of beer and sake bottles outside. Since *izakaya* food is casual fare to go with drinking, it is usually fairly inexpensive. Depending on how much you drink, you can expect to get away with spending ¥2500 to ¥5000 per person.

SUSHI & SASHIMI

There are two main types of sushi: *nigiri-zushi* (served on a small bed of rice – the most common variety) and *maki-zushi* (served in a seaweed roll). Sushi without rice is known as sashimi or *tsukuri* (or, politely, *o-tsukuri*).

Sushi is not difficult to order. If you sit at the counter of a sushi restaurant you can simply point at what you want, as most of the selections are visible in a refrigerated glass case between you and the sushi chef. You can also order à la carte from the menu. When ordering, you usually order *ichi-nin mae* (one portion), which usually means two pieces of sushi. Be careful, since the price on the menu will be that of only one piece.

If ordering à la carte is too daunting, you can take care of your whole order with just one or two words by ordering *mori-awase,* an assortment plate of *nigiri-zushi.* These usually come in three grades: *futsū nigiri* (regular *nigiri*), *jō nigiri* (special *nigiri*) and *toku-jō nigiri* (extra-special *nigiri*). The difference is in the type of fish used. Most *mori-awase* contain six or seven pieces of sushi.

Before popping the sushi into your mouth, dip it very lightly in *shōyu* (soy sauce), which you pour from a small decanter into a low dish specially provided for the purpose. If you're not good at using *hashi* (chopsticks), don't worry – sushi is one of the few foods in Japan that it's perfectly acceptable to eat with your hands. Slices of *gari* (pickled ginger) will also be served to help refresh the palate. The beverage of choice with sushi is beer or sake (hot in winter and cold in summer), with a cup of green tea at the end of the meal.

RĀMEN

The Japanese imported this dish from China and put their own spin on it to make what is one of the world's most delicious fast foods. *Rāmen* dishes are big bowls of noodles in a meat broth, served with a variety of toppings, such as sliced pork, bean sprouts and leeks.

In some restaurants you may be asked if you'd prefer *kotteri* (thick and fatty) or *assari* (thin and light) soup. Other than this, ordering is simple: just sidle up to the counter and say *rāmen*, or ask for any of the other choices usually on offer. Expect to pay between ¥500 and ¥900 for a bowl. Since *rāmen* is derived from Chinese cuisine, some *rāmen* restaurants also serve *chāhan* or *yaki-meshi* (both dishes are fried rice), *gyōza* (dumplings) and *kara-age* (deep-fried chicken pieces).

Rāmen restaurants are easily distinguished by their long counters lined with customers hunched over steaming bowls. You can sometimes *hear* a *rāmen* shop as you wander by – it's considered polite to slurp the noodles and aficionados claim that slurping brings out the full flavour of the broth.

SOBA & UDON

Soba (thin, brown buckwheat noodles) and *udon* (thick, white wheat noodles) are Japan's answer to Chinese-style *rāmen*. Most Japanese noodle shops serve both *soba* and *udon* in a variety of ways.

Noodles are usually served in a bowl containing a light, bonito-flavoured broth, but you can also order them served cold and piled on a bamboo screen with a cold broth for dipping (this is called *zaru soba*). If you order *zaru soba*, you'll receive a small plate of wasabi and sliced spring onions – put these into the cup of broth and eat the noodles by dipping them in this mixture. At the end of your meal, the waiter will give you some hot broth to mix with the leftover sauce, which you drink like a kind of tea. As with *rāmen*, you should feel free to slurp as loudly as you please.

Soba and *udon* places are usually quite cheap (about ¥800 a dish), but some fancy places can be significantly more expensive (the decor is a good indication of the price).

OKONOMIYAKI

Sometimes described as Japanese pizza or pancake, the resemblance is in form only. Actually, *okonomiyaki* are various forms of batter and cabbage cakes cooked on a griddle.

At an *okonomiyaki* restaurant you sit around a *teppan* (iron hotplate), armed with a spatula and chopsticks to cook your choice of meat, seafood and vegetables in a cabbage and vegetable batter.

Some restaurants will do most of the cooking and bring the nearly finished product over to your hotplate for you to season with *katsuo bushi* (bonito flakes), *shōyu* (soy sauce), *ao-nori* (an ingredient similar to parsley), Japanese Worcestershire-style sauce and mayonnaise. Cheaper places, however, will simply hand you a bowl filled with the ingredients and expect you to cook it for yourself. If this happens, don't panic. First, mix the batter and filling thoroughly, then place it on the hotplate, flattening it into a pancake shape. After five minutes or so, use the spatula to flip it and cook for another five minutes. Then dig in.

Most *okonomiyaki* places also serve *yaki-soba* (fried noodles with meat and vegetables) and *yasai-itame* (stir-fried vegetables). All of this is washed down with mugs of draught beer.

One final word: don't worry too much about preparation of the food – as a foreigner you will be expected to be awkward, and the waiter will keep a sharp eye on you to make sure no real disasters occur.

Vegetarians & Vegans

Travellers who eat fish should have almost no trouble dining in Kyoto: almost all *shokudō*, *izakaya* and other common restaurants offer a set meal with fish as the main dish. Vegans and vegetarians who don't eat fish will have to get their protein from tofu and other bean products. Note that most *misoshiru* (miso soup) is made with *dashi* (stock) that contains fish, so if you want to avoid fish, you'll also have to avoid *misoshiru*.

Kyoto has several vegetarian and/or organic restaurants that serve dishes suitable for vegetarians and vegans. See the Eating sections of the Explore chapters for specific recommendations. Reviews that include the icon throughout this guide indicate places that have a good vegetarian selection.

The following is a list of restaurants that specialise in vegetarian or vegan cuisine:

Machapuchare (p88) The *obanzai* (Kyoto-style home cooking) set here is the best veggie meal in Kyoto.

Cafe Proverbs 15:17 (p101) Another great organic spot near Kyoto University.

Kailash (p101) This is a true organic spot in a nice traditional old house.

Shizenha Restaurant Obanzai (p60) For all you can eat veggie, this is the spot.

Biotei (p60) High-quality veggie right downtown.

Kerala (p62) The best Indian restaurant in Kyoto – try the veggie lunch set.

Eating with Kids

For information on eating with children in Japan, see p24.

Cooking Courses

If you want to learn how to cook some of the delightful foods you've tried in Kyoto, we recommend **Uzuki** (www.kyotouzuki.com; 3hr class per person ¥4000), a small cooking class conducted in a Japanese home for groups of two to four people. You will learn how to cook a variety of dishes and then sit down and enjoy the fruits of your labour. You can consult beforehand if you have particular dishes you'd like to cook. The fee includes all ingredients. Reserve via the website.

Department Store Dining

Yes, we know: the idea of dining in a department store sounds as appetising as dining in a petrol station. However, Japanese department stores, especially those in a large city like Kyoto, are loaded with good dining options. And, unlike many street-level shops, they're usually fairly comfortable with foreign diners (if there's any communication trouble, they can always call down to the bilingual ladies at the information counter).

On their basement floors, you'll find *depa-chika* (from the English word 'department' and the Japanese word *chika*, which means 'underground'). A good *depa-chika* is like an Aladdin's cave of gustatory delights that rivals the best gourmet shops in any Western city. Meanwhile, on their upper floors, you'll usually find a *resutoran-gai* ('restaurant city') that includes restaurants serving all the Japanese standards – sushi, noodles, *tonkatsu* (deep-fried breaded pork cutlet), tempura – along with a few international restaurants, usually French, Italian and Chinese.

If you find yourself feeling peckish in Downtown Kyoto, here are some good department dining options:

➡ **Takashimaya** (p65) At the corner of Shijō and Kawaramachi streets, this elegant department store has an incredible food floor (on the B1 level) and the best department store *resutoran-gai* in the city (on the 7th floor).

➡ **Daimaru** (p65) On the north side of Shijō, between Kawaramachi and Karasuma streets, Daimaru has a food floor that rivals the one at Takashimaya (note the awesome Japanese sweet section) and a solid *resutoran-gai* on the 8th floor.

➡ **Daimaru** (p65) On the south side of the Shijō-Teramachi intersection, the Tavelt food floor on the B1 level of this department store is the cheapest of the three listed here. They've usually got a great selection of take-away sushi/sashimi and fruit.

Lonely Planet's Top Choices

Omen (p100) Brilliant noodles and great atmosphere near Ginkaku-ji.

Kane-yo (p59) Perfect *unagi* (eel) in classic 'old Kyoto' surroundings.

Yoshikawa (p58) Great tempura and a breathtaking garden.

Kiyamachi Sakuragawa (p58) A superb introduction to *kaiseki*.

Uosue (p59) Hidden gem downtown serving great *kaiseki*.

Ōzawa (p87) Cross the bridge to dine on sublime tempura.

Café Bibliotec HELLO! (p59) A cafe with style to spare.

Best by Budget

¥

Musashi Sushi (p63)

Goya (p100)

Ippūdō (p58)

Café de 505 (p102)

¥¥

Tōsuirō (p58)

Ganko Zushi (p58)

Tagoto Honten (p59)

Shibazaki (p87)

¥¥¥

Hinaka (p59)

Gion Karyō (p88)

Mishima-tei (p59)

Hyōtei (p100)

Best Rāmen

Ippūdō (p58)

Karako (p101)

Rāmen Kairikiya (p61)

Best Sushi

Den Shichi (p77)

Tsukiji Sushisei (p61)

Ganko Zushi (p58)

Best for a Break from Japanese

Kerala (p62)

Liberte (p63)

Din Tai Fung (p61)

Hati Hati (p62)

Best Noodles (Soba/ Udon)

Honke Tagoto (p62)

Hinode Udon (p101)

Din Tai Fung (p61)

Omen Kodai-ji (p88)

Best Kaiseki

Kiyamachi Sakuragawa (p58)

Hinaka (p59)

Gion Karyō (p88)

Uosue (p59)

Hinode Udon (p101)

Best for Kids

Ganko Zushi (p58)

Capricciosa (p60)

Warai (p61)

Best Cafes

Prinz (p77)

Lugol (p61)

Café Independants (p63)

Drinking & Nightlife

Take a stroll down Kyoto's main nightlife strip, Kiyamachi-dōri, and you might think that there's one bar for every resident of Kyoto. Sure, some can only seat three at a squeeze, but there's no shortage of watering holes. And the variety is astonishing – everything from rough-and-ready student hangouts to impossibly chic spots where you just might spot a geisha.

Kyoto Nightlife

Like its restaurant scene, Kyoto has a deeper nightlife scene than most cities of its size, Japanese or foreign. Indeed, visitors from much bigger cities often remark on the sophistication and scope of the nightlife here in the 'Old Capital'. One reason must surely be the number of visitors the city keeps happy after sightseeing hours are over. Another must be the sheer variety of influences the city absorbs from all these visitors.

Of course, there's more to Kyoto nightlife than just bars and clubs. For starters, there are *izakaya,* which are Japanese-style restaurants that serve a variety of sake and beer (or sake and beer bars joints that happen to serve a variety of Japanese food – sometimes it's hard to tell).

In addition to these traditional establishments, you can indulge in another 'traditional' Japanese form of nightlife: karaoke. Indeed, it would be a shame to come all the way to Japan and not belt out a few numbers in one of Kyoto's seemingly endless 'karaoke boxes'. Even if you shy away from karaoke back home, where you're forced to climb up on a stage and sing in front of strangers, you'll probably enjoy karaoke Japanese-style. Here, you and your friends cram into a small room and entertain (or torment) each other with your very own musical styling.

HOTEL BARS

Some of the best bars in Kyoto are inside hotels. These are usually very easy to enter and you will have no communication problems. Here are our favourites:

➡ **Orizzonte** (Kyoto Hotel Ōkura; p144) This is a restaurant by day, lounge by night (usually from 8.30pm to 11pm). The view over Kyoto here is stunning.

➡ **Tōzan Bar** (Hyatt Regency Kyoto; p145) We love this cosy and cool underground retreat below one of Kyoto's best hotels. It's worth going just to marvel at the design.

Drinking & Nightlife by Neighbourhood

➡ **Southern Higashiyama** (p89) A mix of high-end (hard to enter) traditional spots, hostess bars and approachable nightspots.

➡ **Downtown Kyoto** (p64) Home to plebeian and raucous Kiyamachi and refined and traditional Pontochō.

➡ **Kyoto Station Area** (p48) Not much of a nightlife destination, but plenty of bars and *izakaya* about if you need them.

Lonely Planet's Top Choices

World (p65) Kyoto's coolest club.

Yoramu (p64) A sake lover's paradise.

Bar Main Higashiyama (p89) A slick haunt in Southern Higashiyama.

Sama Sama (p64) A cosy cave on Kiyamachi.

Best Cheap Bars

A-Bar (p64)

Ing (p64)

Rub-a-Dub (p64)

Best for Meeting Locals

Kisui (p90)

A-Bar (p64)

Rub-a-Dub (p64)

Gael Irish Pub (p89)

Best Upmarket Bars

Tōzan Bar (p36)

Gion Finlandia Bar (p90)

Atlantis (p64)

Best Gaijin (Expat) Bars

McLoughlin's Irish Bar & Restaurant (p64)

Gael Irish Pub (p89)

Pig & Whistle (p90)

NEED TO KNOW

Opening Hours

➡ **Izakaya** Around 6pm to midnight

➡ **Bars and clubs** Around 7pm to 2am or later

➡ **Karaoke boxes** Afternoon to midnight or later

Get the Scoop

➡ **Kansai Scene (www.kansaiscene.com)** This magazine has listings of foreigner-friendly bars as well as detailed event listings. It's available at major bookshops and foreigner-friendly businesses. See the website for places where you can grab a copy.

➡ **Deep Kyoto (www.deepkyoto.com)** This website has listings on little-known Kyoto bars, cafes and restaurants, as well as some event information.

Door Policy

Most bars have no door policy per se, but some places may be uncomfortable if you just walk in (it's not necessarily discrimination – Kyoto bars are famous for requiring guests to be introduced by an established patron). As for clubs, they usually admit all comers, as long as you aren't obviously addled or inappropriately dressed.

Entertainment

If you've never seen the otherworldly spectacle of kabuki (stylised Japanese theatre) or the colourful extravagance of a geisha dance, then you've come to the right place: Kyoto is the best city in Japan to enjoy traditional Japanese performing arts. In addition, you'll find a lively music scene, plenty of cinemas and modern performances of all sorts.

Traditional Performing Arts

KABUKI

Performances of *kabuki* (p168), Japan's most colourful and popular traditional form of performance art, are regularly held at the Minami-za Theatre (p90). It's easiest to get tickets to the year-end Kao-mise ('Face Showing') performances, but you can also get tickets to other events throughout the year. The best place to check for upcoming events is in the *Kyoto Visitor's Guide,* which is available at bookshops and foreigner-friendly accommodation around town. Tour companies can also help with tickets.

GEISHA DANCE

Each year, Kyoto's geisha (or, properly speaking, *geiko* and *maiko* – fully fledged and trainee geisha respectively) perform fantastic dances (known as *odori*), usually on seasonal themes. Three of the geisha districts perform their dance in April, to coincide with the cherry blossoms, one performs in May, and the final one performs its dance in November, to coincide with the autumn foliage. For a small additional fee, you can participate in a brief tea ceremony before the show.

We *highly* recommend seeing one of these dances if you are in town when they are being held. Ask at the Tourist Information Center or at your lodgings for help with ticket purchase. Tour companies can also help with tickets.

GEISHA ENTERTAINMENT

In addition to geisha dances, it's possible to arrange private geisha entertainment. While it's not cheap – expect to pay around ¥70,000 for two hours with two geisha, not including dinner and drinks – it can be the memory of a lifetime, and if you're part of a group you can share the costs. Various Kyoto tour companies arrange geisha entertainment, including **Kyoto Culture.org** (www.kyotoculture.org).

Another way to experience geisha entertainment is to join a regularly scheduled geisha event. One of the best is put on by Gion Hatanaka, a Gion ryokan; for details, see p90.

Cinema

You'll find a large number of movie theatres in Downtown Kyoto. These theatres are dominated by Hollywood films, which are screened in their original language, with Japanese subtitles. Tickets average around ¥1800.

Nightlife by Neighbourhood

➡ **Downtown Kyoto** (p65) This is the place to go for cinemas.

➡ **Southern Higashiyama** (p90) Home to Gion, this is the place for geisha entertainment and *kabuki*.

➡ **Northern Higashiyama** (p102) This district is your best bet for performances of nō.

Lonely Planet's Top Choices

Kabuki at Minami-za (p90) The most mesmerising theatrical performances in the city.

Takigi Nō (p22) Primeval drama after dark.

Kyoto Cinema (p65) The best indie films from round the world.

Gion Hatanaka's Kyoto Cuisine & Maiko Evening (p90) One of the best ways to actually meet a geisha.

Best Geisha Dances

Kyō Odori (p91) Held between first and third Sunday in April.

Miyako Odori (p91) Held throughout April.

Kitano Odori (p21) Held between 15 and 25 April.

Kamogawa Odori (p65) Held between 1 and 24 May.

Gion Odori (p91) Held between 1 and 10 November.

Best Arthouse Cinemas

Kyoto Cinema (p65)

Kyoto Minami Kaikan (p78)

Best Classical Music Venues

Kyoto Concert Hall (p78)

ALTI (p78)

Best Live Music Venues

Taku-Taku (p78)

Jittoku (p111)

NEED TO KNOW

Get the Scoop

➡ **Kansai Scene (www.kansaiscene.com)** This magazine has listings of foreigner-friendly bars as well as detailed event listings. It's available at major bookshops and foreigner-friendly businesses. See the website for places where you can grab a copy.

➡ **Deep Kyoto (www.deepkyoto.com)** This website has listings on little-known Kyoto bars, cafes and restaurants, as well as some event information.

Dress Code

➡ **Bars** Whatever you happen to be wearing is fine at most places. Go smart casual at hotel bars and upmarket places in Gion and Pontochō.

➡ **Classical Music Halls** Smart casual.

➡ **Clubs** Casual and comfortable or absolutely fabulous.

➡ **Geisha Dances** Smart casual.

➡ **Private Geisha Entertainment** Smart casual or semi-formal.

➡ **Kabuki and nō** Smart casual.

Shopping

Kyoto has a fantastic variety of both traditional and modern shops. Most of these are located in the Downtown area, making the city a very convenient place to shop. Whether you're looking for fans and kimono or the latest electronics and cameras, Kyoto has plenty to offer.

Shopping in Kyoto

Kyoto has a long history as Japan's artistic and cultural workshop: it's the place where the country's finest artisans used their skills to produce the goods used in tea ceremonies, calligraphy, flower arrangement and religious ceremonies, as well as in kimono fabrics and other textiles. Indeed, Kyoto is the best place to find traditional arts and crafts in all of Japan.

Of course, Kyoto has far more to offer than just traditional items. You will also find the latest fashions in the Shijō-Kawaramachi shopping district, the latest electronics on Teramachi-dōri and a wondrous assortment of food products in markets such as Nishiki. And if you're lucky enough to be in town on the 21st or the 25th of the month, you should make every effort to visit one of the city's excellent flea markets.

PLAN TO SHOP?

Many travellers plan their trips around the cherry blossoms or one of Kyoto's great festivals. Few, however, plan their trips around Kyoto's brilliant markets. This is a shame because Kyoto's two monthly markets are among the best flea markets in all of Asia. The dates to keep in mind are the 21st of the month for the Kōbō-san Market (p78) at Tō-ji, and the 25th of the month for the Tenjin-san Market (p111) at Kitano Tenman-gū. Note that these are close enough together to hit on one slightly extended stay in Kyoto.

Shopping Strips

Shopping neighbourhoods in Kyoto tend to be organised by specialities, which certainly makes things easier if you're after specific items. The following is a list of some of Kyoto's most important shopping streets and what you'll find there.

- **Teramachi-dōri, north of Oike-dōri** (Map p216) Traditional Japanese crafts, tea-ceremony goods, green tea and antiques.
- **Teramachi-dōri, south of Shijō-dōri** (Map p216) Electronics and computers.
- **Shijō-dōri, between Kawaramachi-dōri and Karasuma-dōri** (Map p216) Department stores, fashion boutiques and traditional arts and crafts.
- **Shinmonzen-dōri** (Map p222) Antiques.
- **Gojō-zaka** (Map p222) Pottery.

Shopping by Neighbourhood

- **Downtown Kyoto** (p65) The entire downtown area is one giant shopping district.
- **Kyoto Station Area** (p52) Big electronics and camera shops surround the station.
- **Southern Higashiyama** (p91) Ceramics and traditional crafts.
- **Northern Higashiyama** (p102) Great traditional craft shops.

Lonely Planet's Top Choices

Ippo-dō (p65) This is *the* place to buy green tea, both *matcha* (powdered) and leaf.

Kyoto Handicraft Center (p103) For one-stop souvenir shopping, this place can't be beaten.

Kyūkyō-dō (p66) A convenient Downtown all-round traditional souvenir shop.

Junkudō (p65) This is Kyoto's best bookshop, hands down.

Morita Washi (p66) The selection of *washi* (Japanese paper) is just mind-boggling here.

Takashimaya (p65) Our favourite department store in Kyoto.

Best for Traditional Arts & Crafts

Zōhiko (p103)

Nijūsan-ya (p66)

Nishiharu (p67)

Best for Electronics

Bic Camera (p52)

Yodobashi Camera (p52)

Taniyama Musen (p68)

Best Department Stores

Daimaru (p65)

Isetan (p53)

Best for Washi

Rakushi-kan (p66)

Kamiji Kakimoto (p66)

Best for Kimono & Yukata

Mimuro (p67)

Erizen (p67)

NEED TO KNOW

Opening Hours

- **Department stores** 10am to 7pm, closed one or two days a month
- **Smaller shops** 9am to 5pm, may be closed Sunday

Bargaining

Bargaining in Japan is just not done. Possible exceptions are antique shops, flea markets, camera and electronics stores (especially second-hand shops). The word 'discount' is usually understood by shop assistants. If they are willing to drop the price, accept the first offer – don't haggle further as it will make things very awkward for the staff.

Payment

Departments stores, modern stores, boutiques etc accept credit cards. Some small traditional shops only accept cash.

Temples & Shrines

Kyoto's temples and shrines are the main draw for many visitors to the city, and for good reason: they are among the best examples of religious architecture on earth. Moreover, temples are where you will find Japan's most superb gardens. With over 1000 Buddhist temples and more than 400 Shintō shrines, exploring these wonders is the work of a lifetime.

What to Do at a Temple

There are no steadfast rituals you must follow when visiting a Buddhist temple. Many temples require that you remove your shoes before climbing the steps into the main hall. If there is a low slatted board *(sunoko)* on the ground, step out of your shoes onto this.

At many temples, you can pay a small fee (usually ¥500) for a cup of *matcha* (powdered green tea) and a Japanese sweet, which you can enjoy while looking over the garden. Few foreigners take advantage of this wonderful way to enjoy a temple.

What to Do at a Shrine

There is a distinct ritual to visiting a shrine, but as long as you behave in a respectful manner, you do not have to follow it closely. If you want to do as the locals do, here is the basic drill: rinse your mouth and hands with pure water at a *temizuya* (small pavilion), using the stone ablution *chōzuya* (basin) and *hishaku* (bamboo ladle) provided for this purpose. Rinse both hands before pouring water into a cupped hand to rinse the mouth. Do not spit the water into the basin; rather, spit it onto the gravel that surrounds the basin.

TEMPLE TIP

Visiting temples usually means removing your shoes at least once. A pair of slip-on shoes will make this a lot easier.

Next, proceed to the *haiden* (worshippers' hall), which stands before the main hall of the shrine. Here, you will find an offering box over which a bell hangs with a long rope attached. Visitors toss a coin into the box, then grab and shake the rope to 'wake the gods', bow twice, clap loudly twice, bow again twice (once deeply, once lightly) and then step back and to the side.

Amulets are popular at shrines. *O-mamori* (special talismans) are purchased to ensure good luck or ward off evil. *O-mikuji* (fortunes) are chosen by drawing a numbered rod from a box and taking the corresponding fortune slip.

Temples & Shrines by Neighbourhood

➡ **Kyoto Station Area** (p51) Two of Kyoto's biggest temples are found here: Nishi Hongan-ji and Higashi Hongan-ji.

➡ **Southern Higashiyama** (p83) Superb temples are thick on the ground here.

➡ **Northern Higashiyama** (p96) A green area rich in temples and shrines.

➡ **Northwest Kyoto** (p108) Several of Kyoto's most famous temples are found here.

➡ **Arashiyama & Sagano** (p114) You'll find several temples among the bamboo here.

➡ **Kitayama Area & Greater Kyoto** (p119) There are interesting temples and shrines scattered all round this area.

Lonely Planet's Top Choices

Nanzen-ji (p96) This is a world of Zen temples and subtemples scattered amid trees.

Ginkaku-ji (p95) The famed 'Silver Pavilion' boasts one of Kyoto's finest gardens.

Kinkaku-ji (p106) A golden apparition rises above a tranquil reflecting pond; it's arguably Kyoto's most impressive single sight.

Tenryū-ji (p114) This temple takes *shakkei* (borrowed scenery) to a new level: it borrows the entire sweep of Arashiyama's beautiful mountains.

Daitoku-ji (p72) Each subtemple at this Zen complex contains a sublime garden – a must for garden lovers with an aversion to crowds.

Myōshin-ji (p110) Like Daitoku-ji, this is a walled complex containing many fine subtemples and one of Kyoto's most famous garden's: Taizō-in.

Kurama-dera (p122) Climb a path lined with towering cedar trees to this mountain temple in the hills north of the city.

Chion-in (p82) A vast Pure Land Buddhist temple – the Vatican of Japanese Buddhism.

Best for Quiet Contemplation

Shōren-in (p87)

Hōnen-in (p97)

Tōfuku-ji (p76)

Manshu-in (p75)

Best Temple Gardens

Ryōan-ji (p109)

Tōfuku-ji (p76)

Saihō-ji (p127)

Best Shrines

Fushimi-Inari-Taisha (p76)

Heian-jingū (p99)

Shimogamo-jinja (p73)

NEED TO KNOW

Shrine Admission Fees

You can enter most shrines for free. Some shrines have treasure houses or other special buildings that require an admission fee. This will usually be around ¥400.

Temple Admission Fees

You can enter the grounds of many temples for free, especially larger ones. Others charge an admission fee, averaging around ¥400. Many temples have gardens or special halls that require an admission charge, which also averages around ¥400.

Temple & Shrine Opening Hours

You can enter many shrines 24 hours a day. The same goes for some larger temples. Otherwise, most temples are open 9am to 5pm, seven days a week.

Explore Kyoto

KYOTO'S TOP SIGHTS

Neighbourhoods at a Glance

1 Kyoto Station Area (p48)

Dominated by the eponymous Kyoto Station, this neighbourhood serves as the gateway to Kyoto. Apart from the impressive station building itself, this area is not particularly attractive. That said, there are a few worthwhile sights here: Higashi Hongan-ji and Nishi Hongan-ji are two vast temples within walking distance of the station.

2 Downtown Kyoto (p54)

If you don't give a hoot about temples, shrines and gardens, you might never leave Downtown Kyoto (which is, naturally, smack in the middle of the city). It has just about everything you need: an incredible variety of accommodation, restaurants, nightlife, shopping and entertainment options. And, yes, there are even a few small temples, shrines and museums, plus the famed Nishiki Market.

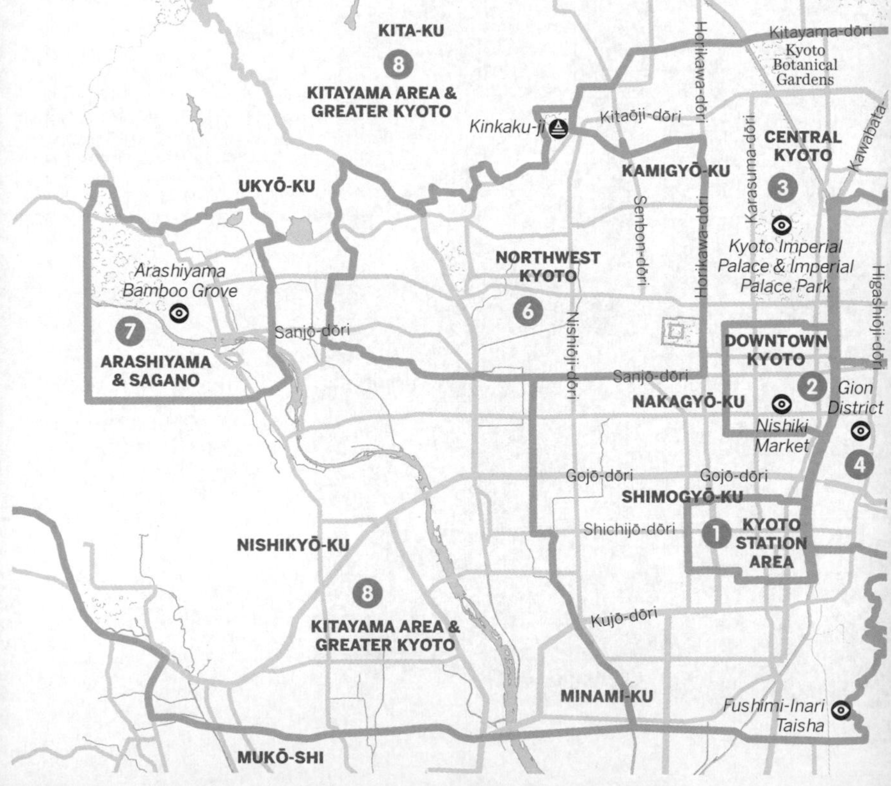

3 Central Kyoto (p69)

Central Kyoto comprises the entire middle of the city (except Downtown Kyoto and the Kyoto Station area). It includes the Kyoto Imperial Palace and its lovely park. To the north is Shimogamo-jinja, a shrine in a forest setting, and to the south Tō-ji, one of Kyoto's oldest temples. Central Kyoto is also home to Daitoku-ji, a self-contained world of Zen temples, gardens and lanes.

4 Southern Higashiyama (p79)

Southern Higashiyama, at the base of the Higashiyama (Eastern Mountains), is Kyoto's richest area for sightseeing. Thick with temples, shrines, museums and traditional shops, it's great to explore on foot, with some pedestrian-only walkways plus parks and expansive temple grounds. It's also home to the Gion entertainment district and some of the city's finest ryokan (Japanese inns).

5 Northern Higashiyama (p92)

At the northern end of the Higashiyama (Eastern Mountains), this area is packed with first-rate attractions and soothing greenery, making it one of the best parts of the city for relaxed sightseeing. It stretches from Nanzen-ji in the south to Ginkaku-ji in the north, two temples linked by the lovely Path of Philosophy (Tetsugaku-no-Michi). Other attractions here include Hōnen-in, a quiet temple overlooked by the crowds, and the museums around Okazaki-kōen.

6 Northwest Kyoto (p104)

Northwest Kyoto contains two of Kyoto's most important temples: Kinkaku-ji, also known as the Golden Pavilion, and Ryōan-ji, home of Japan's most famous Zen garden. Other sights here include the Shōgun's castle of Nijō-jō and the enclosed world of the Myōshin-ji temple.

7 Arashiyama & Sagano (p112)

Arashiyama and Sagano, two adjoining neighbourhoods at the base of Kyoto's western mountains, form the city's second-most-popular sightseeing district. Foreign and domestic tourists flock here to see Tenryū-ji, a temple with a stunning mountain backdrop, and the famous Arashiyama Bamboo Grove. There are also several small temples and a fine hilltop villa.

8 Kitayama Area & Greater Kyoto (p119)

The Kitayama (Northern Mountains) contain several quaint villages that make great day trips out of the city: Kurama, Kibune and Ōhara. Other attractions in the Greater Kyoto area include Uji, famous for tea and temples; Katsura, famous for its imperial villa; Takao, famous for three mountain temples; and Hiei-zan, famous for the mountain temple of Enryaku-ji.

Kyoto Station Area

Neighbourhood Top Five

❶ Feeling the power of Japanese Buddhism expressed in the soaring main halls and their glittering interiors at **Higashi Hongan-ji** (p50). The recently refurbished main hall here is one of the largest wooden buildings on earth.

❷ Climbing to the roof of the **Kyoto Station** (p51).

❸ Savouring the views from the top of **Kyoto Tower** (p51).

❹ Immersing yourself in the grandeur of **Nishi Hongan-ji** (p51).

❺ Escaping the concrete jungle and taking a breather in **Shōsei-en** garden (p51).

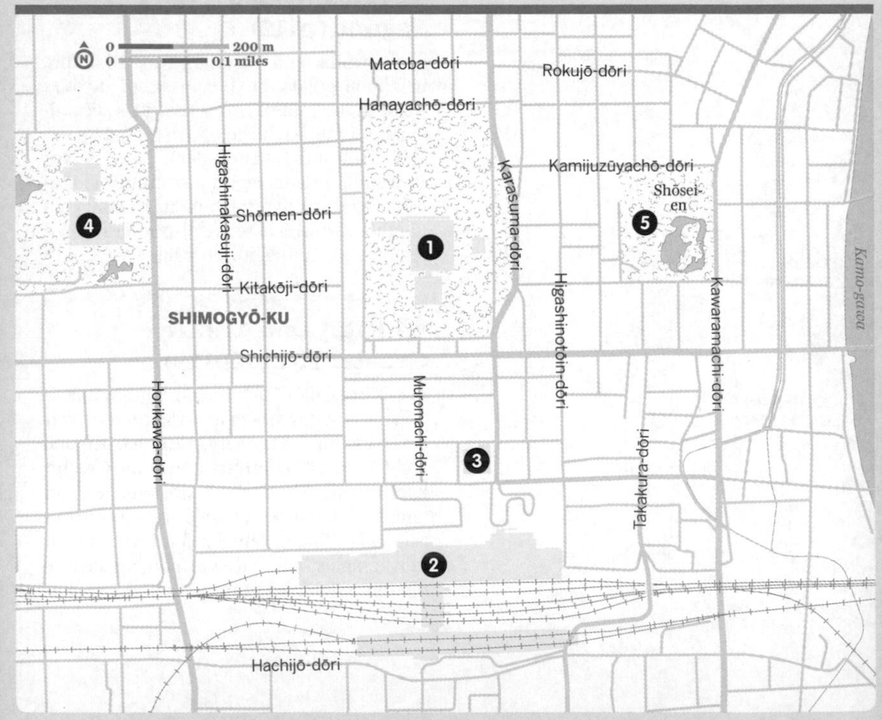

For more detail of this area, see Map p220

Explore: Kyoto Station Area

For most travellers to Kyoto, the Kyoto Station Area serves as the entry point to the city. Odds are, your first step in Kyoto will be onto one of the train platforms in Kyoto Station. This being the case, we should warn you that your first glimpse of the city is likely to be an anticlimax at best, a rude shock at worst: the area around the station is a sea of concrete, neon and billboards. But, rest assured, there is good stuff in every direction.

Like the areas around most train stations in Japan, the Kyoto Station Area is chock-a-block with hotels. However, many people choose to stay in other parts of the city, so they usually hightail it to their digs and skip sightseeing in the Kyoto Station area entirely. This is a shame, since there are some worthwhile sights here, including two of Kyoto's largest and most impressive temples: Higashi Hongan-ji and Nishi Hongan-ji.

Of course, this being the city's main transport hub, the focus here is less on sightseeing and more on meeting your basic needs. The station building itself is packed with restaurants and shops, as are the streets surrounding the buildings. There's a lot of good food here, but few people would head here just to eat, given the offerings in other parts of the city.

Local Life

➡ **Hangout** (p51) The steps leading up to the roof of the station on the west side of the main concourse of Kyoto Station are where local youths congregate.

➡ **Shopping in a hurry** Bic Camera (p52), one of the city's largest and cheapest electronics and camera shops, is connected directly to Kyoto Station by the Nishinotō-in gate.

➡ **Food for the trip** Porta (p53), the shopping area underneath the north side of the station, is crammed with shops that sell take-away food.

Getting There & Away

➡ **Train** The JR lines, including the *shinkansen* (bullet train), and the private Kintetsu line operate to/from Kyoto Station.

➡ **Bus** Many city buses, JR buses and other bus lines operate to/from the Kyoto Station Bus Terminal (on the north side of the station).

➡ **Subway** The Karasuma subway line stops directly underneath Kyoto Station (the Kyoto Station stop is called simply 'Kyoto').

Lonely Planet's Top Tip

During high seasons for tourism (cherry blossom season in April and foliage season in November), the taxi ranks on the south and north side of Kyoto Station can be very long. If you're in a hurry, walk a few blocks north of the station and hail a cab off the street.

Best Things to See

➡ Higashi Hongan-ji (p50)

➡ Nishi Hongan-ji (p51)

➡ Shōsei-en Garden (p51)

For reviews, see p51 ➡

Best Places to Eat

➡ Cube (p52)

➡ Eat Paradise (p52)

➡ Kyoto Rāmen Kōji (p52)

For reviews, see p52 ➡

Best Places to Shop

➡ Bic Camera (p52)

➡ Yodobashi Camera (p52)

➡ Isetan Department Store (p53)

For reviews, see p52 

JTB PHOTO / PHOTOLIBRARY ©

TOP SIGHTS
HIGASHI HONGAN-JI

A short walk north of Kyoto Station, Higashi Hongan-ji is the focus of worship for millions of followers of Jōdo Shin-shū (True Pure Land Buddhism), the most populist and inclusive of all Japanese Buddhist sects. The halls are suitably vast, with glittering interiors that call to mind the Pure Land to which the followers of the sect aspire. The soothing traditional contours of the main gate and main hall are usually the first traditional sights glimpsed by the visitor to Kyoto – heartening symbols that 'Old Kyoto' can still be found amid the neon and concrete of the modern city.

Higashi Hongan-ji (Eastern Temple of the True Vow) was established in 1602 by Shōgun Tokugawa Ieyasu in a 'divide and conquer' attempt to weaken the power of the enormously popular Jōdo Shin-shū (True Pure Land) school. The temple is now the headquarters of the Ōtani branch of Jōdo Shin-shū.

The temple is dominated by the vast Founder's Hall (Goei-dō), which is said to be the second-largest wooden structure in Japan. Standing 38m high, 76m long and 58m wide, the recently refurbished hall contains an image of Shinran, the founder of the sect, although the image is often hidden behind sumptuous gilded doors.

A wooden passageway connects the Founder's Hall with the adjoining Amida-dō Hall (south/left of the Founder's Hall), which contains an image of Amida, the Buddha of the Western Paradise (also known as 'the Pure Land'). While you can enter the hall, the entire structure is presently being refurbished and the hall is covered by a vast superstructure.

There's a tremendous coil of rope made from human hair on display in the passageway. Following the destruction of the temple in the 1880s, a group of female temple devotees donated their locks to make the ropes that hauled the massive timbers used for reconstruction.

DON'T MISS...

- The coil of human-hair rope

PRACTICALITIES

- Map p220
- ☎371-9181
- Shichijō agaru, Karasuma-dōri, Shimogyō-ku
- admission free
- ⏲5.50am-5.30pm Mar-Oct, 6.20am-4.30pm Nov-Feb
- 🚉Kyoto Station, JR & Kintetsu lines & Karasuma subway line

SIGHTS

KYOTO STATION — NOTABLE BUILDING

Map p220 (京都駅; ☎JR West 0570-00-2486, 078-382-8686; Shimogyō-ku, Karasuma-dōri, Shiokōji sagaru, Higashishiokō-ji-chō; Ⓜ Kyoto Station) The Kyoto Station building is a striking steel-and-glass structure – a kind of futuristic cathedral for the transport age. Unveiled in September 1997, the building met with some decidedly mixed reviews. Some critics assail the building as being not in keeping with the traditional architecture of Kyoto; others love its wide-open spaces and dramatic lines.

Whatever the case, you are sure to be impressed by the tremendous space that arches above you as you enter the main concourse. Moreover, you will probably enjoy a brief exploration of the many levels of the station, all the way up to the 15th-floor observation level. And be sure to take the escalator from the 7th floor on the east side of the building up to the 11th-floor glass corridor that runs high above the main concourse of the station – though it's not a good spot for those with a fear of heights!

Located in the station building, you will discover several food courts, as well as the Isetan Department Store and the Kyoto Tourist Information Center (TIC; p196). The station is on the JR and Kintetsu lines and the Karasuma subway line.

KYOTO TOWER — NOTABLE BUILDING

Map p220 (京都タワー; (☎361-3215; Shichijō sagaru, Karasuma, Shimogyō-ku; admission ¥770; ⏲9am-9pm, last entry 8.40pm; Ⓜ 5min walk from Kyoto Station central exit) If you want to orient yourself as soon as you arrive in town, this is the place to do so. Located right outside the Karasuma (north) gate of the station, this retro tower looks like a rocket perched atop the Kyoto Tower Hotel. The tower provides excellent views in all directions and you can really get a sense for the Kyoto *bonchi* (flat basin). There are free mounted binoculars to use, and these allow ripping views over to Kiyomizu-dera (p81) and as far south as Osaka.

FREE NISHI HONGAN-JI — TEMPLE

Map p220 (西本願寺; ☎371-5181; Hanaya-chō sagaru, Horikawa-dōri, Shimogyō-ku; ⏲6am-5pm Nov-Feb, 5.30am-5.30pm Mar, Apr, Sep & Oct, to 6pm May-Aug; Ⓜ 15min walk from Kyoto Station central exit) In 1591 Toyotomi Hideyoshi built this temple, known as Hongan-ji, as the new headquarters for the Jōdo Shin-shū (True Pure Land) school of Buddhism, which had accumulated immense power. Later, Tokugawa Ieyasu saw this power as a threat and sought to weaken it by encouraging a breakaway faction of this school to found Higashi Hongan-ji (*higashi* means 'east') in 1602. The original Hongan-ji then became known as Nishi Hongan-ji (*nishi* means 'west'). It now functions as the headquarters of the Hongan-ji branch of the Jōdo Shin-shū school, with over 10,000 temples and 12 million followers worldwide.

The temple contains five buildings, featuring some of the finest examples of architecture and artistic achievement from the Azuchi-Momoyama period (1568–1600). The **Goei-dō** (main hall) is a marvellous sight. Another must-see building is the **Daisho-in Hall**, which has sumptuous paintings, carvings and metal ornamentation. A small garden and two nō (stylised Japanese dance-drama) stages are connected with the hall. The dazzling **Kara-mon** has intricate ornamental carvings.

FIRST IMPRESSIONS

Your first impression of Kyoto will probably be a bit of a letdown. While Kyoto Station itself is an impressive building, when you see the sea of drab buildings that surround the station, you'll probably wonder if you've gotten off at the right stop. Don't despair: Kyoto *is* a beautiful city, it's just that its beauty is hidden away in corners and pockets of the city, often behind walls. As soon as you get into the sightseeing districts of Southern Higashiyama, Northern Higashiyama and Arashiyama, you'll see what we mean. Even near Kyoto Station, you'll see the lovely pagoda at Tō-ji temple, which will give you faith that there is plenty of beauty to be found in the 'Old Capital'.

HIGASHI HONGAN-JI — TEMPLE

See p50.

SHŌSEI-EN — GARDEN

Map p220 (渉成園; ☎371-9210; Shichijō agaru, Karasuma-dōri, Shimogyō-ku; admission ¥500; ⏲9am-3.30pm; Ⓜ 15min walk from Kyoto Station central exit) About five minutes' walk east of Higashi Hongan-ji, this garden is a nice green island in a vast expanse of concrete. While it's not on par with many other gardens in Kyoto, it's worth a visit if you find yourself in need of something to do near the station, perhaps paired with a visit to the temple. The lovely grounds, incorporating the Kikoku-tei villa, were completed in 1657.

EATING

TOP CHOICE EAT PARADISE — JAPANESE ¥

Map p220 (イートパラダイス; ☎352-1111; Higashi Shiokōji-chō, Shiokōji sagaru, Karasuma dōri, Shimogyō-ku; ⌚11am-10pm; Ⓜ2min walk from Kyoto Station) Up on the 11th floor of the Kyoto Station building, you'll find this collection of decent restaurants. Among the choices here are **Tonkatsu Wako** for *tonkatsu* (deep-fried breaded pork cutlet), **Tenichi** for sublime tempura, and **Wakuden** for approachable *kaiseki* (Japanese haute cuisine). Take the west escalators from the main concourse to get here – Eat Paradise is in front of you when you get to the 11th floor. Note that the restaurants here can be crowded, especially at lunchtimes on weekends.

TOP CHOICE CUBE — JAPANESE ¥

Map p220 (ザ キューブ; ☎371-2134; 11F Kyoto Station Bldg, 901 Higashi Shiokōji-chō, Shiokōji sagaru, Karasuma dōri, Shimogyō-ku; ⌚11am-10pm; Ⓜ2min walk from Kyoto Station) On the same floor as Eat Paradise, this is another good collection of restaurants. You'll see it on your left as you get to the 11th floor.

KYOTO RĀMEN KŌJI — RĀMEN ¥

Map p220 (京都拉麺小路; ☎361-4401; 10F Kyoto Station Bldg, Higashi Shiokōji-chō, Shiokōji sagaru, Karasuma dōri, Shimogyō-ku; ⌚11am-10pm; rāmen ¥700-1000; Ⓜ2min walk from Kyoto Station) If you love your noodles, do not miss this collection of seven *rāmen* restaurants on the 10th floor (underneath the Cube). Buy tickets from the machines, which have pictures but no English writing. In addition to *rāmen*, you can get green-tea ice cream and other Japanese desserts at **Chasen**, and *tako-yaki* (battered octopus pieces) at **Miyako**.

JŌJŌ — IZAKAYA ¥¥

Map p220 (乗々; ☎371-2010; Shimogyō-ku, Nishinotoin, Shichijō-sagaru; dinner from ¥2500; ⌚5.30pm-1am; Ⓡ5min walk from JR Kyoto Station) Jōjō is a funky modern *izakaya* within walking distance of Kyoto Station. Sit at the counter or at one of the tables. There's an excellent variety of sake to choose from and a wide variety of dishes to go with it.

IIMURA — JAPANESE ¥

Map p220 (いいむら; ☎351-8023; Shimogyō-ku, Shichijō-dōri, Higashinotōin Nishi iru, Maoya-chō 216; lunch sets ¥650; ⌚11.30am-2pm; Ⓜ5min walk from Kyoto Station) Try this classic little restaurant for its ever-changing set lunch – usually simple Japanese home-style cooking. Dishes might include a bit of fish or meat and the usual accompaniments of rice, miso soup and pickles. It's in a traditional Japanese house set back a bit from the street, next to a new five-storey building (look for the black-and-white sign).

SHOPPING

TOP CHOICE BIC CAMERA — ELECTRONICS

Map p220 (ビックカメラ; ☎353-1111; Kyoto Station Bldg, 927 Higashi Shiokōji-chō, Shimogyō-ku; ⌚10am-9pm; ⓂKyoto Station) This vast new shop is directly connected to Kyoto Station via the Nishinotō-in gate; otherwise, it's accessed by leaving the north (Karasuma) gate and walking west. You will be amazed by the sheer amount of goods this store has on display. Just be sure that an English operating manual is available for your purchases. For computer peripherals/software, keep in mind that not all items on offer will work with English operating systems.

TOP CHOICE YODOBASHI CAMERA — ELECTRONICS

Map p220 (ヨドバシカメラ; ☎351-1010; 590-2 Higashi Shiokōji-chō, Shimogyō-ku; ⌚9.30am-10pm; ⓂKyoto Station) A major new rival for Bic Camera, this mammoth shop sells a similar range of electronics, camera and computer goods and also has a restaurant floor, supermarket, bookshop, cafe and, well, the list goes on. It's a few minutes' walk north of Kyoto Station.

AVANTI DEPARTMENT STORE

Map p220 (アバンティ; ☎682-5031; Minami-ku, Higashikujō Nishisannō-chō 31; ⏰10am-9pm; Ⓜ1min walk from Kyoto Station, Hachijōguchi exit) This department store has a decent bookshop on its 6th floor, and a food court and supermarket on its B1 floor. It's geared mostly to younger Kyoto shoppers but it's good for browsing if you have time to kill while waiting for a train. Take the underground passage from Kyoto Station.

TOP CHOICE **ISETAN DEPARTMENT STORE** DEPARTMENT STORE

Map p220 (伊勢丹百貨店; ☎352-1111; Shimogyō-ku, Karasuma-dōri, Shiokō-ji sagaru, Higashi shiokō-ji-chō; ⏰10am-8pm, closed irregularly; 🚉JR Kyoto Station) This large, elegant department store is located inside the Kyoto Station building, making it perfect for a last-minute spot of shopping before hopping on the train to the airport. Don't miss the B1 and B2 food floors.

KYŌSEN-DŌ JAPANESE CRAFTS

Map p220 (京扇堂; ☎371-4151; Shimogyō-ku, Higashinotōin-dōri, Shōmen agaru, Tsutsuganechō 46; ⏰9am-5pm Mon-Sat, 10am-6pm Sun & public holidays; Ⓜ10min walk from Kyoto Station) Kyōsen-dō sells a colourful variety of paper fans; here you can see the process of assembling the fans and even paint your own.

KUNGYOKU-DŌ JAPANESE CRAFTS

Map p220 (薫玉堂; ☎371-0162; Shimogyō-ku, Horikawa-dōri, Nishihonganji-mae; ⏰9am-5.30pm, closed 1st & 3rd Sun each month; Ⓜ15min walk from Kyoto Station) A haven for the olfactory sense, this place has sold incense and aromatic woods (for burning, similar to incense) for four centuries. It's opposite the gate of Nishi Hongan-ji.

PORTA SHOPPING MALL SHOPPING CENTRE

Map p220 (ポルタ; ☎365-7528; 902 Higashi Shiokōji-chō, Shiokōji sagaru, Karasuma dōri, Shimogyō-ku; ⏰10am-8pm; ⓂKyoto Station) Located under the front (north side) of Kyoto Station (take the escalators down from just outside the central gate), you'll find this utilitarian shopping mall that's crammed with restaurants, cafes, clothing stores and electronics/camera shops. It's good for a quick bite before a long trip.

KŌJITSU SANSŌ OUTDOOR EQUIPMENT

Map p220 (好日山荘; ☎708-5178; 5F Kyoto Yodobashi, 590-2 Higashi shiokōji-chō, Karasuma dōri Shichijō sagaru, Shimogyō-ku ⏰9.30am-10pm; ⓂKyoto Station) On the 5th floor of Yodobashi Camera (p52), this is one of Kyoto's biggest outdoor goods shops. If you're heading up to the Japan Alps to do some hiking, you might want to stop here before getting on the train.

Downtown Kyoto

Neighbourhood Top Five

❶ Walking through **Nishiki Market** (p56), marvelling at all the weird and wonderful ingredients that go into Kyoto cuisine. Nishiki is the perfect way to spend a rainy day in Kyoto, and it's a good antidote to an overdose of temples.

❷ Taking an evening stroll along **Pontochō** (p57).

❸ Delving into the world of manga at the **Kyoto International Manga Museum** (p57).

❹ Getting lost in the department store food floors at **Takashimaya** (p65) or **Daimaru** (p65).

❺ Shopping for the perfect gift in the shopping district around Shijō and Kawaramachi streets.

For more detail of this area, see Map p216

Explore: Downtown Kyoto

The downtown area is two subway stops north of Kyoto Station (about 2km). Downtown Kyoto is bounded by the Kamo-gawa (the river) to the east, Karasuma-dōri to the west, Oike-dōri to the north and Shijō-dōri to the south. In this relatively small square area, you will find the thickest selection of restaurants, shops, hotels and businesses in all of Kyoto.

While Downtown Kyoto does contain a handful of first-rate sights, sightseeing here is more about soaking up the vibe. Downtown Kyoto is easily reached from almost anywhere in town: the city's two subway lines serve the area, as does the private Hankyū line, and the private Keihan line, which stops just across the river. You could even walk from Kyoto Station to Downtown Kyoto in about half an hour.

The main streets of Shijō and Kawaramachi hold some of the biggest shops, but you'll also find a huge selection of shops in the area's four covered shopping streets (known as *shōtengai*): Sanjō (good for restaurants), Teramachi (a mix of art, religious items and tat), Shinkyōgoku (mostly tacky souvenirs for kids) and Nishiki Market (the city's main food market). But don't just explore these main shopping streets: also head into the maze of smaller streets west of Teramachi, where you'll find a great array of interesting boutiques and restaurants.

Local Life

➡ **Hangout** (p67) The new Mina shopping complex, with branches of Uniclo and Loft stores, is popular with everyone.

➡ **Meeting Point** The Starbucks at Sanjō-Ōhashi is the preferred meeting spot for locals and foreigners alike.

➡ **Romantic Spot** Paris has the Seine and Kyoto has the Kamo-gawa. This is where local couples go for a bit of 'quality time'.

Getting There & Away

➡ **Subway** The Karasuma subway line stops at Shijō and Karasuma-Oike stations.

➡ **Train** The Hankyū line stops at Karasuma and Kawaramachi.

➡ **Bus** Many city buses stop in Downtown Kyoto.

Lonely Planet's Top Tip

Finding a good place to eat in Downtown Kyoto can be confusing (there are almost *too many* places to choose from). If you want a lot of choices in a small area, hit one of the *resutoran-gai* (restaurant floors) at Takashimaya (p65) or Daimaru (p65).

Best Places to Eat

➡ Ippūdō (p58)
➡ Kane-yo (p59)
➡ Yoshikawa (p58)

For reviews, see p58 ➡

Best Places to Drink

➡ McLoughlin's Irish Bar & Restaurant (p64)
➡ Sama Sama (p64)
➡ World (p65)

For reviews, see p64 ➡

Best Places to Shop

➡ Mina (p67)
➡ OPA (p67)
➡ Takashiyama (p65)
➡ Daimaru (p65)
➡ Teramachi *shōtengai* (p56)

For reviews, see p65 ➡

GREG ELMS / LONELY PLANET IMAGES ©

TOP SIGHTS
NISHIKI MARKET

Nishiki Market (*Nishiki-kōji Ichiba* in Japanese) is one of Kyoto's real highlights, especially if you have an interest in cooking and eating. Commonly known as *Kyoto no daidokoro* ('Kyoto's Kitchen') by locals, Nishiki is where a lot of Kyoto's high-end restaurateurs and wealthy individuals do their food shopping. If you want to see all the weird and wonderful foods that go into Kyoto cuisine, this is the place.

Nishiki Market is right smack in the centre of town, one block north of Shijō-dōri, running from Teramachi *shōtengai* to Takakura-dōri (ending almost behind Daimaru department store). Covered for its entire length, this pedestrian-only market is home to 126 shops (at last count). It's said that there were stores here as early as the 14th century, and it's known for sure that the street was a wholesale fish market in the Edo Period (1600–1868). After the end of Edo, as Japan entered the modern era, the market became a retail market, which it remains today.

The emphasis is on locally produced Japanese food items like *tsukemono* (Japanese pickles), tea, beans, rice, seaweed and fish (if you know how to read Japanese or know what to look for, you'll even see the odd bit of whale meat). In recent years, the market has been evolving from a strictly local food market into a tourist attraction, and you'll now find several souvenir shops selling Kyoto-style souvenirs mixed in among the food stalls.

The Aritsugu knife shop (p65) turns out some of the most exquisite knives on earth. Take some time to pick the perfect one for your needs, then watch as the craftsmen carefully put a final edge on the knife with the giant round sharpening stone – the final product will be so sharp it will scare you.

DON'T MISS...

- Aritsugu

PRACTICALITIES

- Map p216
- ☎211-3882
- Nishikikōji-dōri btwn Teramachi & Takakura
- ⏲9am-5pm
- Ⓜ Shijō Station, Karasuma subway line; Kawaramachi or Karasuma stations, Hankyū line

SIGHTS

KYOTO INTERNATIONAL MANGA MUSEUM — MUSEUM

Map p216 (京都国際マンガミュージアム; ☎25 4-7414; www.kyotomm.com/english; Oike agaru, Karasuma-dōri, Nakagyō-ku; adult/child ¥800/300; ⏲10am-6pm, closed Wed; Ⓜ3min walk from Karasuma-Oike Station, Karasuma & Tōzai subway lines) This fine museum has a collection of some 300,000 manga (Japanese comic books). Located in an old elementary school building, the museum is the perfect introduction to the art of manga. While most of the manga and displays are in Japanese, the collection of translated works is growing.

In addition to the galleries that show both the historical development of manga and original artwork done in manga style, there are beginners' workshops and portrait drawings on weekends. Visitors with children will appreciate the children's library and the occasional performances of *kami-shibai* (humorous traditional Japanese sliding-picture shows), not to mention the AstroTurf lawn where the kids can run free. The museum hosts six month-long special exhibits yearly: check the website for details.

PONTOCHŌ — NEIGHBOURHOOD

Map p216 (先斗町; Nakagyō-ku; 🅁2min walk from Kawaramachi Station, Hankyū line) There are few streets in Asia that rival this narrow pedestrian-only walkway for atmosphere. Not much to look at by day, the street comes alive by night, with wonderful lanterns, traditional wooden exteriors and elegant Kyotoites disappearing into the doorways of elite old restaurants and bars.

Pontochō is between the Kamo-gawa and Kiyamachi-dōri. Many of the restaurants and teahouses can be difficult to enter, but several reasonably priced, accessible places can be found. Even if you have no intention of patronising one of the businesses here, it makes a nice stroll in the evening, perhaps combined with a walk in nearby Gion.

Pontochō is also a great place to spot *geiko* (geisha) and *maiko* (apprentice geisha) making their way between appointments, especially on weekend evenings at the Shijō-dōri end of the street.

NISHIKI MARKET — MARKET

See p56.

MUSEUM OF KYOTO — MUSEUM

Map p216 (京都文化博物館; ☎222-0888; Takakura-dōri, Sanjō agaru, Nakagyō-ku; admission ¥500, extra for special exhibitions; ⏲10am-7.30pm, special exhibitions to 6pm Sat-Thu, 7.30pm Fri; Ⓜ3min walk from Karasuma-Oike Station, Karasuma & Tōzai subway lines) This museum is worth visiting if a special exhibition is on (the regular exhibits are not particularly interesting and don't have much in the way of English explanations). On the 1st floor, the Roji Tempō is a reconstruction of a typical merchant area in Kyoto during the Edo period (this section can be entered free; some of the shops sell souvenirs and serve local dishes). Check the *Kyoto Visitors Guide* or *Kansai Time Out* for upcoming special exhibitions.

KYOTO COMMON SENSE

Common sense varies from place to place. In New York, you take the subway. In Kathmandu, you avoid drinking the tap water. In Russia, you don't challenge the locals to drinking contests. In Kyoto, even if you dispense with common sense, you don't run the risk of serious trouble, but there are a few things to keep in mind that will make everything easier and perhaps a little safer:

- **Look both ways** when exiting a shop or hotel onto a pavement – there is almost always someone on a bicycle coming tearing your way. This is especially important if you have young ones in tow.
- **Don't take a taxi** in the main Higashiyama sightseeing district during cherry blossom season – the streets will be so crowded that it will be faster to walk or cycle.
- **Never wait in line for food** even in the busy season. There are so many restaurants in Kyoto that it never makes sense to wait in line to get into a crowded restaurant (you'll see local tourists queuing at popular spots, but there's no need to follow their example).

KALEIDOSCOPE MUSEUM OF KYOTO MUSEUM

Map p216 (京都万華鏡ミュージアム; ☎254-7902; Nakagyō-ku, Aneyakōji, Takakura; adult/child ¥300/200, special exhibits extra; ⌚10am-5.30pm, closed Mon; Ⓜ3min walk from Karasuma-Oike Station, Karasuma & Tōzai subway lines) This one-room museum is filled with unexpected wonders. Frankly, we had no idea of the variety and complexity in the field of kaleidoscopes. We don't know who will enjoy this more, children or the adults trying to keep them entertained. It's right behind the Museum of Kyoto.

SHIORI-AN MUSEUM

Map p216 (紫織庵; ☎241-0215; Nakagyō-ku, Aneyakōji, Takakura; admission ¥500; ⌚10am-5pm; Ⓜ5min walk from Karasuma-Oike Station, Karasuma & Tōzai subway lines) Located in a large traditional merchant's house, this kimono-shop/museum is a great place to learn about kimono and the history of kimono. You can also see the way part of the traditional building was converted into a Western-style building around the turn of last century (when Japan became fascinated with all things Western). There is an English brochure available.

EATING

TOP CHOICE YOSHIKAWA TEMPURA ¥¥¥

Map p216 (吉川; ☎221-5544; Oike sagaru, Tominokōji, Nakagyō-ku; lunch ¥3000-25,000, dinner ¥6000-25,000; ⌚11am-2pm & 5-8.30pm; 🗐; Ⓜ5min walk from Karasuma-Oike Station, Karasuma & Tōzai subway lines) This is the place to go for delectable tempura. It offers table seating, but it's much more interesting to sit and eat around the small counter and observe the chefs at work. It's near Oike-dōri in a fine traditional Japanese-style building. Reservation required for tatami room; counter and table seating unavailable on Sunday.

TOP CHOICE IPPŪDŌ RĀMEN ¥

Map p216 (一風堂; ☎213-8800; 653-1 Bantōya-chō, Nishikikōji higashiiru, Higashinotōin, Nakagyō-ku; rāmen around ¥750-950; ⌚11am-2am; 🗐; Ⓜ1min walk from Shijō Station, Karasuma subway line or Karasuma Station, Hankyū line) There's a reason that there's usually a line outside this *rāmen* joint at lunchtime: the *rāmen* is awesome and the bite-sized *gyōza* (Chinese dumplings) are to die for. We recommend the *gyōza* set meal, which costs ¥750 or ¥850 depending on your choice of *rāmen*. It's on Nishiki-dōri, next to a post office and diagonally across from a Starbucks.

TŌSUIRŌ TOFU ¥¥

Map p216 (豆水楼; ☎251-1600; Nakagyō-ku, Kiyamachi-dōri, Sanjō agaru, Kamiōsaka-chō 517-3; lunch/dinner ¥2000/5000; ⌚11.30am-2pm & 5-9.30pm Mon-Sat, noon-8.30pm Sun; Ⓜ5min walk from Kyoto-Shiyakusho-mae Station, Tōzai subway line) We really like this specialist tofu restaurant. It's got great traditional Japanese decor and in summer you can sit on the *yuka* (dining platform) outside and take in a view of the Kamo-gawa. You will most probably be amazed by the incredible variety of dishes that can be created with tofu. At lunch, the *machiya-zen* (tofu set; ¥2205) is highly recommended. At dinner, we suggest the Higashiyama tofu set (¥3858). Tōsuirō is at the end of an alley on the north side.

GANKO ZUSHI SUSHI ¥¥

Map p216 (がんこ寿司; ☎255-1128; 101 Nakajima-chō, Kawaramachi Higashi iru, Sanjō-dōri, Nakagyō-ku; lunch/dinner ¥1500/3000 per person; ⌚11am-11pm; 🗐; Ⓜ5min walk from Kyoto-Shiyakusho-mae Station, Tōzai subway line) This giant four-storey dining hall is part of Kansai's biggest sushi chain. The ground floor is the sushi area (you can order non-sushi dishes here as well); it has a long sushi counter and plenty of tables (and room for a stroller if you have tots in tow). Despite the fact that it looks a bit touristy, it's actually quite good. There's an extensive English/picture menu and the set meals are good value. Downstairs is an *izakaya* (pub-eatery) and upstairs has rooms for parties. This place may have the most plastic-looking food models of any restaurant window in Kyoto. It's near the Sanjō-Ōhashi bridge.

KIYAMACHI SAKURAGAWA KAISEKI ¥¥¥

Map p216 (木屋町　櫻川; ☎255-4477; Nakagyō-ku, Kiyamachi-dōri, Nijō sagaru, Kamikoriki-chō 491 1F; ⌚11.30am-2pm & 5-9pm, closed Sun; lunch/dinner sets from ¥5000/10,000; Ⓜ3min walk from Kyoto Shiyakusho-mae Station, Tōzai subway line) This elegant restaurant behind the Hotel Okura on Kiyamachi-dōri, is an excellent place to try *kaiseki* (Japanese haute cuisine). The modest but fully satisfying food is beautifully presented and it's a joy to watch the chef in action. The warmth of the reception adds to the quality of the food. Reservations are recommended and smart casual is the way to go here.

UOSUE JAPANESE ¥¥

Map p216 (うをすえ; 351-1437; Shimogyō-ku, Ayakōji-dōri, Higashinotōin Higashi iru, Shinmei-chō 724; lunch & bentō ¥1050, dinner from ¥3990; 11am-2pm & 5-10pm, closed Sun; 1min walk from Karasuma Station, Karasuma subway line) Uosue is one of the best-value Japanese places in town. It's a traditional Kyoto-style restaurant with a clean interior and friendly proprietors. For lunch, try the wonderful *nijū bentō* for ¥1000. At dinner, the *omakase ryōri kōsu* is a great way to sample *kaiseki ryōri* without breaking the bank: it costs just ¥3800. It's next to a tiny shrine – keep an eye out for the sake barrels out the front.

TOP CHOICE **KANE-YO** UNAGI ¥

Map p216 (かねよ; 221-0669; Rokkaku, Shinkyōgoku, Nakagyō-ku; unagi from ¥950; 11.30am-8.30pm; ; 6min walk from Sanjō Station exit 6, Keihan line) This is a good place to try *unagi,* that most sublime of Japanese dishes. You can choose to either sit downstairs with a nice view of the waterfall, or upstairs on the tatami. The *kane-yo donburi* (eel over rice; ¥890) set is excellent value. Look for the barrels of live eels outside and the wooden facade.

TAGOTO HONTEN KAISEKI ¥¥

Map p216 (田ごと本店; 221-1811; 34 Otabi-chō, Shijō dōri Kawaramachi Nishiiru, Shimogyō-ku; lunch/dinner from ¥1600/3700; 11am-3pm & 4.30-9pm; 1min walk from Kawaramachi Station, Hankyū line) Across the street from Takashimaya department store, this long-standing Kyoto restaurant serves approachable *kaiseki* fare in a variety of rooms, both private and common. Their *kiku* set (¥1890) includes some sashimi, a bit of tempura and a variety of other nibblies. *Kaiseki* dinner courses start at ¥6300 and you must make reservations in advance. This is a good spot for those who want a civilised meal downtown in relaxing surroundings. There's an English sign.

MISHIMA-TEI SUKIYAKI ¥¥¥

Map p216 (三嶋亭; 221-0003; 405 Sakurano-chō, Sanjō sagaru, Teramachi-dōri, Nakagyō-ku; sukiyaki lunch & dinner from ¥8700; 11.30am-10pm, closed Wed; ; 5min walk from Kyoto-Shiyakusho-mae Station, Tōzai subway line) This is an inexpensive place to sample sukiyaki. The quality of the meat here is very high, which is hardly surprising when you consider there is a butcher right downstairs. There is an English menu, a special lunch (¥4505) served until 3pm and a discount for foreign travellers! It's in the intersection of the Sanjō and Teramachi covered arcades.

CAFÉ BIBLIOTEC HELLO! CAFE ¥

Map p216 (カフェビブリオティック ハロー; 231-8625; 650 Seimei-chō, Yanaginobanba higashi iru, Nijō, Nakagyō-ku; meals from ¥850, coffee ¥450; 11.30am-midnight; ; 10min walk from Kyoto-Shiyakusho-mae Station, Tōzai subway line) As the name suggests, books line the walls of this cool cafe located in a converted *machiya* (traditional Japanese town house). You can get the usual range of coffee and tea drinks here, as well as light cafe lunches. It's popular with young ladies who work nearby and it's a great place to relax with a book or magazine. Look for the plants out the front.

HINAKA JAPANESE ¥¥

Map p216 (旬肴ひなか; 231-5525; Nakagyō-ku, Nabeya-chō 214-1, Asahi Pontochō Bldg 1F; dishes ¥700-1000; 5pm-11pm, closed Mon; 3min walk from Kawaramachi Station, Hankyū line) Hinaka is a small locals' favourite on Pontochō, one of Kyoto's most atmospheric walkways. The menu includes Kyoto specialities like tofu and *yuba* (tofu skim), as well as fresh seasonal vegetables and fish. The chef hails from one of Kyoto's best known restaurants. He opened here in the spring of 2010 and has already attracted a loyal following, who come here to dine at the counter or at tables with sunken floors (no knee strain here).

TSUKIMOCHIYA NAOMASA SWEETS ¥

Map p216 (月餅家 直正; 231-0175; Nakagyō-ku, Kiyamachi-dōri, Sanjō agaru, Kamiōsaka-chō 530; tsukimochi ¥150; 9.30am-7pm, closed Thu; 5min walk from Sanjō Station, Keihan line) This classic old sweet shop, about 50m north of Sanjō-dōri on Kiyamachi-dōri, is a great place to get acquainted with traditional Kyoto sweets. Just point at what looks good and they'll wrap it up nicely for you. There's no English sign; look for the traditional Kyoto exterior and the sweets in the window. It's closed on the third Wednesday of the month.

TOMIZUSHI SUSHI ¥¥

Map p216 (とみ寿司; ☎231-3628; Nakagyō-ku, Shinkyōgoku-dōri, Shijō agaru, Nakano-chō 578-5; dinner ¥3000; ⊙5pm-midnight, closed Thu; 5min walk from Kawaramachi Station, Hankyū line) For good sushi in lively surroundings, try Tomizushi, where you can rub elbows with your neighbours at a long marble counter and watch as some of the fastest sushi chefs in the land do their thing. Go early or be prepared to wait in a queue. It's near the Shijō-Kawaramachi crossing; look for the lantern and the black-and-white signs.

ZU ZU IZAKAYA ¥¥

Map p216 (厨厨; ☎231-0736; Nakagyō-ku, Pontochō, Takoyakushi agaru, Nishi gawa; dinner ¥3000-4000; ⊙6pm-2am, to midnight Sun, closed Tue; 5min walk from Kawaramachi Station, Hankyū line) This Pontochō *izakaya* is a fun place to eat. The best bet when ordering is to ask the waiter for a recommendation. The fare is sort of nouveau Japanese, with menu items such as shrimp with tofu and chicken with plum sauce. Look for the white stucco exterior and black bars on the windows.

MUKADE-YA JAPANESE ¥¥

Map p216 (百足屋; ☎256-7039; Nakagyō-ku, Shinmachi-dōri-Nishikikōji; lunch/dinner from ¥3150/5250; ⊙11am-2pm & 5-9pm, closed Wed; M5min walk from Shijō Station, Karasuma subway line) Mukade-ya is an atmospheric restaurant located in an exquisite *machiya* west of Karasuma-dōri. For lunch try the special *bentō* (box meal): two rounds (five small dishes each) of delectable *obanzai* (Kyoto-style home cooking) fare. *Kaiseki* courses start at ¥5250.

MERRY ISLAND CAFÉ INTERNATIONAL ¥¥

Map p216 (メリーアイランド カフェ; ☎213-0214; Oike agaru, Kiyamachi-dōri, Nakagyō-ku; lunch from ¥1050; ⊙11.30am-11pm; ; M5min walk from Kyoto-Shiyakusho-mae Station, Tōzai subway line) This popular restaurant strives to recreate the atmosphere of a tropical resort. The menu is *mukokuseki* (without nationality) and most of what is on offer is pretty tasty. It does a good risotto and occasionally offers a nice piece of Japanese steak. In warm weather the front doors are opened and the place takes on the air of a pavement cafe (and it doesn't hurt that it's located on one of the prettiest streets in Kyoto).

SHIZENHA RESTAURANT OBANZAI OBANZAI ¥¥

Map p216 (自然派レストランおばんざい; ☎223-6623; 199 Shimomyōkaku-ji-chō, Oike agaru, Koromonotana-dōri, Nakagyō-ku; lunch/dinner ¥840/2100; ⊙11am-2pm & 5-9pm, closed dinner Wed; ; M5min walk from Karasuma-Oike Station, Karasuma & Tōzai subway lines) A little out of the way, but nevertheless good value, this place serves a decent buffet-style lunch and dinner of mostly organic Japanese vegetarian food. It's northwest of the Karasuma-Oike crossing, set back a bit from the street.

CAPRICCIOSA ITALIAN ¥¥

Map p216 (カプリチョーザ; ☎221-7496; Nakagyō-ku, Kawaramachi-dōri-Sanjō sagaru; lunch/dinner from ¥1000/1500; ⊙11.30am-11pm; ; 5min walk from Sanjō Station, Keihan line) For heaped portions of pasta at rock-bottom prices you won't do much better than this long-time student favourite. Pasta dishes start at around ¥800 and you can try pizzas, salads, and various meat and fish dishes. It will definitely not be the best Italian you've ever had, but you'll probably leave full and happy. It's near the Sanjō-Kawaramachi crossing; look for the red-brick steps and the green awning. There's an English menu and an English sign.

OMEN NIPPON JAPANESE, UDON ¥¥

Map p216 (おめんNippon; ☎253-0377; Nakagyō-ku, Shijō-dōri, Pontochō Nishi iru; Omen ¥1050; ⊙11.30am-3pm & 5-10pm, closed Thu; ; 2min walk from Kawaramachi Station exit 1, Hankyū line) This is one of two Downtown branches of the famous Ginkaku-ji noodle restaurant. It serves a variety of healthy set meals, including a good ¥1900 lunch set that includes noodles and a few sides. It's a small, calm place that's a nice oasis amid the Downtown mayhem, good for a light lunch while out shopping, and it has an English menu to boot. Look for the word 'Nippon' on the sign.

BIOTEI VEGETARIAN ¥

Map p216 (びお亭; ☎255-0086; 2F M&I Bldg, 28 Umetada-chō, Higashinotōin Nishi iru, Sanjō-dōri, Nakagyō-ku; lunch from ¥840; ⊙11.30am-2pm Tue-Fri, 5-8.30pm Tue, Wed, Fri & Sat; ; M5min walk from Karasuma-Oike Station, Karasuma & Tōzai subway lines) Located diagonally across from the Nakagyō post office, this is a favourite of Kyoto vegetarians and has an English menu. It serves daily sets of Japanese vegetarian food (the occasional bit of meat is offered as an option, but you'll be asked your preference). The seating is rather cramped but the food is very good and carefully made from quality ingredients. It's up the metal spiral steps.

SOMUSHI KOCHAYA KOREAN TEAHOUSE ¥

Map p216 (素夢子 古茶家; ☎253-1456; Nakagyō-ku, Karasuma, Sanjō Nishi iru; tea/meals from ¥500/1000; ⊙11am-9pm, closed Wed; Ⓜ3min walk from Karasuma-Oike Station, Karasuma & Tōzai subway lines) This is the only Korean teahouse we've ever seen in Japan. It's a good place to go when you need a change from the creeping monoculture of coffee chain stores. It's a dark, woodsy and atmospheric spot with a variety of herbal teas (the menu details what they're good for). The teahouse also serves a few light meals, including some unusual Korean favourites (just don't expect Korean barbecue).

DIN TAI FUNG TAIWANESE ¥¥

Map p216 (鼎泰豐; ☎221-8811; 3F Kyoto Takashimaya Department Store, Shimogyō-ku, Shijo-Kawaramachi; lunch & dinner sets from ¥2000; ⊙10.30am-8pm Mon-Sat; 🚉1min walk from Kawaramachi Station, Hankyū line) If you're downtown and you feel like a break from Japanese food, head to this popular Taiwanese place on the 3rd flood of Takashimaya (p65). You have to drop about ¥2000 to get full here, but it's worth it: the dumplings are superb!

TSUKIJI SUSHISEI SUSHI ¥¥

Map p216 (築地寿司清; ☎252-1537; Nakagyō-ku, Takakura-dōri, Nishikikōji sagaru, Obiya-chō 581; lunch & dinner set menu ¥1365-3150; ⊙11.30am-3pm & 5-10pm Mon-Fri, 11.30am-10pm Sat & Sun; Ⓜ3min walk from Shijō Station, Karasuma subway line or Hankyū Karasuma Station) On the basement floor, next to Daimaru (p65), this simple sushi restaurant serves excellent sushi at their counter and tables. You can order a set or just point at what looks good. You can see inside the restaurant from street level, so it should be easy to spot.

WARAI OKONOMIYAKI ¥

Map p216 (わらい; ☎257-5966; 1F Mizukōto Bldg, 597 Nishiuoya-chō, Takakura Nishiiru, Nishikikōji-dōri, Nakagyō-ku; okonomiyaki from ¥600; ⊙11.30am-1am; 📄; Ⓜ5min walk from Shijō Station, Karasuma subway line) This Nishiki-dōri restaurant is a great place to try *okonomiyaki* (literally 'cook what you like', often called Japanese pancake) in casual surroundings. It can get a little smoky, but it's a fun spot to eat. They've got sets from as little as ¥650 at lunch. It's about 20m west of the west end of Nishiki Market; look for the English sign in the window.

RĀMEN KAIRIKIYA RĀMEN ¥

Map p216 (ラーメン魁力屋; ☎251-0303; 1F Hijikata Bldg, 435-2 Ebisu-chō, Sanjō agaru, Kawaramachi-dōri, Nakagyō-ku; rāmen from ¥600; ⊙11am-3am; 📄; 🚉5min walk from Sanjō Station, Keihan line) Not far from the Sanjō–Kawaramachi intersection, this popular *rāmen* specialist welcomes foreigners with an English menu and friendly staff. They've got several types of *rāmen* (noodles in a meat broth with meat and vegetables) to choose from and tasty sets that include things like fried rice, fried chicken or *gyōza* (Chinese dumplings), all for about ¥800. It's pretty easy to spot: look for the red-and-white sign and the words 'There is an English menu.'

IKE TSURU JUICE BAR ¥

Map p216 (池鶴; ☎221-3368; Nishikikōji-dōri, Yanaginobanba-Higashi-iru, Nakagyō-ku; juice ¥450; ⊙9am-6.30pm, closed Wed; 🚉5min walk from Kawaramachi Station, Hankyū line) We love this fruit-juice specialist in Nishiki Market. In addition to all the usual favourites, they sometimes have durian on hand and can whip up a very unusual durian juice. Look for the fruit on display – it's on the south side of the market, a little east of Yanaginobanba-dōri.

PARK CAFÉ CAFE ¥

Map p216 (パークカフェ; ☎211-8954; 1F Gion Bldg, 340-1 Aneyakō-ji kado, Gokomachi-dōri, Nakagyō-ku; drinks from ¥450; ⊙noon-11pm; Ⓜ5min walk from Kyoto-Shiyakusho-mae Station, Tōzai subway line) This cool little cafe always reminds us of a Melbourne coffee shop. It's on the edge of the Downtown Kyoto shopping district and is a convenient place to take a break. The comfy seats invite a nice long linger over a cuppa and the owner has an interesting music collection.

LUGOL CAFE ¥

Map p216 (ルゴール; ☎213-2888; Nakagyō-ku, Shinmachi-dōri, Oike agaru, Nakano-chō 50-1; lunch sets ¥900; ⊙11.30am-11pm; Ⓜ5min walk from Karasuma-Oike Station, Karasuma & Tōzai subway lines) For a quick cuppa or a snack in groovy surroundings, this cosy coffee shop on the west side of Downtown Kyoto is a very nice choice. We go there for decorating ideas as much as for the drinks. It's closed on the third Wednesday of the month.

HONKE TAGOTO SOBA ¥

Map p216 (本家 田毎; ☎221-3030; Nakagyō-ku, Sanjō Teramachi Higashi iru; dishes ¥1000-1600, courses ¥3000-6000; ⏰11am-9pm; 📋; 🚉5min walk from Sanjō Station, Keihan line) This casual restaurant in the Sanjō covered arcade serves a variety of *soba* (thin brown buckwheat noodle) and *udon* (thick white wheat noodle) dishes. It can get crowded at lunchtime and the service can be rather brusque, but the noodles are very good and the English/picture menu helps with ordering. The tempura *teishoku* (set-course meal) makes a great lunch.

KYŌ-HAYASHIYA CAFE ¥

Map p216 (京はやしや; ☎231-3198; Nakagyō-ku, Sanjō-dōri, Kawaramachi Higashi iru, Takase Bldg 6F; matcha sweets ¥950; ⏰11.30am-9.30pm; 🚉3min walk from Sanjō Station exit 6, Keihan line) If you need a change from large international coffee chains and want to try some good Japanese green tea – and enjoy a nice view over the mountains while you're at it – this is the place for it. There's a handy picture menu.

KŌSENDŌ-SUMI JAPANESE ¥

Map p216 (光泉洞寿み; ☎241-7377; Nakagyō-ku, Aneyakōji-dōri, Sakaimachi Higashi iru; daily lunch ¥980; ⏰11.30am-3.30pm Mon-Sat; Ⓜ5min walk from Karasuma-Oike Station, Karasuma & Tōzai subway lines) For a pleasant lunch downtown, try this unpretentious little restaurant located in an old Japanese house. The daily lunch special, which is usually simple and healthy Japanese fare, is always displayed out the front for your inspection. It's near the Museum of Kyoto, next to a small car park.

KERALA INDIAN ¥

Map p216 (ケララ; ☎251-0141; 2F KUS Bldg, Sanjō agaru, Kawaramachi, Nakagyō-ku; lunch/dinner from ¥850/2500; ⏰11.30am-2pm & 5-9pm; 🌿📋; 🚉5min walk from Sanjō Station exit 6, Keihan line) This narrow restaurant upstairs on Kawaramachi-dōri is Kyoto's best Indian restaurant. The ¥850 lunch set menu is an excellent deal, as is the vegetarian lunch, and the English menu is a bonus. Dinners run closer to ¥2500 per head and are of very high quality. Finish off the meal with the incredibly rich and creamy coconut ice cream. Kerala is located on the 2nd floor; look for the display of food down on street level.

KATSU KURA TONKATSU ¥

Map p216 (かつくら; ☎212-3581; Nakagyō-ku, Kawaramachi-dōri, Sanjō Nishi iru; tonkatsu from ¥890; ⏰11am-9.30pm; 📋; 🚉5min walk from Sanjō Station, Keihan line) This restaurant in the Sanjō covered arcade is a good place to sample *tonkatsu* (deep-fried breaded pork cutlets). Most of the cutlets come with a set that includes rice, miso soup and cabbage (extra helpings of these are free). It's not the best in Kyoto but it's relatively cheap and casual, and it has an English menu.

YAK & YETI NEPALESE ¥

Map p216 (ヤック&イェティ; ☎213-7919; Nakagyō-ku, Gokomachi-dōri, Nishikikōji sagaru; curry lunch sets from ¥750; ⏰11.30am-3pm & 5-11pm Tue-Sun; 📋; Ⓜ5min walk from Shijō Station, Karasuma subway line) This tiny joint serves more than just the *dal bhaat* (rice and lentil curry) that most people associate with Nepalese cuisine. In fact, the fare (good curries and tasty nan bread) is probably closer to Indian. There is counter seating, but we like to sit on the comfortable cushions here. English menus are available. The staff is pretty chuffed about being listed in our guides and has posted a picture of an old edition out the front – should be no trouble finding it.

HATI HATI INDONESIAN ¥

Map p216 (ハチハチ; ☎212-2228; Nishikiyamachi-dōri-Takoyakushi; dishes from ¥630; ⏰4pm-midnight, to 1am Sat & Sun; 🚉7min walk from Kawaramachi Station, Hankyū line) Hati Hati offers some of the best Indonesian food in Kyoto, including all the standard favourites such as *nasi goreng* (fried rice) and *mee goreng* (fried noodles). It's on the basement floor of the Kankō building; look for the green stairwell. It also doubles as a bar-club – stop by and see what's up if you're in the area.

INODA COFFEE CAFE ¥

Map p216 (イノダコーヒー; ☎221-0507; Nakagyō-ku, Sakaimachi-dōri, Sanjō sagaru; coffee from ¥500; ⏰7am-8pm; Ⓜ5min walk from Karasuma-Oike Station, Karasuma & Tōzai subway lines) This chain is a Kyoto institution and has branches across the city. Though slightly expensive, the old-Japan atmosphere makes it worth a try, especially if you want something Japanese rather than international.

CAFÉ INDEPENDANTS CAFE ¥

Map p216 (カフェ　アンデパンダン; ☎255-4312; B1F 1928 Bldg, Sanjō Gokomachi kado, Nakagyō-ku; salads/sandwiches from ¥400/800; ⏲11.30am-midnight; 🚉7min walk from Sanjō Station, Keihan line) Located beneath a gallery, this cool subterranean cafe offers a range of light meals and cafe drinks in a bohemian atmosphere (after you eat, you can check out the gallery space upstairs). A lot of the food offerings are laid out on display for you to choose from. The emphasis is on healthy sandwiches and salads. Take the stairs on your left before the gallery.

MUSASHI SUSHI SUSHI ¥

Map p216 (むさし寿司; ☎222-0634; Kawaramachi-dōri, Sanjō agaru, Nakagyō-ku; all plates ¥137; ⏲11am-10pm; 📖; 🚉5min walk from Sanjō Station, Keihan line) If you've never tried *kaiten-zushi* (conveyor-belt sushi restaurant), don't miss this place – all the dishes are a mere ¥137. It's not the best sushi in the world, but it's a heckuva lot better than most 'sushi trains' outside Japan. Needless to say, it's easy to eat here: you just grab what you want off the conveyor belt. If you can't find what you want on the belt, there's also an English menu. Musashi is just outside the entrance to the Sanjō covered arcade; look for the miniature sushi conveyor belt in the window.

OOTOYA SHOKUDŌ ¥

Map p216 (大戸屋; ☎255-4811; 2F Goshoame Bldg, Sanjō-dōri, Kawaramachi higashi iru, Nakagyō-ku; meals from ¥600; ⏲11am-11pm; 🚉7min walk from Sanjō Station, Keihan line) Ootoya is a clean, modern Japanese restaurant that serves a range of standard Japanese dishes at bargain-basement prices. It's popular with Kyoto students and young office workers. The large picture menu makes ordering a breeze. Look for the English sign just west of Ganko Sushi.

KARAFUNEYA COFFEE HONTEN CAFE ¥

Map p216 (☎254-8774; Kawaramachi-dōri Sanjō sagaru, Nakagyō-ku; simple meals ¥800-900; ⏲9am-1am; 📖; 🚉7min walk from Sanjō Station, Keihan line) Japan is famous for its plastic food models, but this place takes them to a whole new level – it's like some futuristic dessert museum. We like the centrepiece of the display: the mother of all sundaes that goes for ¥10,000-18,000 and requires advance reservation to order. Lesser mortals can try the tasty *matcha* (powdered green tea) parfait for ¥780 or any of the cafe drinks and light meals on offer.

SHI-SHIN SAMURAI CAFE AND BAR CAFE ¥¥

Map p216 (士心; ☎231-5155; Nakagyō-ku, Koromonotana-dōri, Oshikōji agaru, Kamimyōkakuji-chō 230-1; lunch/dinner from ¥1000/2500; ⏲noon-11pm, closed Tue; 📖; Ⓜ5min walk from Karasuma Oike Station, Karasuma & Tōzai subway lines) We're not entirely sure about the connection between samurai and world peace, but there's no doubting the young owner's wish to improve the world through interesting food, drinks and atmosphere. He's happy to show you his samurai sword and armour and talk to you about world peace in perfect English. The food is quite good, including some of the best *eda-mame* (soybeans in the pod) and garlic fried noodles in Kyoto. The first floor has latticed-windows and an English sign and menu out the front.

LIBERTE FRENCH ¥

Map p216 (リベルテ; ☎253-0600; Nakagyō-ku, Teramachi Nijō agaru, Tokiwagi-chō 65-2; dishes from ¥600, lunch set ¥1000, drinks from ¥320; ⏲8am-9pm Tue-Sun; Ⓜ6min walk from Kyoto Shiyakusho-mae Station, Tōzai subway line) With a bakery downstairs and a simple bistro-style restaurant upstairs, this charming French spot is a great place to stop for lunch while perusing the shops on Teramachi-dōri. The daily lunch specials are simple but sufficient and the clean, well-lit space is very relaxing.

MEW'Z CAFÉ ASIAN FUSION ¥

Map p216 (ミューズカフェ☎212-2911; Nakagyō-ku, Teramachi Nijō agaru, Yōhōjimae-chō 717-1; lunch/dinner sets from ¥750/1160; ⏲11.30am-10pm Thu, Fri & Sun-Tue, noon-11pm Sat; Ⓜ5min walk from Kyoto Shiyakusho-mae Station, Tōzai subway line) This pan-Asian cafe-restaurant on Teramachi-dōri is a great place to relax between bouts of antique hunting in the nearby shops. The place is pleasantly spacious, the music is usually good and the food is generally tasty.

FUJINO-YA JAPANESE ¥¥

Map p216 (藤の家; ☎221-2446; Nakagyō-ku, Pontochō, Shijō agaru; tempura sets ¥2700; ⏲4.30pm-11pm, closed Wed; 🚉3min walk from Kawaramachi Station, Hankyū line) This is one of the easiest places for non-Japanese to enter on Pontochō, a street where many of the other restaurants turn down even unfamiliar Japanese diners. Here you can feast on tempura, *okonomiyaki*, *yaki-soba* (fried noodles) and *kushikatsu* (deep-fried skewers of meat, seafood and vegetables) in tatami rooms overlooking the Kamo-gawa.

GANKO NIJŌ-EN JAPANESE ¥¥

Map p216 (がんこ二条苑; ☎223-3456; Nakagyō-ku, Kiyamachi-dōri, Nijō sagaru; lunch & dinner course from ¥3000; ⊙11am-10pm; Ⓜ3min walk from Kyoto-Shiyakusho-mae Station, Tōzai subway line) This is an upmarket branch of the Ganko Zushi chain that serves sushi and simple *kaiseki* sets. There's a picture menu and you can stroll in the stunning garden before or after your meal. It's near the Nijō–Kiyamachi crossing; you can't miss the grand entrance or the food models in the glass window.

DRINKING & NIGHTLIFE

TOP CHOICE **MCLOUGHLIN'S IRISH BAR & RESTAURANT** BAR

Map p216 (マクラクランズ　アイリッシュバー＆　レストラン; ☎212-6339; 8F The Empire Bldg, Kiyamachi, Sanjō-agaru, Nakagyō-ku; ⊙6pm-1am, closed Tue; @☜; Ⓜ5min walk from Kyoto-Shiyakusho-mae Station, Tōzai subway line) This is our favourite expat bar in town. It has ripping views over the Higashiyama mountains, great craft beers on tap, good food and a nice, open feeling. It also hosts some excellent music events and is an ideal spot to meet some local folks, both expat and Japanese. There is wi-fi internet access in case you want to do some surfing while drinking your beer.

TOP CHOICE **SAMA SAMA** BAR

Map p224 (サマサマ; ☎241-4100; 532 Kamiōsaka-chō, Sanjō-agaru, Kiyamachi, Nakagyō-ku; ⊙6pm-2am, to 4am Fri & Sat, closed Tue; 🚉5min walk from Kawaramachi Station, Hankyū line) This place seems like a very comfortable cave somewhere near the Mediterranean. Scoot up to the counter or make yourself at home on the cushions on the floor and enjoy a wide variety of drinks, some of them from Indonesia (like the owner). It's down an alley just north of Sanjō; the alley has a sign for Sukiyaki Komai Tei.

ING BAR, IZAKAYA

Map p216 (イング; ☎255-5087; Nishikiyamachi-dōri, Takoyakushi agaru, Nakagyō-ku; ⊙6pm-2am Mon-Thu, to 5am Fri-Sun; 🚉5min walk from Kawaramachi Station, Hankyū line) This *izakaya*-cum-bar on Kiyamachi is one of our favourite spots for a drink in Kyoto. It offers cheap bar snacks (¥250 to ¥700) and drinks (from ¥500), good music, and friendly staff. It's in the Royal building on the 2nd floor; you'll know you're getting close when you see all the hostesses out trawling for customers on the streets nearby.

YORAMU BAR

Map p224 (ヨラム; ☎213-1512; 2F Ōtō Bldg, Nijō-dōri, Nakagyō-ku; ⊙6pm-midnight Wed-Sat; Ⓜ10min walk from Karasuma-Oike Station, Karasuma & Tōzai subway lines) Named for Yoramu, the Israeli sake expert who runs it, this place is highly recommended for anyone who wants an education in sake (sake tasting sets cost from ¥1200). It's very small and can only accommodate a handful of people. By day, it's a soba restaurant.

A-BAR BAR

Map p216 (居酒屋　A (あ) ; ☎213-2129; Nishiki yamachi-dōri; ⊙6pm-1am; 🚉5min walk from Kawaramachi Station, Hankyū line) This is a raucous student *izakaya* with a log-cabin interior located in the Kiyamachi area. There's a big menu to choose from and everything's cheap (dishes from ¥160 to ¥680). The best part comes when they add up the bill – you'll swear they've undercharged you by half. It's a little tough to find – look for the small black-and-white sign at the top of a flight of concrete steps above a place called Reims.

ATLANTIS BAR

Map p216 (アトランティス; ☎241-1621; Shijō-Pontochō agaru; ⊙6pm-2am, to 1am Sun; 🚉5min walk from Kawaramachi Station, Hankyū line) This is one of the few bars on Pontochō that foreigners can walk into without a Japanese friend. It's a slick, trendy place that draws a fair smattering of Kyoto's beautiful people, and wannabe beautiful people. In summer you can sit outside on a platform looking over the Kamo-gawa. It's often crowded here so you may have to wait a bit to get in, especially if you want to sit outside.

RUB-A-DUB BAR

Map p216 (ラブアダブ; ☎256-3122; Kiyamachi-dōri-Sanjō; ⊙7pm-2am, to 5am Sat; 🚉5min walk from Sanjō Station, Keihan line) At the northern end of Kiyamachi-dōri, Rub-a-Dub is a funky little reggae bar with a shabby tropical look. It's a good place for a quiet drink on weekdays, but on Friday and Saturday nights you'll have no choice but to bop along with the crowd. Look for the stairs heading down to the basement beside the popular (and delightfully 'fragrant') Nagahama Rāmen shop.

TOP CHOICE WORLD CLUB

Map p216 (ワールド; ☎213-4119; 97 Shinmachi Shijō-agaru Nishi-Kiyamachi Shimogyō-ku; admission ¥2500-3000; 10pm-5am, closed Mon, bar only Tue; 5min walk from Kawaramachi Station, Hankyū line) World is Kyoto's largest club and it naturally hosts some of the biggest events. It has two floors, a dance floor and lockers where you can leave your stuff while you dance the night away. Events include everything from deep soul to reggae and techno to salsa.

ENTERTAINMENT

KAMOGAWA ODORI GEISHA DANCE

Map p216 (鴨川をどり; ☎221-2025; Pontochō-Sanjō sagaru; shows 12.30pm, 2.20pm & 4.10pm; 5min walk from Sanjō Station, Keihan line) Geisha dances from 1 to 24 May at Pontochō Kaburen-jō Theatre, Pontochō. It costs ¥2000/4000/4500 for normal/special seat/special seat with tea.

KYOTO CINEMA CINEMA

Map p216 (京都シネマ; ☎353-4723; Shimogyō-ku, Karasuma dōri Shijō sagaru, Suiginya-chō 620, Cocon Karasuma 3F; 10am-9pm; 2min walk from Shijō Station, Karasuma subway line) This new art-house theatre right downtown is a tremendously welcome addition to the Kyoto cultural scene. It's in the Cocon Karasuma Building, directly connected to Shijō Station; take exit 2.

SHOPPING

TOP CHOICE JUNKUDŌ BOOKSHOP

Map p216 (ジュンク堂書店; ☎253-6460; Kyoto BAL Bldg, 2-251 Yamazaki-chō, Sanjō sagaru, Kawaramachi-dōri, Nakagyō-ku; 11am-8pm; 10min walk from Kawaramachi Station, Hankyū line) On the 5th to 8th floors of the BAL building, right downtown, this is one of Kyoto's best bookshops. The 7th floor has a good selection of English books and a smaller selection of books in other European languages. It also stocks English-language manga, magazines, Lonely Planet travel guides, and Japanese-language textbooks and reference books. There is an excellent cafe on the top floor which has a great view over Kyoto to the Higashiyama mountains. You can get light meals here as well as drinks.

TOP CHOICE IPPO-DŌ TEA

Map p216 (一保堂; ☎211-3421; Teramachi-dōri, Nijō, Nakagyō-ku; 9am-7pm Mon-Sat, to 6pm Sun & holidays, cafe 11am-5pm; 10min walk from Kyoto-Shiyakusho-mae Station, Tōzai subway line) This old-style tea shop sells the best Japanese tea in Kyoto. Its *matcha* (powdered green tea used in tea ceremonies) makes an excellent and lightweight souvenir. Try a 40g container of *wa-no-mukashi* (meaning 'old-time Japan') for ¥1600, which makes 25 cups of excellent green tea. Ippo-dō is north of the city hall, on Teramachi-dōri. It has an adjoining teahouse.

ARITSUGU KNIVES, KITCHENWARE

Map p216 (有次; ☎221-1091; 219 Kajiya-chō, Gokomachi nishi iru, Nishikikōji-dōri, Nakagyō-ku; 9am-5.30pm; 5min walk from Kawaramachi Station, Hankyū line) While you're in the Nishiki Market, have a look at this store – it's where you can find some of the best kitchen knives in the world. It also carries a selection of excellent and unique Japanese kitchenware.

TOP CHOICE TAKASHIMAYA DEPARTMENT STORE

Map p216(高島屋; ☎221-8811; Shimogyō-ku, Shijō-dōri, Kawaramachi Nishi iru, Shin-chō 52; 10am-8pm, restaurants to 9.30pm; 1min walk from Kawaramachi Station, Hankyū line) The grande dame of Kyoto department stores, Takashimaya is almost a tourist attraction in its own right, from the mind-boggling riches of the basement food floor to the wonderful selection of lacquerware and ceramics on the 6th floor. And don't miss the kimono!

TOP CHOICE DAIMARU DEPARTMENT STORE

Map p216 (大丸; ☎211-8111; Shimogyō-ku, Shijō-dōri, Takakura Nishi iru, Tachiuri Nishi-machi 79; 10am-8pm, restaurants 11am-8pm; 1min walk from Shijō Station, Karasuma subway line or Karasuma Station, Hankyū line) Daimaru gives Takashimaya a run for its money with fantastic service, a brilliant selection of goods and a basement food floor that will make you want to move to Kyoto.

FUJII DAIMARU DEPARTMENT STORE

Map p216 (藤井大丸; ☎221-8181; Shimogyō-ku, Shijō-dōri Teramachi; ⏲10.30am-8pm; 🚉2min walk from Kawaramachi Station, Hankyū line) This smallish department store on Shijō-dōri is very popular with local young ladies who flock here to peruse the interesting selection of up-to-the-minute fashions and jewellery. Older Kyotoites head to the basement food floor here to snag great bargains on a wide selection of food, including great take-away sushi and tropical fruit.

KYOTO MARUI DEPARTMENT STORE

Map p216 (丸井; ☎257-0101; Shimogyō-ku, Shijō-dōri, Kawaramachi Higashi iru, Shin-chō 68; ⏲10.30am-8.30pm, restaurants to 10pm; 🚉above Kawaramachi Station, Hankyū line) This new youth-oriented department store hails from Tokyo and brings some of that fashion sense with it. It's a good place to see what's hot with the local *fashionistas*.

NIJŪSAN-YA ACCESSORIES

Map p216 (二十三や; ☎221-2371; Shimogyō-ku, Shijō-dōri, Kawaramachi higashi iru; ⏲10am-8pm; 🚉1min walk from Kawaramachi Station, Hankyū line) Boxwood combs and hair clips are one of Kyoto's most famous traditional crafts, and they are still used in the elaborate hairstyles of the city's geisha and *maiko* (apprentice geisha). This tiny hole-in-the-wall shop has a fine selection for you to choose from (and if you don't like what's on view, you can ask if it has other choices in stock – it usually does).

TANAKAYA HANDICRAFTS

Map p216 (田中彌; ☎221-1959; Shimogyō-ku, Shijō-dōri, Yanaginobanba higashi iru, Tachiurihigashi-chō 9; ⏲10am-6pm, closed Wed; Ⓜ5min walk from Shijō Station, Karasuma subway line) Tanakaya is one of the best places in Kyoto to buy *kyō-ningyō* (Kyoto dolls). In addition to the full range of *kyō-ningyō*, the shop sells display stands and screens, Japanese traditional shell game pieces and miniature Gion Matsuri (p22) floats. It occupies a wide stretch of Shijō-dōri and is easy to spot by its dolls in the window.

MEIDI-YA FOOD

Map p216 (明治屋; ☎221-7661; Nakagyō-ku, Sanjō-dōri, Kawaramachi higashi iru, Nakajima-chō 78; ⏲10am-9pm; 🚉5min walk from Sanjō Station, Keihan line) This famous Sanjō-dōri gourmet supermarket has an outstanding selection of imported food and an excellent selection of wine. Prices are high.

TOP CHOICE **MORITA WASHI** JAPANESE PAPER

Map p216 (森田和紙; ☎341-1419; 1F Kajioha Bldg, 298 Ōgisakaya-chō, Bukkō-ji agaru, Higashinotōin-dōri, Shimogyō-ku; ⏲9.30am-5.30pm Mon-Fri, to 4.30pm Sat; Ⓜ10min walk from Shijō Station, Karasuma subway line) A short walk from the Shijō-Karasuma crossing, this place sells a fabulous variety of handmade *washi* for reasonable prices. It's one of our favourite shops in Kyoto for souvenirs.

KAMIJI KAKIMOTO JAPANESE PAPER

Map p216 (紙司柿本; ☎211-3481; 54 Tokiwagi-chō, Nijō agaru, Teramachi, Nakagyō-ku; ⏲9am-6pm; Ⓜ10min walk from Kyoto-Shiyakusho-mae Station, Tōzai subway line) A close second to Morita Washi as our favourite *washi* (Japanese paper) shop in Kyoto. It's got such unusual items as *washi* computer printer paper and *washi* wallpaper. It's very close to Ippo-dō tea shop, with which it makes a very good double bill.

RAKUSHI-KAN JAPANESE PAPER

Map p216 (楽紙舘; ☎221-1070; Takoyakushi-dōri Takakura nishi iru, Nakagyō-ku; ⏲10.30am-6pm Tue-Sun; Ⓜ5min walk from Shijō Station, Karasuma subway line) On the 1st floor of the Museum of Kyoto, this fine little shop sells a variety of *washi* goods and traditional Japanese stationery. There are several interesting items here that make good souvenirs, including fine letter-writing paper and cards. You can also pick up blank *washi* business cards to have printed up when you get back home.

KYŪKYO-DŌ SOUVENIRS

Map p216 (鳩居堂; ☎231-0510; 520 Shimo honnōjimae-chō, Aneyakōji agaru, Teramachi, Nakagyō-ku; ⏲10am-6pm Mon-Sat; Ⓜ5min walk from Kyoto-Shiyakusho-mae Station, Tōzai subway line) This old shop in the Teramachi covered arcade sells a selection of incense, *shodō* (Japanese calligraphy) goods, tea-ceremony supplies and *washi*. Prices are on the high side but the quality is good.

MINAKUCHI-YA TEXTILES

Map p216 (水口弥; ☎221-3076; Nakagyō-ku, Takakura-dōri-Nishikikōji agaru, Kaiya-chō 558-1; ⏰10am-6pm Tue-Sat, 11am-5pm Sun; Ⓜ10min walk from Shijō Station, Karasuma subway line) This shop sells *noren* (curtains that hang in the entry of Japanese restaurants) and a wide variety of other fabric goods such as placemats, *tenugui* (small hand towels), handkerchiefs and bedding. It's near Daimaru.

TOP CHOICE **OPA** SHOPPING CENTRE

Map p216 (オーパ; ☎255-8111; Nakagyō-ku, Kawaramachi-dōri, Shijō agaru; ⏰11am-9pm; 🚉1min walk from Kawaramachi Station, Hankyū line) This youth-oriented shopping centre is the place to go to see swarms of *ko-gyaru* (brightly clad Japanese girls) and their mates. It's also a decent spot for those who want to check out a wide variety of fashion boutiques and other trendy shops.

SHIN-PUH-KAN SHOPPING CENTRE

Map p216 (新風館; ☎213-6688; Nakagyō-ku, Karasuma dōri, Aneyakōji sagaru, Bano-chō 586-2; ⏰shops 11am-8pm Sun-Thu, to 9pm Fri & Sat, restaurants 11am-11pm; Ⓜ1min walk from Karasuma-Oike Station, Karasuma & Tōzai subway lines) This interesting shopping complex has a variety of boutiques and restaurants clustered around a huge open-air atrium. The offerings here run to the trendy and ephemeral, which seems to appeal to all the young folk who congregate here. Occasional art and music performances are held in the atrium.

ERIZEN TEXTILES

Map p216 (ゑり善; ☎221-1618; Shimogyō-ku, Shijō Kawaramachi, Otabi-chō; ⏰10am-7pm Tue-Sun; 🚉1min walk from Kawaramachi Station, Hankyū line) Roughly opposite Takashimaya department store, Erizen is one of the best places in Kyoto to buy a kimono or kimono fabric. It has a great selection of *kyō-yūzen* (Kyoto dyed fabrics) and other kimono fabrics. Prices are not cheap but the service is of a high level. Staff can measure you for a kimono and are happy to post it to your home later.

TSUJIKURA JAPANESE CRAFTS

Map p216 (辻倉; ☎221-4396; Nakagyō-ku, Kawaramachi-dōri, Shijō agaru higashi gawa, 7F Tsujikura Bldg; ⏰11am-8pm, closed Wed; 🚉2min walk from Kawaramachi Station, Hankyū line) A short walk north of the Shijō-Kawaramachi crossing, Tsujikura has a good selection of waxed-paper umbrellas and paper lanterns with traditional and modern designs.

NISHIHARU JAPANESE CRAFTS

Map p216 (西春; ☎211-2849; Nakagyō-ku, Teramachj-dōri, Sanjō, east-south cnr; ⏰2-6.30pm; 🚉10min walk from Sanjō Station, Keihan line) This is an attractive shop dealing in wood-block prints. All the prints are accompanied by English explanations and the owner is happy to take the time to find something you really like.

ART FACTORY CLOTHING

Map p216; (アートファクトリー; ☎213-3131; 498 Higashigawa-chō, Teramachi, Takoyakushi agaru, Nakagyō-ku; ⏰11am-8pm; 🚉10min walk from Kawaramachi Station, Hankyū line) A T-shirt with your name written in kanji, katakana or hiragana across the chest is a great souvenir, and this place can make them in just a few minutes. If you don't fancy your own name on the shirt, you can also get the name of your country or choose from a variety of Japanese words and slogans. Look for the T-shirts displayed outside (strangely, there is no sign in English or Japanese, but they call themselves 'Art Factory').

MIMURO CLOTHING

Map p216 (みむろ; ☎344-1220, 0120-366529; Shimogyō-ku, Karasuma-dōri, Matsubara Nishi iru, Kita gawa; ⏰10am-6.30pm; Ⓜ5min walk from Shijō Station or Gojō Station, Karasuma subway line) With four floors of kimono and *yukata* (lightweight Japanese robes), this is a must-stop for anyone in the market for one of these garments. The quality of the goods rises with each floor and you should be able to find something that appeals to you, regardless of your budget. You can find washable kimono here from about ¥5000.

TOP CHOICE **MINA** SHOPPING CENTRE

Map p216 (ミーナ京都; ☎222-8470; Nakagyō-ku, Kawaramachi-dōri, Sanjō sagaru, Daikoku-chō 58; ⏰11am-9pm, 7F restaurants 11am-midnight; 🚉5min walk from Sanjō Station, Keihan line or 6min walk from Kawaramachi Station, Hankyū line) One of Kyoto's newest shopping centres (they seem to be sprouting all over the place), Mina has branches of two of Japan's most interesting chains: Uniclo, a budget clothing brand that has spread overseas, and Loft, an interesting department store that stocks all manner of curio and gift items.

COCON KARASUMA SHOPPING CENTRE

Map p216 (古今烏丸; ☎352-3800; Shimogyō-ku, Karasuma dō-ri Shijō sagaru, Suiginya-chō 620; ⏲10am-midnight; Ⓜconnected to Shijō Station Exit 2, Karasuma subway line) Located in the midst of Kyoto's banking district, this new shopping, dining and entertainment complex is always worth a look. The offerings range from books to furniture, with an art-house cinema and several restaurants in between.

TANIYAMA MUSEN ELECTRONICS

Map p216 (タニヤマムセン; ☎343-0221; Shimogyō-ku, Teramachi-dōri-ShijoDji sagaru, Teianmaeno-chō 589; ⏲10am-9pm; 🚉5min walk from Kawaramachi Station, Hankyū line) It's hard not to feel sorry for the electronics shops of Teramachi-dōri: they've been having a hard go of things since the opening of Tokyo-based megastores around Kyoto Station. But Taniyama Musen (*musen* is the old Japanese word for 'radio') is hanging on. The prices here are often just as good as the bigger places near the station and you can actually speak to the clerks here (well, that is, if you can muster a bit of Japanese).

KYOTO ANTIQUE CENTER ANTIQUES

Map p216 (京都アンティークセンター; ☎222-0793; Nakagyō-ku, Teramachi-dōri, Nijōji agaru higashi gawa; ⏲10.30am-7pm, closed Tue; Ⓜ5min walk from Kyoto Shiyakushmae Station, Tōzai subway line) A collection of semi-independent antique shops under one roof, this Teramachi-dōri emporium has oddities, curios and treasures to make those yen burn a hole in your pocket. If you're in the market for an interesting (and possibly pricey) gift for the folks back home, you might find it here.

Central Kyoto

For more detail of this area, see Map p219

Neighbourhood Top Five

❶ Enter the hidden world of the **Kyoto Imperial Palace** (p71) and marvel at the splendour of the Japanese court. In addition to the stunning buildings and interiors, the gardens are lovely and make for pleasant strolling

❷ Wander through the hypnotic arcades of *torii* (Shintō shrine gates) at **Fushimi-Inari-Taisha** (p76).

❸ Stroll through the expansive grounds of **Tōfuku-ji** (p76).

❹ Visit the many subtemples at **Daitoku-ji** (p72).

❺ Take a stroll through the long tree-lined approach to **Shimogamo-jinja** (p73).

Lonely Planet's Top Tip

During cherry blossom season (early April), the city's main tourist sites will be mobbed. If you want to enjoy the blossoms without the crowds, head to the banks of the Kamo-gawa or Takano-gawa, north of Imadegawa-dōri.

Best Places to Eat

- Cocohana (p77)
- Prinz (p77)
- Hiragana-kan (p77)

For reviews, see p76

Best Places for a Stroll

- Kyoto Imperial Palace Park (p71)
- Shimogamo-jinja (p73)
- Fushimi-Inari-Taisha (p76)

For reviews, see p72

Best Places for Kids

- Umekōji Steam Locomotive Museum (p74)
- Fushimi-Inari-Taisha (p76)
- Kyoto Botanical Gardens (p73)

For reviews, see p72

Explore: Central Kyoto

The area we refer to as Central Kyoto in this book is not so much a distinct neighbourhood as it is a vast swath of the city that surrounds the better known sightseeing districts of Downtown Kyoto (p54), the Kyoto Station Area (p48), Southern Higashiyama (p79) and Northern Higashiyama (p92). Central Kyoto runs from the hills that form the northern border of the city proper to the flat suburbs south of Kyoto Station. As such, it is not an area that one would attempt to explore in one day.

The best way to enjoy Central Kyoto is to choose one or two sights that are relatively close to each other and focus on them. You can often link sights in Central Kyoto up with sights in other nearby sightseeing districts, like Downtown Kyoto or the Southern Higashiyama area.

There are many possible routes that take advantage of the offerings here. For example, you could start in the southeast region of the area with a visit to Fushimi-Inari-Taisha and Tōfuku-ji, then head north into the Southern Higashiyama area. Or, you could visit the sights in the Northern Higashiyama Area, like Ginkaku-ji, and continue north to the lesser visited sights of Manshū-in and Shisendō.

Likewise, you might pay a visit to the walled-in Zen world of Daitoku-ji, with its wonderful subtemples, and then continue into Northwest Kyoto (p104) to visit the shining apparition of Kinkaku-ji – the famed Golden Pavilion.

Needless to say, because of its size, this area lends itself to being explored by bicycle.

Local Life

- **Hangout** Kyoto families with children gather on sunny weekend days along the banks of the Kamo-gawa, just north of Kamo-Ōhashi.
- **Jogging Route** (p71) Local runners favour the many paths of the Kyoto Imperial Palace Park.
- **Picnic Spot** (p73) Spread a blanket and eat al fresco is in the expansive fields of the Kyoto Botanical Gardens.

Getting There & Away

- **Train** Take the JR or Keihan lines to sights in the southeast.
- **Bus** Take buses to sights in the northeast.
- **Subway** Take the Karasuma subway line to sights in the north and centre. Take the Tōzai subway line to Nijō-jō.

TOP SIGHTS KYOTO IMPERIAL PALACE & IMPERIAL PALACE PARK

The Kyoto Imperial Palace and its park is the heart of Kyoto, both spatially and metaphorically. It occupies a huge expanse of Central Kyoto – a green haven amid a sea of concrete. The palace recalls the city's proud heritage as the capital of the country and seat of the imperial court for over 1000 years. While the palace itself is grand and steeped in history, for many visitors, the surrounding Imperial Palace Park is the real draw. Here, you can stroll for hours on wide pedestrian avenues or narrow paths through the forest.

The Kyoto Imperial Palace (Kyoto Gosho; 京都御所) served as the official residence of the emperor of Japan from the late 12th century until the 19th century and the palace remains an imperial household property. The park is also home to another walled enclosure known as the Sentō Gosho (p72).

In spring and autumn, it is possible to enter the palace without reservation. Otherwise, you can visit the palace as part of a guided tour (see p72). The tour takes about an hour and covers the various halls inside the palace, including the Shishin-den (Ceremonial Hall), Ko Gosho (Small Palace), Tsune Gosho (Regular Palace) and Oike-niwa (Pond Garden). Regrettably, it is forbidden to enter any of these.

The Imperial Palace is surrounded by a spacious park with a welcome landscape of trees and open lawn – it's Kyoto's very own Central Park. If you're here in early April, do not miss the wonderful cherry trees at the northern end of the park. These *shidare-zakura* (weeping cherry trees) are some of the best in the city.

DON'T MISS

- Cherry trees

PRACTICALITIES

- Map p219
- ☎211-1215
- Kamigyō-ku, Kyoto gyōen 3
- admission free
- Ⓜ10min walk from Imadegawa Station, Karasuma subway line

SIGHTS

SENTŌ GOSHO NOTABLE BUILDING

Map p219 (仙洞御所; ☎211-1215; Kamigyō-ku, Kyoto gyōen; Ⓜ10min walk from Imadegawa Station, Karasuma subway line) A few hundred metres southeast of the Imperial Palace is the Sentō Gosho. It was originally constructed in 1630 during the reign of Emperor Go-Mizunō as a residence for retired emperors. The palace was repeatedly destroyed by fire and reconstructed; it continued to serve its purpose until a final blaze in 1854, after which it was never rebuilt. Today only two structures, the Seika-tei and Yūshin-tei teahouses, remain. The magnificent gardens, laid out in 1630 by renowned landscape designer Kobori Enshū, are the main attraction.

Visitors must obtain advance permission from the Imperial Household Agency (see the boxed text, p72) and be more than 20 years old. One-hour tours (in Japanese) start daily at 11am and 1.30pm. The route takes you past lovely ponds and pathways and, in many ways, a visit here is more enjoyable than a visit to the Gosho, especially if you are a fan of Japanese gardens.

FREE **DAITOKU-JI** TEMPLE

(大徳寺; ☎491-0019; 53 Daitokuji-chō, Murasakino, Kita-ku; ⏲dawn-dusk; Ⓜ20min walk from Kitaōji Station, Karasuma subway line) Daitoku-ji is a separate world within Kyoto – a world of Zen temples, perfectly raked gardens and wandering lanes. It is one of the most rewarding destinations in this part of the city, particularly for those with an interest in Japanese gardens.

Daitoku-ji, the headquarters of the Rinzai Daitoku-ji school, contains an extensive complex of 24 subtemples – including Daisen-in (p72), Kōtō-in (p73), Ōbai-in (p73), Ryōgen-in (p73) and Zuihō-in (p73). If you want an intensive look at Zen culture, this is the place to visit.

The eponymous Daitoku-ji is on the eastern side of the grounds. It was founded in 1319, burnt down in the next century and rebuilt in the 16th century. The San-mon gate (1589) has a self-carved statue of its erector, the famous tea-master Sen no Rikyū, on its 2nd storey.

Some sources say that Toyotomi Hideyoshi was so angry when he discovered he'd been demeaning himself by walking under Rikyū's effigy that he forced the master to commit *seppuku* (ritual suicide) in 1591.

The Karasuma subway line is the best way to get here. From the station, walk west along Kitaōji-dōri for about 20 minutes. You'll see the temple complex on your right. The main entrance is bit north of Kitaōji. If you enter from the main gate, which is on the east side of the complex, you will soon after find Daitoku-ji on your right.

DAISEN-IN TEMPLE

(大仙院; ☎491-8346; 54-1 Daitokuji-chō, Murasakino, Kita-ku; admission ¥400; ⏲9am-5pm Mar-Nov, to 4.30pm Dec-Feb; Ⓜ20min walk from

RESERVATION & ADMISSION TO KYOTO'S IMPERIAL PROPERTIES

Permission to visit the Gosho, Sentō Gosho, Katsura Rikyū and Shūgaku-in Rikyū is granted by the Kunaichō, the **Imperial Household Agency** (宮内庁京都事務所; Map p219; ☎211-1215; ⏲8.45am-noon, 1-5pm Mon-Fri), which is inside the Imperial Palace Park (Kyoto Gyōen), the park that surrounds the Kyoto Imperial Palace (Kyoto Gosho). The agency office is a short walk from Imadegawa Station on the Karasuma line. You have to fill out an application form and show your passport. Children can visit if accompanied by adults over 20 years of age (but are forbidden entry to the other three imperial properties of Katsura Rikyū, Sentō Gosho and Shūgaku-in Rikyū). Permission to tour the palace is usually granted the same day (try to arrive at the office at least 30 minutes before the start of the tour you'd like to join). Guided tours, sometimes in English, are given at 10am and 2pm from Monday to Friday. The tour lasts about 50 minutes. Reservations can also be made online at the Imperial Household Agency's website: http://sankan.kunaicho.go.jp/english/.

The Gosho can be visited without reservation during two periods each year, once in the spring and once in the autumn. The dates vary each year, but as a general guide, the spring opening is around the last week of April and the autumn opening is in the middle of November. Check with the Tourist Information Center (p196) for exact dates.

Kitaōji Station, Karasuma subway line) The two small Zen gardens in this subtemple of Daitoku-ji are elegant examples of 17th-century *karesansui* (dry-landscape rock garden) style. Here the trees, rocks and sand are said to represent and express various spectacles of nature, from waterfalls and valleys to mountain lakes. It's one of the more popular subtemples here, but not as rewarding as Kōtō-in (p73) or Ōbai-in (p73).

KŌTŌ-IN TEMPLE

(高桐院; ☎492-0068; 73-1 Daitokuji-chō, Murasakino, Kita-ku; admission ¥400; ⊙9am-4.30pm; Ⓜ20min walk from Kitaōji Station, Karasuma subway line) On the far western edge of the Daitoku-ji complex (you may have to ask directions to find it), this sublime garden is one of the best in all Kyoto and it's worth a special trip. It's located within a fine bamboo grove that you traverse via a moss-lined path. Once inside there is a small stroll garden which leads to the centrepiece: a rectangle of moss and maple trees, backed by bamboo. Take some time on the veranda here to soak it all up.

ZUIHŌ-IN TEMPLE

(瑞峯院; ☎491-1454; Kita-ku, Murasakino, Daitokuji-chō; admission ¥400; ⊙9am-5pm; Ⓜ20min walk from Kitaōji Station, Karasuma subway line) Another subtemple of Daitoku-ji (p72), Zuihō-in enshrines the 16th-century Christian *daimyō* (domain lord) Ōtomo Sōrin. In the early 1960s, a landscape architect named Shigemori Misuzu rearranged the stones in the back rock garden into the shape of a crucifix! More interesting is the main rock garden, which is raked into appealing patterns reminiscent of water ripples. It's roughly in the middle of the complex; once again, you may have to ask for directions.

ŌBAI-IN TEMPLE

(黄梅院; ☎231-7015; Kita-ku, Murasakino, Daitokuji-chō; admission ¥600; ⊙end Mar–early May & early Oct–early Dec; Ⓜ20min walk from Kitaōji Station, Karasuma subway line) If you are lucky enough to be in Kyoto during autumn when this subtemple of Daitoku-ji is opened to the public, then you should make an effort to visit. The subtemple is a world of interlinked gardens, including an incredibly rich moss garden and a starkly simple *karesansui*. Along with nearby Kōtō-in (p73), we rank this as one of the finest gardens in Kyoto. When you enter the Daitoku-ji complex via the east (main) gate, it's on the left.

RYŌGEN-IN TEMPLE

(龍源院; ☎491-7635; Kita-ku, Murasakino, Daitokuji-chō; admission ¥350; ⊙9am-4.30pm; Ⓜ20min walk from Kitaōji Station, Karasuma subway line) Ryōgen-in is yet another fine subtemple in the Daitoku-ji complex. It has two pleasing gardens, one moss and one *karesansui*. The *karesansui* has an interesting island in its midst that invites lazy contemplation. When you enter the Daitoku-ji complex via the east (main) gate, it's on the left, just before Ōbai-in (p73).

FREE **SHIMOGAMO-JINJA** SHRINE

Off Map p219 (下鴨神社; ☎781-0010; 59 Izumigawa-chō, Shimogamo, Sakyō-ku; ⊙6.30am-5pm; 🚆10min walk from Demachiyanagi Station, Keihan line) This shrine, dating from the 8th century, is a Unesco World Heritage Site. It is nestled in the fork of the Kamo-gawa and Takano-gawa rivers, and is approached along a shady path through the lovely Tadasu-no-mori. This wooded area is said to be a place where lies cannot be concealed and is considered a prime location to sort out disputes. The trees here are mostly broadleaf (a rarity in Kyoto) and they are gorgeous in the springtime.

The shrine is dedicated to the god of harvest. Traditionally, pure water was drawn from the nearby rivers for purification and agricultural ceremonies. The *hondō* (main hall) dates from 1863 and, like the Haiden hall at its sister shrine, Kamigamo-jinja, is an excellent example of *nagare*-style shrine architecture. The annual *yabusame* (horseback archery) event here is spectacular. It happens on 3 May in Tadasu-no-mori.

KYOTO BOTANICAL GARDENS BOTANICAL GARDEN

(京都府立植物園; ☎701-0141; Shimogamohangi-chō, Sakyō-ku; gardens adult ¥200, child ¥80-150, greenhouse adult ¥200, child ¥80-150; ⊙gardens 9am-5pm, greenhouse 9am-4pm; Ⓜ5min walk from Kitayama Station, Karasuma subway line) The Kyoto Botanical Gardens, opened in 1914, occupy 240,000 sq metres and feature 12,000 plants, flowers and trees. It is pleasant to stroll through the rose, cherry and herb gardens or see the rows of camphor trees and the large tropical greenhouse. This is a good spot for a picnic or a bit of frisbee throwing. It's also a great spot for a *hanami* (cherry blossom viewing) party and the blossoms here tend to hold on a little longer than those elsewhere in the city.

SUMIYA PLEASURE HOUSE NOTABLE BUILDING

(角屋もてなしの文化美術館; ☎351-0024; Shimogyō-ku, Nishishinyashikiageya-chō 32; adult ¥1000, child ¥500-800; ⏰10am-4pm Tue-Sun; 🚉7min walk from JR Tanbaguchi Station; 🚌10min walk from Umekōji-kōen-mae bus stop, bus 205 from Kyoto Station) Shimabara, a district northwest of Kyoto Station, was Kyoto's original pleasure quarters. At its peak during the Edo period (1600–1867) the area flourished, with more than 20 enormous *ageya* – magnificent banquet halls where artists, writers and statesmen gathered in a 'floating world' ambience of conversation, art and fornication. Geisha were often sent from their *okiya* (living quarters) to entertain patrons at these restaurant-cum-brothels. By the start of the Meiji period, however, such activities had drifted north to the Gion district and Shimabara had lost its prominence.

Though the traditional air of the district has dissipated, a few old structures remain. The tremendous **Shimabara-no-Ōmon** gate, which marked the passage into the quarter, still stands, as does the Sumiya Pleasure House, the last remaining *ageya*, which is now designated a National Cultural Asset. Built in 1641, this stately two-storey, 20-room structure allows a rare glimpse into Edo-era nirvana. With its delicate latticework exterior, Sumiya has a huge open kitchen and an extensive series of rooms (including one extravagantly decorated with mother-of-pearl inlay).

Special tours in Japanese (requiring advance reservations in Japanese, booked through Sumiya Pleasure House) allow access to the 2nd storey and are conducted daily. An English pamphlet is provided.

FREE **MIBU-DERA** TEMPLE

(壬生寺; ☎841-3381; Nakagyō-ku, Bōjō, Bukkō-ji Kita iru; ⏰8.30am-4.30pm; 🚉10min walk from Ōmiya Station, Hankyū line) Mibu-dera was founded in 991 and belongs to the Risshū school. In the late Edo period, it became a training centre for samurai. Mibu-dera houses tombs of pro-shōgunate Shinsengumi members, who fought bloody street battles resisting the forces that succeeded in restoring the emperor in 1868. Except for an unusual stupa covered in Jizō statues, visually the temple is of limited interest. It is, however, definitely worth visiting during Mibu *kyōgen* (comic drama) performances in late April, or the Setsubun (p21) celebrations in early February.

TŌ-JI TEMPLE

(東寺; ☎691-3325; 1 Kujō-chō, Minami-ku; admission to grounds free, kondō & treasure hall ¥500; ⏰8.30am-5.30pm, to 4.30pm 20 Sep–19 Mar; 🚉5min walk from Tō-ji Station, Kintetsu Kyoto line) One of the main sights south of Kyoto Station, Tō-ji is an appealing complex of halls and a fantastic pagoda that makes a fine backdrop for the monthly flea market held on the grounds.

This temple was established in 794 by imperial decree to protect the city. In 823 the emperor handed it over to Kūkai (known posthumously as Kōbō Daishi), the founder of the Shingon school of Buddhism. Many of the temple buildings were destroyed by fire or fighting during the 15th century, and most of the remaining buildings were destroyed in the Momoyama period.

The Nandai-mon (main gate) was transported here in 1894 from Sanjūsangen-dō (p83) in Southern Higashiyama. The *kōdō* (lecture hall) dates from the 1600s and contains 21 images representing a Mikkyō (esoteric Buddhist) mandala. The *kondō* (main hall), which was rebuilt in 1606, combines Chinese, Indian and Japanese architectural styles and contains statues depicting the Yakushi (Healing Buddha) trinity.

In the southern part of the garden stands the **gojū-no-tō**, a five-storey pagoda that, despite having burnt down five times, was doggedly rebuilt in 1643. Standing at 57m, it is now the highest pagoda in Japan.

The **Kōbō-san** market fair is held here on the 21st of each month. There is also a regular market that runs on the first Sunday of each month.

UMEKŌJI STEAM LOCOMOTIVE MUSEUM MUSEUM

(梅小路蒸気機関車館; ☎314-2996; Kankiji-chō, Shimogyō-ku; adult/child ¥400/100, train ride ¥200/100; ⏰9.30am-5pm Tue-Sun; 🚌Umekō-ji Kōen-mae stop, bus 33, 205 or 208 from Kyoto Station) A hit with steam-train buffs and kids, this excellent museum features 18 vintage steam locomotives (dating from 1914 to 1948) and related displays. It is in the former JR Nijō Station building, which was recently relocated here and thoughtfully reconstructed. You can take a 10-minute ride on one of the smoke-spewing choo-choos (departures at 11am, 1.30pm and 3.30pm).

SHISEN-DŌ TEMPLE

(詩仙堂; ☎781-2954; Sakyō-ku, Ichijōji, Monguchi -chō 27; adult ¥500, child ¥200-400; ⌚9am-4:45pm; 🚌5min walk from Ichijōji-kudari-matsumachi bus stop, bus 5 from Kyoto Station) Most travellers to Kyoto don't venture beyond Ginkaku-ji (p95) when exploring the northern reaches of Higashiyama, but there are several other worthwhile temples in this part of town, including Shisen-dō and Manshu-in (p75). These two temples make a nice combination and are usually ignored by the masses who descend on Kyoto's more popular temples. Note that it's too far to walk here from Ginkaku-ji; consider a taxi or the bus.

With a name meaning 'house of poet-hermits', Shisen-dō was built in 1641 by Ishikawa Jōzan, a scholar of Chinese classics and a landscape architect who wanted a place to retire. Formerly a samurai, Jōzan abandoned his warrior status after a rift with Tokugawa Ieyasu and became a recluse, living here until his death in 1672 at the age of 90.

The hermitage is noted for its display of poems and portraits of 36 ancient Chinese poets, which can be found in the Shisen-no-ma room. The white-sand *karesansui* (dry-landscape rock garden) is lined with azaleas, which are said to represent islands in the sea. The garden also reflects Jōzan's distinct taste for Chinese aesthetics. It's a tranquil place to relax.

In the garden, water flows from a small waterfall to the *shishi-odoshi*, or *sōzu*, a device designed to scare away wild boar and deer. It's made from a bamboo pipe into which water slowly trickles, fills up and swings down to empty. On the upswing to its original position the bamboo strikes a stone with a 'thwack' – just loud enough to interrupt your snooze – before starting to refill.

MANSHU-IN TEMPLE

(曼殊院; ☎781-5010; Sakyō-ku, Ichijōji, Takeno uchi-chō 42; adult ¥500, child ¥400-500; ⌚9am-4.30pm; 🚉20min walk from Shūgakuin Station, Eizan line) About 30 minutes' walk north of Shisen-dō (p75) you'll reach the stately gate of Manshu-in, a popular retreat of former emperors and a great escape from the crowds. The temple was originally founded by Saichō on Hiei-zan (p128) but was relocated here at the beginning of the Edo period by Ryōshōhō, the son of Prince Hachijōnomiya Tomohito (who built Katsura Rikyū; p126).

The graceful temple architecture is often compared with Katsura Rikyū for its detailed woodwork and rare works of art, such as *fusuma-e* sliding doors painted by Kanō Eitoku, a famed artist of the Momoyama period. The *karesansui* garden by Kobori Enshū features a sea of gravel intended to symbolise the flow of a waterfall and stone islands representing cranes and turtles.

FREE SHŪGAKU-IN RIKYŪ IMPERIAL VILLA NOTABLE BUILDING

(修学院離宮; ☎211-1215; Sakyō-ku, Shūgaku-in, Yabusoe; 🚌10min walk from Shūgakuinrikyū-michi bus stop, bus 5 from Kyoto Station) Lying at the foot of Hiei-zan (p128), this superb villa was begun in the 1650s by Emperor Go-Mizunō, following his abdication; work was continued by his daughter Akeno-miya after his death in 1680. It was designed as a lavish summer retreat for the imperial family. The gardens here, with their views down over the city of Kyoto, are worth the trouble it takes to visit.

The villa grounds are divided into three enormous garden areas on a hillside – lower, middle and upper. Each has superb tea-ceremony houses: the upper, Kami-no-chaya, and lower, Shimo-no-chaya, were completed in 1659, and the middle teahouse, Naka-no-chaya, was completed in 1682. The gardens' reputation rests on their ponds, pathways and impressive use of *shakkei* (borrowed scenery) in the form of the surrounding hills. The view from Kami-no-chaya is particularly impressive.

One-hour tours (in Japanese) start at 9am, 10am, 11am, 1.30pm and 3pm; try to arrive early. A basic leaflet in English is provided and more detailed literature is for sale in the tour waiting room.

You must make reservations through the Imperial Household Agency – usually several weeks in advance. See the boxed text, p72, for details.

TAKARA-GA-IKE-KŌEN PARK

(宝ケ池公園; Sakyō-ku, Iwakura, Matsugasaki; Ⓜ10min walk from Kokusaikaikan Station exit 5, Karasuma subway line) This expansive park is an excellent place for a stroll or picnic in natural surroundings. Far from the throngs in the city centre, it is a popular place for bird-watching and has spacious gardens. There is a 1.8km loop around the main pond, where rowing boats can be hired for ¥1000 per hour.

In the northeast of the park, the Kyoto International Conference Hall is an unfortunate attempt at replicating Japan's traditional thatched-roof *gasshō-zukuri* style in concrete. Behind the conference hall, the Hosho-an Teahouse (designed by Soshitsu Sen, Grand Tea-Master XV of the Urasenke school) is worth a look.

TŌFUKU-JI TEMPLE

(東福寺; ☎561-0087; 15-778 Honmahi, Higashiyama-ku; admission to garden/grounds ¥400/free; ⏲9am-4pm Dec-Oct, 8.30am-4.30pm Nov; 10min walk from JR Tōfuku-ji Station, JR Nara line, 10min walk from Keihan Tōfuku-ji Station, Keihan line) Founded in 1236 by the priest Enni, Tōfuku-ji belongs to the Rinzai sect of Zen Buddhism. As this temple was intended to compare with Tōdai-ji and Kōfuku-ji in Nara, it was given a name combining characters from the names of each of these temples.

The present temple complex includes 24 subtemples; at one time there were 53. The huge San-mon is the oldest Zen main gate in Japan. The Hōjō (abbot's hall) was reconstructed in 1890. The gardens, laid out in 1938, are well worth a visit. The northern garden has stones and moss neatly arranged in a chequerboard pattern. From a viewing platform at the back of the gardens, you can observe the Tsūten-kyō (Bridge to Heaven), which spans a valley filled with maples.

Tōfuku-ji offers regular **Zen meditation sessions** for beginners, but don't expect coddling or English-language explanations: this is the real deal. Get a Japanese speaker to inquire at the temple about the next session (they hold about four a month for beginners).

Note that Tōfuku-ji is one of Kyoto's most famous autumn-foliage spots, and it is invariably packed during the peak of colours in November. Otherwise, it's often very quiet.

FREE **FUSHIMI-INARI-TAISHA** SHRINE

(伏見稲荷大社; ☎641-7331; 68 Yabunouchi-chō, Fukakusa, Fushimi-ku; ⏲dawn-dusk; 5min walk from JR Inari Station, JR Nara line, 10min walk from Keihan Fushimi-Inari Station, Keihan line) With seemingly endless arcades of vermilion *torii* (shrine gates) spread across a thickly wooded mountain, this vast shrine complex is a world unto its own. It is, quite simply, one of the most impressive and memorable sights in all of Kyoto.

The shrine was dedicated to the gods of rice and sake by the Hata family in the 8th century. As the role of agriculture diminished, deities were enrolled to ensure prosperity in business. Nowadays, the shrine is one of Japan's most popular, and is the head shrine for some 40,000 Inari shrines scattered the length and breadth of the country.

The entire complex, consisting of five shrines, sprawls across the wooded slopes of Inari-san. A pathway wanders 4km up the mountain and is lined with hundreds of red *torii*. There are also dozens of stone foxes. The fox is considered the messenger of Inari, the god of cereals, and the stone foxes, too, are often referred to as Inari. The key often seen in the fox's mouth is for the rice granary. On an incidental note, the Japanese traditionally see the fox as a sacred, somewhat mysterious figure capable of 'possessing' humans – the favoured point of entry is under the fingernails.

The walk around the upper precincts of the shrine is a pleasant day hike. It also makes for a very eerie stroll in the late afternoon and early evening, when the various graveyards and miniature shrines along the path take on a mysterious air. It's best to go with a friend at this time.

On 8 April there's a **Sangyō-sai festival** with offerings and dances to ensure prosperity for national industry. During the first few days in January, thousands of believers visit this shrine as their *hatsu-mōde* (first shrine visit of the New Year) to pray for good fortune.

EATING

MANZARA HONTEN MODERN JAPANESE ¥¥

Map p219 (まんざら本店; ☎253-1558; Nakagyō-ku, Kawaramachi-dōri, Ebisugawa agaru; dinner courses from ¥5000; ⏲5pm-midnight; M10min walk from Marutamachi Station, Karasuma subway line) Located in a converted *machiya* (traditional Japanese town house), Manzara represents a pleasing fusion of traditional and modern Japanese culture. The fare here is creative modern Japanese and the surroundings are decidedly stylish. The *omakase* (chef's recommendation) course is good value, with eight dishes for ¥4000, and à la carte dishes are available from ¥500. Last orders are at 11.30pm.

DEN SHICHI SUSHI ¥¥

(傳七; ☎323-0700; Ukyō-ku, Saiin, Tatsumi-chō 4-1; lunch/dinner from ¥480/2500; ⏲11.30am-2pm & 5-10.30pm Tue-Sun; 🚉3min walk from Saiin Station, Hankyū line) This is our favourite sushi restaurant in Kyoto. It's a classic: long counter, bellowing sushi chefs and great fresh fish. The lunch sets are unbelievable value and the glass sushi cases make ordering a little easier than at some other places. It's almost always hopping and doesn't take reservations, so you may have to give your name and wait – but it will definitely be worth it. Look for the black-and-white sign about 100m west of Saiin Station on Shijō-dōri.

TOP CHOICE **PRINZ** CAFE ¥

(プリンツ; ☎712-3900; Sakyō-ku, Tanakatakahara-chō 5; lunch from ¥840; ⏲11.30am-midnight Mon-Fri, 8.30am-midnight Sat & Sun; 🚉2min walk from Chayama Station, Eizan line) Behind the blank white facade of Prinz, you'll find a cafe-restaurant, gallery, bookshop, garden and library – a chic island of coolness in an otherwise bland residential neighbourhood. You can sit at the counter and request music from the CDs that line the walls. The lunch set usually includes a light assortment of Western and Japanese dishes, generally on the healthy side of things. Coffee starts at ¥300. All in all, this is a very interesting stop while you're in the northeast part of town.

DIDI INDIAN ¥

(ディディ; ☎791-8226; Sakyō-ku, Tanaka-Ōkubo-chō 22; lunch & dinner ¥1000-2000; ⏲11am-9.30pm, closed Wed; 🚭📵; 🚉1min walk from Mototanaka Station, Eizan line) A cosy little spot in the north of town past Hyakumamben and Kyoto University, this friendly smoke-free restaurant serves passable Indian lunch and dinner sets. There are plenty of vegetarian choices on the menu, which is available in English.

TOP CHOICE **HIRAGANA-KAN** SHOKUDŌ ¥

(ひらがな館; ☎701-4164; Sakyō-ku, Tanakahino kuchi-chō 44; lunch & dinner from ¥800; ⏲11.30am-3.30pm & 6-10.30pm, closed Tue; 🚉8min walk from Mototanaka Station, Eizan line) This place, popular with Kyoto University students, dishes up creative variations on chicken, fish and meat. Most mains come with rice, salad and miso soup. The menu is in Japanese only, but if you're at a loss for what to order try the tasty 'roll chicken *katsu*', a delectable and filling creation of chicken and vegetables. Look for the words 'Casual Restaurant' on the white awning.

HONYARADŌ JAPANESE ¥

Map p219 (ほんやら洞; ☎222-1574; Kamigyō-ku, Imadegawa, Teramachi Nishi iru; lunch ¥700; ⏲noon-10pm; 🚉10min walk from Demachiyanagi Station, Keihan line) This woodsy place overlooking the Kyoto Imperial Palace Park is an institution. It was something of a gathering spot for Kyoto's countercultural elite during the hippy days. It has the lived-in feeling of an eccentric friend's house, with stacks of books and magazines and interesting decorations. The lunch deal (a daily stew set) is good value. Surprisingly, considering the ambience, there aren't many veggie options. It's a good place to relax over coffee.

TOP CHOICE **COCOHANA** KOREAN ¥

(ここはな; ☎525-5587; Higashiyama-ku, Honmachi 13-243-1; lunch from ¥800; ⏲10am-10pm Wed-Sun, to 6pm Mon & Tue; 🚉2min walk from Tōfukuji Station, Keihan line) This place is one of a kind: a Korean cafe in a converted old Japanese house. Dishes here include *bibimbap* (a Korean rice dish) and *kimchi* (Korean pickles). A full range of coffee and tea is also available. It's a woody, rustic place with both table and tatami seating. There is no English menu but the friendly young staff will help with ordering. This makes a great stop while exploring southeastern Kyoto.

KAZARIYA SWEETS ¥

(かざりや; ☎491-9402; Kita-ku, Murasakino Imamiya-chō sweets ¥500; ⏲10am-5pm, closed Wed;; 🚌1min walk from Imamiya-jinja bus stop, bus 46 from Kyoto Station) For more than 300 years, Kazariya has been specialising in *aburi-mochi* (grilled rice cakes coated with soya-bean flour) and served with *miso-dare* (sweet-bean paste). It's a nice place to go for some tea and a sweet after exploring the grounds of Daitoku-ji (p72).

BON BON CAFÉ CAFE ¥

Map p219 (ボンボンカフェ; ☎213-8686; Sakyō-ku, Kawaramachi, Imadegawa, Higashi iru-Kita gawa; coffee/sandwiches from ¥350/500; ⏲11am-10.30pm; 🚉3min walk from Demachiyanagi Station, Keihan line) If you find yourself in need of a light meal or drink while you're in the Demachiyanagi area, this casual open-air cafe is an excellent choice. There is a variety of cakes and light meals on offer. While there is no English menu, much of the ordering can be done by pointing, and the young staff can help you figure out what's not on display. It's on the west bank of the Kamo-gawa and outdoor seats here are very pleasant on warm evenings.

ENTERTAINMENT

CLUB ŌKITSU KYOTO CULTURAL

Map p219 (411-8585; www.okitsu-kyoto.com; in the Kōdōkan, 524-1 Mototsuchimikado-chō, Shinmachi, Kamigyō-ku; 10min walk from Marutamachi Station, Karasuma subway line) offers an upmarket introduction to various aspects of Japanese culture including tea ceremony and the incense ceremony. They also offer kimono dressing upon request (note that kimono dressing is not offered alone: it must be part of a package including tea ceremony and/or incense ceremony). The introduction is performed in an exquisite Japanese villa near the Kyoto Gosho and participants get a real sense of the elegance and refinement of traditional Japanese culture.

KYOTO CONCERT HALL CONCERT HALL

(京都コンサートホール; 711-2980, ticket counter 711-3231/3090; Sakyō-ku, Shimogamo, Hangi-chō 1-26; 3min walk from Kitayama Station, Karasuma subway line) This is Kyoto's main classical music venue. It's a lovely hall with excellent acoustics and it never fails to draw an appreciative crowd of knowledgeable Kyotoites. Check *Kyoto Visitors Guide* or *Kansai Scene* for upcoming concerts.

ALTI CONCERT HALL

Map p219 (京都府立府民ホール アルティ; 441-1414; Karasuma-dōri-Ichijō sagaru; 5min walk from Imadegawa Station, Karasuma subway line) Occasional classical music and dance performances are held at this midtown concert hall. Check *Kyoto Visitors Guide* or *Kansai Scene* for upcoming concerts.

TAKU-TAKU LIVE MUSIC

(磔磔; 351-1321; Tominokōji-dōri-Bukkōji; admission ¥1500-3500; 7-9pm; 10min walk from Shijō Station, Hankyū Kyoto line) This is one of Kyoto's most atmospheric clubs, located in an old *sakagura* (sake brewery). It often hosts major acts (the Neville Brothers, Los Lobos and Dr John have all performed here).

KYOTO MINAMI KAIKAN CINEMA

(京都みなみ会館; 661-3993; Minami-ku, Nishi kujō, Higashihieijō-chō 79; Tōji Station, Kintetsu line) Try this theatre for lesser-known foreign art house and eclectic Japanese films, including Japanese *anime* (animation). It's on Kujō-dōri.

SHOPPING

TOP CHOICE **KŌBŌ-SAN MARKET** FLEA MARKET

(弘法さん(東寺露天市); 691-3325; Minami-ku, Kujō-chō 1 Tō-ji; 5min walk from Tō-ji Station, Kintetsu Kyoto line) This market is held at Tō-ji (p74) on the 21st of each month to commemorate the death of Kōbō Taishi, who in 823 was appointed abbot of the temple. If you're after used kimono, pottery, bric-a-brac, plants, tools and general Japanalia, this is the place.

Southern Higashiyama

Neighbourhood Top Five

❶ Climbing to the top of the Southern Higashiyama district to visit one of Kyoto's most colourful temples: **Kiyomizu-dera** (p81). This temple is almost always crowded but there's plenty of room to move about and the throngs add to the energy of the place.

❷ Letting your soul be soothed by the chanting monks at **Chion-in** (p82).

❸ Sipping a cup of green tea while looking over the sublime garden at **Shōren-in** (p87).

❹ Clapping your hands to awaken the gods at **Yasaka-jinja** (p84).

❺ Taking an evening stroll through the world of geisha in the **Gion District** (p87).

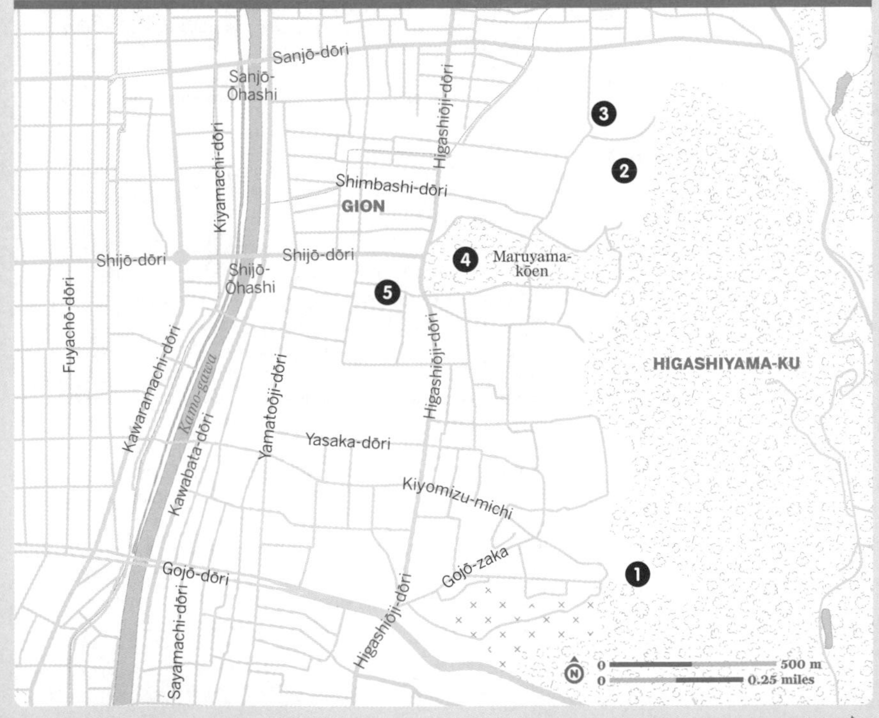

For more detail of this area, see Map p222

Lonely Planet's Top Tip

During the cherry blossom season in early April, the streets of Southern Higashiyama will be choked with traffic. *Do not* get in a taxi or bus in this area at this time unless you just want to sit there. Walking or taking the train/subway is the way to go during peak season.

Best Places to Eat

- Ōzawa (p87)
- Omen Kodai-ji (p88)
- Kasagi-ya (p89)

For reviews, see p87

Best Places to Drink

- Gael Irish Pub (p89)
- Gion Finlandia Bar (p90)
- Bar Main Higashiyama (p89)

For reviews, see p89

Best Places for a Stroll

- Gion District (p87)
- Ninen-zaka & Sannen-zaka (p84)
- Maruyama-kōen (p84)

For reviews, see p83

Explore: Southern Higashiyama

Stretching along the base of the Higashiyama (Eastern Mountains) from the top of Shichijō-dōri to the top of Sanjō-dōri, Southern Higashiyama comprises the thickest concentration of sights in all of Kyoto and is the place you should begin your exploration of the city.

The well-established sightseeing route through this district is covered in our Hills, Temples & Lanes in Southern Higashiyama walking tour (p85). Following this route is the best way to get a good introduction to the area. It's best to do this route in the order presented (south to north), since you'll be going slowly downhill most of the way, but it's perfectly possible to do it from north to south. Keep in mind that the walking tour does not cover some of the sights at the southern end of this district, like Sanjūsangen-dō, a fine temple, and the Kyoto National Museum.

A half day is usually sufficient to cover the main walking route in Southern Higashiyama, but if you eat lunch en route and take your time, you could easily spend a full day in this area. Note that this is Kyoto's most popular sightseeing district, so it will be crowded during peak seasons. Also, don't forget that the lanes here are almost deserted in the evening and a stroll through the darkened streets can be magical.

Downhill from the main sightseeing route, you'll find Gion, Kyoto's high-end entertainment and geisha district. The best way to explore this area is to follow our Night Walk Through the Floating World walking tour (p86).

Local Life

- **Hangouts** Maruyama-kōen (p84), a green oasis in the middle of Southern Higashiyama, is popular with locals for picnics, strolls and dates.
- **Eating** The scenic lanes of Ninen-zaka and Sannen-zaka (p84) are lined with tea shops and restaurants.
- **Expat's favourite** Kyoto expats who crave a proper Western breakfast or a proper pizza head to the restaurants at the Hyatt Regency Kyoto (p145).

Getting There & Away

- **Train** The private Keihan line provides access to Southern Higashiyama. Get off at Gion-shijō or Shichijō stations and walk uphill (east).
- **Bus** Kyoto city buses serve various stops in the district and are a good way to access Kiyomizu-dera.
- **Subway** The Tōzai subway line's Higashiyama Station offers easy access to the northern end of the district.

TOP SIGHTS
KIYOMIZU-DERA

With a commanding position overlooking Kyoto, the superb Buddhist temple of Kiyomizu-dera is the city's spiritual heart and soul. Built around a holy spring (Kiyomizu means 'pure water'), the temple has been drawing pilgrims since the 8th century AD. In addition to halls holding fine Buddhist images, the complex includes a small Shintō shrine that is associated with matters of the heart – buy a prayer plaque here to assure success in romance. There's even a secret underground passage that allows you to experience symbolic rebirth by passing through the womb of a Bodhisattva.

First built in 798, Kiyomizu-dera (清水寺) belongs to the Hossō sect of Buddhism. The present buildings are reconstructions dating from 1633. The main hall (Hondō), which houses a Jūichi-men (11-headed) Kannon figure, features a huge veranda that juts out over the hillside, supported by 139 15m-high wooden pillars. Just below this veranda is **Otowa-no-taki** spring, where visitors drink the sacred waters believed to bestow health and long life.

After exiting the main hall/veranda, up to your left, you will find **Jishu-jinja**, where visitors try to ensure success in love by closing their eyes and walking about 18m between a pair of 'Love Stones'.

Before you enter the actual temple precincts, visit one of the oddest sights in Japan: the **Tainai-meguri**. By entering the hall, you are figuratively entering the womb of Daizuigu Bosatsu, a female Bodhisattva who has the power to grant any human wish.

During the cherry blossom season, autumn foliage season and the summer *obon* season, Kiyomizu-dera holds evening 'light ups', when the trees and buildings are illuminated. Dates are: 12 to 21 March, 25 March to 10 April, 6 to 16 August, 11 November to 4 December.

DON'T MISS

- Cherry blossom, autumn and *obon* light-ups
- Tainai-meguri

PRACTICALITIES

- Map p222
- 1-294 Kiyomizu, Higashiyama-ku
- main hall ¥300, Tainai-meguri ¥100
- main hall 6am-6pm, Tainai-meguri 9am-4pm
- bus 202 or 100 from Kyoto Station to Gojō-zaka or Kiyomizu-michi

CHRISTIAN KOBER / LONELY PLANET IMAGES ©

TOP SIGHTS
CHION-IN

Called by some 'the Vatican of Pure Land Buddhism', this vast temple is one of the most impressive sights in all of Kyoto. The headquarters of one of Japan's most popular Buddhist sects, Chion-in receives millions of pilgrims annually, and it's one of the best places to see Japanese religious faith in action. Enter the enormous main hall and soak up the spiritual energy of the place: chanting monks, praying pilgrims and incense slowly spirally to the heavens. Then set off and explore the many subtemples and halls.

The single most impressive sight in Southern Higashiyama, Chion-in (知恩院) is a must-see for those with a taste for the grand and glorious. It was built by the monk Genchi in 1234 on the site where his mentor, Hōnen, had once taught and eventually fasted to death. Today it is still the headquarters of the Jōdo school, which was founded by Hōnen, and it is a hive of religious activity.

The oldest of the present buildings date from the 17th century. The two-storey **San-mon** gate at the main entrance is the largest in Japan, and prepares the visitor for the massive scale of the temple. The immense main hall (Miei-dō Hall), which measures 35m wide and 45m long, houses an image of Hōnen and is connected with the Dai Hōjō hall by a 'nightingale' floor that squeaks as one walks over it.

After visiting the main hall, with its fantastic gold altar, walk around the back to see the temple's gardens. On the way, you'll pass a darkened hall with a small statue of Amida Buddha glowing eerily in the darkness. It's a nice contrast to the splendour of the main hall.

Chion-in's **temple bell** was cast in 1633. It is the largest temple bell in Japan. It's up a flight of steps at the southeastern corner of the temple precincts.

DON'T MISS

- The temple bell

PRACTICALITIES

- Map p222
- 400 Rinka-chō, Higashiyama-ku
- grounds free, inner buildings & garden ¥400
- 9am-4.30pm
- M 15min walk from Higashiyama Station, Tōzai subway line

SIGHTS

SANJŪSANGEN-DŌ TEMPLE

Map p222 (三十三間堂; ☎525-0033; 657 Sanjūsangendōmawari-chō, Higashiyama-ku; admission ¥600; ⏲8am-4.30pm Apr–Mid-Nov, 9am-3.30pm mid Nov–Mar; 🚌Sanjūsangen-dō-mae stop, bus 206; 🚉10min walk from Shichijō Station, Keihan line) The sheer number of Buddhist images at this temple make it among the more interesting and visually arresting sights in Kyoto. It makes a logical starting point to a full-day exploration of Southern Higashiyama.

The original temple, called Rengeō-in, was built in 1164 at the request of the retired emperor Go-shirakawa. After it burnt to the ground in 1249, a faithful copy was constructed in 1266.

The temple's name refers to the 33 *sanjūsan* (bays) between the pillars of this long, narrow building. The building houses 1001 wooden statues of Kannon (the Buddhist goddess of mercy); the chief image, the 1000-armed Senjū-Kannon, was carved by the celebrated sculptor Tankei in 1254. It is flanked by 500 smaller Kannon images, neatly lined in rows.

There are an awful lot of arms, but if you are picky and think the 1000-armed statues don't have the required number, you should remember to calculate according to the nifty Buddhist mathematical formula, which holds that 40 arms are the equivalent of 1000 because each saves 25 worlds.

At the back of the hall are 28 guardian statues in a variety of expressive poses. The gallery at the western side of the hall is famous for the annual **Tōshiya festival**, held on 15 January, when archers shoot arrows along the length of the hall. The ceremony dates from the Edo period, when an annual contest was held to see how many arrows could be shot from the southern to northern end in 24 hours. The all-time record was set in 1686, when an archer successfully landed more than 8000 arrows at the northern end.

KYOTO NATIONAL MUSEUM MUSEUM

Map p222 (京都国立博物館; ☎531-7509; www.kyohaku.go.jp/eng/index_top.html; 527 Chaya-machi, Higashiyama-ku; adult/student ¥500/250; ⏲9.30am-6pm Tue-Thu, Sat & Sun, to 8pm Fri; 🚌Sanjūsangen-dō-mae stop, bus 206; 🚉10min walk from Shichijō Station, Keihan line) The Kyoto National Museum is housed in two buildings opposite Sanjūsangen-dō temple. It was founded in 1895 as an imperial repository for art and treasures from local temples and shrines. There are 17 rooms with displays of over a thousand artworks, historical artefacts and handicrafts. The permanent collection is excellent but somewhat poorly displayed; unless you have a particular interest in Japanese traditional arts, we recommend visiting this museum only when a special exhibition is on (admission extra). Note that the museum is presently undergoing a partial reconstruction; you can still enter the museum but construction will be going on until late 2013.

KAWAI KANJIRŌ MEMORIAL HALL MUSEUM

Map p222 (河井寛次郎記念館; ☎561-3585; 569 Kanei-chō, Gojō-zaka, Higashiyama-ku; admission ¥900; ⏲10am-5pm; 🚉15min walk from Kiyomizu-gojō Station, Keihan line) This small memorial hall is one of Kyoto's most commonly overlooked little gems; it's worth a look, though, especially if you have an interest in Japanese crafts such as pottery and furniture. The hall was the home and workshop of one of Japan's most famous potters, Kawai Kanjirō (1890–1966). The 1937 house is built in rural style and contains examples of Kanjirō's work, his collection of folk art and ceramics, his workshop and a fascinating *nobori-gama* (a stepped kiln). The museum is near the intersection of Gojō-dōri and Higashiōji-dōri.

ROKUHARAMITSU-JI TEMPLE

Map p222 (六波羅蜜寺; ☎561-6980; Higashiyama-ku, Gojō-dōri-Yamatoōji agaru Higashi; treasure house adult/child ¥600/400; ⏲8.30am-4.30pm; 🚌5min walk from Kiyomizu-michi bus stop, bus 206 from Kyoto Station) An important Buddhist pilgrimage stop, this temple was founded in 963 by Kūya Shōnin, who carved an image of an 11-headed Kannon and installed it in the temple in the hope of stopping a plague that was ravaging Kyoto at the time.

The temple itself is unremarkable but the treasure house at the rear contains a rare collection of 15 fantastic statues; the most intriguing is a standing likeness of Kūya, staff in hand and prayer gong draped around his neck, with a string of tiny figurines parading from his gums. Legend holds that while praying one day, these manifestations of the Buddha suddenly ambled out of his mouth.

KENNIN-JI TEMPLE

Map p222 (建仁寺; ☎561-6363; Higashiyama-ku, Shijō-sagaru; admission ¥500; ⏰10am-4.30pm; 🚉10min walk from Gion Shijō Station, Keihan line) Founded in 1202 by the monk Eisai, Kennin-ji is the oldest Zen temple in Kyoto. It is an island of peace and calm on the border of the boisterous Gion nightlife district and it makes a fine counterpoint to the worldly pleasures of that area. The highlight at Kennin-ji is the fine and expansive *kare-sansui* (dry-landscape rock garden). The painting of the twin dragons on the roof of the Hōdō hall is also fantastic; access to this hall is via two gates with rather puzzling English operating instructions (you'll see what we mean).

KIYOMIZU-DERA TEMPLE

See p81.

NINEN-ZAKA & SANNEN-ZAKA NEIGHBOURHOOD

Map p222 (Higashiyama-ku, Kiyomizu; 🚌10min walk from Higashiyama-yasui bus stop, bus 206 from Kyoto Station) Just downhill from and slightly to the north of Kiyomizu-dera, you will find one of Kyoto's loveliest restored neighbourhoods, the Ninen-zaka-Sannen-zaka area. The name refers to the two main streets of the area: Ninen-zaka and Sannen-zaka, literally 'Two-Year Hill' and 'Three-Year Hill' (the years referring to the ancient imperial years when they were first laid out). These two charming streets are lined with old wooden houses, traditional shops and restaurants. If you fancy a break, there are many tea houses and cafes along these lanes.

KŌDAI-JI TEMPLE

Map p222 (☎526 Shimokawara-chō, Kōdai-ji, Higashiyama-ku; admission ¥600; ⏰9am-5pm; Ⓜ20min walk from Higashiyama Station, Tōzai subway line) This temple was founded in 1605 by Kita-no-Mandokoro in memory of her late husband, Toyotomi Hideyoshi. The extensive grounds include gardens designed by the famed landscape architect Kobori Enshū, and tea houses designed by the renowned master of the tea ceremony, Sen no Rikyū.

The temple holds three annual special night-time illuminations, when the gardens are lit by multicoloured spotlights. The illuminations are held from mid-March to early May, 1 to 18 August, and late October to early December.

MARUYAMA-KŌEN PARK

Map p222 (円山公園; Higashiyama-ku; 🚌1min walk from Gion bus stop, bus 206 from Kyoto Station; Ⓜ20min walk from Higashiyama Station, Tōzai subway line) Maruyama-kōen is a favourite of locals and visitors alike. This park is the place to come to escape the bustle of the city centre and amble around gardens, ponds, souvenir shops and restaurants. Peaceful paths meander through the trees and carp glide through the waters of a small pond in the park's centre.

For two weeks in early April, when the park's cherry trees come into bloom, the calm atmosphere is shattered by hordes of drunken revellers having *hanami* (cherry-blossom viewing) parties under the trees. The centrepiece is a massive *shidare-zakura* cherry tree; this is one of the most beautiful sights in Kyoto, particularly when lit up from below at night. For those who don't mind crowds, this is a good place to observe the Japanese at their most uninhibited. Arrive early and claim a good spot high on the east side of the park, from where you can peer down on the mayhem below.

FREE YASAKA-JINJA SHRINE

Map p222 (八坂神社; ☎625 Gion-machi Kita gawa, Higashiyama-ku; ⏰24hr; 🚌1min walk from Gion bus stop, bus 206 from Kyoto Station; Ⓜ15min walk from Higashiyama Station, Tōzai subway line) This colourful and spacious shrine is down the hill from Maruyama-kōen. It's considered the guardian shrine of Gion. The present buildings, with the exception of the older, two-storey west gate, date from 1654. The granite *torii* (shrine gate) on the south side was erected in 1666 and stands 9.5m high, making it one of the tallest in Japan. The roof of the main shrine is covered with cypress shingles. Among the treasures here are a pair of carved wooden *koma-inu* (guardian lion-dogs) attributed to the renowned sculptor Unkei.

This shrine is particularly popular as a spot for *hatsu-mōde* (first shrine visit of the New Year). If you don't mind a stampede, come here around midnight on New Year's Eve or on any of the days following. Surviving the crush is proof that you're blessed by the gods!

Yasaka-jinja sponsors Kyoto's biggest festival, Gion Matsuri (p22).

CHION-IN TEMPLE

See p82.

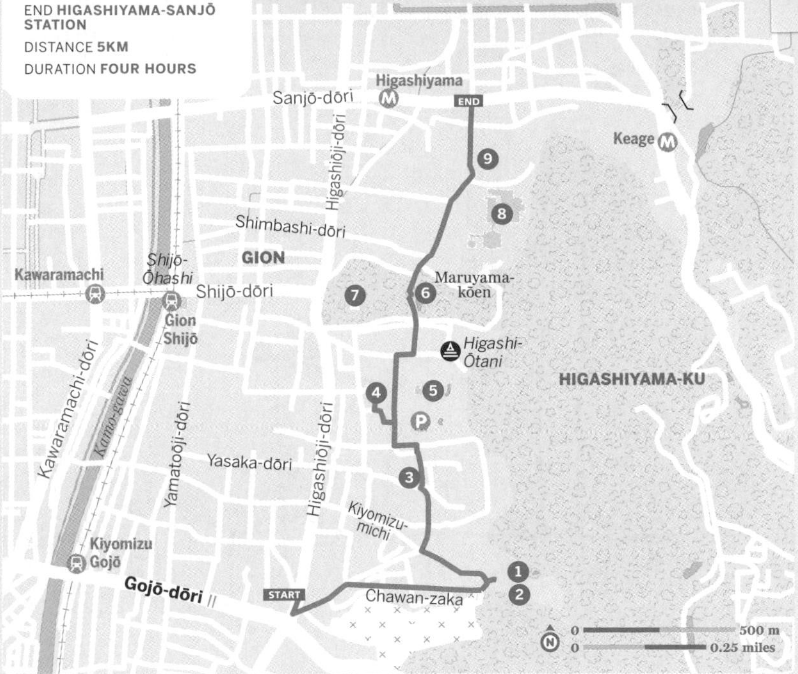

Neighbourhood Walk

Hills, Temples & Lanes in Southern Higashiyama

From the starting point at the Gojō-zaka bus stop on Higashiōji-dōri (bus 18, 100, 206 or 207), walk up Gojō-zaka slope. Head uphill until you reach the first fork in the road; bear right and continue up Chawan-zaka (Teapot Lane). At the top of the hill, you'll come to Kiyomizu-dera. Before you enter the temple, we recommend that you pay ¥100 to descend into the 1 **Tainai-meguri**, the entrance to which is just to the left of the main temple entrance. Next, enter 2 **Kiyomizu-dera**.

After touring Kiyomizu-dera, exit down Kiyomizu-michi. Continue down the hill and take a right at the four-way intersection down stone-paved steps. This is Sannen-zaka, where you will find tiny little 3 **Kasagi-ya**, which has been serving tea and Japanese-style sweets for as long as anyone can remember. It is on the left, just below a vending machine.

Halfway down Sannen-zaka, the road curves to the left. Follow it a short distance, then go right down a flight of steps into Ninen-zaka. At the end of Ninen-zaka zigzag left (at the vending machines) then right (just past the car park), and continue north. Very soon, on your left, you'll come to the entrance to 4 **Ishibei-kōji** – perhaps the most beautiful street in Kyoto. Take a detour to explore this, then retrace your steps and continue north, passing almost immediately the entrance to 5 **Kōdai-ji** on the right up a long flight of stairs.

After Kōdai-ji continue north to the T-junction; turn right at this junction and then take a quick left. You'll cross the wide pedestrian arcade that leads to Ōtani cemetery and then descend into 6 **Maruyama-kōen**. In the centre of the park, you'll see the giant Gion shidare-zakura, Kyoto's most famous cherry tree.

From the park, you can head west into the grounds of 7 **Yasaka-jinja**. Then return to the park and head north to tour the grounds of the impressive 8 **Chion-in**. From here it's a quick walk to 9 **Shōren-in**. From Shōren-in walk down to Sanjō-dōri.

Neighbourhood Walk

Night Walk Through the Floating World

Start on the steps of 1 **Yasaka-jinja** (at the intersection of Shijō-dōri and Higashiōji-dōri), a 10-minute walk from Shijō (Keihan line) or Kawaramachi (Hankyū line) stations. Cross to the south side of Shijō-dōri and just after passing the Gion Hotel turn left. Walk 150m and take the second right. Another 100m brings you to Hanami-kōji, a picturesque street of high-class *ryōtei* (traditional, high-class restaurants). Take a look then walk back north to Shijō-dōri.

Cross Shijō-dōri and go west (left) for about 20m then turn right into Kiri-dōshi. As you continue along Kiri-dōshi, you'll cross Tominagachō-dōri, which is lined with buildings containing hundreds of hostess bars.

Kiri-dōshi crosses another street and then narrows to a tiny alley. You are now about to enter Gion's most lovely area, which lies just across 2 **Tatsumi-bashi bridge**. This is the Shimbashi district, which features some of Kyoto's finest traditional architecture, most upmarket restaurants and exclusive hostess bars.

At the fork in the road you will find a small 3 **Tatsumi shrine**. Take a left and walk west along the canal. Just before you come to the end of the street, on your left, across a bridge, you'll find 4 **Ōzawa**, a fine tempura restaurant.

At the end of Shimbashi, take a left onto gaudy Nawate-dōri. Just before you reach Shijō-dōri, you'll pass 5 **Issen Yōshoku**, a popular *okonomiyaki* (Japanese pancake) restaurant.

Head west on Shijō-dōri, passing 6 **Minami-za**, Kyoto's main kabuki theatre. Cross the Kamo-gawa on the north side of Shijō-ōhashi and walk to the *kōban* (police box) on your right. You are now standing at the intersection of Shijō-dōri and 7 **Pontochō**. Heading north brings you into an entirely different world of upmarket restaurants, bars, clubs and cafes.

At the north end of Pontochō at Sanjō-dōri, take a left and another left on Kiyamachi-dōri. This is a much more casual and inexpensive entertainment district.

GION DISTRICT NEIGHBOURHOOD

Map p222 (祇園; Higashiyama-ku, Gion-machi; 1min walk from Gion Shijō Station, Keihan line) Gion is the famous entertainment and geisha quarter on the eastern bank of the Kamo-gawa. While Gion's true origins were in teahouses catering to weary visitors to Yasaka-jinja (p84), by the mid-18th century the area was Kyoto's largest pleasure district. Despite the looming modern architecture, congested traffic and contemporary nightlife establishments that have compromised its historical beauty, there are still some places left in Gion for an enjoyable walk. It looks quite drab by day, but comes alive with people and lights in the evening.

Hanami-kōji runs north to south and bisects Shijō-dōri. The southern section is lined with 17th-century traditional restaurants and teahouses, many of which are exclusive establishments for geisha entertainment. At the south end you reach Gion Corner (p90) and **Gion Kōbu Kaburen-jō Theatre** (祇園甲部歌舞練場).

If you walk from Shijō-dōri along the northern section of Hanami-kōji and take your third left, you will find yourself on **Shimbashi** (sometimes called Shirakawa Minami-dōri), which is one of Kyoto's most beautiful streets and, arguably, the most beautiful street in all of Asia, especially in the evening and during cherry-blossom season. A bit further north lie Shinmonzen-dōri and Furumonzen-dōri, running east to west. Wander in either direction along these streets, which are packed with old houses, art galleries and shops specialising in antiques – but don't expect flea-market prices here.

SHŌREN-IN TEMPLE

Map p222 (青蓮院; 561-2345; 69-1 Sanjōbō-chō, Awataguchi, Higashiyama-ku; admission ¥500; 9am-5pm; 5min walk from Higashiyama Station, Tōzai subway line) This temple is hard to miss, with its giant camphor trees growing just outside the walls. Fortunately, many tourists manage to do just that, leaving the lovely garden relatively quiet, even when nearby attractions are mobbed.

Shōren-in, commonly called Awata Palace after the road it faces, was originally the residence of the chief abbot of the Tendai school. Founded in 1150, the present building dates from 1895 and the main hall has sliding screens with paintings from the 16th and 17th centuries. This is a pleasant place to sit and think while gazing out over one of Kyoto's finest landscape gardens.

MAIKO COSTUME

If you ever wondered how *you* might look as a *maiko* (apprentice geisha), Kyoto has many organisations in town that offer the chance. **Maika** (舞香; Map p222; 551 1661; Higashiyama-ku, Miyagawa suji; 9.30am-4.30pm Mon-Fri, 9am-7pm holidays; 10min walk from Shijō Station, Keihan line) is in the Gion district. Here you can be dressed up to live out your *maiko* fantasy. Prices begin at ¥6720 for the basic treatment, which includes full make-up and formal kimono (studio photos cost ¥500 per print and you can have stickers made from these). If you don't mind spending some extra yen, it's possible to head out in costume for a stroll through Gion (and be stared at like never before!). The process takes about an hour. Call to reserve at least one day in advance.

EATING

SHIBAZAKI NOODLES ¥¥

Map p222 (柴崎; 525-3600; 4-190-3 Kiyomizu, Higashiyama-ku; soba from ¥1000; 11am-6pm, closed Tue; ; Gojō-zaka or Kiyomizu-michi bus stop, bus 202 or 100 from Kyoto Station) For excellent *soba* noodles and well-presented tempura sets (among other things) in the area of Kiyomizu-dera, try this comfortable and spacious restaurant. After your meal, head upstairs to check out the sublime collection of Japanese lacquerware. Look for the low stone wall and the *noren* curtains hanging in the entryway.

TOP CHOICE **ŌZAWA** TEMPURA ¥¥

Map p222 (おおざわ; 561-2052; Minami gawa, Gion Shirakawa Nawate Higashi iru, Higashiyama-ku; meals from ¥3990; 5-10pm, closed Thu; ; 10min walk from Gion-Shijō Station, Keihan line) Sited on one of the most beautiful streets in Gion – Shirakawa-minami-dōri (also known as Shimbashi) – this charming restaurant offers excellent tempura in refined surroundings. Unless you choose a private tatami room, you'll sit at the counter and watch as the chef prepares each piece of tempura individually before your eyes. Considering the location and the quality of the food, this place is great value. The restaurant is across a bridge; look for the sign on the street. Lunch is available with advance request.

GION KARYŌ KAISEKI ¥¥¥

Map p222 (祇園迦陵; ☎532-0025; Higashiyama-ku, Gion-machi minamigawa 570-235; lunch & dinner courses from ¥3800; ⊙11.30am-3.30pm & 5.30-11pm, closed Wed; 📄; 🚉7min walk from Gion Shijō Station, Keihan line) Take an old Kyoto house, renovate it to make it comfortable for modern diners, serve reasonably priced and excellent *kaiseki* and you have Karyō's recipe for success. The chef and servers are welcoming here and an English menu makes ordering a snap. There are counter seats where you can watch the chef working and rooms with *hori-kotatsu* (sunken floors) for groups.

TOP CHOICE **OMEN KODAI-JI** NOODLES ¥¥

Map p222 (おめん　高台寺店; ☎541-5007; Higashiyama-ku, Kōdaiji-dōri, Shimokawara Higashi iru, Masuya-chō 358; omen from ¥1100, set menu ¥2980; ⊙10.30am-8.30pm; Ⓜ5min walk from Higashiyama-Yasui bus stop, bus 206 from Kyoto Station) This branch of Kyoto's famed Omen noodle chain is the best place to stop while exploring the Southern Higashiyama district. It's in a remodelled Japanese building with a light, airy feeling. The signature udon noodles are delicious and there are many other à la carte offerings.

HISAGO NOODLES ¥

Map p222 (ひさご; ☎561-2109; 484 Shimo kawara-chō, Higashiyama-ku; ⊙11.30am-7.30pm Tue-Sun; 📄; 🚌10min walk from Higashiyama-yasui bus stop, bus 206 from Kyoto Station) If you need a quick meal while in the main Southern Higashiyama sightseeing district, this simple noodle and rice restaurant is a good bet. It's within easy walking distance of Kiyomizu-dera and Maruyama-kōen. *Oyakodonburi* (chicken and egg over rice; ¥980) is the speciality of the house. There is no English sign; look for the traditional front and the small collection of food models on display. In the busy seasons, there's almost always a queue outside.

BAMBOO IZAKAYA ¥¥

Map p222 (晩boo; ☎771-5559; Higashiyama-ku, Higashiyama Sanjō Higashi iru, Minami gawa 1st fl; meals ¥4000-5000; ⊙5.30pm-midnight; Ⓜ5min walk from Higashiyama Station, Tōzai subway line) Bamboo is one of Kyoto's more approachable *izakaya* (Japanese pub/eatery). It's on Sanjō-dōri, near the mouth of a traditional, old shopping arcade. You can sit at the counter here and order a variety of typical *izakaya* dishes, watching as the chefs do their thing.

YAGURA NOODLES ¥

Map p222 (やぐ羅; ☎561-1035; Higashiyama-ku, Shijō-dōri, Yamatoōji Nishi iru; soba ¥1100; ⊙11.30am-9pm, 11am-8.30pm Sun, closed Thu; 🚉1min walk from Gion Shijō Station, Keihan line) Across from Minami-za kabuki theatre, this noodle specialist is an unassuming and casual spot for a nice bowl of noodles while exploring Gion. We recommend the *nishin soba* (*soba* noodles topped with fish; ¥1100). Yagura is located between a *rāmen* joint and a Japanese gift shop – look for the bowls of noodles in the window.

ASUKA CAFETERIA ¥

Map p222 (明日香; ☎751-9809; 144 Nishi-machi, Jingū-michi Nishi iru, Sanjō-dōri, Higashiyama-ku; meals from ¥850; ⊙11am-10pm Tue-Sun; 📄; Ⓜ2min walk from Higashiyama Station, Tōzai subway line) With an English menu, and a staff of friendly Kyoto *mama-sans* who are at home with foreign customers, this is a great place for a cheap lunch or dinner while sightseeing in the Higashiyama area. The tempura *mori-awase* (assorted tempura set) is a big pile of tempura for only ¥1000. Look for the red lantern and pictures of the set meals.

RYŪMON CHINESE ¥¥

Map p222 (龍門; ☎752-8181; Kita gawa, Higashiōji Nishi iru, Sanjō-dōri, Higashiyama-ku; dinner set from ¥3000; ⊙5pm-5am; Ⓜ5min walk from Higashiyama Station, Tōzai subway line) This place may look like a total dive but the food is reliable and authentic, as the crowds of Kyoto's Chinese residents will attest. There's no English menu but there is a picture menu and some of the waitresses can speak English. Decor is strictly Chinese kitsch, with the exception of the deer head over the cash register – still trying to figure that one out. Look for the food pictures out the front.

MACHAPUCHARE JAPANESE, NEPALESE ¥

Map p222 (マチャプチャレ; ☎525-1330; 290 Kamihorizume-chō, Sayamachi-dōri Shōmen sagaru, Higashiyama-ku; obanzai lunch set ¥1050; ⊙11.30am-2pm, closed Tue; 🥕; 🚉10min walk from Shichijō Station, Keihan line) This organic vegetarian restaurant serves a sublime vegetarian *obanzai* (Kyoto home-style cooking) set. The post-and-beam construction of the place and the friendly owner are added attractions. The problem is that the restaurant keeps somewhat irregular hours and the *obanzai* is not always available. Get a Japanese speaker to call and check before trekking here. It's opposite Shōmen-yu *sento* (public bath).

SANTŌKA RĀMEN ¥

Map p222 (山頭火; ☎532-1335; Higashiyama-ku, Sanjō sagaru Higashi gawa; rāmen from ¥790; ⊙11am-11.30pm; 1min walk from Sanjō Station, Keihan line) The young chefs at this sleek restaurant dish out some seriously good Hokkaidō-style *rāmen* (noodles in a meat broth with meat and vegetables). You will be given a choice of three kinds of soup when you order: *shio* (salt), *shōyu* (soy sauce) or miso – we highly recommend you go for the miso soup. For something totally decadent, try the *tokusen toroniku rāmen,* which is made from pork cheeks, of which only 200g can be obtained from one animal. The pork will come on a separate plate from the *rāmen* – just shovel it all into your bowl. The restaurant is located on the east side and ground floor of the new Kyōen restaurant and shopping complex. They keep serving until they run out of soup.

ISSEN YŌSHOKU OKONOMIYAKI ¥

Map p222 (壱銭洋食; ☎533-0001; Higashiyama-ku, Gion, Shijō Nawate kado; okonomiyaki ¥630; ⊙11am-3am Mon-Sat, 10.30am-10pm Sun; 5min walk from Shijō Station, Keihan line) Heaped with red ginger and green scallions, the *okonomiyaki* at this Gion institution is a garish snack – which somehow seems fitting considering the surrounding neighbourhood. It's open to the elements and you can't miss the griddles out the front.

TOP CHOICE KASAGI-YA SWEETS ¥

Map p222 (かさぎ屋; ☎561-9562; 349 Masuya chō, Kōdai-ji, Higashiyama-ku; ⊙11am-6pm, closed Tue; ; 10min walk from Higashiyama-yasui bus stop, bus 206 from Kyoto Station) At Kasagi-ya, on Sannen-zaka near Kiyomizu-dera (p81), you can enjoy a nice cup of *matcha* (powdered green tea) and a variety of sweets. This funky old wooden shop has atmosphere to boot and friendly staff – which makes it worth the wait if there's a queue. Highly recommended. It's hard to spot – you may have to ask one of the local shop owners.

SENMONTEN CHINESE ¥

Map p222 (泉門天; ☎531-2733; Higashiyama-ku, Hanami-kōji-dōri, Shimbashi sagaru Higashi gawa; per 10 dumplings ¥520; ⊙6pm-3am Mon-Sat; M5min walk from Gion Shijō Station, Keihan line) This place serves one thing only: crisp fried *gyōza* (Chinese dumplings), which come in lots of 10 and are washed down with beer or Chinese *raoshu* (rice wine). If you can break the record for the most *gyōza* eaten in one sitting, your meal will be free and you'll receive – guess what? – more *gyōza* to take home. The last time we were here, the men's record was around 150 *gyōza*. Look for the red-and-white sign and the glass door.

KAGIZEN YOSHIFUSA SWEETS, TEA ¥

Map p222 (鍵善良房; ☎561-1818; 264 Gion machi Kita gawa, Higashiyama-ku; kuzukiri ¥900; ⊙9.30am-6pm Tue-Sun; ; 5min walk from Shijō Station, Keihan line) This Gion institution is one of Kyoto's oldest and best-known *okashi-ya* (sweet shops). It sells a variety of traditional sweets and has a lovely tea room out the back where you can sample cold *kuzukiri* (transparent arrowroot noodles) served with a *kuro-mitsu* (sweet black sugar) dipping sauce, or just a nice cup of *matcha* and a sweet. All in all, it's one of the best spots in Gion for a rest. Look for the sweets in the window, the wide front and the *noren* curtains.

DRINKING & NIGHTLIFE

TOP CHOICE BAR MAIN HIGASHIYAMA BAR

Map p222 (バー メイン ヒガシヤマ; ☎541-3331; Garden Oriental Kyoto; Higashiyama-ku, Yasaka-dōri, Shimokawara Higashi iru, Yasaka-kami-machi 366; ⊙8pm-midnight; M10min walk from Higashiyama-Yasui bus stop, bus 206 from Kyoto Station) This slick and elegant bar in the Garden Oriental complex, right in the heart of the Southern Higashiyama sightseeing district is a real stunner. You can choose from counter or table seating and the atmosphere is completely relaxing. Smart casual is the way to go here.

TOP CHOICE GAEL IRISH PUB BAR

Map p222 (ゲール・アイリッシュ・パブ; ☎525-0680; 2F Ōtō Bldg, Nijūikken-chō, Yamatoōji-dōri agaru, Shijō, Higashiyama-ku; ⊙5pm-1am, later Thu-Sun; 3min walk from Gion Shijō Station, Keihan line) A cosy little Irish bar on the doorstep of Gion. It offers good food, excellent beer and friendly staff, as well as occasional live music. It's a great place to meet local expats and see what's going on in town. It's up a flight of steps.

GION S BAR, CAFE

Map p222 (ギヲン エッセ; ☎525-0585; Shirakawa Nawate; ⏲noon-11pm, to 10pm Sun; 🚉5min walk from Shijō Station, Keihan line) Not exactly a bar, not exactly a cafe, this is a fine spot to sip a drink and watch the characters of Gion stroll by. It's near the Shira-kawa canal and right alongside some of Kyoto's best cherry trees.

KISUI IZAKAYA

Map p222 (器粋; ☎585-6639; 1F 2-239 Miyagawa-suji, Higashiyama-ku; ⏲6pm-midnight Mon-Sat; 📄; 🚉5min walk from Gion Shijō Station, Keihan line) This little one-counter *izakaya* at the north end of the Miyagawa geisha district is a good place to knock a few back. The cheerful owner is sure to make you welcome and you can order food from the upstairs restaurant to eat. It's on the first floor, opposite a park, on the corner. There is no English sign.

PIG & WHISTLE PUB

Map p222 (ピッグ&ホイッスル; ☎761-6022; Kawabata-dōri-Sanjō; ⏲5pm-2am Sun-Thu, to 5am Fri & Sat; 🚉1min walk from Sanjō Station, Keihan line) The Pig is a British-style pub with darts, pint glasses, and fish and chips. While many of its patrons have moved on to other venues, we still like this place for its relaxed layout and homey interior. The two main drawcards are Guinness on tap and friendly bilingual staff. The Pig's on the 2nd floor of the Shobi building near the Sanjō-Kawabata crossing.

TOP CHOICE GION FINLANDIA BAR BAR

Map p222 (ぎをん フィンランディアバー; ☎541-3482; Higashiyama-ku, Gion-machi minamigawa; ⏲6pm-3am Mon-Fri, 4pm-3am Sat, 4pm-1am Sun; 🚉5min walk from Gion Shijō Station, Keihan line) This stylish Gion bar in an old geisha house is a great place for a civilised drink in Southern Higashiyama. The 1st floor is decorated with Finnish touches while the upstairs retains a Japanese feeling, with sunken floors and tatami mats. There's a wide selection of vodka on offer here. The cover charge is ¥500 and you can expect to pay around ¥3000 for a few drinks.

ENTERTAINMENT

GION CORNER THEATRE

Map p222 (ギオンコーナー; ☎561-1119; Yasaka Hall, 570-2 Gionmachi Minamigawa, Higashiyama-ku; ⏲nightly 1 Mar–30 Nov, Fri, Sat & Sun from 7pm Dec-Feb; 🚉10min walk from Gion-Shijō Station, Keihan line) Gion Corner presents regularly scheduled shows that include a bit of tea ceremony, koto (Japanese zither) music, ikebana (flower arrangement), *gagaku* (court music), *kyōgen* (ancient comic plays), *kyōmai* (Kyoto-style dance) and *bunraku* (classical puppet theatre). It's geared to a tourist market and is fairly pricey for what you get.

KYOTO CUISINE & MAIKO EVENING GEISHA ENTERTAINMENT

Map p222 (京料理と舞妓の夕べ; ☎541-5315; www.kyoto-maiko.jp; Yasaka Jinja Minamimon-mae, 505 Minamigawa, Gion-machi, Higashiyama-ku; ⏲Mon, Wed, Fri & Sat; 🚌1min walk from Gion bus stop, bus 206 from Kyoto Station; Ⓜ20min walk from Higashiyama Station, Tōzai subway line) If you want to witness geisha perform and then actually speak with them, one of the best opportunities is at Gion Hatanaka, a Gion ryokan (traditional Japanese inn) that offers a regularly scheduled evening of elegant Kyoto *kaiseki* food and personal entertainment by real Kyoto *geiko* (fully fledged geisha) as well as *maiko* (apprentice geisha).

EN TEA CEREMONIES

Map p222 (☎080-3782-2706; 272 Matsubara-chō, Higashiyama-ku; tea ceremony per person ¥2000; ⏲3-6pm, closed Wed; 🚌1min walk from Chion-in-mae bus stop, bus 206 from Kyoto Station) This is a small tea house near Gion where you can experience the Japanese tea ceremony with a minimum of fuss or expense. English explanations are provided and tea ceremonies are held at 3pm, 4pm, 5pm or 6pm (check the website for latest times, as these may change). Reservations are recommended in high season. It's a little tricky to find: it's down a little alley off Higashiōji-dōri – look for the sign just south of Tenkaippin Rāmen.

MINAMI-ZA THEATRE

Map p222 (南座; ☎561-0160; Shijō-Ōhashi; 🚉Gion-Shijō Station, Keihan line) The oldest kabuki theatre in Japan is the Minami-za theatre in Gion. The major event of the year is the **Kaomise festival** (1 to 26 December), which features Japan's finest kabuki actors. Other performances take place on an irregular basis – check with the Tourist Information Center. The most likely months for performances are May, June and September.

MIYAKO ODORI GEISHA DANCE

Map p222 (都をどり; ☎561-1115; Higashiyama-ku-Gion-chō South; 10min walk from Gion-Shijō Station, Keihan line) Presented by the Gion Kōbu geisha district, this is our favourite geisha dance in Kyoto. It's a real stunner and the colourful images will remain with you long after the curtain falls. It's held throughout April at the Gion Kōbu Kaburen-jō Theatre, on Hanami-kōji, just south of Shijō-dōri.

KYŌ ODORI GEISHA DANCE

Map p222 (京おどり; ☎561-1151; Kawabata-dōri-Shijō sagaru; 10min walk from Gion-Shijō Station, Keihan line) Put on by the Miyagawa-chō geisha district, this is a wonderful geisha dance, on a slightly more intimate scale than the Miyako Odori. It's held from the first to the third Sunday in April at the **Miyagawa-chō Kaburen-jō Theatre** (宮川町歌舞練場), east of the Kamo-gawa between Shijō-dōri and Gojō-dōri.

GION ODORI GEISHA DANCE

Map p222 (祇園をどり; ☎561-0224; Higashiyama-ku-Gion; 3min walk from Gion bus stop, bus 206 from Kyoto Station) This is a quaint and charming geisha dance put on by the geisha of the Gion Higashi geisha district. It's held from 1 to 10 November at the **Gion Kaikan Theatre** (祇園会館), near Yasaka-jinja.

SHOPPING

KAGOSHIN BAMBOO CRAFTS

Map p222 (かご新; ☎771-0209; 4 chō-me, Sanjō-Ōhashi higashi, Higashiyama-ku; 9am-6pm Tue-Sun; 3min walk from Sanjō Station, Keihan line) Kagoshin is a small semi-open bamboo craft shop on Sanjō-dōri, only a few minutes' walk east of the Kamo-gawa. It has a good selection of baskets, chopstick holders, bamboo vases, decorations and knick-knacks. The baskets make a good, light souvenir and look great in alcove displays.

TAKEMATSU BAMBOO CRAFTS

Map p222 (竹松; ☎751-2444; Higashiyama-ku, Sanjō-dōri, Ōhashi higashi iru 3-39; 10am-7pm; 3min walk from Sanjō Station, Keihan line) With a name that even residents find hard to pronounce, this fine little specialist store stocks a selection of bamboo crafts. It's only a few steps away from its main competition, Kagoshin, which allows for easy comparison shopping. Like Kagoshin, it stocks baskets, bamboo vases, decorations and knick-knacks.

TESSAI-DŌ ARTS & CRAFTS

Map p222 (てっさい堂; ☎531-9566; Higashiyama-ku, Shimokawara-chō 463; 10am-5pm; 7min walk from Higashiyamayasui bus stop, bus 206 from Kyoto Station) While exploring the lovely Nene-no-Michi lane in Higashiyama's main sightseeing district, you might want to step into this fine little wood-block print shop. This shop specialises in original prints, some of which are quite old. Prices average ¥10,000 per print and the owner will be happy to consult with you about what sort of print you are after.

Northern Higashiyama

Neighbourhood Top Five

❶ Immersing yourself in the green world of **Nanzen-ji** (p94). With wonderful gardens, intimate subtemples and a hidden grotto waiting in the woods, Nanzen-ji is one of Kyoto's most appealing temples.

❷ Taking the bamboo-lined path to see **Ginkaku-ji** (p95), Kyoto's famed 'Silver Pavilion'.

❸ Getting lost in thought on the flower-strewn **Path of Philosophy** (p97).

❹ Escaping the crowds and find yourself at the superb Buddhist sanctuary of **Hōnen-in** (p97).

❺ Checking out the exhibits in Kyoto's museum district of **Okazaki-kōen** (p99).

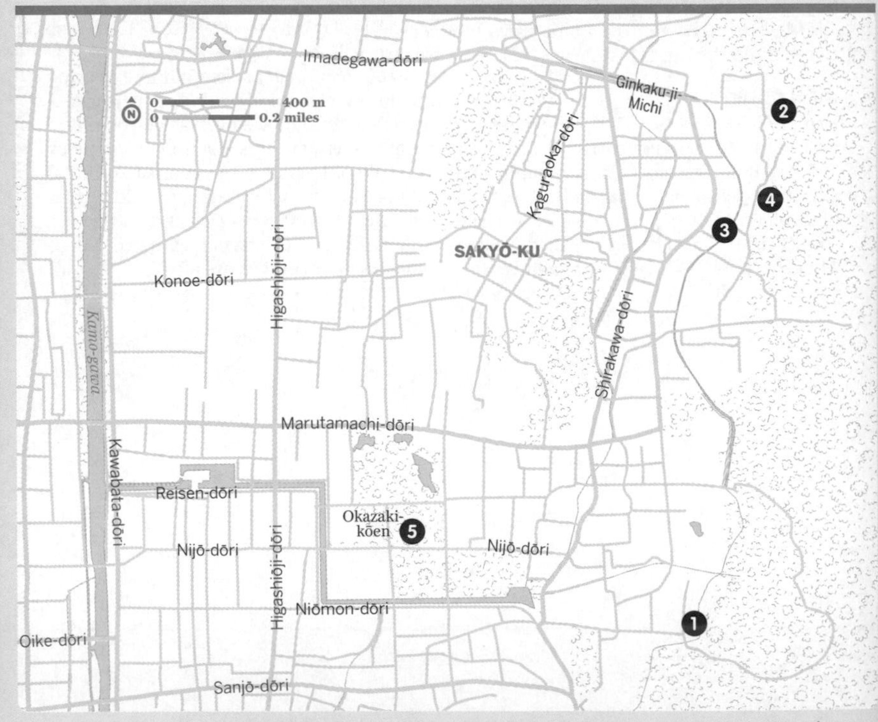

For more detail of this area, see Map p224

Explore: Northern Higashiyama

Running along the base of the Higashiyama (Eastern Mountains) from Sanjō-dōri in the south to Imadegawa-dōri in the north, the Northern Higashiyama area is one of Kyoto's most important sightseeing areas. It comprises a fairly large area and can be explored on foot, mostly over car-free walkways, making it one of the most pleasant areas for sightseeing in Kyoto.

Northern Higashiyama can be divided into two main sections: the strip of temples located directly at the base of the mountains, most of which are accessible from the lovely Path of Philosophy and the museums/shrine district known as Okazaki-kōen (Okazaki Park), which occupies a wide swath of the area between the mountains and the river.

You can explore each section of Northern Higashiyama in about half a day, but a full day allows a more leisurely pace.

Many people use Kyoto city bus 5 to access this area – and this is certainly convenient since this bus traverses the entire district – but keep in mind that this bus is often crowded and it can be slow. If coming from Kyoto Station or Downtown, it's probably better to take the subway here. The Tōzai subway line will get you to Higashiyama Station, which is convenient for Okazaki-kōen, and Keage Station, which is convenient for Nanzen-ji and sights north.

Unfortunately, there are no trains or subways convenient to the northern end of this district. A variety of buses will take you to Downtown and Kyoto Station.

This is the best area in Kyoto for bicycling and a rental cycle is one of the best ways to explore Northern Higashiyama.

Local Life

- **Hangout** (p99) The pond behind the Metropolitan Museum of Art is popular with local parents and couples for picnics and lazy afternoon naps.
- **Exercise** (p97) Local fitness buffs and nature lovers make a daily pilgrimage up Daimonji-yama.
- **Freebie** (p99) The Kyoto Municipal Museum of Art hosts all kinds of special free exhibits.

Getting There & Away

- **Train** The Keihan line stops at stations on the west side of the district.
- **Bus** Kyoto bus 5 traverses the district. Several other city buses stop here as well.
- **Subway** The Tōzai subway line is the best way to access Northern Higashiyama.

Lonely Planet's Top Tip

Visit the big-name sights here (Ginkaku-ji, Eikan-dō and Nanzen-ji) early on a weekday morning to avoid the crowds. Alternatively, go right before closing.

Best Places to Eat

- Omen (p100)
- Goya (p100)
- Falafel Garden (p101)

For reviews, see p100

Best Places to Shop

- Kyoto Handicraft Center (p103)
- Tōzandō (p103)
- Zōhiko (p103)

For reviews, see p102

Best Places for Kids

- Okazaki-kōen (p99)
- Kyoto City Zoo (p99)
- Path of Philosophy (p97)

For reviews, see p96 

JTB PHOTO / PHOTOLIBRARY ©

TOP SIGHTS
NANZEN-JI

Nanzen-ji, a complex of Zen temples and subtemples tucked against the Higashiyama (Eastern Mountains), is the Platonic form of Japanese Buddhist temple. It's got it all: a fine little *karesansui* (Zen) garden, soaring main halls, great gardens and an incredibly scenic location. Despite its popularity it doesn't feel crowded, even during the autumn foliage season (November), when the maples turn crimson and stand in beautiful contrast to the moss beneath their boughs.

Nanzen-ji (南禅寺) began its life as a retirement villa for Emperor Kameyama. Upon his passing in 1291, it was dedicated as a Zen temple. It operates now as the headquarters of the Rinzai school.

At the entrance to the temple stands the San-mon gate (1628), its ceiling adorned with Tosa and Kanō school murals of birds and angels. Beyond the San-mon is the Honden (main hall) with a dragon painting on the ceiling.

Beyond the Honden, the Hōjō hall contains the Leaping Tiger Garden, a classical *karensansui* (dry gravel landscape, or Zen) garden. Sadly, a tape loop in Japanese detracts from the experience of the garden. You can enjoy a cup of tea (¥400) as you sit on tatami mats gazing at a small waterfall; ask at the reception desk.

After visiting the main hall and the Hōjō Garden, walk under the aqueduct and take a hard left and walk up the hill. Climb the steps to Kōtoku-an, a fine subtemple nestled at the base of the mountains. It's free to enter and you will have the place to yourself about half the time.

Several fine subtemples that surround the complex: Nanzen-in (p96), Konchi-in (p96) and Tenju-an (p96).

DON'T MISS

- Kōtoku-an

PRACTICALITIES

- Map p224
- ☎771-0365
- Fukuchi-chō, Nanzen-ji, Sakyō-ku
- grounds free, Hōjō garden ¥500, San-mon gate ¥300-400
- 8.40am-5pm Mar-Nov, to 4.30pm Dec-Feb
- 10min walk from Keage Station, Tōzai subway line

TOP SIGHTS
GINKAKU-JI

JUDY BELLAH / LONELY PLANET IMAGES ©

At the northern end of the Path of Philosophy, Kyoto's famed 'Silver Pavilion', or Ginkaku-ji, is an enclosed paradise of ponds, thick moss, classical Japanese architecture and swaying bamboo groves. It is unquestionably one of the most luxurious gardens in the city and belongs near the top of any Kyoto sightseeing itinerary. Just be sure to visit when the crowds are likely to be thin: early on a weekday morning or just before closing. Or wait for a rainy day: the moss here is superb under a light rain.

In 1482 shōgun Ashikaga Yoshimasa constructed a villa at this fine mountainside location, which he used as a genteel retreat from the turmoil of civil war. Although Ginkaku-ji (銀閣寺) translates as Silver Pavilion, this is simply a nickname to distinguish it from Kinkaku-ji (the 'Golden Pavilion' on the other side of town). The main hall, which overlooks the pond, was originally covered in black lacquer. After Yoshimasa's death it was converted to a temple. The temple belongs to the Shōkoku-ji sect of the Rinzai school of Zen.

You will find walkways leading through the gardens, which were laid out by painter and garden designer Sōami. The gardens include meticulously raked cones of white sand known as *kōgetsudai*, designed to reflect moonlight and enhance the beauty of the garden at night.

In addition to the Buddha image in the main hall, the Tōgudō (residence of Yoshimasa) houses an effigy of Yoshimasa dressed in monk's garb.

Don't miss the footpath that leads to a viewpoint over Kyoto and all the way to the western mountains. The path starts at the northeast corner of the garden and can be climbed in a few minutes.

DON'T MISS

- Footpath to views over Kyoto

PRACTICALITIES

- Map p224
- ☎771-5725
- 2 Ginkaku-ji-chō, Sakyō-ku
- admission ¥500
- ⏲8.30am-5pm Mar-Nov, 9am-4.30pm Dec-Feb
- 🚌10min walk from Ginkaku-ji-michi bus stop, bus 5 from Kyoto Station

SIGHTS

NANZEN-JI TEMPLE
See p94.

FREE **NANZEN-IN** TEMPLE
Map p224 (南禅院; ☎771-0365; ⊙dawn-dusk; Ⓜ10min walk from Keage Station, Tōzai subway line) This subtemple of Nanzen-ji is up the steps after you pass under the aqueduct. It has an attractive garden designed around a heart-shaped pond. This garden is best seen in the morning or around noon, when sunlight shines directly into the pond and illuminates the colourful carp.

TENJU-AN TEMPLE
Map p224 (天授庵; ☎771-0365; 86-8 Fukuchi-chō, Nanzen-ji, Sakyō-ku; admission ¥400; ⊙9am-5pm Mar–mid-Nov, to 4.30pm mid-Nov–Feb; Ⓜ10min walk from Keage Station, Tōzai subway line) Another subtemple of Nanzen-ji, Tenju-an is located on the south side of San-mon, the main gate of Nanzen-ji. Constructed in 1337, Tenju-an has a splendid garden and a great collection of carp in its pond.

KONCHI-IN TEMPLE
Map p224 (金地院; ☎771-3511; 86-12 Fukuchi-chō, Nanzen-ji, Sakyō-ku; admission ¥400; ⊙8.30am-5pm Mar-Nov, to 4.30pm Dec-Feb; Ⓜ10min walk from Keage Station, Tōzai subway line) Just southwest of the main precincts of Nanzen-ji, this fine subtemple has a wonderful garden designed by Kobori Enshū. If you seek a good example of the technique of *shakkei* (borrowed scenery), look no further.

FREE **NANZEN-JI OKU-NO-IN** SHRINE
Map p224 (南禅寺奥の院; Nanzen-ji, Sakyō-ku; ⊙dawn to dusk; Ⓜ10min walk from Keage Station, Tōzai subway line) Perhaps the best part of Nanzen-ji is overlooked by most visitors: Nanzen-ji Oku-no-in, a small shrine hidden in a forested hollow behind the main precinct. To get here, walk up to the red-brick aqueduct in front of Nanzen-in. Follow the road that runs parallel to the aqueduct up into the hills, and walk past (or through) **Kōtoku-an**, a small subtemple on your left. Continue up the steps into the woods until you reach a waterfall in a beautiful mountain glen. It's here at Nanzen-ji Oku-no-in that pilgrims pray while standing under the falls, sometimes in the dead of winter. Hiking trails lead off in all directions from this point; by going due north for 5km (about two hours' walk) you'll arrive at the top of Daimonji-yama (see p97); go east and you'll get to the town of Yamashina (also about two hours).

NOMURA MUSEUM MUSEUM
Map p224 (野村美術館; ☎751-0374; Sakyō-ku, Nanzen-ji, Shimokawara-chō 61; admission ¥700; ⊙10am-4.30pm Tue-Sun early Mar–early Jun & early Sep–early Dec; Ⓜ10min walk from Keage Station, Tōzai subway line) This museum is a 10-minute walk north of Nanzen-ji. Exhibits include scrolls, paintings, implements used in tea ceremonies and ceramics that were bequeathed by business magnate Nomura Tokushiki. If you have an abiding interest in the tea ceremony or in Japanese decorative techniques such as lacquer and *maki-e* (decorative lacquer technique using silver and gold powders), this museum makes an interesting break from temple hopping.

MURIN-AN VILLA GARDEN
Map p224 (無鄰菴; ☎771-3909; Sakyō-ku, Nanzen-ji, Kusakawa-chō; admission ¥400; ⊙9am-4.30pm; Ⓜ7min walk from Keage Station, Tōzai subway line) Often overlooked by the hordes that descend on the Higashiyama area, this elegant villa was the home of prominent statesman Yamagata Aritomo (1838–1922) and the site of a pivotal 1902 political conference as Japan was heading into the Russo-Japanese War.

Built in 1896, the grounds contain well-preserved wooden buildings, including a fine Japanese tearoom. The Western-style annexe is characteristic of Meiji-period architecture and the serene garden features small streams that draw water from the Biwa-ko Sosui canal. For ¥300 you can savour a bowl of frothy *matcha* (powdered green tea) while viewing the *shakkei* backdrop of the Higashiyama Mountains. It's particularly beautiful in the maple-leaf season of November.

EIKAN-DŌ TEMPLE
Map p224 (永観堂; ☎761-0007; 48 Eikandō-chō, Sakyō-ku; admission ¥600; ⊙9am-5pm; Ⓜ15min walk from Keage Station, Tōzai subway line) Perhaps Kyoto's most famous (and most crowded) autumn foliage destination, Eikan-dō should probably be avoided in November, but is worth a visit at other times of year.

This temple is made interesting by its varied architecture, its gardens and its works of art. A fabulous spot for viewing the autumn colours, the temple was found-

DAIMONJI-YAMA CLIMB

Time: two hours
Distance: five km
Located directly behind Ginkaku-ji (p97), Daimonji-yama is the main site of the the Daimon-ji Gozan Okuribi (p22). From almost anywhere in town the Chinese character for 'great' (大; *dai*) is visible in the middle of a bare patch on the face of this mountain. On 16 August, this character is set ablaze to guide the spirits of the dead on their journey home. The view of Kyoto from the top is unparalleled.

Take bus 5 to the Ginkaku-ji Michi stop and walk up to Ginkaku-ji. Here, you have the option of visiting the temple or starting the hike immediately. To find the trailhead, turn left in front of the temple and head north for about 50m toward a stone *torii* (shrine gate). Just before the torii, turn right up the hill.

The trail proper starts just after a small car park on the right. It's a broad avenue through the trees. A few minutes of walking brings you to a red banner hanging over the trail (warning of forest fires). Soon after this you must cross a bridge to the right then continue up a smaller, switchback trail. When the trail reaches a saddle not far from the top, go to the left. You'll climb a long flight of steps before coming out at the top of the bald patch. The sunset from here is great, but bring a torch.

ed as Zenrin-ji in 855 by the priest Shinshō, but the name was changed to Eikan-dō in the 11th century to honour the philanthropic priest Eikan.

In the Amida-dō hall at the southern end of the complex is a famous statue of Mikaeri Amida Buddha glancing backwards.

From Amida-dō, head north to the end of the curving covered *garyūrō* (walkway). Change into the sandals provided, then climb the steep steps up the mountainside to the **Tahō-tō pagoda**, from where there's a fine view across the city.

PATH OF PHILOSOPHY (TETSUGAKU-NO-MICHI) NEIGHBOURHOOD

Map p224 (哲学の道; Sakyō-ku, Ginkaku-ji; 7min walk from Ginkakuji-michi bus stop, bus 5 or 17 from Kyoto Station) The Tetsugaku-no-Michi is one of the most pleasant walks in all of Kyoto. Lined with a great variety of flowering plants, bushes and trees, it is a corridor of colour throughout most of the year. The path takes its name from one of its most famous strollers: 20th-century philosopher Nishida Kitarō, who is said to have meandered lost in thought along the path. Follow the traffic-free route along a canal lined with cherry trees that come into spectacular bloom in early April. It only takes 30 minutes to do the walk, which starts at Nyakuōji-bashi, above Eikan-dō, and leads to Ginkaku-ji (p95). During the day you should be prepared for crowds (especially in the cherry blossom season); a night stroll will definitely be quieter.

REIKAN-JI TEMPLE

Map p224 (霊鑑寺; 771-4040; Sakyō-ku, Shishigatani goshonodan-chō 12; admission ¥500; 10am-4pm spring & autumn; 7min walk from Ginkaku-ji-Michi bus stop, bus 5 or 17 from Kyoto Station) Only open to the public in spring and autumn, Reikan-ji is one of Kyoto's great lesser-visited attractions. During the spring opening, you will find the grounds positively rioting with camellia. In autumn, the brilliant reds of the maples will dazzle the eye. The small collection of artworks in the main building is almost as good as the colours outside. Check with the Tourist Information Center (p196) for exact opening dates, as they vary by year.

GINKAKU-JI TEMPLE

See p95.

FREE HŌNEN-IN TEMPLE

Map p224 (法然院; 771-2400; 30 Goshono dan-chō, Shishigatani, Sakyō-ku; 6am-4pm; 10min walk from Ginkaku-ji-michi bus stop, bus 5 or 17 from Kyoto Station) One of Kyoto's hidden pleasures, this temple was founded in 1680 to honour the priest Hōnen. It's a lovely, secluded temple with carefully raked gardens set back in the woods. The temple buildings include a small gallery where frequent exhibitions featuring local and international artists are held. If you need to escape the crowds that positively plague nearby Ginkaku-ji, come to this serene refuge.

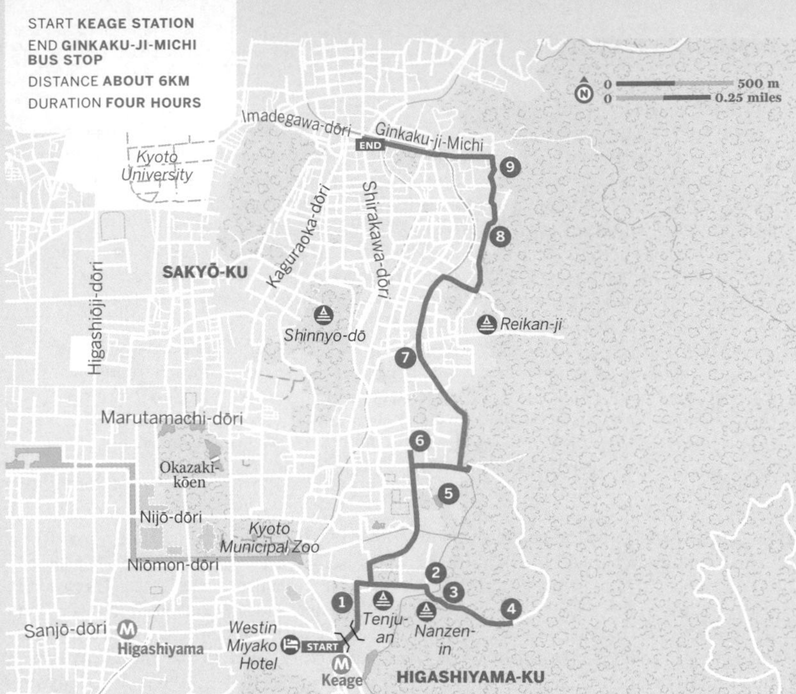

Neighbourhood Walk

A Philosophical Meander

Start at Keage Station on the Tōzai subway line, walk downhill, cross the pedestrian overpass, head back uphill and go through the tunnel under the old funicular tracks. This leads to a narrow street that winds toward 1 **Konchi-in**.

Just past Konchi-in, take a right on the main road and walk up through the gate into 2 **Nanzen-ji**. Continue east, up the slope and you'll soon see the brick Sōsui aqueduct on your right; cross under this, take a quick left and walk up the hill toward the mountains. You'll come first to the lovely 3 **Kōtoku-an** subtemple. Beyond this, the trail enters the woods. Follow it up to the secluded 4 **Nanzen-ji Oku-no-in**, a tiny shrine built around a waterfall.

Return the way you came and exit the north side of Nanzen-ji, following the road through a gate. You'll soon come to 5 **Eikan-dō**, a large temple famous for its artworks and pagoda. At the corner just beyond Eikan-dō, a sign in English and Japanese points up the hill (right) to the Path of Philosophy. If you're hungry, take a short detour north to 6 **Hinode Udon**, a fine noodle restaurant. Otherwise, head up the hill to the 7 **Path of Philosophy (Tetsugaku-no-michi)**, which is the pedestrian path that heads north along the canal.

From here, it's a straight shot up the lovely tree-lined canal for about 800m until you reach a small sign in English and Japanese pointing up the hill to 8 **Hōnen-in**. Follow the sign, take a left at the top of the hill, walk past a small park and you'll see the picturesque thatched gate of Hōnen-in. After checking out the temple (free), exit via the thatched gate and take a quick right downhill.

From here, follow the narrow side streets north to 9 **Ginkaku-ji**, the famed Silver Pavilion. Ginkaku-ji-Michi bus stop is near the intersection of Shirakawa-dōri and Imadegawa-dōri (bus 5, 56, 100, 203 or 204 from Kyoto Station).

Hōnen-in is a 12-minute walk from Gin kaku-ji, on a side street above the Tetsugaku-no-Michi (p97); you may have to ask for directions.

OKAZAKI-KŌEN PARK

Map p224 (岡崎公園; Sakyō-ku, Okazaki; Kyoto Kaikan/Bijyutsukan-mae bus stop, bus 5 from Kyoto Station; M10min walk from Higashiyama Station, Tōzai subway line) Okazaki-kōen is an expanse of parks and canals that lies between Niōmon-dōri and Heian-jingū. Two of Kyoto's significant museums can be found here, as well as two smaller museums and a zoo. If you find yourself in Kyoto on a rainy day and need to do some indoor sightseeing, this area has enough to keep you sheltered for most of the day. The following five sights are all in the Okazaki-kōen Area.

NATIONAL MUSEUM OF MODERN ART MUSEUM

Map p224 (京都国立近代美術館; 761-4111; www.momak.go.jp/English; Enshōji-chō, Okazaki, Sakyō-ku; admission ¥420; 9.30am-5pm Tue-Sun; Kyoto Kaikan/Bijyutsukan-mae bus stop, bus 5 from Kyoto Station; M10min walk from Higashiyama Station, Tōzai subway line) This museum is renowned for its Japanese ceramics and paintings. There is an excellent permanent collection, which includes many pottery pieces by Kawai Kanjirō. The coffee shop here overlooks a picturesque canal.

KYOTO MUNICIPAL MUSEUM OF ART MUSEUM

Map p224 (京都市美術館; 771-4107; 124 Enshōji-chō, Okazaki, Sakyō-ku; 9am-5pm Tue-Sun; Kyoto Kaikan/Bijyutsukan-mae bus stop, bus 5 from Kyoto Station; M10min walk from Higashiyama Station, Tōzai subway line) This fine museum holds several major exhibitions a year (admission varies), as well as a variety of free shows. It's always worth stopping by to see if something is on while you are in town. The pond behind the museum is a great place for a picnic.

FREE **FUREAI-KAN KYOTO MUSEUM OF TRADITIONAL CRAFTS** MUSEUM

Map p224 (京都伝統産業ふれあい館; 762-2670; 9-1 Seishōji-chō, Okazaki, Sakyō-ku; 9am-5pm; Kyoto Kaikan/Bijyutsukan-mae bus stop, bus 5 from Kyoto Station; M10min walk from Higashiyama Station, Tōzai subway line) This multipurpose hall has excellent displays of Kyoto crafts on its basement floor. Exhibits include wood-block prints, lacquerware, bamboo goods and gold-leaf work. It's located in the basement of Miyako Messe (Kyoto International Exhibition Hall).

KYOTO CITY ZOO ZOO

Map p224 (京都市動物園; Kyoto-shi Dōbutsu-en; 771-0210; Okazaki, Hōshōji-chō; adult/child ¥600/free; 9am-5pm Tue-Sun Mar-Nov, to 4.30pm Dec-Feb; Kyoto Kaikan/Bijyutsukan-mae bus stop, bus 5 from Kyoto Station; M10min walk from Higashiyama Station, Tōzai subway line). While we aren't thrilled about the conditions in which the animals are kept here – the cages and enclosures are pretty small – this is a sure-fire hit with kids. All the usual big mammals are present here. Don't miss the Japanese giant salamander *(sanshō uō).*

HEIAN-JINGŪ SHRINE

Map p224 (平安神宮; 761-0221; Nishitennō-chō, Okazaki, Sakyō-ku; shrine precincts/garden free/¥600; 6am-5pm Nov-Feb, 6am-6pm Mar-Oct; Kyoto Kaikan/Bijyutsukan-mae bus stop, bus 5 from Kyoto Station; M10min walk from Higashiyama Station, Tōzai subway line) One of Kyoto's more popular sights, this shrine was built in 1895 to commemorate the 1100th anniversary of the founding of Kyoto. The shrine buildings are colourful replicas, reduced to a two-thirds scale, of the Imperial Court Palace of the Heian period (794–1185).

About 500m in front of the shrine is a massive steel *torii* (shrine gate). Although it appears to be entirely separate, this is actually considered the main entrance to the shrine itself.

The vast garden here, behind the shrine, is a fine place for a wander and particularly lovely during the cherry-blossom season. With its large pond and Chinese-inspired bridge, the garden is a tribute to the style that was popular in the Heian period. It is well known for its wisteria, irises and weeping cherry trees.

One of Kyoto's biggest festivals, the Jidai Matsuri (p22) is held here on 22 October. On 2 and 3 June, Takigi Nō is also held here. Takigi nō is a picturesque form of nō performed in the light of blazing fires. Tickets cost ¥3000 if you pay in advance (ask at the tourist information office for the location of ticket agencies) or you can pay ¥4000 at the entrance gate.

EATING

TOP CHOICE OMEN

NOODLES ¥¥

Map p224 (おめん; ☎771-8994; 74 Jōdo-ji Ishibashi-cho, Sakyō-ku; noodles from ¥1100; ⏰11am-9pm; 📄; 🚌10min walk from Ginkaku-ji-michi bus stop, bus 5 or 17 from Kyoto Station) This elegant noodle shop is named after the thick white noodles that are served in a hot broth with a selection of seven fresh vegetables. Just say *omen* and you'll be given your choice of hot or cold noodles, a bowl of soup to dip them in and a plate of vegetables (you put these into the soup along with some sesame seeds). It's a great bowl of noodles but that's not the end of the story: everything on the frequently changing menu is delicious. You can get a fine salad here, brilliant *tori sansho yaki* (chicken cooked with Japanese mountain spice), good tempura and occasionally a nice plate of sashimi. Best of all, there's a menu in English. It's about five minutes' walk from Ginkaku-ji (p95) in a traditional Japanese house with a lantern outside. It's highly recommended.

TOP CHOICE GOYA

JAPANESE ¥

Map p224 (ゴーヤ; ☎752-1158; 114-6 Nishida-chō, Jōdo-ji, Sakyō-ku; ⏰noon-4.30pm & 5.30pm-midnight, closed Wed; 📄; 🚌3min walk from Ginkakuji-michi bus stop, bus 5 or 17 from Kyoto Station) We love this Okinawan-style restaurant for its tasty food, stylish interior and comfortable upstairs seating. It's perfect for lunch while exploring northern Higashiyama and it's just a short walk from Ginkaku-ji. At lunch they serve simple things like taco rice (¥880) and *gōya champurū* (bitter melon stir-fry; ¥680), while dinners are more à la carte affairs with a wide range of *izakaya* (Japanese pub) fare.

HYŌTEI

KAISEKI ¥¥¥

Map p224 (瓢亭; ☎771-4116; Sakyō-ku, Nanzen-ji Kusagawa-chō 35; ⏰11am-7.30pm; kaiseki lunch/dinner from ¥23,000/27,000, shōkadō bentō lunch ¥5000; Ⓜ10min walk from Keage Station, Tōzai subway line) The Hyōtei is considered to be one of Kyoto's oldest and most picturesque traditional restaurants. In the main building you can sample exquisite *kaiseki* (Japanese *haute cuisine*) courses in private tea rooms. Set meals are available from ¥5000.

OKUTAN

TOFU ¥¥

Map p224 (奥丹; ☎771-8709; Sakyō-ku, Nanzen-ji, Fukuchi-chō 86-30; set meals ¥3150; ⏰11am-4.30pm Mon-Fri, to 5pm Sat & Sun, closed Thu; 🖉; Ⓜ10min walk from Keage Station, Tōzai subway line) Just outside the precincts of Nanzen-ji (p94), you'll find Okutan, a restaurant sited within the luxurious garden of Chōshō-in. This is a popular place that has specialised in vegetarian temple food for hundreds of years. Try a course of *yudōfu* (bean curd cooked in an iron pot) together with vegetable side dishes (¥3150). But be warned: it can get crowded here in the cherry-blossom and autumn-foliage seasons.

GROTTO

JAPANESE ¥¥

Map p224 (ぐろっと; ☎771-0606; 114 Jōdo-ji Nishida-chō, Sakyō-ku; dinner course ¥4750; ⏰6pm-midnight Mon-Sat; 📄; 🚌5min walk from Ginkaku-ji-michi bus stop, bus 5 or 17 from Kyoto Station) This stylish little place on Imadegawa-dōri serves a fine dinner set menu that will take you through the major tastes in the Japanese gastronomy. The atmosphere is slick and subdued. Reservations are highly recommended and last orders are at 10pm.

OKARIBA

WILD GAME ¥¥

Map p224 (お狩り場; ☎751-7790; Sakyō-ku, Okazaki, Higashitenno-chō 43-3; ⏰5-10.30pm Tue-Sun; dinner ¥4000; 🚌1min walk from Higashitenno-chō bus stop, bus 203 from Kyoto Station) For an experience you won't soon forget, try Okariba. If it crawls, walks or swims, it's probably on the menu. The *inoshishi* (wild boar) barbecue is a good start. Those who don't eat meat can try the fresh *ayu* (Japanese trout). Look for the sign of the hunting pig out the front.

TORITO

YAKITORI ¥¥

Map p224 (とりと; ☎752-4144; Sakyō-ku, Higashi Marutamachi 9-5; ⏰5.30pm-midnight, closed Tue; dinner ¥3500-4000; 🚆2min walk from Marutamachi Station, Keihan line) This is part of the new wave of *yakitori* (skewers of grilled chicken and vegetable) restaurants in Kyoto that are updating the old standards in interesting and tasty ways. It's a crowded spot, with a counter and a few small tables. The food is very good and will likely appeal to non-Japanese palates. Dishes include *negima* (long onions and chicken; ¥315 for two sticks) and *tsukune* (chicken meatballs; ¥462). It's near the corner of Marutamachi and Kawabata-dōri; you can see inside to the counter.

KAILASH ORGANIC ¥

Map p224 (カイラス; ☎752-3127; Sakyō-ku, Shōgoin Sannō-chō 19-2; ⌚10.30am-7pm Fri-Tue; lunch sets ¥880; ; 10min walk from Marutamachi Station, Keihan line) In an atmospheric old Japanese town house, this new organic restaurant is a very welcome addition to the Kyoto restaurant scene. The set lunch here usually includes a salad, rice, *tsukemono* (Japanese pickles), soup and a main dish. It has an English menu. We like to relax at the low tables upstairs. Look for the plants.

EARTH KITCHEN COMPANY BENTŌ ¥

Map p224 (アースキッチンカンパニー; ☎771-1897; 9-7 Higashi Maruta-chō, Kawabata, Marutamachi, Sakyō-ku; lunch ¥735; ; ⌚10.30am-6.30pm Mon-Fri; 1min walk from Marutamachi Station, Keihan line) Located on Marutamachi-dōri near the Kamo-gawa, this tiny spot seats just two people but does a bustling business serving tasty takeaway lunch *bentō* (boxed meals). If you fancy a picnic lunch for your temple-hopping and the ease of an English menu, this is the place.

AYATORI CAFETERIA ¥

Map p224 (あやとり; ☎752-2468; Sakyō-ku, Yoshida Izumiden-chō 1-86; ⌚11.30-2pm & 5.30-9.30pm Mon-Fri, 5.30-9.30pm Sat; katsudon ¥730; ; 10min walk from Demachiyanagi Station, Keihan line) Very close to the Hyakumamben intersection, this place is your classic *shokudō* (Japanese-style cafeteria/cheap restaurant). It's a friendly spot that is popular with local workers, resident foreigners and university students. A variety of standard fish and meat set dishes are served, which average around ¥800. In winter, the *kaki furai teishoku* (fried oyster set meal; ¥1050) is lovely. Strangely, considering this is a Japanese restaurant, Ayatori also serves a wonderful potato salad. English menus are available. To find this place, look for the big red-and-black sign.

TOP CHOICE **KARAKO** RĀMEN ¥

Map p224 (唐子; ☎752-8234; 12-3 Tokusei-chō, Okazaki, Sakyō-ku; rāmen from ¥630; ⌚11.30am-2pm & 4.30pm-midnight, closed Tue; 10min walk from Marutamachi Station, Keihan line) Karako is our favourite *rāmen* (noodles in a meat broth with meat and vegetables) restaurant in Kyoto. While it's not much on atmosphere, the *rāmen* here is excellent – the soup is thick and rich and the *chashū* (pork slices) melt in your mouth. We recommend that you ask for the *kotteri* (thick soup) *rāmen*. Look for the lantern outside.

CAFE PROVERBS 15:17 VEGETARIAN ¥

Map p224 (カフェプロバーブス; ☎707-6856; Domus Hyakumanben 3F, 28-20 Tanakamonzen-chō, Sakyō-ku; drinks/food from ¥300/750; ⌚11:45am-10pm, from noon Sun, to 6pm Wed, closed Mon; ; 10min walk from Demachiyanagi Station, Keihan line) This is a pleasant spot for a cuppa or a light organic vegetarian meal. It's a little cramped but the soothing decor makes up for this. Lunch sets include green curry, sandwiches and Japanese fare. The English menu will help with ordering. Café Peace is on the 3rd floor but there's a small sign at street level.

TOP CHOICE **FALAFEL GARDEN** ISRAELI ¥

Map p224 (ファラフェルガーデン; ☎712-1856; Sakyō-ku, Tanaka Shimoyanagi-chō 3-16; ⌚11.30am-9.30pm; falafel from ¥670; 2min walk from exit 7, Demachiyanagi Station, Keihan line) Close to the Keihan and Eizan lines' Demachiyanagi Station, this funky Israeli-run place has excellent falafel and a range of other dishes, as well as offering a set menu (from ¥1150). We like the style of the open-plan, converted Japanese house and the small garden out the back, but the main draw is those tasty falafels! It's easy to spot, across the street from a post office.

ZAC BARAN INTERNATIONAL ¥

Map p224 (ザックバラン; ☎751-9748; Sakyō-ku, Shōgo-in, Sannō-chō 18; ⌚6pm-4am, closed Tue; meals ¥1500; 5min walk from Kumanojinja-mae bus stop, bus 206 from Kyoto Station) Near the Kyoto Handicraft Center (p103), this is a good spot for a light meal or a drink. It serves a variety of spaghetti dishes as well as a good lunch special. Look for the picture of the Freak Brothers near the downstairs entrance. If you fancy dessert, step upstairs to the Second House Cake Works.

HINODE UDON NOODLES ¥

Map p224 (日の出うどん; ☎751-9251; 36 Kitanobō-chō, Nanzenji, Sakyō-ku; noodles from ¥450; ⌚11am-5pm Mon-Sat; ; M15min walk from Keage Station, Tōzai subway line) Filling noodle and rice dishes are served at this pleasant shop with an English menu. Plain *udon* (thick white wheat noodles) are only ¥400, but we recommend you spring for the *nabeyaki udon* (pot-baked *udon* in broth) for ¥800. This is a good lunch spot when temple-hopping in the Northern Higashiyama area.

SHINSHINDŌ NOTRE PAIN QUOTIDIEN CAFE ¥

Map p224 (進々堂; ☎701-4121; Sakyō-ku, Kitashirakawa, Oiwake-chō 88; ⏰8am-6pm, closed Tue; coffee from ¥340; 📋; 🚌2min walk from Hyakumamben bus stop, bus 206 from Kyoto Station) This atmospheric old Kyoto coffee shop is a favourite of Kyoto University students for its curry and bread lunch set (¥780), which is kind of an acquired taste. It's located near the university. Look for the glazed tile bricks and the big window out the front. There's a small English sign and English menus are available.

AU TEMPS PERDU CAFE ¥

Map p224 (オ　タン　ペルデュ; ☎762-1299; Higashiyama-ku, Okazaki Enshōji-chō 64; ⏰11.30am-2.30pm & 5.30-9.30pm Tue-Sun; dishes from ¥500; Ⓜ10min walk from Higashiyama Station, Tōzai subway line) Overlooking the Shirakawa Canal, just across the street from the National Museum Modern of Art (p99), this tiny indoor/outdoor French-style cafe offers some of the best people watching in Northern Higashiyama. It's easy to pull a baby stroller up to these outdoor tables.

CAFE TERRAZZA CAFE ¥

Map p224 (カフェ　テラッツァ; ☎751-7931; Sakyō-ku, Shishigatani Hōnenin-chō 72; ⏰9am-8pm, closed Wed dinner; dishes ¥1500; 🚌7min walk from Ginkakuji-michi bus stop, bus 5 or 17 from Kyoto Station) You won't find a cafe with a better location than this: right on the Path of Philosophy (p97). Sit outside and admire the view. In early April, there's a cherry tree here that turns the entire terrace into a mini-*hanami* (cherry blossom viewing party).

CAFÉ DE 505 CAFE ¥

Map p224 (カフェ　ド　ゴマルゴ; ☎771-5086; National Museum of Modern Art, Sakyō-ku, Okazaki, Enshōji-chō; ⏰9.30am-4.30pm Tue-Sun; dishes ¥1000-1500; Ⓜ10min walk from Higashiyama Station, Tōzai subway line) At the National Museum of Modern Art (p99), this indoor/outdoor cafe is a great spot for a pick-me-up while museum hopping in Okazaki.

GALLERY COEUR CAFE ¥

Map p224 (ギャラリークー; ☎708-2737; 40-7 Minamigosho-chou Okazaki Sakyo-ku; ⏰10am-4.30pm; drinks ¥400; Ⓜ15min walk from Higashiyama Station, Tōzai subway line) Just around the corner from Heian-jingu (p99), this cosy little cafe-gallery is a nice spot for a cuppa in the Okazaki-kōen area. There are comfy couches and tables upstairs, along with an interesting selection of English books.

DRINKING & NIGHTLIFE

METRO CLUB

Map p224 (メトロ; ☎752-4765; BF Ebisu Bldg, Marutamachi sagaru, Kawabata, Sakyō-ku; ⏰10pm-3am; 🚉Marutamachi Station, Keihan line) Metro is part disco, part 'live house' (small concert hall) and it even hosts the occasional art exhibition. It attracts an eclectic mix of creative types and has a different theme every night, so check ahead in *Kansai Scene* to see what's going on. Some of the best gigs are Latin night and the popular Non-Hetero-at-the-Metro night, which draws gay and lesbian clubbers and everyone in between. Metro is inside exit 2 of the Marutamachi Station.

KICK UP BAR

Map p224 (キックアップ; ☎761-5604; Higashiyama-ku, Higashikomonoza-chō 331; ⏰7pm-midnight, closed Wed; Ⓜ1min walk from Keage Station exit 1, Tōzai subway line) Located just across the street from the Westin Miyako, Kyoto (p147), this wonderful bar attracts a regular crowd of Kyoto expats, local Japanese and guests from the Westin. It's subdued, relaxing and friendly.

ENTERTAINMENT

KANZE KAIKAN NŌ THEATRE NŌ THEATRE

Map p224 (観世会館; ☎771-6114; Sakyō-ku-Okazaki; ⏰10.30am-5pm Tue-Sun) This is your best bet for performances of nō (p168).

SHOPPING

CHION-JI TEZUKURI-ICHI HANDICRAFTS

Map p224 (知恩寺手作り市; ☎781-9171; Sakyō-ku, Tanaka Monzen-chō 103; 🚌1min walk from Hyakumamben bus stop, bus 206 from Kyoto Station) This 'handmade market' is held at Chion-ji from dawn to dusk on the 15th of the month. Wares include food and handmade clothes. This is a good chance to see Kyoto's alternative community out in force.

TOP CHOICE KYOTO HANDICRAFT CENTER JAPANESE CRAFTS

Map p224 (京都ハンディクラフトセンター; ☎761-5080; 21 Entomi-chō, Shōgoin, Sakyō-ku; ⏲10am-7pm; 🚉10min walk from Marutamachi Station, Keihan line) The Kyoto Handicraft Center is a huge cooperative that exhibits and sells a wide range of Japanese arts and crafts. It also has demonstrations of woodblock printmaking and a corner where you can try your hand at making some of your own prints. All in all, this is the best one-stop emporium in the whole of Kyoto.

TŌZANDŌ SWORDS

Map p216 (東山堂; ☎762-1341; 24 Shōgoin Entomi-chō, Sakyō-ku; ⏲10am-7pm; 🚉10min walk from Marutamachi Station, Keihan line) If you're a fan of Japanese swords and armour, you have to visit this wonderful shop on Marutamachi (which is diagonally opposite the Kyoto Handicraft Center). They have authentic swords, newly made Japanese armour, martial arts goods etc, and there's usually someone on hand who can speak English.

TOP CHOICE ZŌHIKO JAPANESE CRAFTS

Map p224 (象彦; ☎752-7777; 10 Okazaki Saishōji-chō, Sakyō-ku; ⏲9.30am-6pm, closed Wed; 🚌Kyoto Kaikan/Bijyutsukan-mae bus stop, bus 5 from Kyoto Station; Ⓜ15min walk from Higashiyama Station, Tōzai subway line) This is our favourite lacquerware shop in Kyoto. While the outside is nondescript, the inside is a treasure trove of beautiful lacquerware and there's a fine gallery upstairs. It's very near Heian-jingū (p99).

Northwest Kyoto

Neighbourhood Top Five

❶ Being dazzled by the single most impressive sight in all of Kyoto: the gold-plated main hall of **Kinkaku-ji** (p106), the famed 'Golden Pavilion'.

❷ Feeling the power of the shōgun at **Nijō-jō** (p107).

❸ Meditating on the 15 magical rocks in the Zen garden at **Ryōan-ji** (p109).

❹ Searching for 'Old Kyoto' in the weaving district of **Nishijin** (p108).

❺ Taking a stroll through the enclosed world of Zen temples at **Myōshin-ji** (p110).

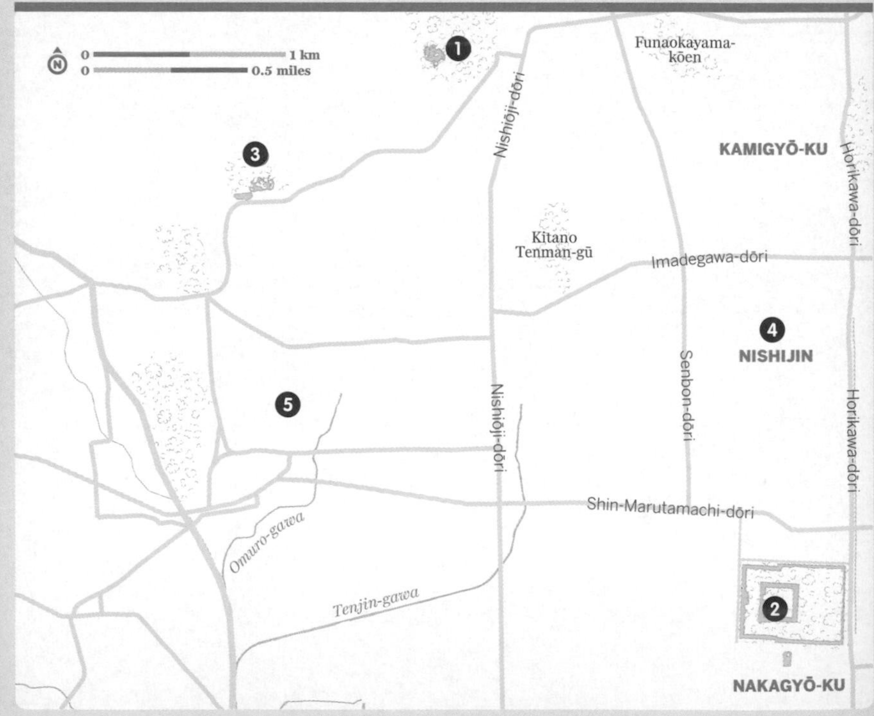

For more detail of this area, see Map p228

Explore: Northwest Kyoto

In this guide, Northwest Kyoto comprises the section of the city that runs from Kyoto's main castle, Nijō-jō, all the way to the base of the mountains in the northwest corner of the city, where you will find Kinkaku-ji, Ryōan-ji and Ninna-ji. Like the Central Kyoto area, the sights here are quite spread out and you shouldn't try to cover them all in one day. Rather, pick a few that are clustered close together and visit them in half a day, then consider spending the rest of the day in an adjoining sightseeing district.

Many people visit Kinkaku-ji and Ryōan-ji in the morning, then continue by taxi down to the Arashiyama and Sagano area, which is also on the west side of the city.

With the exception of sights in the inner part of this district (like Nijō-jō, which is on the Tōzai subway line), it's a bit time consuming to see the sights in Northwest Kyoto. Most sights are best accessed by city bus. Myōshin-ji and nearby sights are also served by the JR line and by the private Randen line. If you're a keen cyclist, you can also explore the area on a bicycle, but keep in mind that there are some hills around Kinkaku-ji and Ryōan-ji, so you'll work up quite a sweat in summer months.

Local Life

➡ **With Kids** Tōei Uzumasa Movie Village (p110) is popular with local families.

➡ **Market Meeting** The Tenjin-san Market (p111) is a popular meeting place for local expats and Kyoto residents.

➡ **Cherry Blossom Spot** In early April, the Randen Kitano line between Narutaki and Utano stations passes through a tunnel of blooming cherry trees.

Getting There & Away

➡ **Train** The JR Sagano/San-in line stops near Myōshin-ji and Tōei Uzumasa Movie Village, while the private Randen Kitano line stops near Ninna-ji.

➡ **Bus** Kyoto city buses serve all the sights in this district.

➡ **Subway** The Tōzai subway line stops very close to Nijō-jō (get off at Nijō-jō-mae).

Lonely Planet's Top Tip

Since Ryōan-ji and Kinkaku-ji (the two most famous sights in Northwest Kyoto) and Arashiyama are all on the west side of town, it makes sense to visit these in one day. Take a taxi between Arashiyama and Kinkaku-ji or Ryōan-ji (or vice versa).

Best Places to Eat

➡ Saraca Nishijin (p110)
➡ Kanei (p111)
➡ Toyouke-jaya (p111)

For reviews, see p110 ➡

Best Places to Meditate on a Garden

➡ Myōshin-ji (p110)
➡ Taizō-in (p110)
➡ Ryōan-ji (p109)

For reviews, see p108 ➡

Best Places to Learn about Kyoto Culture

➡ Nishijin (p108)
➡ Orinasu-ken (p108)
➡ Urasenke Chadō Research Center (p108)

For reviews, see p108 ➡

SEAN CAFFREY / LONELY PLANET IMAGES ©

TOP SIGHTS
KINKAKU-JI

Kyoto's famed 'Golden Pavilion', Kinkaku-ji is one of the world's most impressive religious monuments. The sight of the gold-plated pavilion rising over its reflecting pool is the kind of image that burns itself into your memory for years to come. Of course, there's more to this temple than just its shiny main hall. The grounds are spacious and include another pond, a tea arbour and some lovely greenery. Just don't expect to have the place to yourself – Kinkaku-ji is on everyone's 'must-see' list.

Originally built in 1397 as a retirement villa for shōgun Ashikaga Yoshi-mitsu, Kinkaku-ji (金閣寺) was converted into Buddhist temple by his son, in compliance with his wishes. Also known as Rokuon-ji, Kinkaku-ji belongs to the Shōkokuji school of Buddhism.

The three-storey pavilion is covered in bright gold leaf and features a bronze phoenix on top of the roof. The mirror-like reflection of the temple in the Kyō-ko pond is extremely photogenic, especially when the maples are ablaze in autumn.

In 1950 a young monk consummated his obsession with the temple by burning it to the ground. The monk's story is fictionalised in Mishima Yukio's 1956 novel *The Temple of the Golden Pavilion.*

In 1955 a full reconstruction was completed, following the original design exactly, but the gold-foil covering was extended to the lower floors.

This quaint teahouse **Sekka-tei** embodies the spirit of *wabi sabi* (rustic simplicity) that defines the Japanese tea-ceremony ethic. It's at the top of the hill shortly before the exit of the temple. Because of the enormous popularity and fame of this temple, it's almost always crowded – try to visit early on a weekday morning.

DON'T MISS

➡ Sekka-tei

PRACTICALITIES

➡ Map p228

➡ ☎461-0013

➡ 1 Kinkaku-ji-chō, Kita-ku

➡ admission ¥400

➡ 9am-5pm

➡ bus 205 from Kyoto Station to Kinkakuji-mae stop

TOP SIGHTS
NIJŌ-JŌ

Standing like a direct challenge to the power of the Emperor in the nearby Imperial Palace, the shōgun castle of Nijō-jō is a stunning monument to the power of the warlords who effectively ruled Japan for centuries. For those with an interest in Japan's feudal past and an eye for magnificent interiors, Nijō-jō is a fascinating destination. In addition to stunning (almost rococo) interiors, the castle grounds contain expansive gardens that are perfect for a relaxing stroll.

Nijō-jō (二条城) was built in 1603 as the official residence of Tokugawa Ieyasu. The ostentatious style was intended as a demonstration of Ieyasu's prestige and to signal the demise of the emperor's power.

To safeguard against treachery, Ieyasu had the interior fitted with 'nightingale' floors (intruders were detected by the squeaking boards) and concealed chambers where bodyguards could keep watch and spring out at a moment's notice.

In 1868 the last Tokugawa shōgun, Yoshinobu, surrendered his power to the newly restored Emperor Meiji inside Nijō-jō.

Nijō-jō is built on land that was originally occupied by the 8th-century Imperial Palace, which was abandoned in 1227. The Shinsen-en Garden, just south of the castle, is all that remains of the original palace. This forlorn garden has small shrines and pond.

The Momoyama-era **Kara-mon** gate, originally part of Hideyoshi's Fushimi-jō in the south of the city, features lavish, masterful woodcarving and metalwork. After passing through the gate, you enter the **Ninomaru** palace, which is divided into five buildings with numerous chambers. Access to the buildings used to depend on rank – only those of highest rank were permitted into the inner buildings. The Ōhiroma Yon-no-Ma (Fourth Chamber) has spectacular screen paintings.

The neighbouring **Honmaru** palace dates from the mid-19th century. After the Meiji Restoration in 1868, the castle became a detached palace of the imperial household and in 1939 it was given to Kyoto City. These days it's only open for a special autumn viewing.

Don't miss **Seiryu-en**, the garden that surrounds the inner castle buildings. This superb garden was designed by Kobori Enshū, Japan's most celebrated garden designer. This vast garden comprises three separate islets spanned by stone bridges and is meticulously maintained. The Ninomaru palace and garden take about an hour to walk through. A detailed fact sheet in English is provided.

Keep in mind that the castle is on the itinerary of every foreign and Japanese tour group and it can be packed. If you're after peace and quiet, try an early-morning or late-afternoon visit. If you must visit during the middle of the day, you might find that touring the buildings quickly and then savouring the gardens is the most relaxing way to enjoy the castle.

DON'T MISS

- Seiryu-en

PRACTICALITIES

- Map p228
- ☎841-0096
- 541 Nijōjō-chō, Horikawa Nishi iru, Nijō-dōri, Nakagyō-ku
- admission ¥600
- ⏲8.45am-5pm, closed Tue in Dec, Jan, Jul & Aug
- Ⓜ5min walk from Nijōjō-mae Station, Tōzai subway line

SIGHTS

NISHIJIN NEIGHBOURHOOD

Map p228 (Kamigyō-ku, Horikawa-dōri, Imadegawa; 1min walk from Horikawa-Imadegawa bus stop, bus 9 from Kyoto Station) Nishijin is Kyoto's traditional textile centre, the source of all those dazzling kimono fabrics and *obi* (kimono sashes) that you see being paraded about town. The area is famous for Nishijin-ori (Nishijin weaving). There are quite a few *machiya* (traditional Japanese town houses) in this district, so it's a good place simply to wander. The next three sights are all in Nishijin.

FREE NISHIJIN TEXTILE CENTER MUSEUM

Map p228 (西陣織会館; 451-9231; Imadegawa Minami iru, Horikawa-dōri, Kamigyō-ku; 9am-5pm; 1min walk from Horikawa-Imadegawa bus stop, bus 9 from Kyoto Station) In the heart of the Nishijin textile district, this is worth a peek before starting a walk around the area. There are also displays of completed fabrics and kimono, as well as weaving demonstrations and occasional kimono fashion shows. Unfortunately, these days, it's often overrun by large tour groups. It's on the southwest corner of the Horikawa-dōri and Imadegawa-dōri intersection.

ORINASU-KAN MUSEUM

Map p228 (織成館; 431-0020; 693 Daikoku-chō, Kamigyō-ku; adult/child ¥500/350; 10am-4pm Tue-Sun; 10min walk from Horikawa-Imadegawa bus stop, bus 9 from Kyoto Station) This museum, housed in a Nishijin weaving factory, has impressive exhibits of Nishijin textiles. It's more atmospheric and usually quieter than the Nishijin Textile Center. The **Susamei-sha** building across the street is also open to the public and worth a look. It's a short walk north of the Nishijin Textile Center.

SHŌSUIKAKU MUSEUM

Map p228 (松翠閣; 431-1670; www.shosuikaku.jp/eng/index.html; Kamigyō-ku, Teranouchi-dōri, Chiekōin Higashi iru, Kita gawa; admission ¥200; 9.30am-5pm Tue-Sun; 10min walk from Horikawa-Imadegawa bus stop, bus 9 from Kyoto Station) One of the most interesting sights in Nishijin is this wonderful little museum located in a traditional Japanese house. The exhibits focus on the local Nishijin weaving techniques (you'll be amazed what can be achieved with it). The museum guide will take you upstairs to a room where the walls are covered with large panels of Nishijin weaving – when the lights are dimmed, it's a magical sight.

URASENKE CHADŌ RESEARCH CENTER CULTURAL BUILDING

Map p228 (茶道資料館; 431-6474; Kamigyō-ku, Horikawa-dōri, Teranouchi agaru; admission ¥500; 9.30am-4.30pm; 15min walk from Kurama-guchi Station, Karasuma subway line) Anyone interested in tea ceremony should make their first stop the Urasenke Chadō Research Center. Urasenke is Japan's largest tea school and hosts hundreds of students annually who come from branch schools worldwide to further their studies in 'the way of tea'.

The gallery located on the 1st and 2nd floors holds quarterly exhibitions on tea-related arts; call to see if there is a show being held during your stay. The entrance fee entitles you to a bowl of *matcha* (powdered green tea) and a sweet.

The **Konnichi-an library** has more than 50,000 books (about 100 in English), plus videos on tea, which can be viewed.

If you'd like more information, contact **Urasenke's Office of International Affairs** (Kokusai Kyoku; 431-3111).

FREE KITANO TENMAN-GŪ SHRINE

Map p228 (北野天満宮; 461-0005; Bakuro-chō, Kamigyō-ku; 5am-6pm Apr-Oct, 5.30am-5.30pm Nov-Mar; Kitano Tenmangū-mae stop, bus 50 or 101 from Kyoto Station) The site of Tenjin-San Market (p111), one of Kyoto's most popular flea markets, this shrine is a nice spot for a lazy stroll and the shrine buildings themselves are beautiful. It's particularly pleasant here in the plum-blossom season of March.

Kitano Tenman-gū was established in 947 to honour Sugawara Michizane (845–903), a noted Heian-era statesman and scholar. It is said that, having been defied by his political adversary Fujiwara Tokihira, Sugawara was exiled to Kyūshū for the rest of his life. Following his death in 903, earthquakes and storms struck Kyoto, and the Imperial Palace was repeatedly struck by lightning. Fearing that Sugawara, reincarnated as Raijin (god of thunder), had returned from beyond to avenge his rivals, locals erected and dedicated this shrine to him.

The present buildings were built in 1607 by Toyotomi Hideyori; the grounds contain an extensive grove of plum and apricot trees, which are said to have been Sugawara's favourite fruits.

IN HOT WATER

After a day spent marching from temple to temple, nothing feels better than a good hot bath. Kyoto is full of *sentō* (public baths), ranging from small neighbourhood baths with one or two tubs to massive complexes offering saunas, mineral baths and even electric baths. The **Funaoka Onsen** (船岡温泉; Map p228; ☎441-3735; Kita-ku, Murasakino, Minami-Funaoka-chō 82-1, Kuramaguchi-dōri; admission ¥390; ⏰3pm-1am Mon-Sat, 8am-1am Sun; 🚌5min walk from Senbon-Kuramaguchi bus stop, bus 206 from Kyoto Station) is one of the best in Kyoto and could even double as an evening's entertainment.

This old bath boasts outdoor bathing and a sauna, as well as some museum-quality woodcarvings in the changing room (apparently carved during Japan's invasion of Manchuria). Bring your own bath supplies (soap, shampoo, a towel to dry yourself and another small towel for washing); if you forget, though, you can buy toiletries and rent towels at the front desk. Washing buckets are available free inside the bathing area.

To find it, head west from Horikawa-dōri along Kuramaguchi-dōri. It's on the left, not far past the Lawson convenience store. Look for the large rocks out the front.

Unless you are trying to avoid crowds, the best time to visit is during the Tenjin-san market fair, held on the 25th of each month – December and January are particularly colourful.

KINKAKU-JI — TEMPLE

See p106.

RYŌAN-JI — TEMPLE

Map p228 (龍安寺; ☎463-2216; 13 Goryōnoshita machi, Ryōan-ji, Ukyō-ku; admission ¥500; ⏰8am-5.30pm Mar-Nov, 8.30am-5pm Dec-Feb; 🚌bus 59 from Sanjō-Keihan to Ryōanji-mae stop) You've probably seen a picture of the rock garden here – it's one of the symbols of Kyoto and one of Japan's better-known sights. There is no doubt that it's a mesmerising and attractive sight, but it's hard to enjoy amid the mobs who come to check it off their 'must-see list'. An early-morning visit on a weekday is probably your best hope of seeing the garden under contemplative conditions. If you go when it's crowded, you'll find the less-famous garden around the corner of the stone garden to be a nice escape.

This temple belongs to the Rinzai school and was founded in 1450. The main attraction is the garden, an oblong of sand with an austere collection of 15 carefully placed rocks, apparently adrift in a sea of sand, enclosed by an earthen wall. The designer, who remains unknown to this day, provided no explanation.

Although many historians believe the garden was arranged by Sōami during the Muromachi period (1333–1576), some contend that it is a much later product of the Edo period. It is Japan's most famous *hira-niwa* (flat garden void of hills or ponds) and reveals the stunning simplicity and harmony of the principles of Zen meditation.

The viewing platform for the garden can become packed solid, but the other parts of the temple grounds are also interesting and less of a target for the crowds. Among these, **Kyoyo-chi** pond is perhaps the most beautiful, particularly in autumn.

FREE NINNA-JI — TEMPLE

Map p228 (仁和寺; ☎461-1155; 33 Omuroōuchi, Ukyō-ku; ⏰9am-5pm Mar-Nov, 9am-4.30pm Dec-Feb; 🚌Omuro Ninnaji stop, bus 59 from Sanjō-Keihan or bus 26 from Kyoto Station) Few travellers make the journey all the way out to this sprawling temple complex, but most who do find it a pleasant spot. It's certainly a good counterpoint to the crowded precincts of Ryōan-ji (p109) and Kinkaku-ji (p106). If you're after something a bit off the beaten track in Northwest Kyoto, this temple may fit the bill.

Originally containing more than 60 structures, Ninna-ji was built in 888 and is the head temple of the Omuro branch of the Shingon school. The present temple buildings, including a five-storey pagoda, date from the 17th century. On the extensive grounds you'll find a peculiar grove of short-trunked, multipetalled cherry trees called Omuro-no-Sakura, which draw large crowds in April.

Separate admission fees (an additional ¥500 each) are charged for both the *kondō* and *reihōkan* (treasure house), which are only open for the first two weeks of October.

MYŌSHIN-JI TEMPLE

Map p228 (妙心寺; ☎461-5226; 64 Myoshin-ji-chō, Hanazono, Ukyō-ku; main temple/other areas ¥500/free; ⏰Myōshin-ji temple halls 9.10am-11.50am & 1-3.40pm, other areas dawn-dusk; 🚌Myōshinji Kitamon-mae stop, bus 10 from Sanjō Keihan; 🚉15min walk from Hanazono Station, JR Sagano-Sanin line) Myōshin-ji is a separate world within Kyoto, a walled-off complex of temples and subtemples that invites lazy strolling. The subtemple of Taizō-in here contains one of the city's more interesting gardens.

Myōshin-ji dates from 1342 and belongs to the Rinzai school. There are 47 subtemples, but only a few are open to the public.

From the north gate, follow the broad stone avenue flanked by rows of temples to the southern part of the complex. The eponymous Myōshin-ji temple here is roughly in the middle of the complex. Your entry fee here entitles you to a tour of several of the buildings of the temple. The ceiling of the *hattō* (lecture hall) here features Tanyū Kanō's unnerving painting *Unryūzu* (meaning 'Dragon glaring in eight directions'). Your guide will invite you to stand directly beneath the dragon; doing so makes it appear that it's spiralling up or down.

Shunkōin (☎462-5488), a subtemple of Myōshin-ji, offers regular *zazen* (seated **Zen meditation**) sessions for foreigners with English explanations for ¥1000. This is highly recommended.

TAIZŌ-IN TEMPLE, GARDEN

Map p228 (退蔵院; ☎463-2855; Ukyō-ku, Hanazono Myōshin-ji 35; admission ¥500; ⏰9am-5pm; 🚉10min walk from JR Hanazono Station) This subtemple is in the southwestern corner of the grounds of Myōshin-ji. The *karesansui* (dry-landscape rock garden) depicting a waterfall and islands is well worth a visit.

TŌEI UZUMASA MOVIE VILLAGE THEME PARK

Map p228 (東映太秦映画村; Tōei Uzumasa Eiga Mura; ☎864-7716; Ukyō-ku, Uzumasa Higashi Hachigaoka-chō 10; adult/child 6-18/under 6 ¥2200/1300/1100; ⏰9am-5pm Mar-Nov, 9.30am-4pm Dec-Feb; 🚉13min walk from Uzumasa Station, JR Sagano-Sanin line) In the Uzumasa area, Tōei Uzumasa Movie Village is a rather touristy affair. It does, however, have some recreations of Edo-period street scenes that give a decent idea of what Kyoto must have looked like before the advent of concrete.

The main conceit of the park is that real movies are actually filmed here. While this may occasionally be the case, more often than not it's a show laid on for the tourists. Aside from this, there are displays relating to various aspects of Japanese movies and regular performances involving Japanese TV and movie characters such as the Power Rangers. This should entertain the kids – adults will probably be a little bored.

KŌRYŪ-JI TEMPLE

Map p228 (広隆寺; ☎861-1461; Ukyō-ku, Uzumasa Hachioka-chō 32; adult ¥700, child ¥400-500; ⏰9am-5pm Mar-Nov, to 4.30pm Dec-Feb; 🚉2min walk from Uzumasa Station, Keifuku line) A bit out of the way, Kōryū-ji is easily paired with nearby Myōshin-ji (p110) to form a half-day tour for those with an interest in Japanese Buddhism. It's notable mostly for its collection of Buddhist statuary and so a visit with a knowledgeable guide is a good way to learn about the different levels of beings in the Buddhist pantheon.

Kōryū-ji, one of the oldest temples in Japan, was founded in 622 to honour Prince Shōtoku, who was an enthusiastic promoter of Buddhism.

The *hattō* (lecture hall) to the right of the main gate houses a magnificent trio of 9th-century statues: Buddha, flanked by manifestations of Kannon.

The *reihōkan* (treasure house) contains numerous fine Buddhist statues, including the Naki Miroku (Crying Miroku) and the renowned Miroku Bosatsu (Bodhisattva of the Future), which is extraordinarily expressive. A national upset occurred in 1960 when an enraptured university student embraced the statue in a fit of passion (at least, that was his excuse) and inadvertently snapped off its little finger.

NIJŌ-JŌ CASTLE

See p107.

TOP CHOICE SARACA NISHIJIN CAFE ¥

Map p228 (さらさ西陣; ☎432-5075; Kita-ku, Murasakino Higashifujinomori-chō 11-1; lunch from ¥900; ⏰noon-11pm, closed Wed; 🚌7min walk from Daitoku-ji-mae bus stop, bus 206 from Kyoto Station) This is one of Kyoto's most interesting cafes – it's built inside an old *sentō* (public bathhouse) and the original tiles have been preserved. Light meals and coffee (¥480) are the staples here. The *hon-jitsu Nishijin* (daily Nishijin lunch; ¥900) plate is decent value. Service can be slow and scattered but the interesting ambience makes it worth a look. It's near Funaoka Onsen (p109) and is easy to spot.

TOP CHOICE KANEI NOODLES ¥

Map p228 (かね井; ☎441-8283; Kita-ku, Murasakino Higashifujinomori-chō 11-1; noodles from ¥900; ⏲11.40am-2.30pm & 5-7pm Tue-Sun; 🚌7min walk from Daitoku-ji-mae bus stop, bus 206 from Kyoto Station) A small traditional place not far from Funaoka Onsen (see p109), Kanei is the place to go if you're a *soba* (thin brown buckwheat noodles) connoisseur – the noodles are made by hand here and are delicious. The owners don't speak much English, so here's what to order: *zaru soba* (¥900) or *kake soba* (*soba* in a broth; ¥1000). Note that handmade *soba* quickly loses its taste and texture, so we recommend that you eat it quickly. The servings are small and the dishes are only likely to please real *soba* fans. Kanei is on the corner, a few metres west of Saraca Nishijin.

TOP CHOICE TOYOUKE-JAYA TOFU ¥

Map p228 (とようけ茶屋; ☎462-3662; Kamigyō-ku, Imadegawa-dōri-Onmae Nishi iru; set meals from ¥680; ⏲11am-3pm, closed Thu; 🚌1min walk from Kitano Tenmangū-mae bus stop, bus 101 from Kyoto Station) Locals line up for the tofu lunch sets at this famous restaurant across from Kitano Tenman-gū (p108). Set meals start at ¥650 and usually include tofu, rice and miso soup. The problem is that it gets very crowded, especially when a market is on at the shrine. If you can get here when there's no queue, pop in for a healthy meal.

CAFÉ BEBE CAFE ¥

Map p228 (カフェベベ; ☎463-1477; Kamigyō-ku, Kamishichiken; tea ¥550, tea & pastry ¥650; ⏲10am-6pm; 🗎; 🚌5min walk from Kitano Tenmangū-mae bus stop, bus 101 from Kyoto Station) In the Kamishichiken geisha district, near the east gate of Kitano Tenman-gū (p108), this intimate little cafe in an old *machiya* is a great place to relax with a cup of tea and a book. There's an English menu.

ENTERTAINMENT

JITTOKU LIVE MUSIC HALL

Map p228 (拾得; ☎841-1691; Ōmiya-dōri-Shimotachiuri; ⏲5.30pm-midnight, live music 7-9pm; Ⓜ10min walk from Nijōjō-mae Station, Tōzai subway line) Juttoku is located in an atmospheric old *sakagura* (sake warehouse). It plays host to a variety of shows – check *Kansai Scene* to see what's on.

SHOPPING

TENJIN-SAN MARKET FLEA MARKET

Map p228 (天神さん　北野天満宮露天市; ☎461-0005; Kamigyō-ku, Bakuro-chō, Kitano Tenman-gū; 🚌1min walk from Kitano Tenmangū-mae bus stop, bus 50 or 101 from Kyoto Station) This market is held from dawn to dusk on the 25th of each month at Kitano Tenman-gū (p108) and marks the birthday (and coincidentally the death) of the Heian-era statesman Sugawara Michizane (845–903). It's pleasant to explore the shrine before or after you do your shopping.

NISHIJIN TEXTILE CENTER KIMONO, OBI

Map p228 (西陣織会館; ☎451-9231; Imadegawa Minami iru, Horikawa-dōri, Kamigyō-ku; ⏲9am-5pm; 🚌1min walk from Horikawa-Imadegawa bus stop, bus 9 from Kyoto Station) The Nishijin Textile Center (see p108) is part museum, part event hall and part shop. Downstairs, it occasionally hosts kimono fashion shows, highlighting the area's distinctive Nishijin-ori weaving. Upstairs there are displays where artisans demonstrate the use of traditional looms and dyeing techniques. A variety of goods, including kimono and *obi* (kimono sashes), are for sale on the 2nd floor. These days, it's a little overrun with big tour groups.

Arashiyama & Sagano

Neighbourhood Top Five

❶ Entering the magical green world of the **Arashiyama Bamboo Grove** (p114). If you've seen *Crouching Tiger, Hidden Dragon*, you'll know what to expect.

❷ Meditating on the garden at **Tenryū-ji** (p114).

❸ Meandering the trails through the garden at the superb **Ōkōchi-sansō Villa** (p116).

❹ Hiking up to the moss garden at **Giō-ji** (p117).

❺ Visiting with our simian cousins at **Arashiyama Monkey Park Iwatayama** (p114).

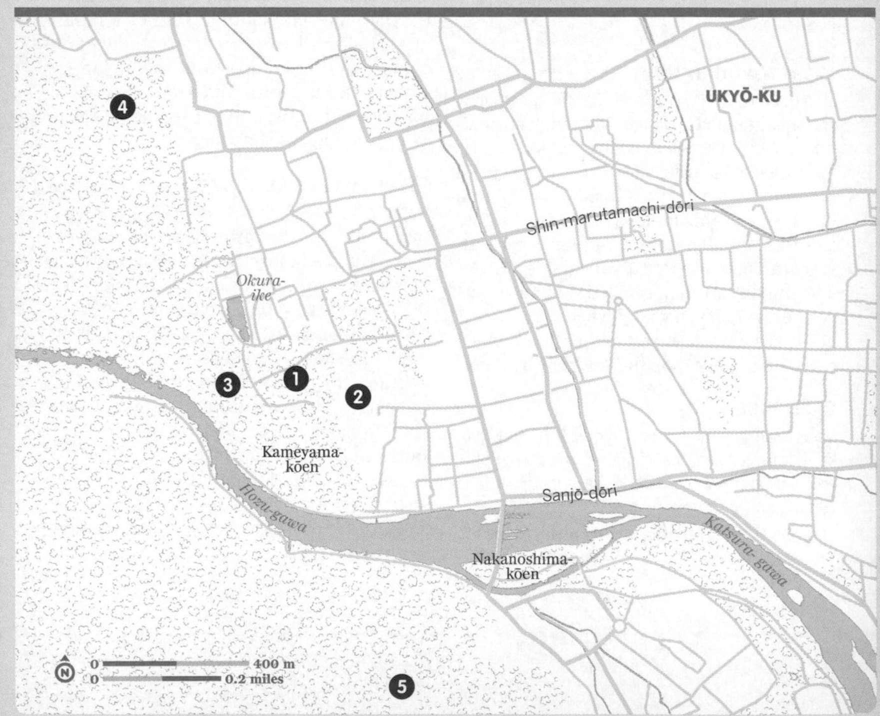

For more detail of this area, see Map p227 ➡

Explore: Arashiyama & Sagano

Located at the base of the mountains on the west side of the city, the Arashiyama and Sagano area is Kyoto's second-most important sightseeing district after Southern Higashiyama. If you're in town for at least two or three days, it's worth making the trek out here to see this superb collection of tourist sites.

A half day is sufficient to do the main route through the area, which we describe in our Ambling Through Bamboo Groves & Temples walking route (p115). Keep in mind that getting out to this area from Downtown Kyoto will take about an hour if you take public transport, and about half an hour if you go by taxi.

Since some of the best sights in Northwest Kyoto (p104), like Kinkaku-ji and Ryōan-ji, are not far from Arashiyama and Sagano, you can make a nice full-day tour of western Kyoto if you are willing to travel between these two areas by taxi.

There are several ways to get to Arashiyama and Sagano from Downtown Kyoto and the Kyoto Station Area. If you're coming from Downtown Kyoto, Kyoto city bus 11 will get you from Shijō-dōri to Tenryū-ji-mae (the main Arashiyama stop). Alternatively, you can take the Tōzai subway line to the westernmost stop, Uzumasa-Tenjin-gawa, and transfer to the Randen street tram, which will take you to central Arashiyama.

From Kyoto Station, you can take the JR Sagano-San-in line and get off at Saga Arashiyama Station (be careful to take only the local train, as the express does not stop in Arashiyama).

Local Life

- **Hangouts** Kameyama-kōen (p114) is popular with locals for picnics.
- **Romantic Strolls** The Hozu-gawa riverbank is favoured for romantic strolls in the early evening.
- **Family Favourite** Arashiyama Monkey Park Iwatayama (p114) is a favourite of Kyoto's kids.

Getting There & Away

- **Train** The JR Sagano-San-in line from Kyoto Station to Saga-Arashiyama Station. The Keifuku Arashiyama, Randen, line from Ōmiya Station to Keifuku Arashiyama Station.
- **Bus** From Marutamachi-dōri: bus 93; from Shijō-dōri: bus 11; from Kyoto Station: bus 28.
- **Subway** The Tōzai subway line stops at Uzumasa-Tenjin-gawa, where you can transfer to the Randen street tram.

Lonely Planet's Top Tip

The main drag of Arashiyama and Sagano is overdeveloped and unlovely. As soon as you can, head west into the hills to escape (via Tenryū-ji or straight through the Arashiyama Bamboo Grove).

Best Places to Eat

- Komichi (p117)
- Shigetsu (p118)
- Hiranoya (p117)

For reviews, see p117

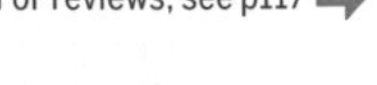

Best Places to Enjoy Nature

- Arashiyama Bamboo Grove (p114)
- Kameyama-kōen (p114)
- Ōkōchi-sansō Villa (p116)

For reviews, see p114

Best Places to Meditate on a Garden

- Tenryū-ji (p114)
- Giō-ji (p117)
- Takiguchi-dera (p116)

For reviews, see p114

SIGHTS

ARASHIYAMA MONKEY PARK IWATAYAMA ZOO

Map p227 (嵐山モンキーパークいわたやま; ☎861-1616; 8 Genrokuzan-chō, Arashiyama, Nishikyō-ku; adult/child ¥550/250; ⏲9am-5pm 15 Mar–15 Nov, to 4pm winter; 🚉20min walk from Keifuku Arashiyama Station, Keifuku Arashiyama, Randen, line) If you want to spend some quality time with our simian cousins or entertain restless children, this park might fit the bill. Just be warned: it's a steep climb up the hill to get to the monkeys. If it's a hot day, you're going to be drenched by the time you get to the spot where they gather.

Though it is common to spot wild monkeys in the nearby mountains, here you can encounter them at a close distance and enjoy watching the playful creatures frolic about. It makes for an excellent photo opportunity, not only of the monkeys but also of the panoramic view over Kyoto. Refreshingly, it is the animals who are free to roam while the humans who feed them are caged in a box!

You enter the park near the south side of Tōgetsu-kyō, through the orange *torii* (shrine gate) of Ichitani-jinja. Buy your tickets from the machine to the left of the shrine at the top of the steps.

TOGETSU-KYŌ BRIDGE

Map p227 (渡月橋; Ukyō-ku, Saga Tenryū-ji, Susukinobaba-chō; 🚉5min walk from Keifuku Arashiyama Station, Keifuku Arashiyama, Randen, line) This bridge is the dominant landmark in Arashiyama and is just a few minutes on foot from either the Keifuku line or Hankyū line Arashiyama Stations. The original crossing, constructed in 1606, was about 100m upriver from the present bridge.

On 13 April *jūsan-mairi*, an important rite of passage for local children aged 13, takes place here. Boys and girls (many in kimono), after paying respects at Hōrin-ji (a nearby temple) and receiving a blessing for wisdom, cross the bridge under strict parental order not to look back towards the temple until they've reached the northern side of the bridge. Not heeding this instruction is believed to bring bad luck for life!

From July to mid-September, this is a good spot from which to watch *ukai* (cormorant fishing) in the evening. If you want to get close to the action, you can pay ¥1700 to join a passenger boat. The Tourist Information Center (p196) can provide more details.

You can also rent boats from the **boat rental stall** (per hr ¥1400; ⏲9am-4.30pm) just upstream from the bridge. It's a nice way to spend some time in Arashiyama and kids love it.

TENRYŪ-JI TEMPLE

Map p227 (天竜寺; ☎881-1235; 68 Susukinobaba-chō, Saga Tenryū-ji, Ukyō-ku; admission ¥600; ⏲8.30am-5pm, to 5.30pm 21 Oct–20 Mar; 🚉2min walk from Keifuku Arashiyama Station, Keifuku Arashiyama, Randen, line) This fine temple has one of the most attractive stroll gardens in all of Kyoto, particularly during the spring cherry-blossom and autumn-foliage seasons. The main 14th-century Zen garden, with its backdrop of the Arashiyama mountains, is a good example of *shakkei* (borrowed scenery). Unfortunately, it's no secret that the garden here is world class, so it pays to visit early in the morning or on a weekday.

Tenryū-ji is a major temple of the Rinzai school. It was built in 1339 on the old site of Go-Daigo's villa after a priest had a dream of a dragon rising from the nearby river. The dream was seen as a sign that the emperor's spirit was uneasy and so the temple was built as appeasement – hence the name *tenryū* (heavenly dragon). The present buildings date from 1900. You will find Arashiyama's famous bamboo grove situated just outside the north gate of the temple.

FREE **ARASHIYAMA BAMBOO GROVE** FOREST

Map p227 (⏲dawn-dusk; 🚉5min walk from Keifuku Arashiyama Station, Keifuku Arashiyama, Randen, line) Walking into this extensive bamboo grove is like entering another world – the thick green bamboo stalks seem to continue endlessly in every direction and there's a strange quality to the light. You'll be unable to resist trying to take a few photos, but you might be disappointed with the results: photos just can't capture the magic of this place. The grove runs from just outside the north gate of Tenryū-ji (p114) to just below Ōkōchi-sansō Villa (p116).

FREE **KAMEYAMA-KŌEN** PARK

Map p227 (亀山公園; ⏲dawn-dusk; 🚉10min walk from Keifuku Arashiyama Station, Keifuku Arashiyama, Randen, line) Just upstream from Tōgetsu-kyō (p114) and behind Tenryū-ji (p114), this park is a nice place to escape the crowds of Arashiyama. It's laced with trails,

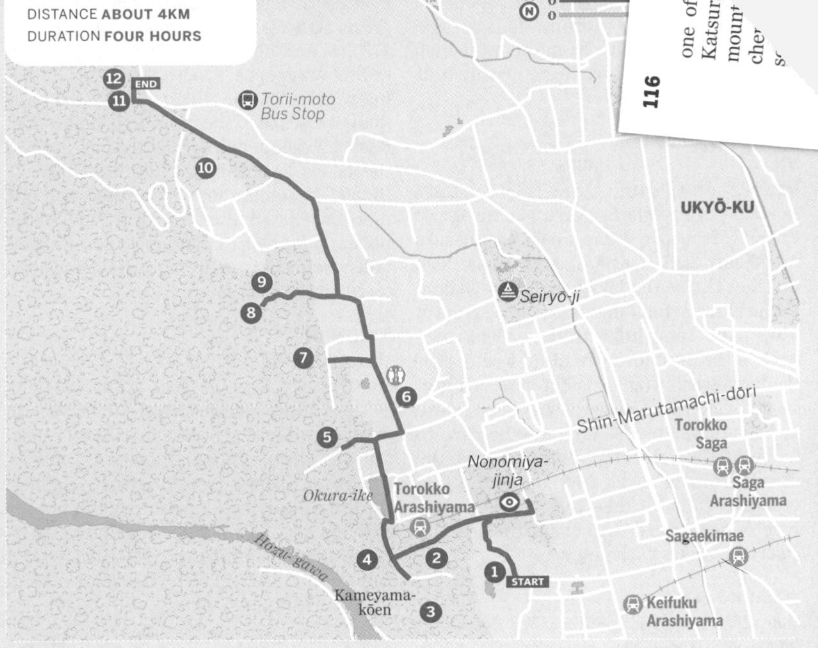

Neighbourhood Walk

Ambling Through Bamboo Groves & Temples

Start at ❶ **Tenryū-ji**, or, if you'd like to skip the temple and save on the entry fee, you can bypass the temple by walking 200m north on the main road and taking a left (turn at the sign that reads 'Nonomiya Shrine etc'). After checking out the temple, exit via the north gate, turn left and enter the famous ❷ **Arashiyama Bamboo Grove**.

At the top of the hill, you can take a quick detour to sample ❸ **Kameyama-kōen** or enter ❹ **Ōkōchi-sansō Villa**, the entrance to which is almost directly in front of you.

Continuing north from Ōkōchi-sansō, head downhill and past Okura-ike pond. From this point on, you'll pass several smaller temples; since it would be costly and time consuming to enter all of them, it's best to choose one and savour it (our vote goes to Giō-ji).

Soon after passing the pond, you'll see the gate of ❺ **Jōjakkō-ji**. After Jōjakkō-ji, walk straight east away from the temple gate, avoiding the temptation to take a left out of the gate and go north. About 100m east of the Jōjakkō-ji gate, take a left (just before a cornfield) and you'll soon come to ❻ **Rakushisha**, a charming poet's hut. After Rakushisha, continue north. About 150m further on brings you to the gate of ❼ **Nison-in**.

Return to the main road from Nison-in and follow it gradually northwest for a few minutes. This will bring you to the turn-off for ❽ **Takiguchi-dera** and ❾ **Giō-ji**, two wonderfully atmospheric little hillside temples (there is no English sign here; look for the four stone way markers). After visiting one or both of these temples, return to the main road and continue walking northwest. You'll soon see the stone steps that lead up to ❿ **Adashino Nembutsu-ji** on your left. From here, it's a short walk onward to the huge orange ⓫ **Atago Torii**. A nice place to refresh yourself after all the walking you've done is ⓬ **Hiranoya**, just north of the *torii*. You can take bus 62 or 72 from Torii-moto bus stop.

…n leads up to a lookout over …awa and up into the Arashiyama …ins. It's especially attractive during …y-blossom and autumn-foliage sea…s. Keep an eye out for monkeys, which …ccasionally descend from the nearby hills to pick fruit.

ŌKŌCHI-SANSŌ VILLA NOTABLE BUILDING, GARDEN

Map p227 (大河内山荘; ☎872-2233; 8 Tabuchi yama-chō, Ogurayama, Saga, Ukyō-ku; admission ¥1000; ⏲9am-5pm; 🚉15min walk from Keifuku Arashiyama Station, Keifuku Arashiyama, Randen, line) This is the lavish estate of Ōkōchi Denjirō, an actor famous for his samurai films. The sprawling stroll gardens may well be the most lovely in all of Kyoto, particularly when you consider the brilliant views eastwards across the city. The house and teahouse are also sublime. Be sure to follow all the trails around the gardens (the standard route is clearly marked). Hold onto the tea ticket they give you when you enter – you'll need it to claim the tea and cake that comes with entry.

JŌJAKKŌ-JI TEMPLE

Map p227 (常寂光寺; ☎861-0435; 3 Ogura-chō, Ogurayama, Saga, Ukyō-ku; admission ¥400; ⏲9am-5pm; 🚉20min walk from Keifuku Arashiyama Station, Keifuku Arashiyama, Randen, line) This temple is perched on top of a mossy knoll and is famed for its brilliant maple trees, which turn a lovely crimson red in November, and its thatched-roof Niō-mon gate. The Hondō was constructed in the 16th century out of wood sourced from Fushimi-jō.

RAKUSHISHA TEMPLE

Map p227 (落柿舎; ☎881-1953; 20 Himyōjin-chō, Ogurayama, Saga, Ukyō-ku; admission ¥200; ⏲9am-5pm Mar-Dec, 10am-4pm Jan & Feb; 🚉20min walk from Keifuku Arashiyama Station, Keifuku Arashiyama, Randen, line) This building was the hut of Mukai Kyorai, the best-known disciple of the illustrious haiku poet Bashō. Legend holds that Kyorai dubbed the house Rakushisha (literally 'House of the Fallen Persimmons') after he woke one morning following a fierce storm to find the persimmons he had planned to sell were all fallen from the trees in the garden and scattered on the ground.

NISON-IN TEMPLE

Map p227 (二尊院; ☎861-0687; 27 Monzenchōjin-chō, Nison-in, Saga, Ukyō-ku; admission ¥500; ⏲9am-4.30pm; 🚉25min walk from Keifuku Arashiyama Station, Keifuku Arashiyama, Randen, line) This is a popular spot with maple-watchers. Nison-in was originally built in the 9th century by Emperor Saga. It houses two important Kamakura-era Buddha statues side by side (Shaka on the right and Amida on the left). The temple features lacquered nightingale floors.

TAKIGUCHI-DERA TEMPLE

Map p227 (滝口寺; ☎871-3929; Ukyō-ku, Saga, Kameyama-chō 10-4; adult/child ¥300/200; ⏲9am-5pm; 🚉35min walk from Keifuku Arashiyama Station, Keifuku Arashiyama, Randen, line) The history of this temple reads like the romance of *Romeo and Juliet*. Takiguchi-dera was founded by Heian-era nobleman Takiguchi Nyūdō, who entered the priesthood

HOZU-GAWA RIVER TRIP

The **Hozu-gawa river trip** (☎0771-22-5846; Kameoka-shi, Hozu-chō; adult/child ¥3900/2500; ⏲9am-3.30pm) is a great way to enjoy the beauty of Kyoto's western mountains without any strain on the legs. With long bamboo poles, boatmen steer flat-bottom boats down the Hozu-gawa from Kameoka, 30km west of Kyoto Station, through steep, forested mountain canyons, before arriving at Arashiyama.

Between 10 March and 30 November there are seven trips daily. During winter the number of trips is reduced to four per day and the boats are heated.

The ride lasts two hours and covers 16km through occasional sections of choppy water – a scenic jaunt with minimal danger. The scenery is especially breathtaking during cherry-blossom season in April and maple-foliage season in autumn.

The boats depart from a dock that is eight minutes' walk from Kameoka Station. Kameoka is accessible by rail from Kyoto Station or Nijō Station on the JR Sagano-San-in main line. The Tourist Information Center (p196) provides an English-language leaflet and timetable for rail connections. The fare from Kyoto to Kameoka is ¥400 one way by regular train (don't spend the extra for the express; it makes little difference in travel time).

after being forbidden by his father to marry his peasant consort Yokobue. One day, Yokobue came to the temple with her flute to serenade Takiguchi, but was again refused by him; she wrote a farewell love sonnet on a stone (in her own blood) before throwing herself into the river to perish. The stone remains at the temple.

GIŌ-JI TEMPLE

Map p227 (祇王寺; ☎861-3574; 32 Kozaka, Saga Toriimoto, Ukyō-ku; admission ¥300; ⊙9am-4.30pm; 35min walk from Keifuku Arashiyama Station, Keifuku Arashiyama, Randen, line) This quiet temple was named for the Heian-era *shirabyōshi* (traditional dancer) Giō, who committed herself here as a nun at age 21 after her romance ended with Taira-no-Kiyomori, the commander of the Heike clan. She was usurped in Kiyomori's affections by a fellow entertainer, Hotoke Gozen (who later deserted Kiyomori to join Giō at the temple). Enshrined in the main hall are five wooden statues: these are Giō, Hotoke Gozen, Kiyomori and Giō's mother and sister (who were also nuns at the temple).

The main attraction here is the lush moss garden outside the thatch-roofed hall of the temple. It's a small spot that is often overlooked by visitors to Arashiyama.

ADASHINO NEMBUTSU-JI TEMPLE

Map p227 (化野念仏寺; ☎861-2221; 17 Adashino-chō,Saga Toriimoto, Ukyō-ku; admission ¥500; ⊙9am-4.30pm; 40min walk from Keifuku Arashiyama Station, Keifuku Arashiyama, Randen, line) This rather unusual temple is where the abandoned bones of paupers without kin were gathered. More than 8000 stone images are crammed into the temple grounds, dedicated to the repose of their spirits. The abandoned souls are remembered with candles each year in the Sentō Kuyō ceremony held here on the evenings of 23 and 24 August. The temple is not a must-see attraction, but it's certainly interesting and the stone images make unusual photographs.

DAIKAKU-JI TEMPLE

Map p227 (大覚寺; ☎871-0071; Ukyō-ku, Saga, Osawa-chō 4; adult/child ¥500/300; ⊙9am-4.30pm; 15min walk from Saga Arashiyama Station, Sagano line) A 25-minute walk northeast of Nison-in (p116) you will find Daikaku-ji, one of Kyoto's less-commonly visited temples. It was built in the 9th century as a palace for Emperor Saga, who then converted it into a temple. The present buildings date from the 16th century and are palatial in style; they also contain some impressive paintings. The large Osawa-no-ike pond was once used by the emperor for boating and is a popular spot for viewing the harvest moon.

EATING

TOP CHOICE **KOMICHI** CAFE ¥

Map p227 (こみち; ☎872-5313; 23 Ōjōin-chō, Nison-in Monzen, Saga, Ukyō-ku; matcha ¥650; ⊙10am-5pm, closed Wed; 20min walk from Keifuku Arashiyama Station, Keifuku Arashiyama, Randen, line) This friendly little teahouse is perfectly located along the Arashiyama tourist trail. In addition to hot and cold tea and coffee, it serves *uji kintoki* (shaved ice with sweetened green tea) in summer and a variety of light noodle dishes year-round. The picture menu helps with ordering. The sign is green and black on a white background.

TOP CHOICE **HIRANOYA** TEA, KAISEKI ¥¥

Map p227 (平野屋; ☎861-0359; Ukyō-ku, Saga Toriimoto Sennō-chō 16; tea ¥840, dinner from ¥15,000; ⊙11.30am-9pm; 5min walk from Otaginenbutsu-ji-mae bus stop, bus 72 from Kyoto Station) Located next to the Atago Torii (a large Shintō shrine gate), this thatched-roof restaurant is about as atmospheric as they get. While you can sample full-course *kaiseki* (Japanese *haute cuisine*) meals here from ¥15,000 (by telephone reservation in Japanese only), we prefer to soak up the atmosphere over a simple cup of *matcha* (powdered green tea) for a relatively modest ¥840 (it comes with a traditional sweet). It's the perfect way to cool off after a long slog around the temples of Arashiyama and Sagano. Just ask for *o-cha* and you're away.

YUDŌFU SAGANO TOFU ¥¥

Map p227 (湯豆腐嵯峨野; ☎871-6946; Ukyō-ku, Saga, Tenryū-ji, Susukinobaba-chō 45; lunch & dinner from ¥3800; ⊙11am-7pm; 10min walk from Keifuku Arashiyama Station, Keifuku Arashiyama, Randen, line) This is a popular place to sample *yudōfu* (bean curd cooked in an iron pot). It's fairly casual, with a spacious dining room. You can usually eat here without having to wait and there's both indoor and outdoor seating. Look for the old cartwheels outside.

TOP CHOICE SHIGETSU VEGETARIAN ¥¥

Map p227 (篩月; ☎882-9725; 68 Susukinobaba-machi, Saga Tenryū-ji, Ukyō-ku; lunch sets ¥3500, ¥5500 & ¥7500; ⏰11am-2pm; ☑; 🚋2min walk from Keifuku Arashiyama Station, Keifuku Arashiyama, Randen, line) To sample *shōjin ryōri* (Buddhist vegetarian cuisine), try Shigetsu in the precincts of Tenryū-ji (p114). This healthy fare has been sustaining monks for more than a thousand years in Japan, so it will probably get you through an afternoon of sightseeing, although carnivores may be left craving something. Shigetsu has beautiful garden views.

MIKAZUKI JAPANESE ¥

Map p227 (三日月; ☎861-0445; Ukyō-ku, Saga, Tenryū-ji, Tsukurimichi-chō 35-2; meals ¥1000; ⏰11am-4pm, closed Tue; 📋; 🚋2min walk from Keifuku Arashiyama Station, Keifuku Arashiyama, Randen, line) The thing that distinguishes this place from its neighbours on the crowded main drag is its English menu and the fact that it is a little more spacious than the others. Dishes include the typical *shokudō* (all-around eatery) noodle and rice classics. The tempura *teishoku* (set-course meal; ¥1600) gives value for money and should power you through a few hours of Arashiyama sightseeing. The sign is in Japanese; it's black-and-white and one of the Japanese characters looks like a bullseye.

KAMEYAMA-YA JAPANESE ¥

Map p227 (亀山家; ☎861-0759; Ukyō-ku, Saga, Kamenoo-chō; ⏰11am-6pm; meals ¥550-1500; 🚋10min walk from Keifuku Arashiyama Station, Keifuku Arashiyama, Randen, line) We love this semi-outdoor restaurant on the banks of the Hozu-gawa. The service can be gruff, the food is only pretty good, but the location is impossible to beat. Dishes include tempura over rice and noodles. There is no English sign but there are a couple of vending machines near the entrance.

YOSHIDA-YA NOODLES ¥

Map p227 (よしだや; ☎861-0213; 20-24 Tsukurimichi-chō, Saga Tenryū-ji, Ukyō-ku; lunch from ¥750; ⏰10.30am-4pm, closed Wed; 🚋1min walk from Keifuku Arashiyama Station, Keifuku Arashiyama, Randen, line) This quaint and friendly little *teishoku-ya* (set-meal restaurant) is the perfect place to grab a simple lunch while in Arashiyama. All the standard *teishoku* favourites are on offer, including things such as *oyakodon* (egg and chicken over a bowl of rice) for ¥1000. You can also cool off here with a refreshing *uji kintoki*(shaved ice with sweetened green tea) for ¥600. There is no English sign; the restaurant is the first place south of the station and it has a rustic front.

ARASHIYAMA YOSHIMURA NOODLES ¥¥

Map p227 (嵐山よしむら; ☎863-5700; Togetsu-kyō kita, Ukyō-ku; soba from ¥1050, set meals from ¥1575; ⏰11am-5pm; 📋; 🚋5min walk from Keifuku Arashiyama Station, Keifuku Arashiyama, Randen, line) For a tasty bowl of *soba* noodles and a million-dollar view over the Arashiyama mountains and the Togetsu-kyō bridge, head to this extremely popular eatery just north of the famous bridge, overlooking the Katsura-gawa. There's an English menu but no English sign; look for the big glass windows and the stone wall.

Kitayama Area & Greater Kyoto

ŌHARA | KURAMA | KIBUNE | SOUTHEAST KYOTO | FUSHIMI | UJI | SOUTHWEST KYOTO | TAKAO AREA | NORTH KYOTO | NORTHEAST KYOTO

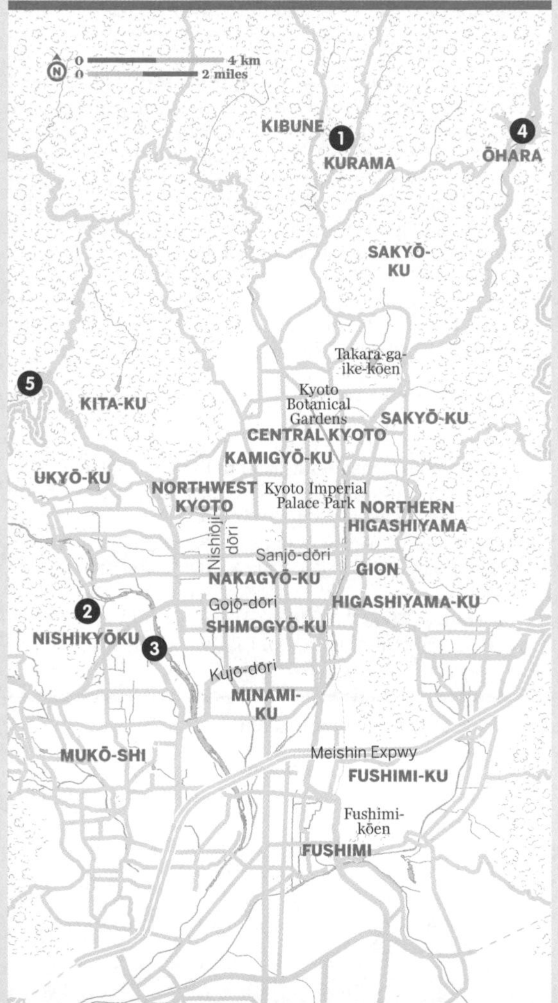

For more detail of this area, see Map p231 and p230 ➡

Neighbourhood Top Five

❶ Ascending to the mountain temple of **Kurama-dera** (p122), one of the best half-day trips in Kyoto. If you have the energy, continue over the top of the mountain and down to the village of Kibune.

❷ Entering the green wonderland of **Saihō-ji** (p127).

❸ Making a pilgrimage to the pinnacle of Japanese architecture, **Katsura Rikyū Imperial Villa** (p126).

❹ Escaping to the quaint rural village of **Ōhara** (p121) to visit the Buddhist paradise of Sanzen-in and then walk the rural footpaths of the village.

❺ Climbing to **Jingo-ji** (p127), a mountain temple where you can play 'karmic frisbee.'

Lonely Planet's Top Tip

Avoid Ōhara on busy autumn foliage weekends in November. There's only one main road up there from Kyoto and you'll spend too much time sitting in traffic (and the temples will be crowded when you get there). Wait until Monday if you can.

Best Places to Eat

- Yōshūji (p123)
- Hirobun (p123)
- Seryō-jaya (p121)

Best Places to Hike

- Kurama-dera (p122)
- Takao (p127)
- Mt Hiei (p128)

Best Gardens

- Katsura Rikyū Imperial Villa (p126)
- Saihō-ji (p127)
- Sanzen-in (p121)

Explore: Kitayama Area & Greater Kyoto

The Kitayama Area & Greater Kyoto area encompass all the sites found at the periphery of the city. This includes four villages in the Kitayama (Northern Mountains) area: Takao, Ōhara, Kurama and Kibune. It also includes two first-rate sights in the southwest corner of the city: Saihō-ji ('Moss Temple') and Katsura Rikyū Imperial Villa. In the south, you'll find the sake-brewing centre known as Fushimi, and still further south you'll find the tea-growing centre known as Uji, which is also home to a fine Buddhist temple, Byōdō-in. Finally, in the northeast corner of the city, you'll find the mountain temple complex of Enryaku-ji, which sits atop Mt Hiei, the mountain that dominates that corner of the city.

Needless to say, due to their location, most of these sights require at least half a day to visit and you shouldn't try to link any of these areas into one day trip (with the exception, perhaps, of Uji and Fushimi).

All of the sights in this chapter can be reached by public transport. Kurama and Kibune are a very easy 30-minute trip from Kyoto via the Eizan Dentetsu line. Likewise, Ōhara is an easy 40-minute bus trip from central Kyoto (longer in autumn foliage season). Fushimi and Uji are both served by the JR line and the private Keihan line. Buses and trains serve the sights in Southwest Kyoto and buses and/or funiculars will get you up Mt Hiei to visit Enryaku-ji.

Local Life

- **Beat the Heat** Locals head to the *yuka* (dining platforms) over the river in Kibune (p123) to cool off when the Kyoto summer heat cranks up.
- **A Taste of Winter** Folks who love winter scenery head up to Kurama-dera (p122) after a snowstorm hits the area.
- **Foliage Treat** The village of Ōhara (p121) is loved by locals and other Japanese for its autumn foliage.

Getting There & Away

- **Train** The Eizan line will get you to Kurama and Kibune. The JR line and the Keihan line serve Fushimi and Uji.
- **Bus** Kyoto City buses and/or Kyoto buses (they're different) serve all the destinations in this chapter. JR buses also serve Takao.
- **Rental Car** A rental car is a good option for exploring the Kitayama area.

SIGHTS

Ōhara

Since ancient times Ōhara, a quiet farming town about 10km north of Kyoto, has been regarded as a holy site by followers of the Jōdo (Pure Land) school of Buddhism. The region provides a charming glimpse of rural Japan, along with the picturesque Sanzen-in, Jakkō-in and several other fine temples. It's most popular in autumn, when the maple leaves change colour and the mountain views are spectacular.

From Kyoto Station, Kyoto buses 17 and 18 run to Ōhara bus stop. The ride takes about an hour and costs ¥580. From Keihan line's Sanjō Station, take Kyoto bus 16 or 17 (¥470, 45 minutes). Be careful to board a tan-coloured Kyoto bus, not a green Kyoto City bus of the same number.

TOP CHOICE SANZEN-IN — TEMPLE

Map p230 (三千院; ☎744-2531; 540 Raigōin-chō, Ōhara, Sakyō-ku; admission ¥700; ⏰8.30am-5pm Mar-Nov, to 4.30pm Dec-Feb; 🚌15min walk from Ōhara bus stop) Famed for its autumn foliage, hydrangea garden and stunning Buddha images, this temple is deservedly popular with foreign and domestic tourists alike.

Founded in 784 by the priest Saichō, Sanzen-in belongs to the Tendai school. Saichō, considered one of the great patriarchs of Buddhism in Japan, also founded Enryaku-ji (p128).

The temple's garden, **Yūsei-en**, is one of the most photographed sights in Japan, and rightly so. Take some time to sit on the steps of the Shin-den hall and admire the garden's beauty. Then head off to see **Ōjō-gokuraku-in** (Temple of Rebirth in Paradise), the hall in which stands the impressive Amitabha trinity, a large Amida image flanked by attendants Kannon and Seishi (god of wisdom). After this, walk up to the garden at the back of the temple where, in late spring and summer, you can walk among hectares of blooming hydrangeas.

The approach to Sanzen-in is opposite the main bus stop; there is no English sign but you can usually just follow the Japanese tourists. The temple is located about 600m up this walk on your left as you crest the hill.

If you're keen for a short hike after leaving the temple, continue up the hill to see the rather oddly named **Soundless Waterfall** (Oto-nashi-no-taki; 音無の滝). Though in fact it sounds like any other waterfall, its resonance is believed to have inspired Shōmyō Buddhist chanting.

A good spot for a snack after your explorations is **Seryō-jaya** (芹生茶屋; Map p230; ☎744-2301; Ōhara Sanzenin hotori, Sakyō-ku; lunch sets from ¥2000; ⏰11am-5pm; 🚌15min walk from Ōhara bus stop), just by the entry gate to Sanzen-in. It serves wholesome *sansai ryōri* (mountain-vegetable cooking), fresh river fish and *soba* (thin brown buckwheat noodles) topped with grated yam. There is outdoor seating in warmer months. To find this place, look for the food models.

JIKKŌ-IN — TEMPLE

Map p230 (実光院; ☎744-2537; Sakyō-ku, Ōhara, Shōrinin-chō 187; adult/child incl green tea & sweets ¥700/300; ⏰9am-4.30pm; 🚌15min walk from Ōhara bus stop) Only about 50m north of Sanzen-in, this small temple is often praised for its lovely garden and *fudan-zakura* cherry tree, which blossoms between October and March. Jikkō-in is worth the visit if you want to escape the crowds that often plague Sanzen-in.

SHŌRIN-IN — TEMPLE

Map p230 (勝林院; ☎744-2537; Sakyō-ku, Ōhara, Shōrinin-chō 187; adult/child ¥300/200; ⏰9am-4.30pm; 🚌15min walk from Ōhara bus stop) This temple is worth a look, even if only through its admission gate, to admire the thatched roof of the main hall. It's also a good option if you're trying to avoid crowds. It's also near Sanzen-in.

HŌSEN-IN — TEMPLE

Map p230 (宝泉院; ☎744-2409; Sakyō-ku, Ōhara, Shōrinin-chō 187; adult ¥800, child ¥600-700; ⏰9am-5pm; 🚌15min walk from Ōhara bus stop) A quieter option than Sanzen-in, this temple is just down the path west of the entry gate to Shōrin-in. The main tatami room offers a view of a bamboo garden and the surrounding mountains, framed like a painting by the beams and posts of the building. There is also a fantastic 700-year-old pine tree in the garden. The blood-stained Chi Tenjō ceiling boards came from Fushimi-jō castle.

JAKKŌ-IN — TEMPLE

Map p230 (寂光院; ☎744-2545; 676 Kusao-chō, Ōhara, Sakyō-ku; admission ¥600; ⏰9am-5pm Mar-Nov, to 4.30pm Dec-Feb; 🚌20min walk from

Ōhara bus stop) Jakkō-in sits on the opposite side of Ōhara from the more famous Sanzen-in (p121). It's reached by a very pleasant walk through a quaint 'old Japan' village. It's a relatively small temple that can't compete with the beauty of its popular neighbour, but it does make an interesting end point to a fine walk in the country.

The history of the temple is exceedingly tragic. The actual founding date of the temple is subject to some debate (it's thought to be somewhere between the 6th and 11th centuries), but it acquired fame as the temple that harboured Kenrei Mon-in, a lady of the Taira clan. In 1185 the Taira were soundly defeated in a sea battle against the Minamoto clan at Dan-no-ura. With the entire Taira clan slaughtered or drowned, Kenrei Mon-in threw herself into the waves with her son Antoku, the infant emperor; she was fished out – the only member of the clan to survive.

She was returned to Kyoto, where she became a nun and lived in a bare hut until it collapsed during an earthquake. Kenrei Mon-in was then accepted into Jakkō-in and stayed there, immersed in prayer and sorrowful memories, until her death 27 years later. Her tomb is located high on the hill behind the temple.

The main building of this temple burned down in May 2000 and the newly reconstructed main hall lacks some of the charm of the original. Nonetheless, it is a nice spot.

Jakkō-in is west of Ōhara. Walk out of the bus station up the road to the traffic lights, then follow the small road to the left. You might have to ask directions on the way.

Kurama & Kibune

Located just 30 minutes north of Kyoto, Kurama and Kibune are a pair of tranquil valleys that have been long favoured as places to escape the crowds and stresses of the city. Kurama's main attractions are its mountain temple and *onsen* (mineral hot spring). Kibune, an impossibly charming little hamlet just over the ridge, is a cluster of ryokan overlooking a mountain river. Kibune is best in summer, when the ryokan serve dinner on platforms built over the rushing waters of Kibune-gawa, providing welcome relief from the heat.

The two valleys lend themselves to being explored together. In winter, you can start from Kibune, walk 30 minutes over the ridge, visit Kurama-dera, then soak in the *onsen* before heading back to Kyoto. In summer, the reverse route is better: start from Kurama, walk up to the temple, then down the other side to Kibune to enjoy a meal suspended above the cool river. Either way, a trip to Kurama and Kibune is probably the single best day or half-day trip possible from Kyoto city.

If you happen to be in Kyoto on the night of 22 October, be sure not to miss the Kurama Hi Matsuri (p23) fire festival. It's one of the most exciting festivals in the Kyoto area.

To get to Kurama and Kibune, take the Eizan line from Kyoto's Demachiyanagi Station. For Kibune, get off at the second-to-last stop, Kibune-guchi, take a right out of the station and walk about 20 minutes up the hill. For Kurama, go to the last stop, Kurama, and walk straight out of the station. Both destinations are ¥410 and take about 30 minutes to reach.

TOP CHOICE **KURAMA-DERA** TEMPLE

Map p231 (鞍馬寺; ☎741-2003; 1074 Kurama Honmachi, Sakyō-ku; admission ¥200; ⊙9am-4.30pm; 2min walk from Kurama Station, Eizan line) Located high on a thickly wooded mountain, Kurama-dera is one of the few temples in modern Japan that still manages to retain an air of real spirituality. This is a magical place that gains a lot of its power from its brilliant natural setting.

The temple also has a fascinating history: in 770 the monk Gantei left Nara's Toshōdai-ji in search of a wilderness sanctuary in which to meditate. Wandering in the hills north of Kyoto, he came across a white horse that led him to the valley known today as Kurama. After seeing a vision of the deity Bishamon-ten, guardian of the northern quarter of the Buddhist heaven, Gantei established Kurama-dera just below the peak of Kurama-yama. Originally belonging to the Tendai school of Buddhism, Kurama has been independent since 1949, describing its own brand of Buddhism as Kurama-kyō.

The entrance to the temple is just up the hill from Kurama Station. A tram goes to the top for ¥100 or you can hike up in about 30 minutes (follow the main path past the tram station). The trail is worth taking (if it's not too hot), since it winds through a forest of towering old-growth cryptomeria trees, passing by **Yuki-jinja**,

OUT TO EAT IN KURAMA & KIBUNE

Most of the restaurants in Kurama are clustered on the main road outside Kurama-dera's main gate.

Visitors to Kibune from June to September should not miss the chance to dine at one of the picturesque restaurants beside the Kibune-gawa. Known as *kawa-doko*, meals are served on platforms suspended over the river as cool water flows underneath. Most of the restaurants offer a lunch special for around ¥3000. For a *kaiseki* (Japanese *haute cuisine;* ¥5000 to ¥10,000) spread, have a Japanese speaker call to reserve it in advance.

Yōshūji (雍州路; Map p231; ☎741-2848; 1074 Honmachi, Kurama, Sakyō-ku; meals from ¥1050; ⊙10am-6pm, closed Tue; ✎ⓘ; 🚉2min walk from Kurama Station, Eizan line) Yōshūji serves superb *shōjin ryōri* (Buddhist vegetarian cuisine) in a delightful old Japanese farmhouse with an *irori* (open hearth). The house special, a sumptuous selection of vegetarian dishes served in red lacquered bowls, is called *kurama-yama shōjin zen* (¥2600). If you're just wanting a quick bite, try the *uzu-soba* (*soba* topped with mountain vegetables; ¥1050). It's halfway up the steps leading to the main gate of Kurama-dera (p122).

Aburaya-shokudō (油屋食堂; Map p231; ☎7741-2009; 252 Honmachi, Kurama, Sakyō-ku; udon & soba from ¥600; ⊙9.30am-4.30pm; 🚉2min walk from Kurama Station, Eizan line) Just down the steps from the main gate of Kurama-dera, this classic old-style *shokudō* (Japanese-style cafeteria/cheap restaurant) reminds us of what Japan was like before it got rich. The *sansai teishoku* (¥1750) is a delightful selection of vegetables, rice and *soba* topped with grated yam. It's on the corner.

Nakayoshi (仲よし; Map p231; ☎741-2000; Sakyō-ku, Kurama, Kibune-chō 71; lunch/kaiseki dinner from ¥3500/8500; ⊙11am-7pm; 🚉5min taxi ride from Kibune-guchi Station, Eizan line) Nakayoshi serves a lunch *bentō* (boxed meal) for ¥3500. It has dining platforms over the river and the food is well prepared.

Tochigiku (栃喜久; Map p231; ☎741-5555; Sakyō-ku, Kurama, Kibune-chō 17; sukiyaki from ¥8000; ⊙11am-7pm; 🚉5min taxi ride from Kibune-guchi Station, Eizan line) Try this lovely riverside restaurant for chicken and beef sukiyaki, wild boar stew and *kaiseki* sets. There is a small English sign.

Hirobun (ひろ文; Map p231; ☎741-2147; 87 Kibune-chō, Kurama, Sakyō-ku; noodles/kaiseki courses from ¥600/8400; ⊙11.30am-9pm; 🚉5min taxi ride from Kibune-guchi Station, Eizan line) Here you can try *nagashi-somen* (¥1200), which are thin noodles that flow to you in globs down a split-bamboo gutter. This dish is served until 5pm. To find Hirobun, look for the black-and-white sign and the lantern. It's at the top of the village.

Beniya (べにや; Map p231; ☎741-2041; Sakyō-ku, Kurama, Kibune-chō 17; meals from ¥2500; ⊙11am-7pm; 🚉5min taxi ride from Kibune-guchi Station, Eizan line) This elegant riverside restaurant serves *kaiseki* sets for ¥7600, ¥10,000 or ¥12,400. There is a wooden sign with white lettering out the front.

Kibune Club (貴船倶楽部; Map p231; ☎741-3039; 76 Kibune-chō, Kurama, Sakyō-ku; coffee from ¥500; ⊙11.30am-6pm summer, 11.30am-5pm winter; 🚉5min taxi ride from Kibune-guchi Station, Eizan line) The exposed wooden beams and open, airy feel of this rustic cafe make it a great spot for a cuppa while exploring Kibune.

a small Shintō shrine, on the way. Near the peak, there is a courtyard dominated by the Honden (Main Hall); behind this a trail leads off to the mountain's peak.

At the top, you can take a brief detour across the ridge to **Ōsugi-gongen**, a quiet shrine in a grove of trees. Those who want to continue to Kibune can take the trail down the other side. It's a 1.2km, 30-minute hike from the Honden to the valley floor of Kibune. On the way down are two mountain shrines, **Sōjō-ga-dani Fudō-dō** and **Okuno-in Maō-den**, which make pleasant rest stops.

KURAMA ONSEN ONSEN

Map p231 (鞍馬温泉; ☎741-2131; 520 Kurama Honmachi, Sakyō-ku; ⊙10am-9pm; 🚇10min walk from Kurama Station, Eizan line) One of the few *onsen* within easy reach of Kyoto, Kurama Onsen is a great place to relax after a hike. The outdoor bath has fine views of Kurama-yama and costs ¥1100/700 per adult/child. For ¥2300/1600 you get to use the indoor bath, sauna and relaxation areas as well. For both baths, buy a ticket from the machine outside the door of the main building (instructions are in Japanese and English).

To get to Kurama Onsen, walk straight out of Kurama Station and continue up the main street, passing the entrance to Kurama-dera on your left. The *onsen* is about 10 minutes' walk on the right. There's also a free shuttle bus between the station and the *onsen*, which meets incoming trains.

Southeast Kyoto

FREE **DAIGO-JI** TEMPLE

(☎571-0002; 22 Higashiōji-chō, Daigo, Fushimi-ku; ⊙9am-5pm Mar-Nov, to 4pm Dec-Feb; Ⓜ10min walk from Daigo Station, Tōzai subway line) Daigo-ji was founded in 874 by Shobo, who gave it the name Daigo (meaning 'the ultimate essence of milk'). This refers to the five periods of Buddha's teaching, which were compared to the five forms of milk prepared in India; the highest form is called *daigo* in Japanese.

The temple was expanded into a vast complex on two levels, Shimo Daigo (lower) and Kami Daigo (upper). Kami Daigo is atop Daigo-yama, behind the temple. During the 15th century those buildings on the lower level were destroyed, with the sole exception of the five-storey pagoda. Built in 951, this pagoda is treasured as the oldest of its kind in Japan and is the oldest existing building in Kyoto.

In the late 16th century, Hideyoshi took a fancy to Daigo-ji and ordered extensive rebuilding. It is now one of the Shingon school's main temples. To explore Daigo-ji thoroughly and at a leisurely pace, mixing some hiking with your temple-viewing, you will need at least half a day.

The subtemple **Sampō-in** (admission ¥600) is a fine example of the amazing opulence of that period. The Kanō paintings and the garden are special features.

From Sampō-in it's a steep and tiring 50-minute climb up to Kami Daigo. To get here, walk up the large avenue of cherry trees, through the Niō-mon gate, out the back gate of the lower temple, up a concrete incline and into the forest, past the pagoda.

To get to Daigo-ji, take the Tōzai line subway east from central Kyoto to the Daigo stop, and walk east (towards the mountains) for about 10 minutes. Make sure that the train you board is bound for Rokujizō, as some head to Hama-Ōtsu instead. Admission to the grounds is free most of year but during the cherry-blossom and autumn-foliage seasons it costs ¥600.

Fushimi

Fushimi, home to 37 sake breweries, is one of Japan's most famous sake-producing regions. Its location on the Uji-gawa made it a perfect location for sake production, as fresh, high-quality rice was readily available from the fields of neighbouring Shiga-ken and the final product could be easily loaded onto boats for export downriver to Osaka.

Despite its fame, Fushimi is one of Kyoto's least-attractive areas. It's also a hard area to navigate due to a lack of English signage. It's probably only worth a visit if you have a real interest in sake and sake production.

To get to Fushimi, take a local or express train (not a limited express) from Sanjō Station on the Keihan line to Chūshojima Station (¥260, 20 minutes). Alternatively, you can take the Kintetsu Kyoto line from Kyoto Station to Momoyama-Goryōmae Station (¥250, 11 minutes). You'll find a useful map on a pillar outside Chūshojima Station that you can use to orient yourself.

GEKKEIKAN SAKE ŌKURA MUSEUM MUSEUM

(☎623-2056; Fushimi-ku, Minamihama-chō 247; adult/child ¥300/100; ⊙9.30am-4.30pm; 🚇10min walk from Chūshojima Station, Keihan line) The largest of Fushimi's sake breweries is Gekkeikan, the world's leading producer of sake. Although most of the sake is now made in a modern facility in Osaka, a limited amount is still handmade in a Meiji-era *sakagura* (sake brewery) here in Fushimi.

The museum is home to a collection of artefacts and memorabilia tracing the 350-year history of Gekkeikan and the sake-brewing process. Giant murals depicting traditional methods of brewing adorn the walls and there is the chance to sample – and of course purchase – some of the local brew.

If you are travelling with a tour group that is larger than 20 people, and if you call two weeks in advance (☎623-2001), you can arrange a guided English tour of the brewery. Otherwise, ask at the Tourist Information Center (p196) about joining a tour given in Japanese.

The museum is a 10-minute walk north-east of Chūshojima Station on the Keihan line. To get here from the station, go right at the main exit, take a right down an unpaved road, a left at the playground, cross the bridge over the canal and follow the road round to the left; the museum is on the left.

FREE KIZAKURA KAPPA COUNTRY SAKE BREWERY

(☎611-9919; Fushimi-ku, Shioya-chō 228; ⏲11.30am-2pm & 5-10pm Mon-Fri, 11am-2pm & 3-10pm Sat & Sun; 🚉6min walk from Chūshojima Station, Keihan line) A short walk from its competitor, Gekkeikan, Kizakura is another sake brewery worth a look while you're in the neighbourhood. The vast complex houses both sake and beer breweries, courtyard gardens and a small gallery dedicated to the mythical (and sneaky) creature Kappa. The restaurant-bar is an appealing option for a bite and a bit of fresh-brewed ale.

TERADAYA MUSEUM MUSEUM

(☎622-0243; Fushimi-ku, Minamihama-chō; adult ¥400, child ¥200-300; ⏲10am-3.40pm; 🚉5min walk from Chūshojima Station, Keihan line) Famed as the inn of choice for rebel samurai Sakamoto Ryōma (1834–67), these days Teradaya operates as a museum. Fans of Ryōma faithfully make the pilgrimage here to see the room where he slept.

You might have to ask a passer-by for directions, as the way is poorly marked. There is a sign out the front in English that reads: 'The site of the Teradaya Feud'.

Uji

About 20 minutes south of Kyoto Station by train, the small city of Uji is rich in Heian-period culture. Its main claims to fame are Byōdō-in and Ujigami-jinja (both Unesco World Heritage sites) and tea cultivation. The Uji-bashi Bridge, originally all wood and the oldest of its kind in Japan (it is now constructed of concrete and wood), has been the scene of many bitter clashes in previous centuries, although traffic jams seem to predominate nowadays.

If you've exhausted the sights in the main part of Kyoto and feel like a pleasant half-day trip out of town, Uji is a decent choice.

Uji can be easily reached by rail from Kyoto on the Keihan Uji line (¥320, 30 minutes) from Sanjō Station (change at Chūshojima) or the JR Nara line (¥230, 20 minutes) from Kyoto Station.

TOP CHOICE BYŌDŌ-IN TEMPLE

(☎0774-21-2861; 116 Uji renge, Uji-shi; admission ¥600; ⏲8.30am-5.30pm; 🚉15min walk from Keihan Uji Station, Keihan Uji line, 10min walk from Uji Station, JR Nara line) If you happen to have a ¥10 coin in your pocket, dig it out now and have a look at it. The building depicted on the coin is the main hall of this pretty temple in the centre of Uji. Overlooking a serene pond, the hall is one of the loveliest Buddhist structures in Japan.

This temple was converted from a Fujiwara villa into a Buddhist temple in 1052. The **Hōō-dō** (Phoenix Hall), the main hall of the temple, was built in 1053 and is the only original building remaining. The phoenix used to be a popular mythical bird in China and was revered by the Japanese as a protector of Buddha. The architecture of the building resembles the shape of the bird and there are two bronze phoenixes perched opposite each other on the roof.

The Hōō-dō was originally intended to represent Amida's heavenly palace in the Pure Land. This building is one of the few extant examples of Heian-period architecture, and its graceful lines make you wish that far more had survived the wars and fires that have plagued Kyoto's past. Inside the hall is the famous statue of Amida Buddha and 52 *bosatsu* (Bodhisattvas) dating from the 11th century and attributed to the priest-sculptor Jōchō.

Nearby, the **Hōmotsukan Treasure House** (admission ¥300; ⏲9am-4pm 1 Apr–31 May & 15 Sep–23 Nov) contains the original temple bell and door paintings and the original phoenix roof adornments. Allow about an hour to wander through the grounds.

To get to Byōdō-in from Keihan Uji Station, cross the river on the bridge right outside the station; immediately after crossing

UJI TEA

The mountains that surround the town of Uji are perfect for growing tea, and the town has always been one of Japan's main tea-cultivation centres. In fact, tea is usually the first thing most Japanese associate with the name Uji. You won't see any of the plantations unless you hire a car and drive into the mountains to the south, but you will see plenty of shops selling tea in Uji town. As you might expect, this is also a great place to try a simple Japanese tea ceremony.

On the river bank behind Byōdō-in stands the delightful **Taihō-an** (☎0774-23-3334; info@kyoto-uji-kankou.or.jp; Uji-shi Uji Araragi-gawa; admission ¥500; ⏰10am-4pm; 🚉10min walk from Uji Station, Keihan Uji line). The friendly staff conduct a 30-minute tea ceremony (ask for the tatami room, unless you have knee trouble). Casual dress is fine here and no reservations are necessary. Buy your tickets at the Uji-shi Kanko centre next door.

Another stop for a taste of Uji's famed green tea is **Tsūen-jaya** (☎0774-21-2243; www.tsuentea.com/engindex.htm; Uji-shi Uji Higashiuchi; ⏰9.30am-5.30pm; 🚉Uji Station, Keihan Uji line), located just across from the station. Japan's oldest surviving tea shop, Tsūen-jaya has been in the Tsūen family for more than 830 years. The present building, near Uji-bashi, dates from 1672 and is full of interesting antiques. You can try fresh *matcha* (powered green tea), including a sweet, for ¥630 or ¥840.

the bridge, take a left past a public toilet (don't take the street with the large stone *torii*, or shrine gate), and continue straight through the park.

FREE UJIGAMI-JINJA SHRINE

(☎0774-21-4634; Uji-shi, Uji Yamada 59; ⏰9am-4.30pm; 🚉5min walk from Uji Station, Keihan Uji line) Ujigami-jinja holds the distinction of being Japan's oldest shrine. Despite its historical significance, the shrine is the least interesting of Kyoto's 17 Unesco World Heritage sites.

According to ancient records, Uji-no-waki-Iratsuko, a 5th-century prince, tragically sacrificed his own life to conclude the matter of whether he or his brother would succeed the imperial throne; needless to say his brother, Emperor Nintoku, won the dispute. The main building was dedicated to the twosome and their father, Emperor Ōjin, and enshrines the tombs of the trio.

The shrine is across the river from Byōdō-in and a short walk uphill; take the orange bridge. On the way, you'll pass through **Uji-jinja** (admission free; ⏰dawn-dusk), which is actually better looking than its more famous neighbour.

Southwest Kyoto

The southwest area of Kyoto is a sprawling residential and commercial area that few foreign tourists ever visit. Despite the relatively drab surroundings, however, there are three very worthwhile sights here: Katsura Rikyū Imperial Villa; the stunning Saihō-ji, Kyoto's famed Moss Temple; and Jizo-in, a quaint little temple with a tiny moss garden.

For transport to and from this area, see the transport information for the following sights.

FREE KATSURA RIKYŪ IMPERIAL VILLA NOTABLE BUILDING

(☎211-1215; Katsura Misono, Nishikyō-ku) Katsura Rikyū, one of Kyoto's imperial properties, is widely considered to be the pinnacle of Japanese traditional architecture and garden design. Set amid an otherwise drab neighbourhood, it is (very literally) an island of incredible beauty. There are those, however, who feel that the troublesome application process, the distance of the villa from Downtown and the need to join a regimented tour detracts from the experience.

The villa was built in 1624 for the emperor's brother, Prince Toshihito. Every conceivable detail of the villa – the teahouses, the large pond with islets and the surrounding garden – has been given meticulous attention.

Tours (in Japanese) start at 10am, 11am, 2pm and 3pm, and last 40 minutes. Try to be there 20 minutes before the start time. An explanatory video is shown in the waiting room and a leaflet is provided in English.

You must make reservations, usually several weeks in advance, through the Imperial Household Agency – see the boxed tex, p72, for details.

To get to the villa from Kyoto Station, take bus 33 and get off at the Katsura Rikyū-mae stop, which is a five-minute walk from the villa. The easiest access from the city centre is to take a Hankyū line train from Kawaramachi Station to Katsura Station line, which is a 15-minute walk from the villa. A taxi from Katsura Station to the villa will cost about ¥700. Note that some *tokkyū* (express) trains don't stop in Katsura.

SAIHŌ-JI TEMPLE, GARDEN

(☎391-3631; 56 Jingatani-chō, Matsuo, Nishikyō-ku; admission ¥3000) The main attraction at this temple is the heart-shaped garden, designed in 1339 by Musō Kokushi. The garden is famous for its luxuriant mossy growth – hence the temple's other name, Koke-dera (Moss Temple). It is a truly lovely garden, but it costs a fair bit and entry is only allowed as part of a tour, with advance reservations (see p127).

Take bus 28 from Kyoto Station to the Matsuo-taisha-mae stop and walk 15 minutes southwest. From Keihan Sanjō Station, take Kyoto bus 63 to Koke-dera, the last stop, and walk for two minutes.

RESERVATIONS FOR SAIHŌ-JI

To visit Saihō-ji (p127) you must make a reservation. Send a postcard at least one week before the date you wish to visit and include your name, number of visitors, address in Japan, occupation, age (you must be over 18) and desired date (choice of alternative dates preferred). The address:

Saihō-ji,
56 Kamigaya-chō,
Matsuo, Nishikyō-ku,
Kyoto-shi 615-8286
JAPAN

Enclose a stamped self-addressed postcard for a reply to your Japanese address. You might find it convenient to buy an Ōfuku-hagaki (send and return postcard set) at a Japanese post office.

JIZŌ-IN TEMPLE

(☎381-3417; Nishikyō-ku, Yamadakitano-chō 23; adult/child ¥500/300; ⏲9am-4.30pm; 🚌5min walk from Koke-dera bus stop, Kyoto bus 78 from Arashiyama Station, Hankyū line) This delightful little temple could be called the 'poor man's Saihō-ji'. It's only a few minutes' walk south of Saihō-ji (p127) in the same atmospheric bamboo groves. While the temple does not boast any spectacular buildings or treasures, it has a nice moss garden and is almost completely ignored by tourists, making it a great place to sit and contemplate.

From the car park near Saihō-ji, there is a small stone staircase that climbs to the road leading to Jizō-in (it helps to ask someone to point the way, as it's not entirely clear).

Takao Area

The Takao area is tucked far away in the northwestern part of Kyoto. It is famed for autumn foliage and a trio of temples: Jingo-ji, Saimyō-ji and Kōzan-ji.

To reach Takao, take bus 8 from Nijō Station to the last stop, Takao (¥500, 40 minutes). From Kyoto Station, take the hourly JR bus to the Yamashiro Takao stop (¥500, 50 minutes).

TOP CHOICE **JINGO-JI** TEMPLE

(☎861-1769; 5 Takao-chō, Umegahata, Ukyō-ku; admission ¥500; ⏲9am-4pm) This mountaintop temple is one of our favourites in all of Kyoto. It sits at the top of a long flight of stairs that stretch from the Kiyotaki-gawa to the temple's main gate. The Kondō (Gold Hall) is the most impressive of the temple's structures, located roughly in the middle of the grounds at the top of another flight of stairs.

After visiting the Kondō, head in the opposite direction along a wooded path to an open area overlooking the valley. Here you'll see people tossing small discs over the railing into the chasm below. These are *kawarakenage*, light clay discs that people throw in order to rid themselves of their bad karma. Be careful, it's addictive and at ¥100 for two it can get expensive (you can buy the discs at a nearby stall). The trick is to flick the discs very gently, convex side up, like a frisbee. When you get it right, they sail all the way down the valley – taking all that bad karma with them (try not to think about the hikers down below).

To get to Jingo-ji, walk down to the river from the the Yamashiro Takao bus stop and climb the steps on the other side.

TOP CHOICE SAIMYŌ-JI TEMPLE

(☎861-1770; 2 Makio-chō, Umegahata, Ukyō-ku; admission ¥500; ⊙9am-5pm) About five minutes upstream from the base of the steps that lead to Jingo-ji, this fine little temple is another one of our favourite spots in Kyoto. See if you can find your way round to the small waterfall at the side of the temple. The grotto here is pure magic.

KŌZAN-JI TEMPLE

(☎861-4204; 8 Toganoo-chō, Umegahata, Ukyō-ku; admission ¥600; ⊙8am-5pm) Hidden amid a grove of towering cedar trees, this temple is the least accessible of the three temples in Takao. It's famous for the *chuju giga* scroll in its collection, an ink-brush depiction of frolicking animals that is considered by many to be the precursor of today's ubiquitous manga. The temple is reached by following the main road north from the Yamashiro Takao bus stop or, more conveniently, by getting off the JR bus at the Toga-no-O bus stop, which is right outside the temple.

North & Northeast Kyoto

In the north of Kyoto lies Kamigamo-jinja, a fine Shintō shrine, and the imposing bulk of Hiei-zan with its mountaintop temple complex of Enryaku-ji. Note that attractions further to the north in the Kitayama mountains are covered earlier in this chapter.

FREE KAMIGAMO-JINJA SHRINE

(☎781-0011; 339 Motoyama, Kamigamo, Kita-ku; ⊙8am-5pm; 🚌5min walk from Kamigamo-misonobashi bus stop, bus 9 from Kyoto Station.) Kamigamo-jinja is one of Japan's oldest shrines and predates the founding of Kyoto. Established in 679, it is dedicated to Raijin, the god of thunder, and is one of Kyoto's 17 Unesco World Heritage sites. The present buildings (more than 40 in all), including the impressive Haiden hall, are exact reproductions of the originals, dating from the 17th to 19th centuries. The shrine is entered from a long approach through two *torii* (shrine gateways). The two large conical white-sand mounds in front of Hosodono hall are said to represent mountains sculpted for gods to descend upon. It's not one of Kyoto's leading sights but it's worth a look if you find yourself in the north.

HIEI-ZAN & ENRYAKU-JI MOUNTAIN, TEMPLE

(☎077-578-0001; 4220 Honmachi, Sakamoto, Ōtsu city, Shiga; admission ¥550; ⊙8.30am-4.30pm, 9am-4pm winter) A visit to 848m-high Hiei-zan and the vast Enryaku-ji complex is a good way to spend half a day hiking, poking around temples and enjoying the atmosphere of a key site in Japanese history.

TRANSPORT: HIEI-ZAN & ENRYAKU-JI

You can reach Hiei-zan and Enryaku-ji by train or bus. The most interesting way is the train/cable-car/funicular route. If you're in a hurry or would like to save money, the best way is a direct bus from Sanjō Keihan or Kyoto Stations. Note that the Japanese word for funicular is *ropeway*.

➡ **Train** Take the Keihan line north to the last stop, Demachiyanagi, and change to the Yase-Hieizanguchi-bound Eizan Dentetsu Eizan-line train (be careful not to board the Kurama-bound train that sometimes leaves from the same platform). Travel to the last stop, Yase-Hieizanguchi (¥260; about 15 minutes from Demachiyanagi Station), then board the cable car (¥530, nine minutes) followed by the funicular (¥310, three minutes) to the peak, from which you can walk down to the temples.

➡ **Bus/Cable Car** Take Kyoto bus (not Kyoto City bus) 17 or 18, both of which run from Kyoto Station to the Yase-ekimae stop (¥390, about 50 minutes). From there it's a short walk to the cable-car station from where you can complete the journey.

➡ **Direct Bus** if you want to save money (by avoiding both the cable car and funicular), there are direct Kyoto buses from Kyoto and Keihan Sanjō Stations to Enryaku-ji, which take about 70 and 50 minutes respectively (both cost ¥800).

Enryaku-ji was founded in 788 by Saichō, also known as Dengyō-daishi, the priest who established the Tenzai school. This school did not receive imperial recognition until 823, after Saichō's death; however, from the 8th century the temple grew in power. At its height, Enryaku-ji possessed some 3000 buildings and an army of thousands of *sōhei* (warrior monks). In 1571 Oda Nobunaga saw the temple's power as a threat to his aims to unify the nation and he destroyed most of the buildings, along with the monks inside. Today only three pagodas and 120 minor temples remain.

The complex is divided into three sections: Tōtō, Saitō and Yokawa. The **Tōtō** (eastern pagoda section) contains the **Kompon Chū-dō** (Primary Central Hall), which is the most important building in the complex. The flames on the three dharma lamps in front of the altar have been kept lit for more than 1200 years. The **Daikō-dō** (Great Lecture Hall) displays life-sized wooden statues of the founders of various Buddhist schools. This part of the temple is heavily geared to group access, with large expanses of asphalt for parking.

The **Saitō** (western pagoda section) contains the Shaka-dō, which dates from 1595 and houses a rare Buddha sculpture of the Shaka Nyorai (Historical Buddha). The Saitō, with its stone paths winding through forests of tall trees, temples shrouded in mist and the sound of distant gongs, is the most atmospheric part of the temple. Hold on to your ticket from the Tōtō section, as you may need to show it here.

The **Yokawa** is of minimal interest and a 4km bus ride away from the Saitō area. The **Chū-dō** here was originally built in 848. It was destroyed by fire several times and has undergone repeated reconstruction (most recently in 1971). If you plan to visit this area as well as Tōtō and Saitō, allow a full day for in-depth exploration.

Day Trips from Kyoto

Nara p131

Thirty minutes away from Kyoto by express train, Nara boasts a compact collection of truly first-rate sights. If you're in Kyoto for more than four days, Nara is a must!

Osaka p134

A short train trip from Kyoto, Osaka is a great place to see modern Japan in all its hyperkinetic intensity. If you aren't going to Tokyo, consider a trip to Osaka.

Miyama-chō p137

If you want to see rural Japan (thatched-roof cottages etc), hire a car and head to these villages in the mountains north of the city.

Nara

Explore

Nara is the most rewarding day trip from Kyoto and it's very easy to reach. Indeed, by taking the Kintetsu limited express *(tokkyū)* from Kyoto Station to Kintetsu Nara Station, you're there in about 30 minutes – less time than it might take you to visit some of the more distant parts of Kyoto itself.

Whether you go by JR or Kintetsu, grab a map at the nearest tourist information centre (there's one at each station) and walk to Nara-kōen (Nara Park), which contains the thickest concentration of must-see sights in the city, including the awesome Daibutsu (Great Budda) at Tōdai-ji. On the way there, don't miss Isui-en, a compact stunner of a garden. With a 9am start, you can see the sights and be back in Kyoto in time for dinner.

The Best...

- **Sight** Tōdai-ji (p131)
- **Place to Eat** Tempura Asuka (p133)
- **Place to Drink** Saka-gura Sasaya (p134)

Top Tip

Unless you're travelling with a Japan Rail Pass, take a comfortable *tokkyū* on the private Kintetsu line from Kyoto Station (south side of the station) to Kintetsu Nara Station.

Getting There & Away

Kintetsu line (train) The Kintetsu line, which runs between Kintetsu Kyoto Station (in Kyoto Station) and Kintetsu Nara Station, is the fastest and most convenient way to travel between Nara and Kyoto. There are *tokkyū* (¥1110, 33 minutes) and *kyūkō* (¥610, 40 minutes). The *tokkyū* trains run directly and are very comfortable; the *kyūkō* usually require a change at Saidai-ji.

JR line (train) The JR Nara line also connects JR Kyoto Station with JR Nara Station (*JR Miyakoji Kaisoku,* ¥690, 41 minutes) and there are several departures an hour during the day. This is good for Japan Rail Pass holders.

Need to Know

- **Area Code** ☎0742
- **Distance from Kyoto** 37km south
- **JR Nara Station Information Center** (☎22-9821; outside the east exit of JR Nara Station; ⏲9am-5pm)

SIGHTS

TŌDAI-JI TEMPLE

(東大寺大仏殿; ☎22-5511; 406-1 Zōshi-chō; admission to Daibutsu-den hall & Sangatsu-dō each ¥500, admission to Nigatsu-dō free; ⏲8am-4.30pm Nov-Feb, 8am-5pm Mar, 7.30am-5.30pm Apr-Sep, 7.30am-5pm Oct) Nara's main attraction – and a must-see for any visitor to the city – is Tōdai-ji, a huge temple complex on the north side of Nara-kōen. On your way to the temple you'll pass through the **Nandai-mon**, which contains two fierce-looking Niō guardians. The gate's recently restored wooden images, carved in the 13th century by the sculptor Unkei, are some of the finest wooden statues in all of Japan, if not the world. These truly dramatic works of art seem ready to spring to life at any moment.

Tōdai-ji's **Daibutsu-den** is the largest wooden building in the world. Unbelievably, the present structure, rebuilt in 1709, is a mere two-thirds the size of the original! The *daibutsu* (Great Buddha) contained within is one of the largest bronze figures in the world and was originally cast in 746. The present statue, recast in the Edo period, stands just over 16m high and consists of 437 tonnes of bronze and 130kg of gold.

As you circle the statue, towards the back of the Buddha you'll see a wooden column with a hole through its base. Popular belief maintains that those who can squeeze through the hole, which is exactly the same size as one of the Great Buddha's nostrils, are ensured of enlightenment. It's fun to watch the kids wiggle through nimbly and the adults get wedged in like champagne corks. A hint for determined adults: it's a lot easier to go through with both arms held above your head.

From the entrance to Daibutsu-den, walk east and climb a flight of stone steps, and continue to your left to reach the following two halls: Nigatsu-dō and Sangatsu-dō halls (almost subtemples) of Tōdai-ji.

Nara
0 520 m
0 0.25 miles
Sacho-gawa
To Kyoto (40km)
To Kyoto (40km)
Kintetsu Nara Line
Kintetsu Nara
Nobori-Ōji
Higashi-muki Arcade
Sanjō-dōri
Sarusawa-ike
JR Nara
JR Nara Line
NARAMACHI
Nara-kōen
Mikasa-yama
1
2
3
4
5
6
7
8
9
10
11
12

Nara

Sights

1 Isui-en........E2
2 Kasuga Taisha........F3
3 Nara National Museum........D2
4 Nigatsu-dō........F1
5 Sangatsu-dō........F1
6 Tōdai-ji Daibutsu-den........E1
7 Tōdai-ji Nandai-mon........E2

Eating

8 Falafel Garden........C2
9 Mellow Café........C2
10 Silk Road........E2
11 Tempura Asuka........C3

Drinking & Nightlife

12 Saka-gura Sasaya........C3

They are an easy walk east (uphill from the Daibutsu-den). You can walk straight east up the hill, but we recommend taking a hard left out of the Daibutsu-den exit, following the enclosure past the pond and turning up the hill. This pathway is among the most scenic walks in all of Nara.

As you reach the plaza at the top of the hill, the **Nigatsu-dō** is the temple hall with the veranda overlooking the plaza. The veranda affords a great view over Nara, especially at dusk. A short walk south of Nigatsu-dō is **Sangatsu-dō**, which is the oldest building in the Tōdai-ji complex.

FREE KASUGA TAISHA SHRINE

(春日大社; 160 Kasugano-chō; dawn-dusk) About 15 minutes' walk roughly south of Sangatsu-dō is Kasuga Taisha, Nara's most important shrine. It was founded in the 8th century by the Fujiwara family and was completely rebuilt every 20 years, according to Shintō tradition, until the end of the 19th century. It lies at the foot of the hill in a pleasant wooded setting with herds of sacred deer awaiting hand-outs. As with similar shrines in Japan, you will find several subshrines scattered around the main hall. The approaches to the shrine are lined with hundreds of lanterns and there are many more hundreds within the shrine itself.

ISUI-EN GARDEN

(依水園; 25-0781; 74 Suimon-chō; admission museum & garden ¥650; 9.30am-4:30pm Wed-Mon (enter by 4pm), closed New Year holidays) Nara's most splendid garden Isui-en is a short walk southwest of Tōdai-ji. The garden dates from the Meiji era and is beautifully laid out with abundant greenery and a pond filled with ornamental carp. It's without a doubt the best garden in the city and is well worth a visit.

NARA NATIONAL MUSEUM MUSEUM

(奈良国立博物館; Nara Kokuritsu Hakubutsukan; 050-5542-8600; 50 Noboriōji-chō; admission ¥500; 9.30am-5pm) The Nara National Museum is devoted to Buddhist art and is divided into two sections, housed in different buildings. Built in 1894, the Nara Buddhist Sculpture Hall & Ritual Bronzes Gallery contains a fine collection of *butsu-zō* (statues of Buddhas and Bodhisattvas). The Buddhist images here are divided into categories, each with an excellent English explanation, making this a great introduction to Mahayana Buddhist iconography. The newer East and West wings, a short walk away, contain the permanent collections (sculptures, paintings and calligraphy) and are used for special exhibitions.

EATING

TEMPURA ASUKA TEMPURA ¥¥

(天ぷら飛鳥; 26-4308; 11 Shōnami-chō; meals ¥1500-5000; 11.30am-2.30pm & 5-9.30pm Tue-Sun;) This reliable restaurant serves attractive tempura and sashimi sets in a relatively casual atmosphere. At lunchtime try the nicely presented *yumei-dono bentō* (a box filled with a variety of tasty Japanese foods) for ¥1600.

SILK ROAD SHOKUDŌ ¥

(シルクロードの終着駅; 25-0231; 16 Kasugano-chō; meals ¥1000; 10am-7pm;) If you have kids in tow, head into the Yumekaze Hiroba dining/shopping complex across from the Nara National Museum to find this wonderful 'train-centric' restaurant. There are two huge model train layouts that your kids can actually control while eating bowls of standard Japanese curry rice and similar favourites. As if Nara wasn't already child-friendly enough!

MELLOW CAFÉ CAFE ¥¥

(メロー　カフェ; 27-9099; 1-8 Konishi-chō; lunch from ¥980; 11am-11.30pm;) Located down a narrow alley (look for the palm tree) not far from Kintetsu Nara Station, this open-plan cafe is a pleasant spot to fuel up for a day of sightseeing. The menu centres on pasta and pizza (there's a brick oven).

FALAFEL GARDEN INTERNATIONAL ¥
(ファラフェルガーデン; ☎24-2722; 13-2 Higashimuki Minamimachi; food from ¥680, lunch from ¥950; ⏰11am-9pm; 📋) About midway along the Konishi shopping arcade, this falafel specialist is a great place for vegetarians and anyone in need of a break from noodles and rice.

DRINKING

FREE **SAKA-GURA SASAYA** SAKE
(☎27-3383; ⏰10am-7pm Wed-Mon) This small sake specialist in the old Naramachi section of town offers tastings of the various types of sake produced in Nara Prefecture (prices range from ¥100 to ¥500 per sample; all sake is also available for purchase). They have a useful English explanation sheet. Look for the barrels and a sign in the window reading 'sake'.

Osaka

Explore

Less than an hour from Kyoto by train, Osaka is the perfect way to experience the energy of a big Japanese city without traipsing all the way to Tokyo. Unlike Kyoto, which contains dozens of discrete tourist sights, Osaka is a city that you experience in its totality. Start with a visit to the castle, Osaka-jō, then head out to Osaka Aquarium (great for kids), and be sure to finish up in Minami (the city's southern hub) to experience the full neon madness that is Osaka after dark.

One day is usually enough to experience Osaka, and trains run late enough to get you back to your lodgings in Kyoto after dinner and a few drinks. Of course, the city is packed with hotels if you are planning a big night out.

The Best...

- **Sight** Osaka-jō (p134)
- **Place to Eat** Imai Honten (p135)
- **Place to Drink** Zerro (p137)

Top Tip

If you're travelling on a Japan Rail Pass, take the *shinkansen* (bullet train) from Kyoto Station to Shin-Osaka Station then head into the city by the Midō-suji subway line.

Getting There & Away

Shinkansen (bullet train) Runs between Kyoto and Shin-Osaka stations (¥2730, 14 minutes).

JR shinkaisoku (train) Runs between Kyoto Station and JR Osaka Station (¥540, 28 minutes).

Hankyū line (train) Runs between Hankyū Umeda Station in Osaka and Hankyū Kawaramachi, Karasuma and Ōmiya Stations in Kyoto (*tokkyū* from Kawaramachi ¥390, 44 minutes).

Keihan line Runs between Sanjō, Shijō or Shichijō Stations in Kyoto and Keihan Yodoyabashi Station in Osaka (*tokkyū* from Sanjō ¥400, 51 minutes).

Getting Around

Train/Subway The JR loop line (known as the JR *kanjō-sen*) circles the city area. There are also seven subway lines; the most useful is the Midō-suji line, which runs north–south, stopping at Shin-Osaka, Umeda (next to Osaka Station), Shinsaibashi, Namba and Tennō-ji Stations.

Need to Know

- **Area Code** ☎06
- **Distance from Kyoto** 45km southwest
- **Umeda Visitors Information Office** (☎6345-2189; outside JR Osaka Station; ⏰8am-8pm, closed 31 Dec–3 Jan)

SIGHTS

OSAKA-JŌ CASTLE
(大阪城; ☎6941-3044; 1-1 Osaka-jō, Chūō-ku; admission grounds free, castle keep ¥600; ⏰9am-5pm, 9am-7pm Aug; 🚉JR Osaka Loop line

to Osaka-jō-kōen) Osaka's most popular attraction is a 1931 concrete reconstruction of the original castle, which was completed in 1583 as a display of power on the part of Toyotomi Hideyoshi. Refurbished at great cost in 1997, today's castle has a decidedly modern look. The interior of the castle houses a museum of Toyotomi Hideyoshi memorabilia, as well as displays relating the history of the castle.

Ōte-mon, the gate that serves as the main entrance to the park, is a 10-minute walk northeast of Tanimachi-yonchōme Station on the Chūō and Tanimachi subway lines. You can also take the Osaka loop line; get off at Osaka-jō-kōen Station and enter through the back of the castle.

OSAKA MUSEUM OF HISTORY MUSEUM

(大阪歴史博物館; Osaka Rekishi Hakubutsukan; ☎6946-5728; 4-1-32 Ōtemae, Chūō-ku; admission ¥600; ⏲9.30am-5pm Sat-Mon & Wed-Thu, 9.30am-8pm Fri; Ⓜ Tanimachi subway line to Tanimachi-yonchōme) Just southwest of Osaka-jō, the excellent Osaka Museum of History is housed in a fantastic new building adjoining the Osaka NHK Broadcast Center. It occupies the 7th to 10th floors of the new sail-shaped building.

The displays are broken into four sections by floor; you start at the top and work your way down, passing through time from the past to the present. The displays are very well done and there are plenty of English explanations; taped tours are available.

The museum is a two-minute walk northeast of Tanimachi-yonchōme Station.

DŌTOMBORI NEIGHBOURHOOD

(Ⓜ Midō-suji subway line to Shinsaibashi or Namba stations) Dōtombori is Osaka's liveliest nightlife area. It's centred on **Dōtombori-gawa** and **Dōtombori Arcade**, a strip of restaurants and theatres where a peculiar type of Darwinism is the rule for both people and shops: survival of the flashiest. In the evening, head to **Ebisu-bashi** bridge to sample the glittering nightscape, which brings to mind a scene from the science-fiction movie *Blade Runner*. Nearby, the banks of the Dōtombori-gawa have recently been turned into attractive pedestrian walkways and this is the best vantage point for the neon madness above.

Only a short walk south of Dōtombori Arcade you'll find **Hōzen-ji**, a tiny temple hidden down a narrow alley. The temple is built around a moss-covered **Fudō-myōō statue**. This statue is a favourite of people employed in *mizu shōbai* (water trade), who pause before work to throw some water on the statue. Nearby, you'll find **Hōzen-ji Yokochō**, a tiny alley filled with traditional restaurants and bars.

To the south of Dōtombori, in the direction of Nankai Namba Station, you'll find a maze of colourful arcades with restaurants, pachinko parlours, strip clubs, cinemas and who knows what else. To the north of Dōtombori, between Midō-suji and Sakai-suji, the narrow streets are crowded with hostess bars, discos and pubs.

OSAKA AQUARIUM AQUARIUM

(Kaiyūkan; ☎6576-5501; www.kaiyukan.com/language/eng; 1-1-10 Kaigan-dōri, Minato-ku; adult/child ¥2000/900; ⏲10am-8pm, enter 1hr prior to the closing, hours vary, check website) The Osaka Aquarium is worth a visit, especially for those who have children in tow. The aquarium is centred on the world's largest aquarium tank, which is home to the star attractions – two enormous whale sharks as well as a variety of smaller sharks, rays and other fish. To get there, take the Chūō subway line to the last stop (Osaka-kō) and from here it's about a five-minute walk to the aquarium. Get there for opening time if you want to beat the crowds – on weekends and public holidays long queues are the norm.

EATING

IMAI HONTEN NOODLES ¥

(☎6211-0319; Chūō-ku, Dōtombori 1-7-22; udon from ¥550) One of the Dōtombori area's oldest and most revered udon specialists, it's our favourite place to eat when we're in Minami. It's an oasis of calm amid the chaos (their no-mobile-phone policy ensures quiet). Try the *tendon* (tempura over rice; ¥1575). It's sandwiched between two pachinko parlours. There's no English sign, but the traditional front stands out among the glitter.

SHINSAIBASHI MADRAS 5 CURRY ¥¥

(マドラス心斎橋店; ☎6213-0858; 2-7-22 Nishi Shinsaibashi, Chūō-ku; ¥1000-2000; ⏲11am-1am; Ⓜ Midō-suji, Yotsubashi or Nagahori Tsurumiryokuchi subway line to Shinsaibashi, Namba or Yotsubashi) If you've never tried Japanese-style curry rice, this new Amerika-Mura

Osaka (Minami Area)

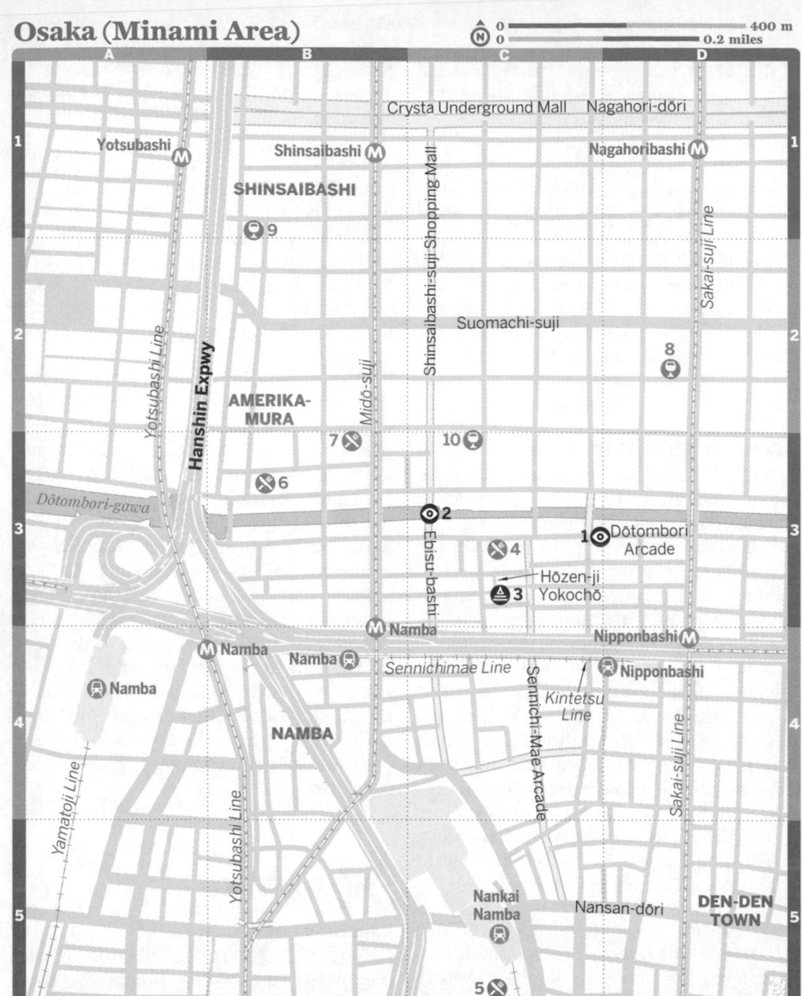

restaurant is a good place to get aquainted with it. A clean, well-lit space with friendly staff, you can choose from tomato-, beef- or chicken-based curries and a variety of toppings. You can even get *genmai* (brown rice) if you wish. The *mikusu furai* (mixed fry; ¥1080) curry is a good choice.

SAI-JI-KI VEGETARIAN ¥¥
(菜蒔季; ☎6636-8123; 6F Namba Parks, 2-10-70 Namba naka, Naniwa-ku; lunch/dinner from ¥1600/2100; ⏰11am-11pm; Ⓜ Midō-suji, Sennichimae, Yotsubashi subway line to Namba) This vegetarian restaurant in the Namba Parks shopping complex in Minami serves an all-you-can eat buffet of mostly Japanese food for ¥1799. If you go at lunchtime, be prepared to wait in line.

SLICES BAR & CAFE PIZZA ¥¥
(☎6211-2231; 1F Yoshimoto Bldg, 2-3-21 Nishi-Shinsaibashi, Chūō-ku; pizza slices/whole from ¥400/2600; ⏰noon-midnight Sun-Fri, noon-2am Sat; 📖; Ⓜ Midō-suji subway line to Namba or Shinsaibashi) If you need a break from Japanese food and want something casual and easy, stop into this foreigner-friendly pizza joint for a slice or two. In addition to pizza, they serve wraps, bagels, salads and fries. There's a big English sign.

Osaka (Minami Area)

Sights

Eating

Drinking & Nightlife

DRINKING

ZERRO BAR

(ゼロ; ☎6211-0439; 2-3-2 Shinsaibashi-suji, Chūō-ku; ⏰7pm-5am; 📵; Ⓜ Midō-suji subway line to Namba or Shinsaibashi) Zerro is the perfect place to start off your evening, with a wide assortment of food and drink, as well as some of the most energetic bartenders around. Live DJs every weekend will have you grooving and shaking until the wee hours of the morning. Check their tasty 'Friday Night Roast' with fresh oven-roasted meat and vegetables.

CINQUECENTO BAR

(チンクエチェント; ☎6213-6788; 2-1-10 Higashi-Shinsaibashi, Chūō-ku; ⏰7:30pm-5am Mon-Sat, 8pm-3am Sun & holidays; 📵; Ⓜ Midō-suji subway line to Namba or Shinsaibashi) This cosy, appropriately named bar is the perfect place to meet local expats and make new friends. Everything on the menu is ¥500, with a hearty selection of food and the most extensive martini selection in the city. Knock back a few before heading off to the nearby clubs.

ROCK ROCK BAR

(ロックロック; ☎6244-6969; 1-8-1 Nishi-Shinsaibashi, Chūō-ku; ⏰7pm-5am; 📵; Ⓜ Midō-suji subway line to Namba or Shinsaibashi) Ever dreamt of running into a famous rock star in a small, intimate setting? Well, you now have your chance, as Rock Rock is the home to official after parties for just about every international act imaginable. Nightly events with a modest cover charge showcase some of Osaka's finest rock DJs. In case you're curious, past visitors to the bar include James Hatfield, Rob Halford, Keanu Reeves, Lady Gaga and a host of others.

Miyama-Chō

Explore

The antidote to the urban centres of Kyoto, Osaka and Nara is a visit to Miyama-chō, a collection of rural hamlets in the Kitayama (Northern Mountains) north of Kurama (p122). Miyama-chō has two great sights: Ashiu, a hiker's paradise; and Kitamura, a collection of thatched-roof houses. En route, you can stop at the temple of Bujō-ji. While you can reach all three by public transport, with a car you can hit all three and even do a quick hike in Ashiu in one long day.

The Best...

- **Sight** Bujōji (p138)
- **Place to Eat** Morishige (p138)
- **Place to Stay** Matabe (p138)

Top Tip

Renting a car is easily the best way to explore this area. Unless there's snow on the ground, the driving is pleasant and stress free.

Getting There & Away

Train/Bus Take a train on the JR Sagano/Saiin line from Kyoto Station to Hiyoshi Station (¥740, 55 minutes), then a bus from Hiyoshi to Kitamura (¥600, 50 minutes).

Car The fastest road to Miyama-chō is Rte 162 (Shūzankaidō), but there is a lovely but longer (two hours) option (routes 38/477) via Kurama and over Hanase-tōgei and Sasari-tōge passes. This route is also good for getting to Bujō-ji.

Bus/Hiking You can also get to Bujō-ji and Ashiu (but not Kitamura) via Kyoto bus 32 from Demachiyanagi Station. If you're only going to Bujō-ji, get off at Daihizan-guchi bus stop (¥900, 90 minutes) and walk 2km east on the narrow road. If you're going to Ashiu, continue to Hirogawara (¥1050, 110 minutes) and hike over Sasari-tōgei Pass. From Hirogawara follow the road to the pass and then take the trail down to Ashiu (use Shobunsha's Yama-to-Kogen series *Kitayama* map).

Need to Know

- **Area Code** ☎0771
- **Distance from Kyoto** 50km north

SLEEPING IN MIYAMA-CHŌ

There are several interesting places in which to stay in the Miyama-chō area. It's best if have a Japanese-speaking person call to make reservations as few lodge-owners speak English. Some owners will pick up guests in Hirogawara.

➡ **Matabe** (またべ; ☎77-0258; Nantan-shi, Miyama-chō, Kita; per person incl 2 meals ¥8500) This quaint *minshuku* (Japanese-style B&B) in Kitamura is in a traditional thatched-roof house.

➡ **Miyama Heimat Youth Hostel** (美山ハイマートユースホステル; ☎/fax 75-0997; Miyama-chō, Obuchi, Nakasai 57; members/nonmembers ¥3350/3950, breakfast/dinner ¥700/1200) One of the cheaper options in the area, this simple youth hostel is in a thatched-roof house on the road to Ōno Dam.

➡ **Yama-no-Ie** (芦生山の家; ☎77-0290; Nantan-shi, Miyama-chō, Ashiu; per person incl 2 meals ¥7350) The only place to stay in Ashiu – other than camping – is in this impressive lodge. It's a few minutes by foot from the forest trailhead.

SIGHTS

BUJŌ-JI — TEMPLE

(峰定寺; Hanase-Harachi-cho, off route 38, 2km east of Daihizan-guchi bus stop; admission ¥500, no children under 12yr; ⏲9am-3.30pm, closed on rainy/snowy days) Bujō-ji is a *shugendo* (mountain asceticism) temple that is also called 'the Northern Omine', a reference to Mt Omine-san in Nara Prefecture, which is a centre for Japan's *yamabushi* (mountain mystics).

It's a 430-step climb to the main hall. First, you surrender your bags and cameras, and get a special pilgrim's bag and staff, plus a printout of a mantra to chant as you climb. Only then can you pass through the gate and climb to the hall. Just before the hall, ring the bell, focus your thoughts and then climb to the veranda to soak up the views.

ASHIU — NEIGHBOURHOOD

(芦生; off route 38 in Miyama-cho, take the turning after descending from Sasari-tōge pass) This quiet and *tiny* village sits on the eastern edge of Miyama-chō. The main attraction is a 4200-hectare virgin forest to the east of the village. Administered by Kyoto University's Department of Agriculture, this is about the only remaining virgin forest in Kansai. Hiking trails enter the forest from above the stone hut at Sarari-tōge Pass and from Ashiu, at the bottom of the pass (note that you should register at the office in Ashiu before entering the forest). The most basic walk follows old train tracks along the undammed Yura-gawa River. More involved hikes continue beyond the tracks up the river or up side valleys. If you intend to do serious hiking here, grab a copy of Shobunsha's Yama-to-Kogen *Kitayama* map at a Kyoto bookshop.

KITAMURA (KAYABUKI-NO-SATO) — NEIGHBOURHOOD

(北村; along route 38 in Miyama-chō, about 20min drive west of Ashiu) Miyama-chō's star attraction is Kitamura (North Village) a hamlet boasting a cluster of some 50 thatched-roof farmhouses. In 1994 the village was designated a national preservation site, and since then the local government has been generously subsidising the exorbitant cost of rethatching the roofs (at an average cost of ¥6 million – around US$50,000).

Sometimes known as 'Kayabuki-no-Sato' (the Village of Thatched-Roof Houses; かやぶきの里), this quaint hamlet is said to contain the thickest concentration of thatched-roof houses in all Japan.

Sights worth seeing here include the **Minzoku Shiryokan** (Folk Museum) and the **Chisana Aibijutsukan** (Little Indigo Museum).

EATING

MORISHIGE — NOODLES ¥

(もりしげ; ☎75-1086; Miyama-chō, Uchikubo, Taninoshimo 15; noodle dishes from ¥750) A thatched-roof place that serves simple but tasty noodle dishes and *nabe* dishes.

YURURI — JAPANESE ¥¥

(厨房 ゆるり; ☎76-0741; Miyama-chō, Morisato; set ¥3000) A wonderfully elegant restaurant occupying a fine thatched-roof house. It's about half an hour north of the centre of Miyama-chō by car. Reservations are required.

Sleeping

When it comes to accommodation, you're spoiled for choice in Kyoto. You can choose from traditional ryokan (Japanese-style inns), luxury hotels, 'business hotels', guesthouses, youth hostels and even capsule hotels. And this being a tourist city, you'll find that most places are perfectly at home with foreign guests.

Ryokan

Ryokan are traditional Japanese inns, with tatami mats on the floor and futons instead of beds. The best places serve sublime Japanese cuisine, have attentive service and beautiful rooms, often with garden views. Note that many places that call themselves ryokan are really just hotels with Japanese-style rooms. That isn't to say they aren't comfortable: they are often friendly and relaxing and may cost less than hotels. Also note that ryokan may not have en suites, and at some places even toilets may be shared; inquire when you make a reservation. Finally, note that some simpler ryokan may not accept credit cards. For more on ryokan, see 'Staying in a Ryokan' on p143.

Business Hotels

In Japan, 'business hotels' are budget or midrange hotels with cramped but efficient rooms and small 'unit baths' (en suite tub/shower/toilet). They usually cost between ¥6000 and ¥12,000 per room and most accept credit cards. There is no room service but some of the nicer places have large shared bathrooms and saunas on their premises. The front desk staff usually speak some English. These are often your best bet in terms of price versus performance, and there is none of the formality and confusion that you might encounter at a ryokan.

Luxury Hotels

There are several four- and five-star luxury hotels in Kyoto, including some of the top international brands (with two others – the Ritz-Carlton and the Four Seasons – rumoured to be opening properties shortly). Kyoto's luxury hotels are similar to their counterparts elsewhere in the world, but some have Japanese decorative touches and attentive Japanese service.

Youth Hostels

Kyoto's youth hostels are much like youth hostels that you'll find elsewhere in the world: not much atmosphere and a mixture of dorms and private rooms. On the plus side, Kyoto's youth hostels are accustomed to foreigners and are cleaner than many of their overseas counterparts. A room in a typical youth hostel costs about ¥3200, cash only. Membership is not necessary.

Guesthouses

Guesthouses are similar to youth hostels, without the regimented atmosphere and with various perks thrown in, like on-site restaurants, bars etc. Guesthouses usually have both dorms, which average ¥2500 per person, and a variety of private rooms, which average ¥3500 per person.

Capsule Hotels

Unlike most capsule hotels, which serve as refuges for sozzled salarymen who've missed the last train home, Kyoto's capsule hotels are geared to travellers, including foreign travellers. You probably already know what a capsule hotel is: a simple hotel where you sleep in a small 'capsule' and use common bathing facilities. They're fun, but be prepared for noise.

NEED TO KNOW

Price Ranges
We've used the following price codes for an en-suite double room in high season. Ryokan often charge per person but this is noted as necessary.

¥	under ¥6000
¥¥	¥6000-15,000
¥¥¥	over ¥15,000

Reservations
Making phone reservations in English is usually possible; providing you speak clearly and simply.

Websites
➡ **International Tourism Center of Japan** (www.itcj.jp) A free reservation service representing hundreds of *minshuku* (Japanese-style B&Bs)

➡ **Lonely Planet** (hotels.lonelyplanet.com) Books accommodation.

High & Low Seasons
Kyoto's accommodation can be booked out in the late-March/early-April cherry-blossom season and the November autumn-foliage season. It can also be hard to find rooms during Golden Week (29 April to 5 May) and O-bon (mid-August).

Tipping
Tipping is not usually done in Japan.

Checking In & Out
Check-in is usually from 2pm or 3pm (sometimes later at ryokan) and is fairly rigid. However, almost all places will store your luggage for you. Check-out is generally 10am or 11am.

Lonely Planet's Favourites

Hyatt Regency Kyoto (p145)
Tawaraya (p143)
Hiiragiya (p143)
Capsule Ryokan Kyoto (p142)
Westin Miyako, Kyoto (p147)

Best by Budget

¥
Tour Club (p142)
Budget Inn (p142)
Utano Youth Hostel (p148)
K's House Kyoto (p142)

¥¥
Dormy Inn Premium Kyoto Ekimae (p142)
Hotel Monterey Kyoto (p144)
Citadines Kyoto Karasuma Gojō (p145)
Kyoto Yoshimizu (p146)

¥¥¥
Yoshikawa (p144)
Kyoto Hotel Ōkura (p144)
Hoshinoya Kyoto (p147)

Best Ryokan

Yoshikawa (p144)
Seikōrō (p146)
Ryokan Ugenta (p148)
Gion Hatanaka (p146)
Shiraume (p146)

Best Hotels

Kyoto Hotel Ōkura (p144)
Hotel Granvia Kyoto (p142)
Citadines Kyoto Karasuma Gojō (p145)
Palace Side Hotel (p145)

Best for Sightseeing

Ryokan Uemura (p146)
Ryokan Motonago (p146)
Gion Hatanaka (p146)
Three Sisters Inn Annex (p147)

Best for Families

Budget Inn (p142)
Sakara Kyoto (p146)
Koto Inn (p147)

Best for Couples

Yoshikawa (p144)
Hoshinoya Kyoto (p147)
Mitsui Garden Hotel Kyoto Sanjō (p144)
Gion Hatanaka (p146)

Best for Backpackers

Tour Club (p142)
Budget Inn (p142)
Ryokan Shimizu (p142)
K's House Kyoto (p142)
Tōyoko Inn Kyoto Gojō Karasuma (p145)
Gojō Guesthouse (p145)

Best Value for Money

Kyoto Hotel Ōkura (p144)
Tōyoko Inn Kyoto Gojō Karasuma (p145)
Palace Side Hotel (p145)
Ryokan Uemura (p146)
Tōyoko Inn Kyoto Gojō Karasuma (p145)

Where to Stay

Neighbourhood	For	Against
Kyoto Station Area	Close to transport; plenty of dining and shopping options; good location if you intend to explore the rest of Kansai	Far from most sightseeing districts; not particularly attractive
Downtown Kyoto	In the heart of everything – shops, restaurants and nightlife; some nice strolls in the area (eg Pontochō)	Can feel a little busy; fairly high ambient noise on street level; crowded pavements and the odd rowdy (but harmless) reveller on the street on weekend evenings
Central Kyoto	Most parts of Central Kyoto are relatively quiet	Depending on location, can be far from sights and rather inconvenient
Southern Higashiyama	In the heart of the city's main sightseeing district; beautiful walks in every direction, including fantastic evening strolls (eg Gion/Shimbashi, Ninen-zaka)	Fewer dining options than downtown; crowded in the cherry-blossom season
Nothern Higashiyama	Lots of sights nearby; peaceful and green; nice day and evening strolls	Few negatives, unless you demand to be right in the heart of the shopping and dining district
Northwest Kyoto	Peaceful and green with some interesting sights	Inconvenient and not well served by trains or subways; few dining or shopping options
Arashiyama & Sagano	One of the main sightseeing districts; magical evening strolls along the river and among the bamboo grove	On the far west side of town, so all sights except those nearby require a long trek; few good dining or shopping options

Kyoto Station Area

TOP CHOICE HOTEL GRANVIA KYOTO HOTEL ¥¥¥

Map p220 (ホテルグランヴィア京都; ☎344-8888; www.granvia-kyoto.co.jp/e/index.html; Shiokōji sagaru, Karasuma-dōri, Shimogyō-ku; d/tw from ¥25,410/28,875; ; Kyoto Station, Karasuma central gate) Imagine being able to step out of bed and straight into the *shinkansen* (bullet train). This is almost possible when you stay at the Hotel Granvia, a fine hotel located directly above Kyoto Station. The rooms are clean, spacious and elegant, with deep bathtubs. This is a very professional operation with some good on-site restaurants, some of which have views over the city.

TOP CHOICE DORMY INN PREMIUM KYOTO EKIMAE BUSINESS HOTEL ¥¥

Map p220 (ドーミーインPREMIUM京都駅前; ☎371-5489; www.hotespa.net/hotels/kyoto, in Japanese; Shimogyō-ku, Higashishiokōji-chō 558-8; tw/d from ¥13,000/11,000; @; 3min walk from Kyoto Station) Located almost directly across the street from Kyoto Station, this clean, efficient new hotel is a great choice. Rooms are clean and well maintained and the on-site spa bath is a nice plus.

TOP CHOICE CAPSULE RYOKAN KYOTO CAPSULE HOTEL ¥

Map p220 (カプセル旅館京都; ☎344-1510; www.capsule-ryokan-kyoto.com; 204 Tsuchihashicho, Shimogyo-ku; capsule bed ¥3500, single ¥4980-6980, tw ¥7980; @; 7min walk from Kyoto Station, Karasuma central gate) This unique new accommodation offers ryokan-style capsules (meaning tatami mats inside the capsules), as well as comfortable, cleverly designed private rooms. Each capsule also has its own TV and cable internet access point, while the private rooms have en-suite bathrooms and all the amenities you might need. Free internet, wi-fi and other amenities are available in the comfortable lounge. It's near the southeast corner of the Horikawa–Shichijo intersection.

BUDGET INN GUESTHOUSE ¥

Map p220 (バジェットイン; ☎344-1510; www.budgetinnjp.com; 295 Aburanokōji-chō, Shichijō sagaru, Shimogyō-ku; tr/q/5-bed r per person ¥3660/3245/2960; @; 7min walk from Kyoto Station, Karasuma central gate) This well-run guesthouse is an excellent choice in this price bracket. It has eight Japanese-style private rooms, all of which are clean and well maintained. All rooms have their own bathroom and toilet, and can accommodate up to five people, making it good for families. The staff here is very helpful and friendly, and internet access, laundry and wi-fi are available. From Kyoto Station, walk west on Shiokōji-dōri and turn north one street before Horikawa and look for the English-language sign out front.

TOP CHOICE TOUR CLUB GUESTHOUSE ¥

Map p220 (旅倶楽部; ☎353-6968; www.kyotojp.com; 362 Momiji-chō, Higashinakasuji, Shōmen-sagaru, Shimogyō-ku; dm ¥2450, d per person ¥3490, tw ¥3490-3885, tr ¥2960-3240; @; 10min walk from Kyoto Station, Karasuma central gate) One of the first international-style guesthouses in Japan, Tour Club was recently refurbished. This clean, well-maintained guesthouse remains a favourite of foreign visitors to Kyoto. Facilities include internet access, a small Zen garden, laundry, wi-fi, and free tea and coffee. Most private rooms have a private bathroom and toilet, and there is a spacious quad room for families. This is probably the best choice in this price bracket. From Kyoto Station turn north off Shichijō-dōri two blocks before Horikawa (at the faux-Greco building) and keep an eye out for the English sign.

RYOKAN SHIMIZU RYOKAN ¥

Map p220 (旅館しみず; ☎371-5538; www.kyoto-shimizu.net; 644 Kagiya-chō, Shichijō-dōri, Wakamiya agaru, Shimogyō-ku; r per person from ¥5250; @; Kyoto Station, Karasuma central gate) A short walk north of Kyoto Station's Karasuma central gate, this friendly ryokan has a loyal following of foreign guests, and for good reason: it's clean, well run and fun. Rooms are standard ryokan style with one difference: all have attached bathrooms and toilets. Bicycle rental is available.

K'S HOUSE KYOTO GUESTHOUSE ¥

Map p220 (ケイズハウス京都; ☎342-2444; http://kshouse.jp/kyoto-e/index.html; 418 Nayachō, Shichijō agaru, Dotemachi-dōri, Shimogyō-ku; dm from ¥2300, s/d/tw per person from ¥3500/2900/2900; @; Kyoto Station, Karasuma central gate, or Shichijō Station, Keihan line) K's House is a large 'New Zealand–style' guesthouse with both private and dorm rooms. The rooms are simple but adequate and there are spacious common areas. The roof-top terrace, patio and attached bar-restaurant make this a very sociable spot and a good place to meet other travellers and share information.

MATSUBAYA RYOKAN RYOKAN ¥

Map p220 (松葉家; ☎351-3727; www.matsubayainn.com; Nishi-iru Higashinotōin, Kamijuzuyamachi-dōri, Shimogyō-ku; r per person from ¥4200; @; Kyoto Station, Karasuma central gate) A short walk from Kyoto Station, this newly renovated ryokan has clean, well-kept rooms and a management that is used to foreign guests. Some rooms on the 1st floor look out on small gardens. Matsubaya also has several serviced apartments in its adjoining Bamboo House section – these would be great for anyone planning a longer stay in the city. Western (¥500 to ¥800) or Japanese breakfast (¥1000) is available.

APA HOTEL KYOTO EKIMAE BUSINESS HOTEL ¥¥

Map p220 (アパ　ホテル; ☎365-4111; www.apahotel.com/hotel/kansai/01_kyoto-ekimae/english/index.html; Shiokōji sagaru, Nishinotōin-dōri, Shimogyō-ku; s/tw per person from ¥9500/9000; @; 5min walk from Kyoto Station, Karasuma central gate) This excellent business hotel is a good midpriced choice. Rooms are on the large size, with firm, clean beds and unit baths. The staff are professional and seem at ease dealing with foreign guests.

Downtown Kyoto

TOP CHOICE TAWARAYA RYOKAN ¥¥¥

Map p216 (俵屋旅館; ☎211-5566; fax 221-2204; Fuyachō-Oike sagaru, Nakagyō-ku; r per person with 2 meals ¥42,263-84,525; @; M Karasuma-Oike Station, exit 3, Tōzai or Karasuma subway lines) Tawaraya has been operating for more than three centuries and is one of the finest places to stay in the world. From the decorations to the service to the food, every thing at the Tawaraya is simply the best available. It's a very intimate, warm and personal place that has many loyal guests. It's centrally located within easy walk of two subway stations and plenty of good restaurants.

TOP CHOICE HIIRAGIYA RYOKAN ¥¥¥

Map p216 (柊家旅館; ☎221-1136; fax 221-139; www.hiiragiya.co.jp/en; Anekōji-agaru, Fuya-chō, Nakagyō-ku; r per person incl 2 meals ¥36,750-81,900; @; M Karasuma-Oike Station, exit 3, Tōzai or Karasuma subway lines) This elegant ryokan has long been favoured by celebrities from round the world. Facilities and services are excellent and the location is hard to beat. Ask for one of the newly re-done rooms if you prefer a polished sheen; alternatively, request an older room if you fancy some 'Old Japan' *wabi-sabi* (imperfect beauty).

STAYING IN A RYOKAN

Due to language difficulties and unfamiliarity, staying in a ryokan is not as straightforward as staying in a Western-style hotel. However, it's not exactly rocket science, and with a little education it can be a breeze, even if you don't speak a word of Japanese. Here's the basic drill.

When you arrive, leave your shoes in the *genkan* (entry area/foyer) and step up into the reception area. Here, you'll be asked to sign in. You'll then be shown around the place and then to your room where you will be served a cup of tea. You'll note that there is no bedding to be seen in your room – your futons are in the closets and will be laid out later. You can leave your luggage anywhere except the *tokonoma* (sacred alcove) that will usually contain some flowers or a hanging scroll. If it's early enough, you can then go out to do some sightseeing.

When you return, you'll change into your *yukata* (lightweight Japanese robe) and be served dinner in your room or in a dining room. After dinner, it's time for a bath. If it's a big place, you can generally bathe anytime in the evening until around 11pm. If it's a small place, you'll be given a time slot. While you're in the bath, some mysterious elves will go into your room and lay out your futon so that it will be waiting for you when you return all toasty from the bath.

In the morning, you'll be served a Japanese-style breakfast (some places these days serve a simple Western-style breakfast for those who can't stomach rice and fish in the morning). You pay at check-out, which is usually around 11am.

KYOTO HOTEL ŌKURA HOTEL ¥¥¥

Map p216 (京都ホテルオークラ; ☎211-5111; http://okura.kyotohotel.co.jp/english; Kawaramachi-dōri, Oike, Nakagyō-ku; s from ¥21,945, d & tw from ¥31,185; ⊖@; ⓂKyoto Shiyakusho-mae Station, exit 3, Tōzai subway line) This towering hotel in the centre of town commands an impressive view of the Higashiyama Mountains. Rooms here are clean and spacious and many have great views, especially the excellent corner suites – we just wish we could open a window to enjoy the breeze. You can access the Kyoto subway system directly from the hotel, which is convenient on rainy days or if you have luggage. You can often find great online rates for the Ōkura and it's one of the better value places in this price bracket.

HOTEL UNIZO BUSINESS HOTEL ¥¥

Map p216 (ホテルユニゾ; ☎241-3351; www.hotelunizo.com/eng/kyoto/index.html; Kawaramachi-dōri-Sanjō sagaru, Nakagyō-ku; s/d/tw from ¥8505/13,650/12,810; ⊖; 🚍Kawaramachi-Sanjō stop, bus 5) They don't get more convenient than this business hotel: it's smack in the middle of Kyoto's nightlife, shopping and dining district – you can walk to hundreds of restaurants and shops within five minutes. It's a standard-issue business hotel, with tiny but adequate rooms and unit bathrooms. Nothing special here, but it's clean, well run and used to foreign guests. Front rooms can be noisy, so see if you can get something on an upper floor or at the back.

YOSHIKAWA RYOKAN ¥¥¥

Map p216 (吉川; ☎221-5544; fax 221-6805; www.kyoto-yoshikawa.co.jp; Tominokōji, Oike-sagaru, Nakagyō-ku; r per person with 2 meals from ¥35,000; @; ⓂKarasuma-Oike Station or Kyoto Shiyakusho-mae Station, Tōzai & Karasuma subway lines) Located in the heart of downtown, within easy walking distance of two subway stations and the entire dining and nightlife district, this superb traditional ryokan has beautiful rooms and a stunning garden. The ryokan is famous for its tempura and its meals are of a high standard. All rooms have en suite bathrooms and toilets.

HOTEL MONTEREY KYOTO BUSINESS HOTEL ¥¥

Map p216 (ホテルモントレ京都; ☎251-7111; www.hotelmonterey.co.jp/en/htl/kyoto/index.html; Nakagyō-ku, Karasuma-dōri, Sanjō sagaru, Manjūya-chō 604; s/tw from ¥15,000/28,000; @; Ⓜ3min walk from exit 6, Karasuma-Oike Station, Karasuma & Tōzai subway lines) Within a few minutes' walk of the Karasuma-Oike subway station (only three stops north of Kyoto Station), this relatively new upmarket business hotel is a great place to stay if you want to be downtown: it's on the western edge of the main shopping and dining district. Some guests have complained about dirty carpets, but most are very happy with the rooms here.

MITSUI GARDEN HOTEL KYOTO SANJŌ HOTEL ¥¥

Map p216 (三井ガーデンホテル京都三条; ☎256-3331; www.gardenhotels.co.jp/eng/sanjo; 80 Mikura-chō, Nishiiru, Karasuma, Sanjō St, Nakagyō-ku; s/d/tw from ¥10,500/17,600/18,800; @; Ⓜ2min walk from exit 6, Karasuma-Oike Station, Tōzai or Karasuma subway lines) Just west of the downtown dining and shopping district, this is a clean and efficient hotel that offers good value for the price and reasonably comfortable rooms.

SUPER HOTEL KYOTO SHIJŌ-KAWARAMACHI BUSINESS HOTEL ¥¥

Map p216 (スーパーホテル京都・四条河原町; ☎255-9000; www.superhoteljapan.com/en; Nakagyō-ku, Shinkyōgoku-dōri, Shijō agaru, Nakanomachi 538-1; s/tw from ¥6480/8480; @; 🚉3min walk from Kawaramachi Station, Hankyū line, 10min walk from Shijō Station, Karasuma subway line) Right in the middle of the main shopping district, a short walk from the Shinkyōgoku shopping arcade and Nishiki Market, this new business hotel is great for those who want a basic place to sleep and a convenient location. The free breakfast and large communal bathroom (rooms also have en suite bathrooms) are nice touches.

BEST WESTERN HOTEL KYOTO BUSINESS HOTEL ¥¥

Map p216 (ベストウェスタンホテル京都; ☎254-4055; www.bwjapan.co.jp/kyoto/en/index.html; Nakagyō-ku, Kawaramachi-Rokkaku, Matsugae-chō 457; s/tw from ¥14,000/28,000; @; 🚉3min walk from Keihan Sanjō Station, Keihan line or Kyoto Shiyakushomae Station, Tōzai subway line) Plunked down right in the middle of Downtown Kyoto's main shopping district, the Best Western claims one of the most convenient locations in Kyoto. It's brand new and off to a good start. Rooms are small but spotless, with everything you might need, including helpful staff.

Central Kyoto

RYOKAN RAKUCHŌ RYOKAN ¥

(旅館洛頂; ☎721-2174; fax 791-7202; 67 Higashi-hangi chō, Shimogamo, Sakyō-ku; s/tw/tr ¥5300/9240/12,600; ⊖@ᯤ; Ⓜ Karasuma subway line to Kitaōji Station; 🚌 Furitsudaigaku-mae stop, bus 205) There is a lot to appreciate about this fine little foreigner-friendly ryokan in the northern part of town: there is a nice little garden; it's entirely nonsmoking; and the rooms are clean and simple. Meals aren't served, but staff can provide you with a good map of local eateries. The downside is the somewhat out-of-the-way location.

PALACE SIDE HOTEL HOTEL ¥¥

Map p219 (パレスサイドホテル; ☎415-8887; www.palacesidehotel.co.jp/english/fr-top-en.html; Kamigyō-ku, Karasuma-dōri, Shimotachiuri agaru; s/tw/d from ¥6000/9000/9800; ⊖@; Ⓜ 3min walk from Marutamachi Station, Karasuma subway line) Overlooking the Kyoto Imperial Palace Park, this excellent-value hotel has a lot going for it, starting with a friendly English-speaking staff, great service, washing machines, an on-site restaurant, well-maintained rooms and free internet terminals. The rooms are small but serviceable.

TŌYOKO INN KYOTO GOJŌ KARASUMA BUSINESS HOTEL ¥¥

(東横INN京都五条烏丸; ☎344-1045; www.toyoko-inn.com/hotel/00040; Shimogyō-ku, Karasuma-dōri, Matsubara sagaru, Gojō Karasuma-chō 393; s/tw from ¥6480/9480; @; Ⓜ 3min walk from Gojō Station exit 2, Karasuma subway line, 5min walk from Shijō Station exit 6, Karasuma subway line) Those familiar with the Tōyoko Inn chain know that this hotel brand specialises in simple, clean, fully equipped but small rooms at the lowest price possible. There are all kinds of interesting extras: free breakfast, free telephone calls inside Japan, and reduced rates on rental cars. They'll even lend you a laptop if you need to do some emailing. It's a little south of the city centre, but easily accessed by subway from Kyoto Station.

KYŌMACHIYA RYOKAN SAKURA BUSINESS HOTEL ¥¥

(京町家旅館さくら; ☎343-3500; www.kyoto-ryokan-sakura.com/index_en.html; Shimogyō-ku, Aburanokōji Hanaya-chō sagaru, Butsuguya-chō 228; s/tw from ¥7000/12,000; @; Ⓜ 10min walk from Kyoto Station) This new ryokan, a relatively short walk from Kyoto Station, has clean, efficient rooms as well as a variety of traveller-friendly extras. They're at home with foreign travellers and English is spoken. It's a bit over to the west side of town, but a bicycle or public transport will get you to the sightseeing spots fairly quickly. The local area retains a lot of charming old Kyoto buildings. For longer stays, ask about the serviced apartment next door.

CITADINES KYOTO KARASUMA GOJŌ BUSINESS HOTEL ¥¥¥

(シタディーン京都 烏丸五条; ☎352-8900; www.citadines.jp/kyoto/index.html; Shimogyō-ku, Gojō-dōri, Karasuma Higashi iru, Matsuya-chō 432; tw & d from ¥23,100; @; Ⓜ 1min walk from Gojō Station, Karasuma subway line) On Gojō-dōri, a bit south of the main downtown district, but within easy walking distance of the Karasuma subway line (as well as the Keihan line), this serviced apartment–hotel is a welcome addition to the Kyoto accommodation scene. The kitchens allow you to do your own cooking and other touches make you feel right at home.

GOJŌ GUESTHOUSE GUESTHOUSE ¥

Map p219 (五条ゲストハウス; ☎525-2299; stay@gojo-guest-house.com; Higashiyama-ku, Gojōbashi higashi 3-396-2; dm ¥2500, s/tw ¥3500/6000; @; 🚆 5min walk from Kiyomizu Gojō Station exit 4, Keihan line) This is a fine guesthouse in an old wooden Japanese house, which makes the place feel more like a ryokan than your average guesthouse. It's a relaxed and friendly place at home with foreign guests. The staff here speak good English and can help with travel advice. Best of all: they have *gaijin* (foreigner) sized futons!

Southern Higashiyama

TOP CHOICE **HYATT REGENCY KYOTO** HOTEL ¥¥¥

Map p222 (ハイアットリージェンシー 京都; ☎541-1234; www.kyoto.regency.hyatt.com; 644-2 Sanjūsangendō-mawari, Higashiyama-ku; r ¥19,000-46,000; ⊖@ᯤ; 🚆 5min walk from Shichijō Station, Keihan line) The Hyatt Regency is an excellent, stylish and foreigner-friendly hotel at the southern end of Kyoto's Southern Higashiyama sightseeing district. Many travellers consider this the best hotel in Kyoto. The staff here are extremely efficient and helpful (there are even foreign staff members – something of a rarity in Japan). The on-site restaurants and bar are excellent. The stylish rooms and bathrooms have lots of neat touches. The concierges are knowledgeable about the city and they'll even lend you a laptop to check your email if you don't have your own.

SEIKŌRŌ RYOKAN ¥¥¥

Map p222 (晴鴨楼; ☎561-0771; http://ryokan.asia/seikoro; 467 Nishi Tachibana-chō, 3 chō-me, Gojō sagaru, Tonyamachi-dōri, Higashiyama-ku; r per person with 2 meals from ¥24,150; ⊜@🛜; 🚌Kawaramachi-Gojō stop, bus 17 or 205) The Seikōrō is a classic ryokan with a grandly decorated lobby. It's fairly spacious, with excellent, comfortable rooms, attentive service and a fairly convenient midtown location. Several rooms look over gardens and all have private bathrooms.

RYOKAN MOTONAGO RYOKAN ¥¥¥

Map p222 (旅館元奈古; ☎561-2087; www.motonago.com; 511 Washio-chō, Kōdaiji-michi, Higashiyama-ku; r per person with 2 meals from ¥17,850; ⊜@; 🚌Gion stop, bus 206) This ryokan may have the best location of any in the city, and it hits all the right notes for one in this class: classic Japanese decor, friendly service, nice bathtubs and a few small Japanese gardens.

RYOKAN UEMURA RYOKAN ¥¥

Map p222 (旅館うえむら; ☎/fax 561-0377; Ishibe-kōji, Shimogawara, Higashiyama-ku; r with breakfast per person ¥9000;⊜; 🚌Higashiyama-Yasui stop, bus 206) This beautiful little ryokan is at ease with foreign guests. It's on a quaint, quiet cobblestone alley, just down the hill from some of Kyoto's most important sights. Book well in advance, as there are only three rooms. Note that the manager prefers bookings by fax and asks that cancellations also be made by fax – with so few rooms, it can be costly when bookings are broken without notice. There's a 10pm curfew.

SAKARA KYOTO INN ¥¥

Map p222 (桜香楽; http://sakarakyoto.com/Home.html; 541-2 Furukawa-cho Higashiyama-ku; r ¥10,000-25,000; @🛜; Ⓜ Higashiyama Station, Tōzai subway line) This modern Japanese-style inn is conveniently located in a covered pedestrian shopping arcade just south of Sanjō-dōri, about 50m from Higashiyama Subway Station. It's great for couples and families and rooms can accommodate up to five people. Each room has bath/shower, kitchenette and laundry facilities. Reservation is by email only.

GION HATANAKA RYOKAN ¥¥¥

Map p222 (祇園畑中; ☎541-5315; www.thehatanaka.co.jp/english/index.html; Yasaka-jinja Minami-mon mae, Higashiyama-ku; r per person with 2 meals from ¥30,000; ⊜🛜; 🚉Keihan Shijō Station or Kawaramachi Station, Hankyū line) Climb a flight of beautiful, stone stairs to reach the entrance to Gion Hatanaka, a fine ryokan right in the heart of the Southern Higashiyama sightseeing district (less than a minute's walk from Yasaka-jinja). Despite being fairly large, this ryokan manages to retain an intimate and private feeling. In addition to bathtubs in each room, there is a huge wooden communal bath. The rooms are clean, well designed and relaxing. This ryokan offers regularly scheduled geisha entertainment that nonguests are welcome to join; for more details see p90.

SHIRAUME RYOKAN ¥¥¥

Map p222 (白梅; ☎561-1459; Higashiyama-ku, Gion Shimbashi, Shirakawa hotori, Shijōnawate agaru, Higashi iru; r per person with 2 meals ¥22,000-35,000; @; 🚉3min walk from Gion Shijō Station, Keihan line, 5min walk from Sanjō Keihan Station, Keihan line & Tōzai subway line) Looking out over the Shirakawa Canal in Shimbashi, a lovely street in Gion, this ryokan offers excellent location, atmosphere and service. The decor is traditional with a small inner garden and nice wooden bathtubs. This is a great spot to sample the Japanese ryokan experience.

KYOTO YOSHIMIZU RYOKAN ¥¥

Map p222 (京都吉水; ☎551-3995; kyoto@yoshimizu.com; Higashiyama-ku, Maruyama kōen, Bentendō ue; from ¥7800 per person incl breakfast only; 🚌10min walk from Gion bus stop, 20min by taxi from Kyoto Station; @) This ryokan, perched at the base of the Higashiyama mountains at the top of Maruyama-kōen is truly special. It's surrounded by greenery and it's like staying in the countryside (but only 15 minutes' walk to Gion). There is one room with Western-style beds for those uncomfortable sleeping on futons. A few rooms look out over soothing maple leaves or bamboo groves. The only drawback here is that some rooms are only divided by thin walls or doors, so you can hear your neighbours talk if they are not considerate.

Northern Higashiyama

TOP CHOICE WESTIN MIYAKO, KYOTO HOTEL ¥¥¥

Map p224 (ウエスティン都ホテル; ☎771-7111; www.westinmiyako-kyoto.com; Keage, Sanjō-dōri, Higashiyama-ku; d & tw from ¥33,500, Japanese-style r from ¥41,500; ; MKeage Station, exit 2, Tōzai subway line) This grande dame of Kyoto hotels occupies a commanding position overlooking the Higashiyama sightseeing district (meaning it's one of the best locations for sightseeing in Kyoto). Rooms are clean and well maintained, and staff are at home with foreign guests. Rooms on the north side have great views over the city to the Kitayama mountains. There is a fitness centre, as well as a private garden and walking trail. The hotel even has its own ryokan section for those who want to try staying in a ryokan without giving up the convenience of a hotel.

KYOTO GARDEN RYOKAN YACHIYO RYOKAN ¥¥¥

Map p224 (八千代旅館; ☎771-4148; www.ryokan-yachiyo.com/top/englishtop.html; 34 Fukuchi-chō, Nanzen-ji, Sakyō-ku; r per person with 2 meals ¥15,000-60,000; ; MKeage Station, exit 2, Tōzai subway line) Located just down the street from Nanzen-ji (p94), this large ryokan is at home with foreign guests. Rooms are spacious and clean, and some look out over private gardens. English-speaking staff are available.

THREE SISTERS INN MAIN BUILDING RYOKAN ¥¥

Map p224 (スリーシスターズイン洛東荘本館; ☎761-6336; fax 761-6338; 18 Higashifukunokawa-chō, Okazaki, Sakyō-ku; s/d/tr from ¥9345/13,650/20,475; ; Dōbutsuen-mae stop, bus 5) Perfectly situated for exploration of eastern Kyoto, this long-time favourite of foreign travellers is a good choice for those who want to try a ryokan without any language difficulties. It's very close to the interesting Yoshida-Yama area and not far from Heian-jingū (p99).

THREE SISTERS INN ANNEX RYOKAN ¥¥

Map p224 (スリーシスターズイン洛東荘別館; ☎761-6333; fax 761-6338; 89 Irie-chō, Okazaki, Sakyō-ku; s/d/tr ¥10,810/18,170/23,805; ; Okazakimichi stop, bus 100, Dōbutsuen-mae stop, bus 5) An annexe of the Three Sisters Inn, this ryokan is well run, comfortable and used to foreigners. It has a pleasant breakfast nook that overlooks a wonderful Japanese garden. The bamboo-lined walkway is another highlight. It's right behind Heian-jingū (p99) and relatively close to the sights of Northern Higashiyama.

KOTO INN GUESTHOUSE ¥¥

Map p224 (古都イン; ☎751-2753; koto.inn@gmail.com; 373 Hori-ike-chō, Higashiyama-ku; d from ¥15,000; ; M2min walk from Higashiyama Station, Tōzai subway line) Conveniently located near the Higashiyama sightseeing district, this vacation rental is good for families, couples and groups who want a bit of privacy. It's got everything you need and is decorated with lovely Japanese antiques. While the building is traditionally Japanese, all the facilities are fully modernised.

Arashiyama & Sagano

HOTEL RAN-TEI HOTEL ¥¥¥

Map p227 (ホテル嵐亭; ☎371-1119; hotelrantei@kyoto-centuryhotel.co.jp; Ukyō-ku, Saga Tenryū-ji, Susukinobaba-chō 12; r per person ¥16,000-34,000; ; 10min walk from Keifuku Arashiyama Station, Keifuku Arashiyama line) The excellent Ran-tei has spacious gardens and both Japanese- and Western-style accommodation. The rooms are spacious and quiet here and there is a great view from the bathroom. The Japanese-style breakfast may not suit all palates but it is filling.

ARASHIYAMA BENKEI RYOKAN ¥¥¥

Map p227 (嵐山辨慶旅館; ☎872-3355; www.benkei.biz/~english; Ukyō-ku, Saga Tenryū-ji, Susukinobaba-chō 34; r per person incl meals from ¥21,000; 6min walk from Keifuku Arashiyama Station, Keifuku Arashiyama line) This elegant ryokan has a pleasant riverside location and serves wonderful *kaiseki* (Japanese haute cuisine). The service is kind and friendly and the river view from the spacious rooms is great.

HOSHINOYA KYOTO RYOKAN ¥¥¥

Map p227 (星のや; ☎871-0001; http://kyoto.hoshinoya.com/en; Nishikyō-ku, Arashiyama Genrokuzan-chō 11-2; r per person incl meals from ¥44,920; 7min walk from Keifuku Arashiyama Station, Keifuku Arashiyama line) Sitting in a secluded area on the south bank of the Hozu-gawa in Arashiyama (upstream from the main sightseeing district), this modern take on the classic Japanese inn is quickly becoming a favourite of well-heeled visitors

AIRPORT HOTELS

If you find yourself in need of a bed close to your flight from Itami or Kansai airports, there are a couple of decent options.

Green Rich Hotel Osaka Airport (グリーンリッチホテル 大阪空港前 ☎06-6842-1100; www.gr-osaka.com; Osaka-fu, Ikeda-shi, Kūkō 1-9-6; s/d from ¥7900/11,000; @) Right across from the airport and within walking distance (10 minutes from the south terminal if you had to), this friendly little hotel is the best deal near Itami. Rooms are small but sufficient for a night before an early departure. The helpful folks at the information counter can also arrange for the hotel's shuttle bus to come and pick you up.

Hotel Nikkō Kansai Airport (ホテル日航関西空港; ☎072-455-1111; www.nikkokix.com/e/top.html; 1 Senshū Kūkō kita, Izumisano-shi; s ¥21,945, d & tw ¥32,340; @; Kansai Kūkō, JR Kansai Kūkō line) The only hotel at the airport is the excellent Hotel Nikkō Kansai Airport, connected to the main terminal building by a pedestrian bridge (you can even bring your luggage trolleys right to your room). The rooms here are in good condition, spacious and comfortable enough for brief stays. Online booking through hotel booking sites can result in much lower rates.

to Kyoto in search of privacy and a unique experience. Rooms feature incredible views of the river and the surrounding mountains. The best part is the approach: you'll be chauffeured by a private boat from a dock near Togetsu-kyō bridge to the inn (note that on days following heavy rains, you'll have to go by car instead). This is easily one of the most unique places to stay in Kyoto.

Northwest Kyoto

UTANO YOUTH HOSTEL YOUTH HOSTEL ¥

Map p228 (宇多野ユースホステル; ☎462-2288; http://yh-kyoto.or.jp/utano/index.html; Ukyō-ku, Uzumasa, Nakayama-chō 29; dm/tw per person ¥3300/4000; 1min walk from Yūsu-Hosuteru-mae bus stop, bus 26 from Kyoto Station) The best hostel in Kyoto, Utano is friendly and well organised and makes a convenient base for the sights of Northwest Kyoto (but keep in mind that it's a hike to reach any other part of town). If you want to skip the hostel food, turn left along the main road to find several coffee shops offering cheap *teishoku* (set-course meals). There is a 10pm curfew.

SHUNKŌIN TEMPLE LODGE ¥

Map p228 (春光院; ☎462-5488; rev.taka.kawakami@gmail.com; Ukyō-ku, Hanazono, Myōshinji-chō 42; per person ¥4000-5000; @; 5min walk from JR Hanazono Station) This is a *shukubō*, or temple lodging, at a subtemple in Myōshin-ji (p110). It's very comfortable and quiet and the main priest here speaks fluent English. For an extra ¥1000 you can try Zen meditation and go on a guided tour of the temple. Being in the temple at night is a very special experience.

Kitayama Area & Greater Kyoto

RYOKAN UGENTA RYOKAN ¥¥¥

Map p231 (旅館右源太; ☎741-2146; www.ugenta.co.jp; Sakyō-ku, Kurama, Kibune-chō 76; r per person incl meals from ¥45,150; @; Kibune-guchi Station, Eizan line) The Ugenta is a superb and stylish inn located in the village of Kibune, about 30 minutes north of Kyoto by taxi or train. There are only two rooms here, one Japanese-style and one Western-style. Both have private cypress-wood outdoor bathtubs. This would be the perfect place for a secluded getaway or honeymoon. We've heard reports that the *nakai-sans* (private maids who bring in your food) can be a little brusque and quick, but we assume that this will improve with time. The Ugenta offers a free shuttle bus to and from the station.

Understand Kyoto

Kyoto Today

For much of its history, Kyoto has been a microcosm of Japan: when Japan prospered, Kyoto prospered; when Japan struggled, Kyoto struggled. Now, as Japan works furiously to recover from the Great East Japan Earthquake of March 2011, the tourist city of Kyoto is reeling from a devastating drop in the number of both international and domestic visitors. And the disaster brought many long-simmering questions to the foreground. Most importantly, just what kind of city does Kyoto want to become?

Classic Kyoto Films

Rashomon (1950) Kurosawa Akira's classic uses the southern gate of Kyoto as the setting for a 12th-century rape and murder story told from several perspectives.

Sisters of Nishijin (1952) The father of a silk-weaving family kills himself as the family is caught between the old and the new.

Lost in Translation (2003) Most of this film takes place in Tokyo, but there's a lovely montage of shots of the heroine's trip to Kyoto.

Kyoto Novels

The Old Capital (Kawabata Yasunari; 1962) A young woman's past is disturbed by the discovery of a twin sister in another family.

The Temple of the Golden Pavilion (Mishima Yukio; 1956) A fictionalised account of a young Buddhist acolyte who burned down Kyoto's famous Golden Pavilion in 1950.

Memoirs of a Geisha (Arthur Golden; 1997) This account of the life of a Kyoto geisha was later turned into a successful movie (most of which was not filmed in Kyoto).

The Lady and the Monk (Pico Iyer; 1991) An account of the author's relationship with a Japanese woman against the backdrop of Kyoto.

Kyoto Suffers with Japan

In March 2011 northern Japan was struck by an earthquake and tsunami of almost apocalyptic proportions. The epicentre of the quake was over 600km northeast of the city and the city suffered no physical damage. Likewise, Kyoto was not affected by radiation fallout from the nuclear plants at Fukushima, which are located over 500km northeast of the city.

Despite the lack of immediate physical damage, Kyoto was economically devastated by the disaster. The quake could not have struck at a worse time: Kyoto was just gearing up for the annual rush of tourists who descend on the city to enjoy its famous cherry blossoms. Travellers, both domestic and foreign, cancelled their visits en masse. Residents of Kyoto were treated to the bizarre spectacle of famous cherry blossom spots almost totally free of tourists at the height of the cherry blossom season (ironically, spring 2011 was one of the best seasons for blossoms in recent years).

Early figures for 2011 showed tourism receipts down about 50% in Kyoto. For a city that depends very heavily on tourism, this is truly a frightening number. Despite slashing prices, the city's hotels and ryokans were barely able to attract customers. Many of those who did come were wealthy Tokyoites fleeing perceived radiation dangers in the capital.

As spring turned to summer in 2011, Kyoto residents were cheered to see tourists starting to trickle back. They did their best to attract even more visitors, stressing that the city is a long way from the affected areas and radiation levels in Kyoto never exceeded normal annual averages (indeed, the wind usually blows west to east here).

By any rational measure, the city of Kyoto, like the rest of Japan, is facing enormous challenges in the wake of the disaster. It is a sad reality that many worthy businesses will be forced to close their doors. Still,

Kyoto has weathered severe crises before. In the long run, the city may even receive more visitors than in the past, due to its distance from the areas most badly damaged by the quake. One can only hope that once travellers experience the beauty and safety of Kyoto, they will be emboldened to explore the rest of the country as well.

Preservation Versus Development

In the last few decades, Kyoto has been gripped by a fierce debate: whether to preserve its traditional cityscape or to demolish it and put up modern buildings. Many city residents and politicians would love to turn Kyoto into a contemporary city like Tokyo or Osaka. In contrast, many Japanese and foreign tourists would prefer that Kyoto remain a kind of living museum for Japan's cultural heritage.

A new wrinkle has been added to the debate since the global financial crisis of 2008. While Western economies were slammed by the crisis, the Chinese economy kept right on growing. City leaders, hoping to cash in, announced plans to develop the city to appeal to Chinese tourists. Most controversially, the city started construction of an aquarium in Kyoto's Umekōji-kōen in 2010. Critics pointed out that Kyoto is not a maritime city and argued that the city should build attractions that highlight the city's cultural traditions. They said that Chinese tourists flock to the city's traditional attractions and can easily find a larger aquarium in nearby Osaka. Still, construction on the aquarium continues.

Moving in the Right Direction

Fortunately, there are grassroots and political forces working to preserve the city and to develop it in creative ways that celebrate its past. The city government recently enacted a law that places height restrictions on new buildings. It has also restricted large and intrusive billboards and neon signs (something you will surely appreciate if you've seen what parts of Tokyo look like).

Better still, there are moves afoot to turn parts of the central Downtown area into pedestrian-only zones during the daytime and early evening. In addition, the city has banned outdoor smoking around Kyoto Station, in the Downtown shopping district and in much of the Southern Higashiyama sightseeing district.

Perhaps the most welcome trend in the city is the so-called '*machiya* boom,' in which traditional Kyoto townhouses are being converted into extremely atmospheric restaurants, cafes, bars and shops. If these *machiya* businesses succeed, it may stem the loss of the lovely traditional structures, a few of which are carted away each day in the back of a truck to be dumped into a landfill on the outskirts of the city.

population per sq km

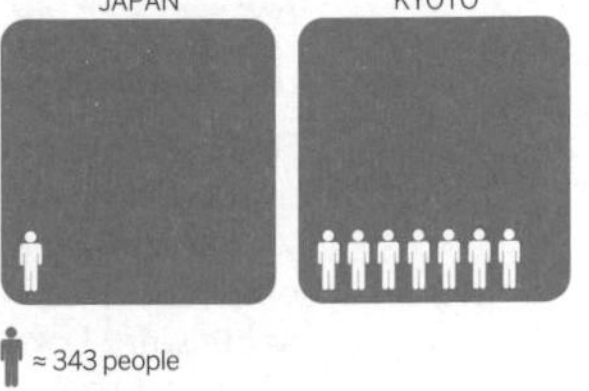

age group
(% of population)

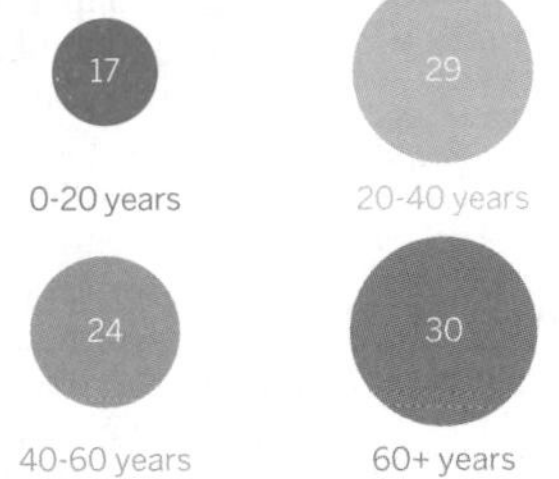

if Kyoto were 100 people

97 would be Japanese
2 would be Korean
1 would be Western or another nationality

History

From the 8th century until the late 19th century, Kyoto's history was almost synonymous with Japanese history. Kyoto was literally the stage where the great events of Japanese history unfolded. This is where emperors and shōguns vied for power. This is where the main religious sects were born and popularised. And this is where the traditional arts of Japan were polished to their present-day perfection. Indeed, it is no exaggeration to say that Kyoto itself forms a vast living textbook of Japanese history: almost everywhere you step, an event took place that shaped the nation we know as Japan.

EARLY HISTORY

Although the origins of the Japanese race remain unclear, anthropologists believe humans first arrived on the islands as early as 100,000 years ago via the land bridges that once connected Japan to Siberia and Korea, and by sea from the islands of the South Pacific. The first recorded evidence of civilisation in Japan is *jōmon* (pottery fragments with cord marks) produced around 10,000 BC. During the Jōmon period (10,000–300 BC), people lived a primitive existence as independent fishers, hunters and food gatherers.

Jōmon pottery vessels dating back some 15,000 years are the oldest known pottery vessels in the world.

This stone age period was gradually superseded by the Yayoi era, dating roughly from 300 BC to AD 300. The Yayoi people are considered to have had a strong connection with Korea. Their most important developments were the wet cultivation of rice and the use of bronze and iron implements, and they also introduced new practices such as weaving and shamanism. The Yayoi period witnessed the progressive development of communities represented in more than 100 independent family clusters dotting the archipelago.

As more and more of these settlements banded together to defend their land, regional groups became larger and by AD 300 the Yamato kingdom had emerged in the region of present-day Nara. Forces were loosely united around the imperial clan of the Yamato court, whose leaders claimed descent from the sun goddess, Amaterasu, and who introduced the title of *tennō* (emperor). The Yamato kingdom established Japan's first fixed capital in Nara, eventually unifying the regional groups into a single state. By the end of the 4th century, official relations with the Korean peninsula

TIMELINE

544

The first Aoi (Hollyhock) Matsuri is held to pray for an end to calamitous weather that had been plaguing the city of Kyoto. The festival is still held today in May.

Early 7th century

The vast, fertile plain of the Kyoto basin (then known as Yamashiro-no-kuni) is first settled by the Hata clan from Korea, along with another clan, the Kamo.

622

Kōryū-ji is established in northwest Kyoto to house a statue given to the Hata clan by Prince Shōtoku. The temple becomes the tutelary temple of the clan.

were established and Japan steadily began to introduce arts and industries such as shipbuilding, leather-tanning, weaving and metalwork.

During the Yamato period a highly aristocratic society with militaristic rulers developed. Its cavalry wore armour, carried swords and used advanced military techniques similar to those of northeast Asia. The Yamato government also sent envoys directly to the Chinese court, where they were exposed to philosophy and social structure.

BUDDHISM & CHINESE INFLUENCE

When Buddhism drifted onto the shores of Japan, Kyoto was barely more than a vast, fertile valley. First introduced from China in 538 via the Korean kingdom of Paekche, Buddhism was pivotal in the evolution of the Japanese nation. It eventually brought with it a flood of culture through literature, the arts, architecture and kanji, a system of writing in Chinese characters. However, initial uptake of Buddhism was slow until Empress Suiko (554–628) encouraged all Japanese to accept the new faith. Widespread temple construction was authorised and in 588, as recorded in the 8th-century *Nihon Shoki* (Chronicle of Japan), Japan's first great temple complex, Asuka-dera, was completed.

Gradually the wealth and power of the temples began to pose a threat to the governing Yamato court, prompting reforms from Prince Shōtoku (574–622), regent for Empress Suiko. He set up the Constitution of 17 Articles, which combined ideas from Buddhism and Confucianism to outline the acceptable behaviour of the people, and laid the guidelines for a centralised state headed by a single ruler. He also instituted Buddhism as a state religion and ordered the construction of more temples, including Nara's eminent Hōryū-ji (p131), the world's oldest surviving wooden structure. Another significant accomplishment of Prince Shōtoku was the first compilation of Japanese history in 620; however, the book was later burned.

Reforms and bureaucratisation of government led to the establishment, in 710, of a permanent imperial capital, known as Heijō-kyō, in Nara, where it remained for 74 years.

The prosperous Nara period (710–94) saw further propagation of Buddhism and, by the end of the 8th century, the Buddhist clergy had become so meddlesome that Emperor Kammu decided to sever the ties between Buddhism and government by again moving the capital. He first moved it to Nagaoka (a suburb of Kyoto) in 784, but due to the assassination of the city's principal architect, several ominous natural disasters and superstitious beliefs regarding the location, a decade later he suddenly shifted the capital to Heian-kyō, present-day Kyoto.

SHINTŌ

The Japanese religion of Shintō is one of the few religions in the world to have a female sun deity, or a female supreme deity.

784

Emperor Kammu moves the capital from Nara to Nagaoka (a suburb of Kyoto) to avoid the powerful Buddhist clergy who had previously meddled in the imperial court.

788

Saichō establishes a monastery atop Hiei-zan (Mt Hiei) to protect the city from the 'dangerous' northeast direction. Saichō starts a school of Buddhism known as Tendai (or Tenzai).

794

Things go poorly in Nagaoka and Emperor Kammu searches in the Kyoto basin for another site for his capital. Late that year, he finds a suitable spot in present-day Kyoto.

794

A pair of temples, Tō-ji and Sai-ji, are built at the southern edge of the city to protect the city and the imperial court. Tō-ji can still be visited today.

ESTABLISHMENT OF HEIAN-KYŌ

The Kyoto basin was first settled in the 7th century when the region was known as Yamashiro-no-kuni. The original inhabitants were immigrants from Korea, the Hata clan, who established Koryū-ji (p110) in 603 as their family temple in what is today the Uzumasa District. A major reason Emperor Kammu proclaimed Heian-kyō the new capital of Japan was his realisation that the city lay within a strategic natural fortress created by the rivers and mountains which surround it on three sides, fulfilling the geomantic requirements derived from proto-feng shui.

As with the previous capital in Nara, the city was laid out in accordance with Chinese geomancy in a grid pattern adopted from the Tang dynasty capital, Chang'an (present-day Xi'an). The rectangle-shaped precincts were established west of where the Kamo-gawa flows. Originally measuring 4.5km east to west and 5.3km north to south, the city was about one-third the size of its Chinese prototype. Running through the centre was Suzaku-ōji, an 85m-wide, willow-lined thoroughfare dividing the eastern (Sakyō-ku) part of the city from the west (Ukyō-ku). The northern tip of the promenade was the site of the ornate Imperial Palace and to the far south stood the 23m-high, two-storey Rajō Gate, over 35m wide and 10m deep. However, to avoid a repeat of the power struggle between the imperial court and Buddhist clergy, only two temples, the West Temple and the East Temple (Tō-ji; p74), were built within the city limits.

The Tale of Genji, written by the court-lady Murasaki Shikibu around 1004, is widely believed to be the world's first novel.

Literally, capital of peace *(hei)* and tranquillity *(an)*, the ensuing Heian period (794–1185) effectively lived up to its name. Over four centuries the city went beyond its post as a political hub to become the country's commercial and cultural centre. Towards the end of the 9th century, contact with China became increasingly sporadic, providing an opportunity for Japan to cultivate an independent heritage. This produced a great flowering in literature, the arts and religious thinking, as the Japanese adapted ideas and institutions imported from China.

The development of hiragana (Japanese characters), whose invention is attributed to the Buddhist priest Kūkai in the 9th century, led to a popular literary trend best recalled by Murasaki Shikibu's legendary saga *Genji Monogatari* (The Tale of Genji). This period in Kyoto's history conjures up romantic visions of riverside moon-gazing parties where literati drew calligraphy and composed poetry while the aristocracy frolicked in their self-imposed seclusion.

Japanese monks returning from China established two new sects, Tendai (or Tenzai, meaning Heavenly Terrace) and Shingon (True Words), that became the mainstays of Japanese Buddhism. Soon other sects were springing up and temples were being enthusiastically built.

798

Kiyomizu-dera is established at the foot of the Higashiyama mountains. It is said that the location was chosen by a priest from Nara who had a vision of a holy spring at the site.

869

The head priest of Yasaka-jinja leads a procession through the streets of Kyoto in an effort to end a series of epidemics that had plagued the city. This is the origin of today's Gion Matsuri.

10th century

The centre of the city gradually shifts east, closer to the Kamo-gawa and the Higashiyama. During this time, imperial properties in the west are abandoned.

1052

The Byōdō-in Buddhist temple is established. The following year, the famous Hōō-dō (Phoenix Hall) is built. The temple is one of the best examples of Heian-era architecture.

The Heian period is considered the apogee of Japanese courtly elegance, but in the provinces a new power was on the rise – the samurai (warrior class), which built up its armed forces to defend its autonomy. Samurai families moved into Kyoto, where they muscled in on the court, and subsequent conflicts between rival military clans led to civil wars. Members of the Fujiwara, Taira and Minamoto families attacked each other, claimed control over conquered tracts of land and set up rival regimes. This was the beginning of a long period of feudal rule by successive shōgunates (samurai families). This feudal system effectively lingered on for seven centuries until imperial power was restored in 1868.

FROM ARISTOCRATIC TO MILITARY RULE

Although Kyoto served as home to the Japanese imperial family from 794 to 1868, it was not always the focus of Japanese political power. During the Kamakura period (1185–1333), Kamakura (near present-day Tokyo) was the national capital, while during the Edo period (1600–1868) the Tokugawa Shōgunate ruled the country from Edo (present-day Tokyo). Still, despite the decline in influence of the imperial court, Kyoto flourished as townspeople continued developing age-old traditions.

In 1192, while the emperor remained nominal ruler in Kyoto, Minamoto Yoritomo, the first shōgun of the Kamakura Shōgunate, set up his headquarters in Kamakura. Yoritomo purged members of his own family who stood in his way, but after fatally falling from his horse in 1199, the Hōjō, his wife's family, eliminated all of Yoritomo's potential successors. In 1213 they became true wielders of power behind the shōguns and warrior lords.

During this era the popularity of Buddhism spread to all levels of society. From the late 12th century, Eisei (1145–1215) and other Japanese monks returning from China introduced a new sect, Zen, which encountered resistance from the established sects in Kyoto but appealed to the samurai class. Meanwhile, as the spiritual fervour grew, Japanese merchants prospered in increased trade dealings with China.

Forces beyond the sea undermined the stability of the Kamakura regime. The Mongols, under Kublai Khan, reached Korea in 1259 and sent envoys to Japan seeking Japanese submission. The envoys were expelled and the Mongols sent an invasion fleet which arrived near present-day Fukuoka in 1274. This first attack was only barely repulsed with the aid of a typhoon that destroyed up to 200 Mongol ships. Further envoys sent by Khan were beheaded in Kamakura as a sign that the government of Japan was not interested in paying homage to the Mongols.

It is commonly believed that the attempted Mongol invasions of Japan were deterred by typhoons before landing on Japanese soil. In fact, there was hard fighting on land (mostly in Kyūshū) in both cases before the supporting fleets were dispersed by typhoons.

Mid-12th century

The name Kyoto (written with two Chinese characters that mean 'capital') starts to replace the original name of the city, Heian-kyo ('peaceful capital').

1168

The priest Eisai travels to China and observes Chang Buddhism. He later introduces this as Zen Buddhism in Japan. He also introduces the practice of tea drinking.

Cast-iron tea kettle

In 1281 the Mongols dispatched an army of over 100,000 soldiers to Japan. After an initial success, the Mongol fleet was almost completely destroyed by yet another massive typhoon that assaulted the shores of Kyushu for two days. Ever since, this lucky typhoon has been known to the Japanese as kamikaze (divine wind) – a name later given to the suicide pilots of WWII.

Although the Kamakura government emerged victorious, it was unable to pay its soldiers and lost the support of the warrior class. Emperor Go-Daigo led an unsuccessful rebellion to overthrow the shōgunate and was exiled to the Oki Islands near Matsue. A year later, he escaped from the island, raised an army and toppled the government, ushering in a return of political authority to Kyoto.

The history of the struggle between the northern and southern courts of the 14th century is detailed in a Japanese historical epic known as the *Taiheiki*. Partial English translations of this work are available.

TAIHEIKI

COUNTRY AT WAR

After completing his takeover, Emperor Go-Daigo refused to reward his warriors, favouring the aristocracy and priesthood instead. In the early 14th century this led to a revolt by the warrior Ashikaga Takauji, who had previously supported Go-Daigo. When Ashikaga's army entered Kyoto, Go-Daigo fled to Mt Hiei and sent the imperial Sacred Treasures to Ashikaga in conciliation. Ashikaga installed a new emperor and appointed himself shōgun, initiating the Muromachi period (1333–1568). Go-Daigo escaped from Kyoto and, the Sacred Treasures he had sent to Ashikaga being counterfeit, set up a rival court at Yoshino in a mountainous region near Nara. Rivalry between the two courts continued for 60 years until the Ashikaga made an unfulfilled promise that the imperial lines would alternate.

Kyoto gradually recovered its position of political significance and, under the control of the art-loving Ashikaga, enjoyed an epoch of cultural and artistic fruition. Talents now considered typically Japanese flourished, including such arts as landscape painting, classical nō drama, ikebana (flower arranging) and *chanoyu* (tea ceremony). Many of Kyoto's famous gardens date from this period, such as Saihōji's famed Moss Garden (p127) and the garden of Tenryū-ji (p114). Kinkaku-ji (Golden Pavilion; p109) and Ginkaku-ji (Silver Temple; p95) were built by the Ashikaga shōguns to serve as places of rest and solitude. Eventually formal trade relations were reopened with Ming China and Korea, although Japanese piracy remained a bone of contention with both.

The Ashikaga ruled, however, with diminishing effectiveness in a land slipping steadily into civil war and chaos. By the 15th century Kyoto had become increasingly divided as *daimyō* (domain lords) and local barons fought for power in bitter territorial disputes that were to last

1192

Minamoto Yoritomo is appointed shōgun and establishes the political capital in Kamakura. While the imperial court remains in Kyoto, the real power centre of the country leaves the city.

1202

Eisai establishes the Zen temple Kennin-ji, under sponsorship of shōgun Minamoto no Yoriie. It remains one of Kyoto's most important Zen temples.

Early 13th century

The priest Hōnen, troubled by divisions between Japan's major Buddhist sects, establishes a new populist sect known as Jōdo (Pure Land) Buddhism. He fasts to death in 1212.

Mid-13th century

The priest Shinran preaches a radical doctrine that becomes known as Jōdo-Shinshū (True Pure Land Buddhism). Followers establish the vast Higashi-Hongan-ji and Nishi-Hongan-ji.

for a century. In 1467 the matter of succession to the shōgunate between two feudal lords, Yamana and Hosokawa, ignited the most devastating battle in Kyoto's history. With Yamana's army of 90,000 camped in the southwest and Hosokawa's force of 100,000 quartered in the north of the city, Kyoto became a battlefield. The resulting Ōnin-no-ran (Ōnin War; 1467–77) wreaked untold havoc on the city; the Imperial Palace and most of the city were destroyed by fighting and subsequent fires, and the populace was left in ruin.

The war marked the rapid decline of the Ashikaga family and the beginning of the Sengoku-jidai (Warring States period), a protracted struggle for domination by individual *daimyō* that spread throughout Japan and lasted until the start of the Azuchi-Momoyama period in 1568.

RETURN TO UNITY

After a succession of power struggles, the country was finally united in the late 16th century by Toyotomi Hideyoshi.

By the late 16th century, Kyoto's population had swelled to 500,000 and Hideyoshi was fascinated with redesigning and rebuilding the city, which had been devastated by more than a century of war. Prior to his death in 1598 he transformed Kyoto into a castle town and greatly altered the cityscape by ordering major construction projects including bridges, gates and the Odoi, a phenomenal earthen rampart designed to isolate and fortify the perimeter of the city, and to provide a measure of flood control. He also rebuilt temples burned by Nobunaga, including the stronghold of the Ikkō sect, the great Hongan-ji.

The first Europeans to arrive in Japan were the Portuguese, who landed on the island of Tanegashima, south of Kyūshū in 1543.

The rebuilding of Kyoto is usually credited to the influence of the city's merchant class, which led a citizens' revival that gradually shifted power back into the hands of the townspeople. Centred on Shimogyō, the commercial and industrial district, these enterprising people founded a *machi-shū* (self-governing body) that contributed greatly to temple reconstruction. Over time, temples of different sects were consolidated in one quarter of the city, creating the miniature Tera-Machi (city of temples), which still exists.

The Azuchi-Momoyama period has been referred to as the 'Japanese Renaissance', during which the arts further prospered. Artisans of the era are noted for their boisterous use of colour and gold-leaf embellishment, which marked a new aesthetic sense in contrast to the more sombre monotones of the Muromachi period. The Zen-influenced tea ceremony was developed to perfection under Master Sen no Rikyū, who also wrote poetry and practised ikebana. The performing arts also

1281

Kublai Khan of Mongolia attempts to conquer Japan for the second time, but the invasion force is destroyed by a massive typhoon (the so-called kamikaze).

1333

The Kamakura Shōgunate is defeated, Emperor Daigo II returns from exile and the political capital is re-established in Kyoto, where it remains until 1868.

1397

Shōgun Ashikaga Yoshimitsu is given a property to serve as a retirement villa. After his death, his son turns the villa into Rokuon-ji, known today as Kinkaku-ji (the Golden Pavilion).

1467

The devastating Ōnin War breaks out in Kyoto between two families competing for shōgunate succession, leading to nationwide war known as the Sengoku-Jidai (Warring States) period.

matured, along with skill in ceramics, lacquerware and fabric-dyeing. A vogue for building castles and palaces on a flamboyant scale was also nurtured, the most impressive examples being Osaka-jō, which reputedly required three years of labour by up to 100,000 workers, and the extraordinary Ninomaru Palace in Kyoto's Nijō-jō (p107).

PEACE & SECLUSION

The supporters of Hideyoshi's young heir, Toyotomi Hideyori, were defeated in 1600 by his former ally, Tokugawa Ieyasu, at the decisive Battle of Sekigahara in Gifu prefecture. Ieyasu set up his *bakufu* (literally, field headquarters) at Edo, marking the start of the Edo (Tokugawa) period (1600–1868). Meanwhile the emperor and court exercised purely nominal authority in Kyoto.

There emerged a pressing fear of religious intrusion (seen as a siphoning of loyalty to the shōgun) and Tokugawa set out to stabilise society and the national economy. Eager for trade, he was initially tolerant of Christian missionary activities but, fearing the Christians would support Hideyori's efforts to resist the *bakufu* military government, he took steps to prohibit Christianity before destroying the Toyotomi family. Japan entered a period of *sakoku* (national seclusion) during which Japanese were forbidden on pain of death to travel to (or return from) overseas or to trade abroad. As efforts to expel foreign influences spread, only Dutch, Chinese and Koreans were allowed to remain, under strict supervision, and trade was restricted to the artificial island of Dejima at Nagasaki.

SAMURAI WILLIAM

Samurai William, by Giles Milton, is one of the most interesting accounts of the early Tokugawa period. It tells the story of William Adams, a shipwrecked English sailor, who gains the confidence of Shōgun Ieyasu.

The Tokugawa family retained large estates and took control of major cities, ports and mines; the remainder of the country was allocated to autonomous *daimyō*. Foreign affairs and trade were monopolised by the shōgunate, which yielded great financial authority over the *daimyō*. Tokugawa society was strictly hierarchical. In descending order of importance were the nobility, who had nominal power; the *daimyō* and their samurai; farmers; and, at the bottom, artisans and merchants. Mobility from one class to another was blocked; social standing was determined by birth.

To ensure political security, the *daimyō* were required to make ceremonial visits to Edo every alternate year, while their wives and children were kept in permanent residence in Edo as virtual hostages of the government. At the lower end of society, farmers were subject to a severe system of rules that dictated in minute detail their food, clothing and housing and land surveys which were designed to extract the greatest tax yield possible.

1482

Shōgun Ashikaga Yoshimasa builds a retreat at the base of the Higashiyama mountains. After his death, the retreat is converted into Jishō-ji, a temple known today as Ginkaku-ji.

GREG ELMS / LONELY PLANET IMAGES ©

Ginkaku-ji temple (p95)

1568

Oda Nobunaga, son of a *daimyō* in Owari Province (now known as Aichi-ken), seizes power from the imperial court in Kyoto and begins to pacify and unify central Japan.

1591

The ruling shōgun, Toyotomi Hideyoshi, orders the construction of a wall around the city of Kyoto. The wall extends for 23km and is traversable by seven gates.

One effect of this strict rule was to create an atmosphere of relative peace and isolation in which the arts excelled. There were great advances in haiku poetry, *bunraku* puppet plays and kabuki theatre. Crafts such as wood-block printing, weaving, pottery, ceramics and lacquerware became famous for their refined quality. Some of Japan's greatest expressions in architecture and painting were produced, including Katsura Rikyū in Kyoto (p95) and the paintings of Tawaraya Sōtatsu, pioneer of the Rimpa school. Furthermore, the rigid emphasis of these times on submitting unquestioningly to rules of obedience and loyalty has lasted in the arts, and society at large, to the present day.

By the turn of the 19th century, the Tokugawa government was characterised by stagnation and corruption. Famines and poverty among the peasants and samurai further weakened the system. Foreign ships started to probe Japan's isolation with increasing insistence and the Japanese soon realised that their outmoded defences were ineffectual. Russian contacts in the north were followed by British and American visits. In 1853 Commodore Matthew Perry of the US Navy arrived with a squadron of 'black ships' to demand the opening of Japan to trade. Other countries also moved in with similar demands.

Despite being far inland, Kyoto felt the foreign pressure, which helped bring to a head the growing power struggle between the shōgun and emperor, eventually pushing Japan back into a state of internal conflict. A surge of antigovernment feeling among the Japanese followed and Kyoto became a hotbed of controversy. The Tokugawa government was accused of failing to defend Japan against foreigners, and of neglecting the national reconstruction necessary for Japan to meet foreign powers on equal terms. In the autumn of 1867, forces led by Satsuma and Chōshū samurai armed with English weapons attacked the palace demanding an imperial restoration. The ruling shōgun, Keiki, offered his resignation to avoid bloodshed, and Emperor Meiji resumed control of state affairs. This development has since been referred to as the Meiji Restoration.

The Coming of the Barbarians, by Pat Barr, is perhaps the most interesting account of the opening of Japan in the mid-19th century.

EMERGENCE FROM ISOLATION

With the Meiji Restoration in 1868, the seat of Japanese national political power was restored to Kyoto, but the following year the capital was transferred to Edo along with the imperial court. Political power now resided in Edo and many great merchants and scholars of the era followed the emperor. After more than a millennium as capital, the sudden changes came as a major blow to Kyoto as the population dropped dramatically and the city entered a state of bitter depression.

1600

Tokugawa Ieyasu defeats Toyotomi at the Battle of Sekigahara. The Tokugawa Shōgunate government is established in Edo (present-day Tokyo), but the capital remains in Kyoto.

1603

The castle known as Nijō-jō was built to serve as the official residence of the first Tokugawa Shōgun, Ieyasu. The castle is a direct challenge to the emperor's power.

1620

Construction starts on Katsura-Rikyū Imperial Villa. The villa was originally built to house an adopted son of Tokugawa Hideyoshi. The imperial family cooperates in the construction.

1646

Omotesenke tea-ceremony school is founded by Sen Sosa, the great-grandson of Sen no Rikyū, Japan's great tea master. The school remains in Kyoto to this day.

Kyoto quickly set its sights on revival, taking steps to secure autonomy and rebuild its infrastructure. It again flourished as a cultural, religious and economic centre, with progressive industrial development. By the late 1800s Kyoto led the country in education reforms, establishing Japan's first kindergarten, primary and junior high schools, and a public library. In 1871 the first Kyoto Exhibition was launched, in which the Maiko and Kamogawa *odori* (dances; p38) originated. In 1880 the nation's first public art school, the Kyoto Prefecture Art School (now the Kyoto City University of Arts) was opened. In the same period the city introduced Japan's first electricity system, water system and fully functioning transport network. In 1885 work began on the monumental Lake Biwa Canal, which made Kyoto the first Japanese city to harness hydroelectric power.

In 1889 a proper city government was finally formed, which helped create an atmosphere in which industry could flourish. As traditional industry pushed on, research developed in the sciences, in particular physics and chemistry. Modern industries such as precision machinery also grew, as did the introduction of foreign technologies such as the automated weaving loom, which bolstered the struggling Nishijin textile industry. To celebrate the 1100th anniversary of the city's founding, Kyoto hosted the 4th National Industrial Exhibition Fair in 1895 and established the country's first streetcar system (fuelled by the Keage Hydroelectric Plant). The same year saw the construction of Heian-jingū (actually a 5:8 scale replica of Daigokuden, the emperor's Great Hall of State; p99), and the birth of the Jidai Matsuri (Festival of the Ages).

Despite the apparent industrial boom, the initial stages of Kyoto's restoration were undermined by a state of virtual civil war. The abolition of the shōgunate was followed by the surrender of the *daimyō,* whose lands were divided into the prefectures that exist today. With the transfer of the capital to Edo, now renamed Tokyo (Eastern Capital), the government was recentralised and European-style ministries were appointed for specific tasks. A series of revolts by the samurai against the erosion of their status culminated in the Saigō Uprising, when they were finally beaten and stripped of their power.

The salaries of the foreign specialists invited to Japan in the Meiji period are believed to have amounted to 5% of all government expenditure during the period.

Despite nationalist support for the emperor under the slogan of *sonnō-jōi* (revere the emperor, repel the barbarians), the new government soon realised it would have to meet the outside world on its own terms, and the economy underwent a crash course in Westernisation and industrialisation. Foreign experts were engaged to provide assistance and Japanese students were sent abroad to acquire expertise in modern technologies. Western-style factories were established and mining was expanded under the management of *zaibatsu* (wealthy groups), such as Mitsui and Sumitomo. In 1889 Japan created a US-style constitution

1662

The first Daimon-ji Gozan Okuribi, in which a giant Chinese character is set alight on the side of a mountain in eastern Kyoto, is held.

1853

American Commodore Matthew Perry's 'black ships' arrive at Uraga Harbour (part of present-day Yokosuka), leading to a treaty allowing American trade with Japan.

1867

An alliance of the Chōshū and Satsuma *daimyō* (domain lords) and the titular Emperor Meiji overthrows the Tokugawa Shōgunate and restores imperial rule (the so-called 'Meiji Restoration').

1869

The 17-year-old Emperor Meiji moves from Kyoto to Edo, renamed Tokyo the year before, where Japan's new political and economic capital is established.

that gave the appearance of a democracy but preserved the authoritarian rule of the emperor and his select group of advisers.

In the 1890s Japan's growing confidence was demonstrated by the abolition of foreign treaty rights and by the ease with which it trounced China in the Sino-Japanese War (1894–95). The subsequent treaty nominally recognised Korean independence from China's sphere of influence and ceded Taiwan to Japan. Friction with Russia over control of Manchuria and Korea led to the Russo-Japanese War (1904–05), in which the Japanese navy stunned the Russians by inflicting a crushing defeat on their Baltic fleet at the Battle of Tsu-shima. For the first time, Japan commanded the respect of the Western powers.

THE PURSUIT OF EMPIRE

Upon his death in 1912, Emperor Meiji was succeeded by his son, Yoshihito, whose period of rule was named the Taishō era. When WWI broke out, Japan sided against Germany but did not become deeply involved in the conflict. While the Allies were occupied with war, Japan took the opportunity to expand its economy at top speed.

The Shōwa period began when Emperor Hirohito ascended to the throne in 1926. A rising tide of nationalism was bolstered by the world economic depression that began in 1929. Popular unrest was marked by political assassinations and plots to overthrow the government, which led to a significant increase in the power of the militarists, who approved the invasion of Manchuria in 1931 and the installation of a Japanese puppet regime, Manchukuo. In 1933 Japan withdrew from the League of Nations and in 1937 entered into full-scale hostilities against China.

As the leader of a new order for Asia, Japan signed a tripartite pact with Germany and Italy in 1940. The Japanese military leaders viewed the USA as the main obstacle to their imperial conquest of Asia, and when diplomatic attempts to gain US neutrality failed, the Japanese drew them into WWII with a surprise attack on the US Pacific Fleet in Pearl Harbor on 7 December 1941. The intent of the strike was to neutralise the fleet, which Japan rightly viewed as its main threat in the region.

At first Japan scored rapid successes, pushing its battle fronts across to India, down to the fringes of Australia and into the mid-Pacific. But eventually the decisive Battle of Midway turned the tide of the war against Japan. Exhausted by submarine blockades and aerial bombing, by 1945 Japan had been driven back on all fronts. In August, the declaration of war by the Soviet Union and the atomic bombs dropped by the USA on Hiroshima and Nagasaki were the final straws: Emperor Hirohito announced Japan's unconditional surrender.

DYNASTIES

The Yamato dynasty is the longest unbroken monarchy in the world, and Hirohito's reign from 1926–1989 the longest of any monarch in Japan.

1871

Japan's first exposition is held in Kyoto. The Miyako and Kamogawa *odori* (dances performed by geisha and apprentice geisha) are first performed at the Kyoto exhibition the following year.

1890

The Sosui Canal, linking Biwa-ko (a lake in nearby Shiga-ken) and Kyoto is completed. The canal is still in use and can be seen running through the grounds of Nanzen-ji.

1895

Kyoto celebrates the 1100th year of its founding; a street tram service begins operation; and Hiean-jingū, one of the city's most popular Shintō shrines, is built.

1915

The first street lamps are installed on Shijō-dōri and the accession of Emperor Taishō is celebrated throughout Japan (although he had officially become emperor three years prior).

WHO REALLY SAVED KYOTO?

Kyoto's good fortune in escaping US bombing during WWII is a well-publicised fact. Still, while it may provide patriotic colour for some Americans to hear that the city was consciously spared out of US goodwill and reverence for Kyoto's cultural heritage, not everyone agrees with the prevailing story.

The common belief is that Kyoto was rescued through the efforts of American scholar Langdon Warner (1881–1955). During the latter half of the war Warner sat on a committee that endeavoured to save artistic and historical treasures in war-torn regions. More than a half-century later, Warner is a household name in Japan and is still alluded to in discussions on the future preservation of Kyoto. He is said to have made a desperate plea to US military authorities to spare the cities of Kyoto, Nara, Kamakura and Kanazawa.

Despite this popular account, other theories have surfaced, along with documentation pointing to an elaborate conspiracy aimed at quelling anti-American sentiment in occupied Japan. The evidence has fuelled a debate as to whether or not it was in fact a well-planned public relations stunt scripted by US intelligence officials to gain the trust of a nation that had been taught to fear and hate the American enemy.

Some historians have suggested that both Kyoto and Nara were on a list of some 180 cities earmarked for air raids. Kyoto, with a population of over one million people, was a prime target (along with Hiroshima and Nagasaki) for atomic annihilation and many avow the choice could easily have been Kyoto. Nara, it has been suggested, escaped merely due to having a population under 60,000, which kept it far enough down the list not to be reached before the unconditional surrender of Japan in September 1945.

POSTWAR RECONSTRUCTION & REVIVAL

Japan was occupied by Allied forces until 1952 under the command of General Douglas MacArthur. The chief aim was a thorough reform of Japanese government through demilitarisation, the trial of war criminals and the weeding out of militarists and ultranationalists from the government. A new constitution was introduced which denounced war and banned a Japanese military, and also dismantled the political power of the emperor, who stunned his subjects by publicly renouncing any claim to divine origins.

At the end of the war, the Japanese economy was in ruins and inflation was running rampant. A programme of recovery provided loans, restricted imports and encouraged capital investment and personal saving. In 1945 the Kyoto Revival Plan was drafted and, again, Kyoto was set for rebuilding. In 1949 physicist Hideki Yukawa was the first in a long line of Nobel Prize winners from Kyoto University, and the city went on to become a primary educational centre.

1941

The Imperial Japanese Navy attacks the US Pacific Fleet in Pearl Harbor, Hawaii, in a strike designed to prevent American interference in Japan's territorial expansion in Asia.

1966

Kyoto International Conference Hall opens at Takaragaike as the first international conference hall in Japan. Takaragaike later serves as the site for the Kyoto Protocol agreement.

1981

Karasuma subway starts between Kyoto and Kitaō-ji stations, allowing easy north–south travel through the city. The line later extends south to Takeda and north to Takaragaike.

1994

Kyoto celebrates the 1200th anniversary of its founding and 17 Historic Monuments of Ancient Kyoto are registered as Unesco World Heritage sites, including Kinkaku-ji and Ginkaku-ji.

By the late '50s trade was flourishing and the Japanese economy continued to experience rapid growth. From textiles and the manufacture of labour-intensive goods such as cameras, the Japanese 'economic miracle' had branched out into virtually every sector of society and Kyoto increasingly became an international hub of business and culture.

Japan was now looking seriously towards tourism as a source of income, and foreign visitors were steadily arriving on tours for both business and pleasure. By this time Kyoto had further developed as a major university centre and during the 'Woodstock era' of the late '60s, antiwar movements and Japanese flower power mirrored those of America and brought student activism out into the streets. The year 1966 saw the enactment of a law to preserve historical sites in the city and the opening of the Kyoto International Conference Hall, where the Kyoto Protocol was drafted in 1997.

During the 1970s Japan faced an economic recession, with inflation surfacing in 1974 and 1980, mostly due to steep price hikes for the imported oil on which Japan is still gravely dependent. By the early '80s, however, Japan had emerged as an economic superpower, and Kyoto's high-tech companies, including Kyocera, OMRON and Nintendo, were among those dominating fields such as electronics, robotics and computer technology. The notorious 'bubble economy' that followed marked an unprecedented era of free spending by Japan's nouveau riche. Shortly after the 1989 death of Emperor Shōwa and the start of the Heisei period (with the accession of Emperor Akihito) the miracle bubble burst, launching Japan into a critical economic freefall from which it has not yet fully recovered.

In 1997, the so-called Kyoto Protocol was adopted at the Takaragaike International Conference Hall in northern Kyoto. The Kyoto Protocol is a United Nations program aimed at limiting greenhouse gas emissions and countering global warming.

KYOTO PROTOCOL

KYOTO TODAY & TOMORROW

In 1994 Kyoto marked the 1200th anniversary of its founding. While the city celebrated its ancient heritage, however, developers celebrated this milestone by building several structures in excess of the height restrictions that had been put in place to maintain the city's traditional skyline. Fortunately, in September 2007, the Kyoto city government enacted new ordinances that restrict building heights and ban all rooftop and blinking advertisements.

Meanwhile, down on street level, there was a revival of interest in the city's *machiya* (traditional wooden town houses; see p178), and many of these fine old structures were turned into shops, restaurants and inns.

As Kyoto heads into the future, the real challenge is to preserve its ancient history while meeting the desires of its citizens for economic development and modern convenience.

1997

The futuristic Kyoto Station building, featuring a 60m-high atrium over the main concourse, opens in the same year as the Tōzai (east–west) line, Kyoto's second subway line.

PHIL WEYMOUTH / LONELY PLANET IMAGES ©

Kyoto Station (p51)

2011

On 11 March, the Great East Japan Earthquake strikes off the northeast coast. While Kyoto suffers no damage, there's a massive decline in tourist numbers.

People & Culture

Kyoto is the cultural heart of Japan. It is the place in which Japanese culture is at its most refined, most intense and most distinctive. Indeed, Kyoto is the place where many Japanese go to learn what it is to be Japanese. The people of Kyoto, whether they be artisans, geisha or typical office workers, bear the stamp of this rich cultural legacy in everything from their language to their manners.

THE CULTURE OF KYOTO

The cultural life of Kyoto was centred on the imperial court for over 1100 years. The court drew to it the finest artisans and craftspeople from across Japan, resulting in an incredibly rich cultural and artistic atmosphere. Today Kyoto is still home to many of Japan's best artists in every field, from textiles and bamboo craft to the tea ceremony. The imperial court also left its mark on the language of the city, and true *Kyoto-ben* (Kyoto dialect) has the lilting tones and formality of the now-departed imperial residents.

In addition to playing host to the imperial court, Kyoto has always been the headquarters of Japan's major religious sects, including Zen, Pure Land and Tendai. The astonishing preponderance of temples and shrines in the present-day city is testament to the role that Kyoto has always played in the spiritual life of the Japanese.

A maiko (apprentice geisha) strolls down Shimbashi, Southern Higashiyama

Kyoto's cultural life is deeply informed by the natural world. Due to its geographic location, Kyoto has always enjoyed four very distinct seasons, which are reflected in, and celebrated by, the yearly procession of Kyoto rituals and festivals. From the hanging of scrolls in people's homes and tableware in *kaiseki* restaurants, to the young lady's *yukata* robe the night before the Gion Matsuri festival (p22), every aspect of Kyoto is a reminder and an echo of the season. This rich and complex culture is still apparent to even the most casual visitor and it seems to embody a certain elegance, refinement and style that has few rivals elsewhere in the world.

THE PEOPLE OF KYOTO

Ask other Japanese about Kyotoites and they will probably say that they are cold, arrogant, conservative, haughty, indirect and two-faced. They'll tell you that Kyotoites act as though the city is still the capital and the imperial seat; that your family has to live there for three generations before it will be accepted; and that they never understand what a Kyotoite really means because they never say what they're feeling.

The good news is that most of this is exaggeration and really only applies a small minority of older folks in traditional neighbourhoods. And, as a visitor, you'll probably never pick up on any of this. In defence of the people of Kyoto, there is a good reason for their famed indirectness: as the seat of Japan's political life for so many centuries, the residents of the city naturally learned to guard their opinions in the presence of shifting political powers. Furthermore, as the seat of Japanese cultural, artistic and spiritual life, it is hardly surprising that Kyotoites feel a certain pride that can easily be mistaken for arrogance. The fact is that they have a lot of culture to guard, so a little conservatism is only natural.

It's difficult to talk of a Kyoto identity, of course, because it is true that there are two different cultures existing in modern-day Kyoto: that of the old and that of the young. While most older Kyotoites cling to the traditional ways of the city, the young identify with the national Japanese culture that has its epicentre somewhere in the shopping malls of Tokyo's Shibuya district. The comparison can be jarring when you see a kimono-clad older Kyoto woman sharing the pavement with a group of gaudily clad *kogals* (fashionable young things). You might conclude that you're looking at two totally different species.

DIALECT

Listen carefully and you'll hear the distinctive Kyoto dialect *(Kyoto-ben)* all around you. *Okini* means 'thank you' and *oideyasu* means 'welcome'.

GEISHA MANNERS

There's no doubt that catching a glimpse of a geisha is an once-in-a-lifetime Japanese experience. Unfortunately, the sport of 'geisha spotting' has really gotten out of hand in Kyoto's Gion district (the city's main geisha district). It's probably best to keep the following in mind if you join the ranks of geisha spotters in Gion:

- The geisha you see in Gion are usually on their way to or from an appointment and cannot stop for photos or conversation.
- Never touch or grab a geisha, or physically block their progress.
- No one likes to be mobbed by photographers or hounded as they walk down the street.
- If you really want to get close to a geisha, private tour agencies and high-end ryokan/hotels can arrange geisha entertainment.
- Finally, if you are intent on getting a few photos of geisha, you will find plenty of 'tourist geisha' in the streets of Higashiyama during the daytime. These are tourists who have paid to be made up as geisha. They look pretty much like the real thing and they are usually more than happy to pose for pictures. For information on how you can look like a *maiko* see p87.

Geisha

No other aspect of Japanese culture is as misunderstood as the geisha. First – and let's get this out of the way – geisha are not prostitutes. Nor is their virginity sold off to the highest bidder. Nor do they have to sleep with regular patrons. Simply put, geisha are highly skilled entertainers who are paid to facilitate and enliven social occasions in Japan.

The origins of geisha are subject to some debate, but most historians believe that the institution started in the Edo Period (1600–1868). At this time, there were various types of prostitutes who served men in the pleasure quarters of the large cities. Some became very accomplished in various arts. Eventually there arose a class of young ladies who specialised exclusively in entertainment and who did not engage in sexual relations with clients. These were the first true geisha, and over their years they became prized for their accomplishments in a wide variety of Japanese arts.

The best way to see geisha – a whole lot of geisha – is to attend one of Kyoto spring or autumn geisha dances. For more information, see p38.

Kyoto is the capital of the geisha world. Confusingly, in Kyoto they are not called geisha; rather, they are called *maiko* or *geiko*. A *maiko* is a girl between the ages 15 and 20 who is in the process of training to become a fully fledged *geiko* (the Kyoto word for geisha). During this five-year period, she lives in an *okiya* (geisha house) and studies traditional Japanese arts, including dance, singing, tea ceremony and shamisen (a Japanese stringed instrument). During this time, she will start to entertain clients, usually in the company of a *geiko,* who acts like an older sister.

Due to the extensive training she receives, a *maiko* or *geiko* is like a living museum of Japanese traditional culture. In addition to her skills, the kimono she wears and the ornaments in her hair and on her *obi* (kimono sash) represent the highest achievements in Japanese arts.

While young girls may have been sold into this world in times gone by, these days, girls make the choice themselves. The proprietor of the *okiya* will meet the girl and her parents to determine if the girl is serious and if her parents are willing to grant her permission to enter the world of the geisha (the *okiya* makes a considerable investment in terms of training and kimonos, so they are loath to take girls who may quit).

Memoirs of a Geisha by Arthur Golden is an entertaining fictional account of the life of a Kyoto geisha.

Once a *maiko* completes her training and becomes a *geiko,* she is able to move out of the *okiya* and live on her own. At this point, she is free to have a boyfriend, but if she gets married she has to leave the world of the geisha. It's easy to spot the difference between a *maiko* and a *geiko* – *geiko* wear wigs with minimal ornamentation (usually just a wooden comb), while *maiko* wear their own hair in an elaborate hairstyle with many bright hair ornaments called *kanzashi*. Also, *maiko* wear elaborate long-sleeve kimono, while *geiko* wear simpler kimono with shorter sleeves.

Maiko and *geiko* entertain their clients in exclusive restaurants, banquet halls, 'teahouses' (more like exclusive traditional bars) and other venues. An evening of *maiko/geiko* entertainment usually starts with a *kaiseki* meal (Japanese haute cuisine). While their customers eat, the *maiko/geiko* enter the room and introduce themselves in Kyoto dialect. They proceed to pour drinks and make witty banter with the guests. Sometimes they even play drinking games and we can tell you from experience that it's hard to beat geisha at their own games! If it's a large party with a *jikata* (shamisen player), the girls may dance after dinner.

As you might guess, this sort of entertainment does not come cheap: a dinner with one *maiko,* one *geiko* and a *jikata* might cost about US$900, but it's definitely worth it for a once-in-a-lifetime experience.

Knowledgeable sources estimate that there are perhaps 100 *maiko* and just over 100 *geiko* in Kyoto. It's impossible to arrange private geisha entertainment without an introduction from an established patron. However, these days, geisha entertainment can be arranged through top-end hotels, ryokan and some cultural organisations in Kyoto.

Arts & Crafts

Rightly described as Japan's cultural heart and soul, Kyoto is famous for keeping alive the flame of Japanese tradition. Almost all of Japan's traditional arts and crafts reached their peak of sophistication and elegance here. From kabuki to textiles, Kyoto's traditional arts and crafts reflect centuries of polishing and refinement in a city that was home to Japan's most discerning citizens for well over 1000 years.

A TRADITION OF VARIED INFLUENCES

While Kyoto is rightly viewed as Japan's cultural storehouse and the capital of its traditional arts, it also boasts a long history of eagerly embracing the new, the exotic and the experimental. A case in point are the Persian carpets and Flemish tapestries which decorate the Gion Festival floats. Kyoto's savvy silk merchants managed to obtain these Silk Road products even after the Tokugawa Shōgunate clamped its lid on the country in the mid-17th century. When the Meiji Restoration of 1868 once again opened Japan to the world, Kyoto's culturally astute citizens quickly demonstrated as much enthusiasm for European classical music and painting as they did for Western science and technology. The present moment finds Kyoto, along with the rest of Japan, showing a renewed interest in the arts and crafts of its Asian neighbours.

GREG ELMS / LONELY PLANET IMAGES ©

Lacquerware on display at a Kitaoji shop

The current artistic scene, for example, shows a new willingness to combine elements previously considered incompatible. In one of the city-sponsored art festivals, for instance, a Brahms quintet might take place on the nō stage of a Shintō shrine, or an Edo-period Buddhist temple might host a performance of *butō* (a form of Japanese modern dance).

One of the best sources of information on upcoming cultural events in Kyoto and Kansai is the magazine *Kansai Scene* (www.kansaiscene.com).

Unfortunately, most of Kyoto's craft traditions are in crisis. The silk weaving industry, which for centuries supported the city's economy and gave work to countless artisans, is in decline as fewer and fewer Japanese wear kimono. In fact, all crafts tied to the traditional Japanese lifestyle are in similar danger of disappearing.

Whatever the future holds, the legacy of Kyoto's glorious past – its temples, shrines and gardens – will remain to delight the visitor. And, in spite of pachinko parlours, car parks and other forms of urban ugliness, such things as the maple leaf garnish on your lunch-set tofu or the *Nishijin-obi* (decorative belt) of your waitress's kimono prove that an artistic sensibility shaped by 1200 years of tradition is still alive.

PERFORMING ARTS

Nō and kabuki, Japan's best known theatrical traditions, can both be viewed in Kyoto. The city is home to several schools of nō and performances are frequent. *Kyōgen* (ancient comic plays, which are an offspring of nō) are also occasionally performed in Kyoto.

Nō

Nō seems to have originated from the happy combination of indigenous Shintō-related dance and mime traditions, and dance forms that originated elsewhere in Asia. It owes its form and its repertory to the artistic dynasty of Kannami Kiyotsugu, which flourished in Kyoto between 1350 and 1450. Rather than a drama in the usual sense, a nō play seeks to express a poetic moment by symbolic and almost abstract means. The actors wear masks and perform before an unchanging set design, which features a painting of a large pine tree. The language used is the elegant language of Kyoto's 14th-century court. Obviously, nō's rather esoteric qualities make having some previous understanding of the play to be performed especially helpful. An exception to this might be the open air Takigi Nō, performed on the evenings of 1 and 2 June in the precincts of Heian-jingū (p99). Here, the play of firelight on brocade costumes will captivate even the most jaded viewer.

Despite the fact that nō masks are carved of wood and are therefore immovable, they are often designed so that tilting the masks at various angles can change the expression of the mask, an effect heightened by the lighting of the stage (which is often firelight).

Kabuki

While nō was patronised by the Ashikaga shōguns who created the Ginkaku-ji and Kinkaku-ji, kabuki, which developed much later, was a plebeian form of entertainment supported by the merchant class which came to prominence during the long and peaceful Edo period. It is as vibrant and brash as the former is austere and refined.

Kabuki evolved mainly in Edo (present-day Tokyo), but Kyoto played a big part in its beginnings. It was here, around 1600, that an Izumo shrine priestess and her troupe of dancers started entertaining crowds on the banks of the Kamo-gawa with a new type of dance people dubbed kabuki, a slang expression that meant 'cool' or 'in vogue'. Okuni, the priestess' name, was the Madonna of her day and knew how to please a crowd. At a time when 'Southern Barbarian' (ie European) fashion was all the rage, she is reported to have sometimes danced in Portuguese garb with a crucifix around her neck.

Okuni's dancers were not above prostituting their talents, and when fights for the ladies' affections became a bit too frequent, the order-obsessed Tokugawa officials declared the entertainment a threat to public morality. When women's kabuki was banned, troupes of adolescent men with unshorn forelocks took over, a development that only fed the flames of samurai ardour. Finally, in 1653, the authorities mandated that only adult men with shorn forelocks could perform kabuki, a development that gave rise to one of kabuki's most fascinating and artistic elements, the *onnagata* (an actor who specialises in portraying women).

Other ingenious features of kabuki include the revolving stage (a kabuki invention), the *hanamichi* (a raised walkway connecting the stage to the back of the theatre and used for dramatic entrances and exits), on-stage assistants *(koken)* and on-stage costume changes *(hiki-nuki)*.

Unlike Western theatre, kabuki is an actor-centred, actor-driven drama. It is essentially the preserve of a small number of acting families, and the Japanese audience takes great enjoyment in watching how different generations of one family perform the same part.

A kabuki program is generally five hours long and is made up of sections of four or five different works. One of the pieces is often a dance-drama. Only the most diehard fans sit through an entire program. Many spectators slip out to enjoy a *bentō* (lunchbox) or a smoke, returning to their seats to catch the scenes they like best.

Kyoto boasted seven kabuki theatres in the Edo period. Now only one, the Minami-za (p90), remains. Completely renovated in 1990, it stands just east of Shijō-Ōhashi, the same site it occupied back in 1615. Every December (and sometimes also November) it hosts *Kaomise,* during which Tokyo's most famous kabuki actors come to Kyoto to show *(mise)* their faces *(kao)*.

A statue of Okuni, fan in hand and with a samurai sword slung over one shoulder, stands at the east end of Shijō-Ōhashi, diagonally across from the Minami-za.

KABUKI

During kabuki performances, diehard kabuki fans may ritually shout out the names of the acting houses to which their favourite performers belong. These shouts are known as *kakegoe*. The men who deliver these *kakegoe* usually lurk in the upper reaches of the theatre.

Kyōgen

Designed to provide comic relief during a program of nō plays, *kyōgen* is farce that takes the spectator from the sublime realm of nō into the ridiculous world of the everyday. Using the colloquial language of the time, *kyōgen* pokes fun at such subjects as samurai, depraved priests and faithless women. Masks are not worn, and costumes tend to feature bold, colourful patterns.

The recent years have witnessed a boom in *kyōgen's* popularity, largely thanks to the influence of the mass media and the appearance of a new generation of photogenic young actors. In Kyoto the Shigeyama family is the foremost practitioner of the art. To see *kyōgen* in its original folk-art form, try to catch a performance of Mibu *kyōgen*. These mimed Buddhist morality plays are performed today at Mibu-dera (p74) just as they were in Kyoto's early medieval period.

TOP FIVE KYOTO MUSEUMS

- Kyoto National Museum (p83)
- National Museum of Modern Art (p99)
- Kyoto Municipal Museum of Art (p99)
- Kawai Kanjirō Memorial Hall (p83)
- Fureai-kan Kyoto Museum of Traditional Crafts (p99)

KYOTO'S BEST CRAFT SHOPS & MARKETS

➡ **Morita Washi** (p66) The selection of *washi* (traditional Japanese paper) at this downtown shop boggles the mind.

➡ **Erizen** (p67) This is the place to go for a custom-made new kimono.

➡ **Kamiji Kakimoto** (p66) Another great *washi* shop with things like washi computer printer paper.

➡ **Kyōsen-dō** (p53). If you're after a classic *kyo-sensu* (Kyoto fan), this is the place.

➡ **Takashimaya** (p65) The 6th floor of this department store has great lacquerware, pottery, wood crafts and so on.

➡ **Kyoto Handicraft Center** (p103) The quality of goods at this one-stop handicraft shop is excellent and the English-speaking salespeople make shopping a breeze.

➡ **Kōbō-san** (p78) This flea market, held on the 21st of each month at Tōji, is a great place to find a wide variety of used craft items.

➡ **Tenjin-san** (p111) Held on the 25th of every month, this is another brilliant flea market.

KYOTO CRAFTS

After becoming capital of Japan in 784, Kyoto attracted the leading craftspeople from all over the country. They have traditionally come to the city to service the needs of Japan's imperial court, which was based in Kyoto for over 1100 years. In addition to the imperial court, Kyoto was home to the headquarters of Japan's main Buddhist sects, the *kizoku* or noble class, the main tea schools, wealthy merchants and cultured samurai. The result was a city of small workshops filled with busy artisans, all competing with each other to tempt the demanding clientele of the city.

It's hardly surprising, then, that the Kyoto 'brand' symbolises elegance, refinement and excellence. Items bearing the prefix *kyo,* as in *kyo-yūzen* (Kyoto Yūzen kimono fabric), are revered in Japan as the apogee of sophistication.

One of the aesthetic principles of traditional Japanese art is known as *wabi-sabi*, which is usually translated as spare, rustic, simple beauty. Many scholars trace the origins of this aesthetic to the tea ceremony, in which rough, irregular tea bowls were sometimes prized more highly than perfectly finished pieces.

There are many ways for the visitor to experience Kyoto's rich craft heritage. To get a full overview of the range of Kyoto crafts, we recommend a visit to the Fureai-kan Kyoto Museum of Traditional Crafts (p99). A short walk away you will find the Kyoto Handicraft Center (p103). Next, we recommend an aimless wander through the heart of Kyoto's downtown area, in the region between Oike-dōri and Shijō-dōri (to the north and south) and Kawaramachi-dōri and Karasuma-dōri (to the east and west). Here, you will find dozens of shops selling traditional Kyoto crafts interspersed with some of Kyoto's trendiest modern shops.

Pottery & Ceramics

Evidence of the first Kyoto wares (*kyō-yaki,* the *yaki* meaning, in this case, 'ware') dates from the reign of Emperor Shōmu in the early 8th century. By the mid-1600s there were more than 10 different kilns active in and around the city. Of these, however, only Kiyomizu-yaki remains today. This kiln first gained prominence through the workmanship of potter Nonomura Ninsei (1596–1660), who developed an innovative method of applying enamel overglaze to porcelain. This technique was further embellished by adding decorative features such as transparent glaze *(sometsuke),* as well as incorporating designs in red paint *(aka-e)* and celadon *(seiji).* Kiyomizu-yaki is still actively produced in Kyoto and remains popular with devotees of tea ceremony.

During the Edo period, many *daimyō* encouraged the founding of kilns and the production of superbly designed ceramic articles. The climbing kiln *(noborigama)* was widely used, and a fine example can be seen at the home of famed Kyoto potter Kawai Kanjirō (p83). Constructed on a slope, the climbing kiln had as many as 20 chambers and could reach temperatures as high as 1400°C.

During the Meiji period, ceramics waned in popularity, but were later part of a general revival in *mingei-hin* (folk arts). This movement was led by Yanagi Sōetsu, who encouraged famous potters such as Kawai, Tomimoto Kenkichi and Hamada Shōji. The English potter Bernard Leach studied in Japan under Hamada and contributed to the folk-art revival. On his return to England, Leach promoted the appreciation of Japanese ceramics in the West.

Those with an interest in Kyoto wares – and Kiyomizu-yaki in particular – should check out the streets below Kiyomizu-dera in Southern Higashiyama (p81). You'll find all manner of shops here selling Kiyomizu-yaki and other types of Japanese pottery. Nearby, on Gojō-dōri, between Higashiōji-dōri and Kawabata-dōri, the Tōki Matsuri (Ceramics Fair) is held on 18–20 July. You can also find a wide variety of ceramics in the shops on Teramachi-dōri, between Marutamachi-dōri and Oike-dōri. Finally, the 6th floor of Takashimaya department store (p65) has a great selection of pottery.

Lacquerware

Lacquerware (*shikki* or *nurimono*) is made using the sap from the lacquer tree *(urushi)*. Once lacquer hardens it becomes inert and extraordinarily durable. The most common colour of lacquer is an amber or brown, but additives are used to produce black, violet, blue, yellow and even white. In the better pieces, multiple layers of lacquer are painstakingly applied and left to dry, and finally polished to a luxurious shine.

Japanese artisans have devised various ways to further enhance the beauty of lacquer. The most common method is *maki-e,* which involves the sprinkling of silver and gold powders onto liquid lacquer to form a picture. After the lacquer dries, another coat seals the picture. The final effect is often dazzling and some of the better pieces of *maki-e* lacquerware are now National Treasures.

There are several places in Kyoto where you can see some stunning examples of lacquerware, including *maki-e* lacquerware. The Nomura Museum (p96) has a fine collection of lacquerware utensils used in the tea ceremony. Those looking to take a bit of lacquerware home will find an excellent selection at Zōhiko (p103).

LACQUERWARE

Real Japanese lacquerware is covered with a varnish made from the *Toxicodendron vernicifluum* plant, which is known colloquially as 'the lacquer tree'. The resin from these trees produces a strong allergic rash in most people, but lifetime lacquer workers usually develop immunity.

Textiles

Kyoto is famous for its *kyō-yūzen* textiles. *Yūzen* is a method of silk-dyeing *(senshoku)* developed to perfection in the 17th century by fan painter Miyazaki Yūzen. *Kyō-yūzen* designs typically feature simple circular flowers *(maru-tsukushi)*, birds and landscapes, and stand out for their use of bright-coloured dyes. The technique demands great dexterity in tracing designs by hand *(tegaki)* before rice paste is applied to fabric like a stencil to prevent colours from bleeding into other areas of the fabric. By repeatedly changing the pattern of the rice paste, very complex designs can be achieved.

Traditionally, when the dyeing process was complete, the material was rinsed in the Kamo-gawa and Katsura-gawa rivers (believed to be particularly effective in fixing the colours) before being hung out to dry.

Every year in mid-August this ritual is re-enacted and the fabrics flap in the wind like rows of vibrant banners.

During the turbulent civil wars of the 15th century, Kyoto's weavers congregated into a textiles quarter near Kitano-Tenman-gū Shrine called Nishijin (literally, 'Western Camp'). The industry was revamped during the Edo period and the popularity of Nishijin workmanship endured through the Meiji Restoration.

Kyoto is also famed for techniques in stencil-dyeing *(kyō-komon)* and tie-dyeing *(kyō-kanoko shibori)*. *Kyō-komon* (*komon* means 'small crest') gained notoriety in the 16th and 17th centuries, particularly among warriors who ordered the adornment of both their armour and kimono, through the stencilling of highly geometric designs onto fine silk with vibrant colours. Typically the patterns incorporate flowers, leaves and other flora.

At the other end of the refined, courtly spectrum, *aizome* (the technique of dyeing fabrics in vats of fermented indigo plants) gave Japan one of its most distinctive colours. Used traditionally in making hardy work clothes for the fields, Japan's beautiful indigo-blue can still be seen in many modern-day textile goods.

Together with Kyoto-dyed fabrics *(kyō-zome)*, Nishijin weaving (Nishijin-*ori*) is internationally renowned and dates to the founding of the city. Nishijin techniques were originally developed to satisfy the demands of the nobility who favoured the quality of illustrious silk fabrics. Over time new methods were adopted by the Kyoto weavers and they began to experiment with materials such as gauze, brocade, damask, satin and crepe. The best known Nishijin style is the exquisite *tsuzure* – a tightly woven tapestry cloth produced with a hand loom *(tebata)* – on which detailed patterns are preset.

In 1915 the Orinasu-kan textile museum (p108) was established to display Nishijin's fine silk fabrics and embroidery. The museum has two halls which display some stunning examples of Nishijin-*ori*. Nearby, the Nishijin Textile Center (p111) has decent, if touristy, displays on Nishijin-ori, including a demonstration loom, a shop selling Nishijin items and occasional kimono fashion shows.

If you'd like to purchase a kimono or an *obi* (kimono sash), you will find the best prices on used items at either the Kōbō-san (p78) or the Tenjin-san markets (p111). If you're after a new kimono, try Erizen (p67) or Takashimaya (p65).

Dolls

Among the finest of Japan's handcrafted dolls *(ningyō)* are Kyoto's *kyō-ningyō*. Elaborate in detail and dressed in fine brocade fabrics, they date from the Heian period and their exquisite costumes reflect the taste and styles of that aristocratic time.

Some other common dolls are daruma dolls, which are based on the figure of Bodhidharma, the religious sage commonly considered to be the founder of Zen Buddhism; *gosho-ningyō,* chubby plaster dolls sometimes dressed as figures in nō dramas; *kiku-ningyō,* large dolls adorned with real chrysanthemum flowers; and *ishō-ningyō,* which is a general term for elaborately costumed dolls, sometimes based on kabuki characters.

If you'd like to purchase a *kyō-ningyō,* you'll find a good selection at Tanakaya (p66) or the Kyoto Handicraft Center (p103).

Fans

As with many of Japan's traditional crafts, fans were first made in Kyoto and continue to be prolifically produced here today. *Kyō-sensu*

GEISHA CRAFTS

Kyoto's geisha, properly known in Kyoto as *geiko* or *maiko* (fully fledged and apprentice geisha, respectively), are walking museums of traditional crafts. In fact, if you want to see several of Kyoto's traditional crafts in one quick glance, the best place to look is at a *geiko* or *maiko* shuffling by on her way to an appointment. Some things to look out for include:

➡ Kimono: The kimono worn by *geiko* and *maiko* are likely made right here in Kyoto, most probably in the workshops in and around the Nishijin textile district. Kimono are the visible capital in the geisha world; they are worth thousands or even hundreds of thousands of dollars and are loaned to maiko by the 'mama-san' of her house.

➡ Obi: The *obi* (kimono sash) worn by *geiko* and *maiko* is where the weaving skills of Kyoto's silk weavers are given their freest rein. They are often wild and almost psychedelic explosions of colour.

➡ Flower hairpins: Known in Japanese as *hana-kanzashi*, these delicate hairpins are made from silk and light metal, usually with seasonal motifs. *Maiko* wear different *hana-kanzashi* in each month.

➡ Boxwood combs: Handmade boxwood combs (*kushi* in Japanese) are indispensable for creating the wonderful hairstyles of the *maiko*. One reason for using these combs, apart from their incredibly pleasing appearance, is the fact that they don't produce static electricity.

➡ Umbrellas: On a rainy day, *maiko* and *geiko* are sheltered from the rain by *wagasa* (traditional Japanese umbrellas). With bamboo frames and paper or silk, these umbrellas are perfectly suited to the geisha wardrobe.

For more on geisha, see page p166.

(Kyoto fans) first found popularity among the early aristocracy, but by the late 12th century their popularity had spread to the general populace. Though fans were originally a practical and fashionable tool to keep oneself cool in Japan's sweltering summers, they gradually took on more aesthetic purposes as Japan's arts flourished from the 15th century onwards, from plain fans used in tea ceremony and incense smelling, to elaborate ones used in nō drama and traditional dance. Fans are still commonly used as decorative items and for ceremonial purposes.

Originally made from the leaves of the cypress tree, fans are now primarily made with elaborately painted Japanese paper fixed onto a skeleton of delicate bamboo ribs. The paper can feature decorations from simple geometric designs to courtly scenes from the Heian period and are often sprinkled with gold or silver leaf powder.

Fans make a lightweight and excellent souvenir of Kyoto and can be purchased at major department stores and at speciality shops like Kyōsen-dō (p53). The latter shop sometimes has demonstrations of fan making.

Like the practice of drinking tea, it is said that the art of papermaking was brought to Japan by Buddhist monks. It is said that the art was introduced into Japan in the early 7th century by monks who used the paper for copying sutras.

Washi

The art of making paper by hand was introduced into Japan from China in the 5th century and it reached its golden age in the Heian era, when it was highly prized by members of the Kyoto court for their poetry and diaries. *Washi* (traditional Japanese paper) is normally produced using mulberry, but it can also be made from mountain shrubs and other plants. One distinctive type of *washi* found in Kyoto is *kyo-chiyogami,* which has traditionally been used by Japanese to wrap special gifts.

Washi was made in large quantities in Japan until the introduction of Western paper in the 1870s. After that time, the number of families involved in the craft plummeted. However, there are still a number of traditional papermakers active in Kyoto city and in country areas north of the city. Recently, *washi* has enjoyed something of a revival (there's even *washi* for computer printers!). There are several fine *washi* shops in Kyoto, including Morita Washi (p66) and Kamiji Kakimoto (p66).

IKEBANA

Ikebana – the art of flower arranging – was developed in the 15th century and can be grouped into three main styles: *rikka* (standing flowers), *shōka* (living flowers), and free-style techniques such as *nageire* (throwing-in) and *moribana* (heaped flowers). There are several thousand different schools, the top three being Ikenobō, Ōhara and Sōgetsu, but they share one aim: to arrange flowers to represent heaven, earth and humanity. Ikebana displays were originally used as part of tea ceremony, but can now be found in private homes – in the *tokonoma* (sacred alcove) – and even in large hotels.

Apart from its cultural associations, ikebana is also a lucrative business. Its schools have millions of students, including many young women who view proficiency in the art as a means to improve their marriage prospects.

Kyoto Culture.org (www.kyotoculture.org) can arrange introductory classes in ikebana. You can also occasionally see shows of ikebana in downtown department stores. Finally, if you stay in a good ryokan, you will probably see ikebana displayed in the entryway and in the *tokonoma* in your room.

Architecture & Gardens

Hidden amid a sea of concrete and neon that looks disappointingly like any other Japanese city, you will find in Kyoto countless pockets of astonishing beauty: ancient temples with graceful wooden halls, traditional townhouses clustered together along narrow streets, colourful Shintō shrines and, best of all, a profusion of gardens unlike anything else in Japan. Indeed, one of the best reasons to come to Kyoto is to immerse yourself in the city's almost limitless collection of gardens and traditional structures.

ARCHITECTURE

Temples

Temples (*tera* or *ji*) vary widely in their construction, depending on the type of school and historical era of construction. From the introduction of Buddhism in the 6th century until the Middle Ages, temples were the most important architectural works in Japan, and hence exerted a strong stylistic influence on all other types of building.

Tōfuku-ji (p76)

Evolution of Temple Design

There were three main styles of early temple architecture: *tenjiku yō* (Indian), *karayō* (Chinese) and *wayō* (Japanese). All three styles were in fact introduced to Japan via China. *Wayō* arrived in the 7th century and gradually acquired local character, becoming the basis of much Japanese wooden architecture. It was named so as to distinguish it from *karayō* (also known as Zen style), which arrived in the 12th century. A mixture of *wayō* and *karayō* (known as *setchuyō*) eventually came to dominate, and *tenjikuyō* disappeared altogether.

Despite the frequent earthquakes in Japan, the pagodas at Buddhist temples almost never fall down. They are designed so that each floor moves in opposition to the others in a movement known as 'the snake dance'.

With their origins in Chinese architecture and with an emphasis on other-worldly perfection, early temples were monumental and symmetrical in layout. A good example of the Chinese influence can be seen in the famous Phoenix Hall at Byōdō-in in Uji (p125), a Tang-style pavilion.

The Japanese affinity for asymmetry eventually affected temple design, leading to the more organic – although equally controlled – planning of later temple complexes. An excellent example in Kyoto is Daitoku-ji (p72), a Rinzai Zen monastery (a large complex containing a myriad of subtemples and gardens).

Architectural Components

Temples generally have four gates, oriented to the north, south, east and west. The *nandai-mon* (southern gate) is usually the largest one. There is also a central gate, *chū-mon,* which is sometimes incorporated into the cloister. The *niō-mon* (guardian gate) houses frightful-looking statues of gods such as Raijin (the god of thunder) and Fū-jin (the god of wind).

The *Gojū-no-tō,* or five-storey pagoda, is a major component of temple design. These are elegant wooden towers, symbolising *Shaka,* the Historical Buddha. Their design is a variation of the Indian stupa, a structure originally intended to hold the remains of *Shaka* (sometimes with an actual tooth or chip of bone, but more often represented by crystal or amber). The spire on top usually has nine tiers, representing the nine spheres of heaven.

Kyoto contains a number of excellent examples of five-storey pagodas, including the pagoda at Tō-ji (p74), the best known and the tallest in Japan.

The word for the Shintō shrine gate *(torii)* is written with the kanji for 'bird' and 'be', forming a compound that means something like 'the place where the bird is'. Scholars have noted that several shamanistic traditions in mainland Asia use bird perches in a ceremonial manner.

Shrines

Shrines can be called *jinja, jingū, gū* or *taisha*. The original Shintō shrine is Izumo Taisha in Shimane Prefecture, which has the largest shrine hall in Japan. It is said to have been modelled on the Emperor's residence, and its style, known as *taisha-zukuri,* was extremely influential on later shrine design. Shrines tend to use simple, unadorned wood construction and are built raised above the ground on posts. The roof is gabled, not hipped as with temple architecture. The entrance is generally from the end, not the side, again distinguishing it from temple design. The distinctive roof line of shrine architecture is due to an elaboration of the structural elements of the roof. The criss-cross elements are called *chigi* and the horizontal elements are called *katsuogi.*

Nagare Style

As Buddhism increased its influence over Shintō, it also affected the architecture. The clean lines of the early shrines were replaced with curving eaves and other ornamental details. Worshippers were provided with shelter by extending the roof or even building a separate worship

BUDDHIST IMAGES

There are dozens of images in the Japanese Buddhist pantheon, varying from temple to temple, depending on the religious school or period of construction. As you explore the temples of Kyoto, keep your eyes peeled for the following figures:

➡ **Nyorai (Buddhas)**: At the top of the Buddhist cosmic hierarchy, you will find *nyorai* (Buddhas). The four most common images are those of Shaka (Sanskrit: Sakyamuni), the Historical Buddha; Amida (Sanskrit: Amitabha), the Buddha of the Western Paradise; Miroku (Sanskrit: Maitreya), the Buddha of the Future; and Dainichi, the Cosmic Buddha.

➡ **Bosatsu (Bodhisattva)**: A *bosatsu* is a Bodhisattva, a being who puts off entry into nirvana in order to help all the beings stuck in the corrupt world of time. The most common *bosatsu* are Kannon (the god – or goddess – of mercy) and Jizō (the protector of travellers and children). Kannon is often depicted as standing in graceful flowing robes or with 1000 arms (the better to help all sentient beings). Jizō is often depicted as a monk with a staff in one hand and a jewel in the other. Other jizō are barely distinguishable from stones with faintly carved faces or bodies. You might see these wearing red bibs, which reflects jizō's role as protector of children.

➡ **Myōō (Kings of Light)**: These fierce looking deities entered the Buddhist pantheon from Hinduism. You might see them arranged beside *nyorai* and *bosatsu* in Buddhist temples. The most common figure is Fudō Myōō, the Immovable God of Light. These figures act as protector figures and their wrathful forms are thought to snap people out of wrongful thinking.

➡ **Tenbu**: Usually directly translated as 'ten' or 'tenbu', these are a group of guardian figures inherited from Indian and Chinese cosmologies. A common example is the four heavenly kings, who guard the Buddha by surrounding him in the four directions.

hall. This led to the *nagare* style, the most common type of shrine architecture. Excellent examples in Kyoto can be found at Shimogamo-jinja (p73) and Kamigamo-jinja (p128).

Gongen Style

The *gongen* style employs a H-shaped plan, connecting two halls with an intersecting gabled roof and hallway called an *ishi no ma*. This element symbolises the connection between the divine and the ordinary worlds. The best example of this architectural style in Kyoto is at Kitano Tenman-gū (p108).

Architectural Components

At the entrance to the shrine is the *torii* (gateway) marking the boundary of the sacred precinct. The most dominant *torii* in Kyoto is in front of Heian-jingū (p99), a massive concrete structure a considerable distance south of the shrine. Fushimi-Inari-Taisha (p76) in southern Kyoto has thousands of bright vermilion gates lining paths up the mountain to the shrine itself.

Neighbourhood Shrines

Every neighbourhood in every Japanese town or city has its own tiny shrine to Jizō. Pieces of clothing or red bibs draped around Jizō figures are an attempt to cover the souls of dead children. An annual August children's festival (Jizō-bon) features two days of praying and playing around the Jizō shrine by the local children dressed in *yukata* (a light kimono for summer or for bathing in a ryokan).

MACHIYA: KYOTO'S TRADITIONAL TOWNHOUSE

One of the city's most notable architectural features are its *machiya,* long and narrow wooden row houses that functioned as both homes and workplaces. The shop area was located in the front of the house, while the rooms lined up behind it formed the family's private living quarters. Nicknamed *'unagi no nedoko'* (eel bedrooms), the *machiya*'s elongated shape came about because homes were once taxed according to the amount of their street frontage.

A *machiya* is a self-contained world, complete with private well, store house, Buddhist altar, clay ovens outfitted with huge iron rice cauldrons, shrines for the hearth god and other deities, and interior mini-gardens.

Although well suited to Kyoto's humid, mildew-prone summers, a wooden *machiya* has a limited lifespan of about 50 years. Thus, as the cost of traditional materials and workmanship rose, and as people's desire for a more Western-style lifestyle increased, fewer and fewer people felt the urge to rebuild the old family home, as had been the custom in the past. Those considerations, plus the city's high inheritance tax, convinced many owners to tear down their *machiya,* build a seven-story apartment building, occupy the ground floor, and live off the rent of their tenants.

The result is that Kyoto's urban landscape – once a harmonious sea of clay-tiled two-storey wooden townhouses – is now a jumble of ferro-concrete offices and apartment buildings.

Ironically, however, *machiya* are making a comeback. After their numbers have drastically declined, the old townhouses have began to acquire an almost exotic appeal. Astute developers began to convert them into restaurants, clothing boutiques and even hair salons. Today such shops are a major draw for the city's tourist trade, and not only foreign visitors – the Japanese themselves (especially Tokyoites) love their old-fashioned charm.

The shrines are located by *fū-sui* (known in Chinese as feng shui), a specifically Asian form of geomancy. It is impossible (or bad luck) to move them, so they are found almost everywhere, often notched into concrete walls or telephone poles.

These shrines are maintained by the local community, with each person contributing a regular small sum of money. The person responsible for the shrine changes on a yearly basis, but everyone in the area will leave offerings for Jizō, usually something they themselves have excess of, such as fruit, chocolate or sake.

GARDENS

Many of Japan's most famous gardens are to be found in Kyoto, and no trip here would be complete without a visit to at least a few of them. Most of the well-known ones, whose characteristics are described below, are connected to temples or imperial villas. In addition to these, Kyoto's traditional dwellings and shops feature another type of garden called *tsubo-niwa* – tiny inner gardens that bring light into the building and provide its inhabitants with a sense of the seasons.

Japanese gardens make use of various ingenious devices to achieve their effect. *Shakkei,* or 'borrowed scenery', is one such clever design ploy, by which a distant object, such as a mountain or volcano cone, is incorporated into garden's design, adding depth and impact. Kyoto's garden designers obviously never anticipated urban sprawl. A nice example of *shakkei* is the garden at Tenryū-ji (p114), which incorporates the Arashiyama mountains into the garden design.

Japanese gardens fall into four basic types: *funa asobi* (pleasure boat), *shūyū* (stroll), *kanshō* (contemplative) and *kaiyū* (varied pleasures).

Funa Asobi

Popular in the Heian period, *funa asobi* gardens featured a large pond used for pleasure boating. Such gardens were often built around noble mansions. The garden which surrounds Byōdō-in (p125) in Uji is a vestige of this style of garden.

Shūyū

The *shūyū* garden is intended to be viewed from a winding path, allowing the garden to unfold and reveal itself in stages and from different vantages. Popular during the Heian, Kamakura and Muromachi periods, *shūyū* gardens can be found around many noble mansions and temples from those eras. A celebrated example is Ginkaku-ji (p95).

The garden at the Zuihō-in subtemple at Daitoku-ji contains stones laid out in the form of the Christian cross. This subtemple was established to honour the Christian Daimyō Ōtomo Sōrin. The stones were arranged in a cross pattern in the 1960s.

Kanshō

The *kanshō* garden is intended to be viewed from one place. Zen rock gardens, also known as *kare-sansui* gardens, are an example of this type, which were designed to aid contemplation. Ryōan-ji (p109) is perhaps the most famous example of this type of garden. Although various interpretations of the garden have been put forth (the rocks 'represent a tiger and her cubs', for example), the garden's ultimate meaning, like that of Zen itself, cannot be expressed in words.

Kaiyū

Lastly, the *kaiyū*, or varied pleasures garden, features many small gardens with one or more tea houses surrounding a central pond. Like the stroll garden, it is meant to be explored on foot and provides the viewer with a variety of changing scenes, many with literary allusions. The imperial villa of Katsura Rikyū (p126) is the classic example of this type of garden.

The Tea Ceremony

Despite all the mystery surrounding it, the tea ceremony is, at heart, simply a way of welcoming a guest with a cup of tea. In Japan, this ritual has been developed and practised for almost 500 years and is properly known as *chadō* (literally 'the way of tea'). Of course, as with most *dō* ('ways') in Japan, the practice has been ritualised and formalised to an almost unimaginable degree. In a typical tea ceremony, both the host and the guests follow a strict set of rules that vary according to the particular school of tea to which the host belongs.

A HISTORY OF TEA IN JAPAN

Tea came to Japan from China as part of a cultural package that included kanji and Buddhism, but the beverage did not become popular until the medieval period. Buddhist monks drank tea for its medicinal and stimulatory properties, a practice that gradually spread to warrior society and then on to commoners. By the 16th century, elite urban commoners such as the merchant and tea master Sen no Rikyū (1522–91) had elevated the preparation, serving and consumption of *matcha* (powdered green tea) to an elaborate ritual. In the 17th century, tea masters established their own schools of tea, and these institutions codified, spread and protected the practice over subsequent centuries.

Tea ceremony at Club Ōkitsu Kyoto (p78)

MATCHA

The tea used in the tea ceremony is called *matcha. Matcha* is powdered green tea made from the best parts of the tea leaf. The tea is hand-picked, steamed, then dried and ground into powder. Most teas are infusions; that is, you put the leaves in the hot water and then take them out before drinking. When you drink *matcha,* however, you actually drink the ground tea. This is one reason it contains so many nutrients and is thought by many to be anti-carcinogenic.

TEA CEREMONIES TODAY

These days the tea ceremony is studied and practised by Japanese who want to deepen their appreciation and mastery of traditional Japanese arts. In particular, many women from good families study the tea ceremony to deepen their aesthetic senses and to improve their marriage prospects.

The tea ceremony is often compared to the world of the geisha in that the tea ceremony is a nexus of traditional Japanese arts; it brings together garden design, architecture, calligraphy, flower arrangement, incense, kimono and many other traditional arts. Not surprisingly, many geisha also practise the tea ceremony.

The tea room is normally entered by walking through a garden. The garden functions as a transitional area where you leave daily life and enter the spiritual world.

THE INS AND OUTS OF TEA CEREMONIES

By this point, you're probably wondering what happens in an actual tea ceremony. First, it must be noted that tea ceremonies can be short and spontaneous or long and extremely formal. They might be held to mark an anniversary, the changing of the seasons or just as an opportunity to see old friends.

In a proper full-length tea ceremony, a group of guests arrive at the location of the gathering, perhaps a home or a temple with its own tea house, and wait in the outer garden, a peaceful and meditative space. Upon entering the tea house, they observe while the host arranges the charcoal and serves a special meal of *kaiseki* (haute Japanese) cuisine. After the meal, guests are served some simple sweets, take a brief intermission, then return for a serving of viscous *koicha* (thick tea) followed in many cases, by a round of *usucha* (thin tea). At certain moments during the gathering, the guests have the chance to admire the hanging scroll, the flower arrangement and the host's careful selection of *chadōgu* (tea utensils).

These days few people have the time or energy to produce or participate in the full-length version, and abbreviated tea ceremonies are often held. These often include just the consumption of one traditional Japanese sweet and a bowl of *usucha,* and the enjoyment of the flowers, scroll and utensils. This is the type of ceremonies that most visitors to Kyoto are likely to participate in.

The stepping stones that lead to the tea room are intentionally placed unevenly: they force you to empty your mind and concentrate on each step: a very Zen idea.

RELAX & HAVE A CUP OF TEA

If you are lucky enough to participate in a tea ceremony, the main thing to remember is this: *relax!* Concentrate on enjoying the tea, the flowers, the scrolls, the scenery and the beauty of the utensils. Don't worry too much about committing some dreadful faux pas. Keep in mind that even most Japanese people don't know the exact rules of the ceremony; just follow the person next to you and savour the experience. The mark of a good tea host is his or her ability to put you at ease and allow you to con-

IF YOU JOIN A TEA CEREMONY...

- Remove your jewellery and watches to avoid scratching the tea bowls.
- Refrain from taking photos with the camera directly over the tea bowls in order to avoid damaging them (by dropping the camera). Tea bowls can be priceless treasures.
- Wear white socks without holes if possible.

centrate on the true meaning of the tea ceremony: hospitality, community and aesthetic enjoyment. In many circumstances, this means relaxing or transcending the rules, rather than rigorously adhering to them.

EXPERIENCING A TEA CEREMONY

There are many places in Kyoto that offer tea ceremonies to foreign guests. It's important to note that, as with many things in life, you get what you pay for when it comes to tea ceremonies. The quality of the tea, the utensils, the sweets, the decorations, the setting, the skill of the host and the depth of his/her explanations vary enormously, usually in direct proportion to price. There are several places in Kyoto that offer tea ceremonies to the foreign travellers, including En (p90), Club Ōkitsu Kyoto (p78) and **Kyoto Culture.org** (www.kyotoculture.org).

Finally, for those who really want to delve deeply into the tea ceremony, a visit to the Urasenke Chadō Research Center (p108) is a must. Urasenke offers courses to foreigners who would like to start down the path to becoming a tea master.

Survival Guide

Transport

GETTING TO KYOTO

Air

While there is no international or domestic airport in Kyoto, the city is within easy reach of three airports: Kansai International Airport (KIX), which is Kyoto's main international entry point; Central Japan International Airport Centrair (NGO), about an hour from Kyoto by train; and Osaka International Itami Airport (ITM), which mostly handles flights from other parts of the country.

The trip between KIX and Kyoto can be expensive and time consuming; if you are flying domestically and have a choice of airports, it is cheaper and easier to fly into Osaka International Itami Airport.

It's sometimes cheaper to fly into Tokyo's Narita International Airport (NRT) or Haneda (IATA) than into KIX.

Flights, tours and rail tickets can be booked online at lonelyplanet.com/bookings.

Kansai International Airport (KIX)

The fastest and most convenient way to move between KIX and Kyoto is the special *haruka* airport express (reserved/unreserved ¥3490/2980, 75 minutes), operated by Japan's main train company, JR. Unreserved seats are almost always available, so you usually don't need to purchase tickets in advance.

First and last departures from KIX to Kyoto are at 6.33am and 10.16pm Monday to Friday (6.42am at weekends); first and last departures from Kyoto to KIX are at 5.46am and 8.16pm.

If you have the time to spare, you can save some money by taking the *kankū kaisoku* (Kansai airport express) between the airport and Osaka Station, and then taking a regular *shinkaisoku* (special rapid train) to Kyoto. The total journey by this route takes about 90 minutes with good connections, and costs ¥1830.

For those travelling on Japanese airlines (JAL and ANA), there is an advance check-in counter inside the JR ticket office in Kyoto Station. This service allows you to check in with your luggage at the station, which is a real bonus for those with heavy bags.

Osaka Airport Transport (☎06-6844-1124; www.okkbus.co.jp/en/index.html) runs direct limousine buses between Kyoto and KIX (adult/child ¥2500/1250, 88 minutes). At KIX the buses leave from the kerb outside the International Arrivals Hall.

In Kyoto, there are pick-up and drop-off points on the southern side of **Kyoto Station** (Map p220; in front of Avanti Department Store), and at **Nijō Station** (Map p228) and **Sanjō Keihan Station** (Map p224).

CLIMATE CHANGE & TRAVEL

Every form of transport that relies on carbon-based fuel generates CO_2, the main cause of human-induced climate change. Modern travel is dependent on aeroplanes, which might use less fuel per kilometre per person than most cars but travel much greater distances. The altitude at which aircraft emit gases (including CO_2) and particles also contributes to their climate change impact. Many websites offer 'carbon calculators' that allow people to estimate the carbon emissions generated by their journey and, for those who wish to do so, to offset the impact of the greenhouse gases emitted with contributions to portfolios of climate-friendly initiatives throughout the world. Lonely Planet offsets the carbon footprint of all staff and author travel.

Perhaps the most convenient option is the **MK Taxi Sky Gate Shuttle limousine van service** (☎778-5489; www.mk-group.co.jp/english/shuttle/index.html), which will drop you off anywhere in Kyoto for ¥3500 – simply go to the staff counter at the south end of the arrivals hall of KIX and they will do the rest. From Kyoto to the airport it is necessary to make reservations two days in advance and they will pick you up anywhere in Kyoto and take you to the airport.

A similar service is offered by **Yasaka Taxi** (☎803-4800). Keep in mind that these are shared taxis (actually vans), so you may be delayed by the driver picking up or dropping off other passengers.

At KIX, the **main tourist information counter** (☎072-456-6025; 1st fl, International Arrivals Hall; ⌚8:30am-8:30pm) is operated by the Osaka prefectural government. It's located roughly in the centre of the international arrivals hall.

If you'd prefer not to lug your bags into Kyoto, there are several luggage delivery services that are located in the arrivals hall.

Osaka International Itami Airport

Osaka Airport Transport (☎06-6844-1124; www.okkbus.co.jp/en/index.html) runs frequent airport limousine buses between Itami and Kyoto Station (¥1280, 55 minutes). There are less frequent pick-ups and drop-offs at some of Kyoto's main hotels. The Itami stop is outside the arrivals hall – buy your ticket from the machine near the bus stop and ask one of the attendants which stand is for Kyoto. The Kyoto Station stop is in front of Avanti Department Store (Map p220).

You can also take the **MK Taxi Sky Gate Shuttle limousine van service** (☎778-5489; www.mk-group.co.jp/english/shuttle/index.html) to/from the city for ¥2300. Call at least two days in advance to reserve or ask at the information counter in the arrivals hall in Osaka.

You'll find an information counter with English-speaking staff in the main arrivals hall. There are several luggage delivery services in the arrivals hall if you don't want to carry your bags to Kyoto.

For information on travelling to/from central Osaka, see p134.

Central Japan International Airport Centrair

The Meitetsu Tokoname Railroad line connects Centrair with Nagoya Station (¥850, 30 minutes), which connects to the Tōkaidō *shinkansen* line. It is therefore quite convenient to use Centrair as your gateway to Kyoto.

The *shinkansen* (¥5640, 36 minutes) goes to/from Nagoya Station. You can save around half the cost by taking regular express trains, but you will need to change trains at least once and can expect the trip to take about three hours.

Narita & Haneda International Airports

As a rule, it will cost about ¥15,000 and take around five hours to get from Narita to Kyoto by train. Note that you will have to first take N'EX express train from Narita into the city and then catch a *shinkansen* from Tokyo Station to Kyoto. It will take about four hours and cost around ¥14,000 to get from Haneda to Kyoto. Thus, if you're not in a hurry or have business in Tokyo and it's cheaper to fly via Tokyo, consider this option.

For those making the trip via Tokyo's Narita Airport, note that Tokyo Station is 66km from Narita Airport. The N'EX special express train is the fastest way to travel from Narita to Tokyo Station (¥2940, one hour); the 'Airport Narita' trains are cheaper and fairly fast (¥1280, 1½ hours).

The JR *shinkansen* is the fastest and most frequent rail link between Tokyo and Kyoto (one way, ¥13,220, two hours and 40 minutes). Take a *hikari* or *nozomi shinkansen* (these are the two fastest types of *shinkansen*).

Avoid the slow *kodama shinkansen*, which stop frequently.

Shinkansen run between Tokyo and Kyoto roughly between 6am and 9pm.

Train

Kyoto is linked to the rest of the country by a multitude of excellent train lines, including the *shinkansen* (bullet train). The city is reached from most places in Japan by JR. If you'll be travelling further afield, consider buying a Japan Rail Pass (see the boxed text, p186).

There are also several private lines connecting Kyoto with Nagoya, Nara, Osaka and Kōbe. Where they exist, private lines are always cheaper than JR.

GETTING AROUND KYOTO

Kyoto has an excellent public transport system. There is a comprehensive bus network, two subway lines, six train lines (two of which can be used like subways for trips around Kyoto) and a huge fleet of taxis.

Furthermore, being largely flat, Kyoto is a great city for cycling – it's perfectly feasible to rent or buy a bicycle on your first day in the city and never have to use the public transport system.

Note that Kyoto was not designed with motor vehicles in mind. There's no need to hire a car; in fact, it's far more trouble than it's worth.

NEGOTIATING JAPAN'S RAIL SYSTEM – PASSES & PHRASES

Japan Rail Pass

The Japan Rail Pass is a must if you're planning extensive train travel within Japan. It will save you both money and the need to carry change each time you board a train (though with a Green Car Pass, you have to make reservations at a ticket office).

The most important thing to note about the pass is that Japan Rail Passes *must be purchased outside Japan.* They are only available to foreign tourists and Japanese overseas residents. The pass cannot be used for the super express *nozomi shinkansen* service, but is OK for everything else (including other *shinkansen* services). Children between the ages of six and 11 qualify for child passes, while those below six ride free.

As a one-way reserved seat Kyoto–Tokyo *shinkansen* ticket costs ¥13,220, travelling Kyoto–Tokyo–Kyoto will make a seven-day pass come close to paying off. Note that the pass is valid only on JR services (ie you still have to pay for private train services).

In order to get a pass, you must first purchase an 'exchange order' outside Japan at JAL and ANA offices or major travel agencies. Once you arrive in Japan, you must bring this order to a JR Travel Service Centre (found in most major JR stations and at Narita and Kansai international airports). When you validate your pass, you'll have to show your passport. The clock starts to tick on the pass as soon as you validate it, so don't do so it if you're just going into Tokyo or Kyoto and intend to hang around for a few days. Instead, validate when you leave those cities to explore the rest of the country.

For more information on the pass and overseas purchase locations, visit the **Japan Rail Pass** (www.japanrailpass.net/eng/en001.html) website.

DURATION (DAYS)	REGULAR ADULT (¥)	REGULAR CHILD (¥)	GREEN ADULT (¥)	GREEN CHILD (¥)
7	28,300	14,150	37,800	18,900
14	45,100	22,550	61,200	30,600
21	57,700	28,850	79,600	39,800

Useful Words & Phrases

TRAIN TYPES

shinkansen	新幹線	bullet train
tokkyū	特急	limited express
shinkaisoku	新快速	JR special rapid train
kyūkō	急行	express
kaisoku	快速	JR rapid or express
futsū	普通	local
kaku-eki-teisha	各駅停車	local

OTHER USEFUL WORDS

jiyū-seki	自由席	unreserved seat
shitei-seki	指定席	reserved seat
green-sha	グリーン車	1st-class car
ōfuku	往復	round trip
katamichi	片道	one way
kin'en-sha	禁煙車	nonsmoking car
kitsuen-sha	喫煙車	smoking car

Bus

Kyoto has an intricate network of bus routes providing an efficient way of getting around at moderate cost. Many of the routes used by visitors have announcements in English. Most buses run between 7am and 9pm, though a few run earlier or later.

The main bus terminals are also train stations: Kyoto Station (Map p220), Sanjō Station (Map p224), Karasuma-Shijō Station (Map p216), and Kitaōji Station. The bus terminal at Kyoto Station is on the north side and has three main departure bays (departure points are indicated by the letter of the bay and number of the stop within that bay).

The main bus information centre (Map p220) is located in front of Kyoto Station. Here you can pick up bus maps, purchase bus tickets and passes (on all lines, including highway buses), and get additional information.

Three-digit numbers written against a red background denote loop lines: bus 204 runs around the northern part of the city and buses 205 and 206 circle the city via Kyoto Station. Buses with route numbers on a blue background take other routes.

The TIC stocks the *Bus Navi: Kyoto City Bus Sightseeing Map*, which shows the city's main bus lines. But this map is not exhaustive. If you can read a little Japanese, pick up a copy of the regular (and more detailed) Japanese bus map available at major bus terminals throughout the city, including the main bus information centre.

Bus stops usually have a map of destinations from that stop and a timetable for the buses serving that stop. Unfortunately, all of this information is in Japanese, so nonspeakers will simply have to ask locals for help.

Entry to the bus is usually through the back door and exit is via the front door. Inner-city buses charge a flat fare (¥220), which you drop into the clear plastic receptacle on top of the machine next to the driver on your way out. A separate machine gives change for ¥100 and ¥500 coins or ¥1000 notes.

On buses serving the outer areas, take a *seiri-ken* (numbered ticket) on boarding. When alighting, an electronic board above the driver displays the fare corresponding to your ticket number (drop the *seiri-ken* into the ticket box with your fare).

When heading for locations outside the city centre, be careful which bus you board. Kyoto City buses are green, Kyoto buses are tan and Keihan buses are red and white.

Bicycle

Kyoto is a great city to explore on a bicycle. With the exception of the outlying areas, it is mostly flat and there is a useful bike path running the length of the Kamo-gawa.

Many guesthouses will rent or lend bicycles to their guests and there are also rental shops around Kyoto Station, in Arashiyama and Sagano, and in Downtown Kyoto. With a decent bicycle and a good map, you can easily make your way all around the city. Dedicated bicycle tours are also available (see p187).

Unfortunately, Kyoto's bike parking facilities must be among the worst in the world – hence the number of bikes you see haphazardly locked up around the city. Many bikes end up stolen or impounded during regular sweeps of the city (particularly those near entrances to train/subway stations). If your bike does disappear, check for a poster (in both Japanese and English) in the vicinity indicating the time of seizure and the inconvenient place you'll have to go to pay the ¥2000 fine and retrieve your bike.

The city does not impound bicycles on Sundays or holidays, so you can park pretty much wherever you wish on those days.

If you don't want to worry about your bike being stolen or impounded, we recommend using one of the city-operated bicycle and motorcycle parking lots. There is one downtown on Kiyamachi-dōri midway between Sanjō-dōri and Shijō-dōri (Map p216), another near Kyoto Station (Map p220), and another in the north of town near the Eizan Densha Station at Demachiyanagi (Map p224). These places charge ¥150 per day (buy a ticket from the machine on your way in or out).

Hire

A great place to rent a bicycle is the **Kyoto Cycling Tour Project** (KCTP; Map p220; ☎354-3636; www.kctp.net/en). The folks here rent out mountain bikes (¥1500 per day), which are perfect for getting around Kyoto, or

KYOTO EVENING BUS TOURS

Those who wish to take an evening tour of the city should consider the **Kyoto Night Cruise Bus Tour** (☎662-1700; www.kyoto-lab.jp/kanko/kyoto_night bus_eng.html; adult/child 7-12/under 7 ¥1600/800/free), operating on Thursday, Friday and Saturday evenings, and evenings before holidays. The route takes in some of Kyoto's main sights, several of which are illuminated specially for the bus. Check the website for departure times and pick-up/drop-off points.

you can pick them up at their shop. KCTP also conducts a variety of bicycle city tours, which are an excellent way to see the city (check the website for details).

The **B.B House Maruni** (B.B Houseマルニ; ☎771-6644; ⊙9am-8pm Mon-Sat) bicycle shop is a good place to rent a bicycle to explore the Northern Higashiyama area. It's within walking distance of Ginkaku-ji, but the closest bus stop is Kinrin-shako-mae. Look for it just south of a Fresco supermarket.

Most rental outfits require you to leave ID such as a passport.

Subway

Kyoto has two efficient subway lines, which operate from 5.30am to 11.30pm. Minimum adult fare is ¥210 (children ¥110).

The quickest way to travel between the north and south of the city is the Karasuma subway line. The line has 15 stops and runs from Takeda in the far south, via Kyoto Station, to the Kyoto International Conference Hall (Kokusaikaikan Station) in the north.

The east–west Tōzai subway line traverses Kyoto from Nijō Station in the west, meeting the Karasuma subway line at Karasuma-Oike Station, and continuing east to Sanjō Keihan, Yamashina and Rokujizō in the east and southeast.

Train

The main train station in Kyoto is Kyoto Station (Map220), which is actually two stations under one roof: JR Kyoto Station and Kintetsu Kyoto Station. This station is in the south of the city, just below Shichijō-dōri. The easiest way to get downtown from this station is to hop on the Karasuma subway line. There is a bus terminal on the north side of the station from where you can catch buses to all parts of town; for more information, see p187.

In addition to the private Kintetsu line that operates from Kyoto Station, there are two other private train lines in Kyoto: the Hankyū line that operates from Downtown Kyoto along Shijō-dōri and the Keihan line that operates from stops along the Kamo-gawa.

Buying a Ticket

All stations are equipped with automatic ticket machines, which are simple to operate. Destinations and fares are all posted above the machines in both Japanese and English – once you've figured out the fare to your destination, just insert your money and press the yen amount. Most of these machines accept paper currency in addition to coins (usually just ¥1000 notes). If you've made a mistake, press the red *tori-keshi* (cancel) button. There's also a help button to summon assistance.

Kansai Thru Pass

This new pass is a real bonus to travellers who plan to do a fair bit of exploration in the Kansai area. It enables you to ride on city subways, private railways and city buses in Kyoto, Nara, Osaka, Kobe and Wakayama. It also entitles you to discounts at many attractions in the Kansai area. A two-day pass costs ¥3800 and a three-day pass costs ¥5000. It is available at the Kansai airport travel counter on the 1st floor of the International Arrivals Hall and at the main bus information centre in front of Kyoto Station, among others. For more information, visit www.surutto.com/conts/ticket/3dayeng.

Discount Ticket Shops

Known as *kakuyasu-kippu-uriba,* these stores deal in discounted tickets for trains, buses, domestic flights, ferries, and a host of other things such as cut-rate stamps and phonecards. Typical savings on *shinkansen* tickets are between 5% and 10%, which is good news for long-term residents who are not eligible for Japan Rail Passes. Discount ticket agencies are found around train stations in medium and large cities. The best way to find one is to ask at the *kōban* (police box) outside the station.

Around Kyoto Station, you'll find **Tōkai Discount Ticket Shop** (Map p220; ☎north side 344-0330, south side 662-6640; ⊙north side 9:30am-7.30pm Mon-Fri, 9am-7pm Sat, Sun & holidays, south side 10am-8pm).

KYOTO BUS & SUBWAY PASSES

To save time and money you can buy a *kaisū-ken* (book of five tickets) for ¥1000. There's also a *shi-basu senyō ichinichi jōshaken cādo* (one-day card) valid for unlimited travel on city buses that costs ¥500. A similar pass *(Kyoto kankō ichinichi jōsha-ken)* that allows unlimited use of the bus and subway costs ¥1200. A *Kyoto kankō futsuka jōsha-ken* (two-day bus/subway pass) costs ¥2000. *Kaisū-ken* can be purchased directly from bus drivers. The other passes and cards can be purchased at major bus terminals and at the bus information centre. Also, be sure to refer to the Kansai Thru Pass entry.

Taxi

Taxis are a convenient, but expensive, way of getting from place to place about town. A taxi can usually be flagged down in most parts of the city at any time. There are also a large number of *takushī noriba* (taxi stands) in town, outside most train/subway stations, department stores etc.

There is no need to touch the back doors of the cars at all – the opening/closing mechanism is controlled by the driver.

Fares generally start at ¥630 for the first 2km. The exception is **MK Taxi** (☎721-2237), where fares start at ¥580. Regardless of which taxi company you go for, there's a 20% surcharge for rides between midnight and 6am. MK Taxi also provides tours of the city with English-speaking drivers. For a group of up to four people, prices start at ¥21,800 for three hours.

Two other companies that offer a similar tour service, English-speaking drivers and competitive prices are **Kyōren Taxi Service** (☎672-5111) and **Kyoto Daiichi Kōtsū** (☎602-8162).

Car & Motorcycle

Kyoto's heavy traffic and narrow roads make driving in the city difficult and stressful. You will almost always do better riding a bicycle or catching public transport. Unless you have specific needs, do not even entertain the idea of renting a car to tour the city – it's far more cost and headache than any traveller needs (plus parking fines start at ¥15,000).

However, it makes sense to rent a car if you plan to explore certain rural areas that aren't serviced by train lines (such as Miyama-chō, p137). Driving is on the left-hand side in Japan. A litre of petrol costs around ¥159.

ONLINE TRANSPORT INFORMATION

The **Kyoto-Navi System** (www.kyoto-navi.org/indexE.html) is a useful website for figuring out transport around Kyoto. The site gives detailed transport directions from downtown Kyoto to various sightseeing spots around town. The creators of the site plan on adding additional starting points in the future. The site is available in English, Korean, Chinese and Japanese.

Driving Licence & Permits

Travellers from most nations are able to drive in Japan with an International Driving Permit backed up by their own regular licence. The international permit is issued by your national automobile association and costs around US$5 in most countries. Make sure it's endorsed for cars and motorcycles if you're licensed for both.

Travellers from Switzerland, France and Germany (and others whose countries are not signatories to the Geneva Convention of 1949 concerning international driving licences) are not allowed to drive in Japan on a regular international licence. Rather, travellers from these countries must have their own licence backed by an authorised translation of the same licence. These translations can be made by their country's embassy or consulate in Japan or by the **Japan Automobile Federation** (JAF; ☎03-6833-9000, 0570-00-2811; www.jaf.or.jp/e/index_e.htm; 2-2-17 Shiba, Minato-ku, Tokyo 105-0014).

Hire

There are several car-rental agencies in Kyoto. **Toyota Rentacar Kyoto Eki Shinkansen-guchi Branch** (Map p220; ☎365-0100; http://rent.toyota.co.jp/en/index.html; Minami-ku, Higashi Kujo Kamitonoda-cho 31-1) is about 200m walk from the south (Hachijō) exit of Kyoto Station. The **Toyota Rentacar Hyakumamben Branch** (Map p224; ☎702-8100; http://rent.toyota.co.jp/en/index.html; Sakyo-ku, Tanakamonzen-cho 103-31) at the Hyakumamben intersection in Northern Higashiyama, is good for those heading north into the Kitayama Area. **Matsuda Rent-a-Car** (☎361-0201; www.mazda-rentacar.com/en; Shimogyo-ku, Gojo-dori Kawaramachi Nishi iru, Hongakujimae-cho 811) is close to the intersection of Kawaramachi-dōri and Gojō-dōri. You'll need to produce an International Driving Permit.

Typical hire rates for a small car are about ¥5000 to ¥7000 for the first day, with reductions for rentals of more than one day. Move up a bracket and you're looking at about ¥9000 to ¥14,000 for the first day, with reductions for rentals of more than one day. On top of the hire charge, there's a ¥1000 per day insurance cost.

Communication can be a major problem when hiring a car. If you cannot find a local to assist you with the paperwork, speaking a little Japanese will help greatly. Some of the offices will have a rent-a-car phrasebook, with questions you might need to ask in English. Otherwise, just speak as slowly as possible and hope for the best.

Directory A–Z

Business Hours

The following are typical business hours in Japan. Reviews in this book don't list business hours unless they differ from these standards. Note that restaurants and shops are often closed irregularly.

Banks 9am to 3pm Monday to Friday

Bars 7pm to late, closed one day per week

Companies 9am to 5pm or 6pm Monday to Friday

Department stores 10am to 7pm, closed one or two days/month

Post offices 9am to 5pm Monday to Friday; central post offices open to 7pm Monday to Friday and 9am to 3pm Saturday

Restaurants 11am to 2pm, 6pm to 11pm, closed one day per week

Smaller shops 9am to 5pm, may be closed Sunday

Customs Regulations

Alcohol	up to 3 760cc bottles
Gifts/souvenirs	up to ¥200,000 in total value
Perfume	2 ounces
Tobacco products	100 cigars/400 cigarettes/500g loose

Electricity

The Japanese electric current is 100V AC. Tokyo and eastern Japan are on 50Hz, and western Japan – including Nagoya, Kyoto and Osaka – is on 60Hz.

Most electrical items from other elsewhere in the world will function on Japanese current.

Both transformers and plug adaptors are readily available in Kyoto's Teramachi-dōri electronics district, running south of Shijō-dōri (Map p216) or at Bic Camera (p52).

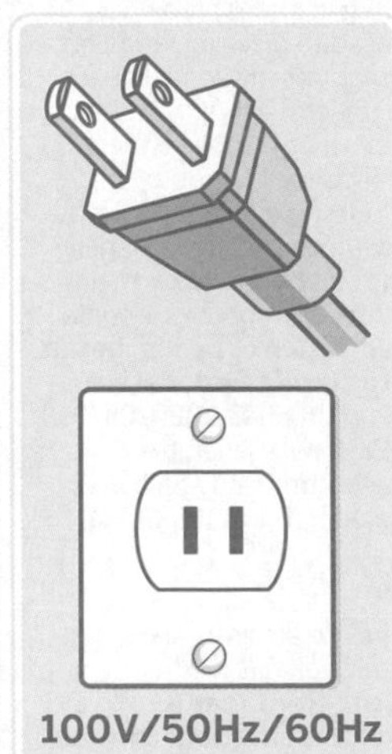

Embassies

Australia (☎03-5232-4111; www.australia.or.jp/en; 2-1-14 Mita, Minato-ku, Tokyo)

Canada (☎03-5412-6200; www.canadanet.or.jp/english.shtml; 7-3-38 Akasaka, Minato-ku, Tokyo)

China (☎03-3403-3388; 3-4-33 Moto-Azabu, Minato-ku)

France (☎03-5798-6000; www.ambafrance-jp.org; 4-11-44 Minami Azabu, Minato-ku, Tokyo)

Germany (☎03-5791-7700; www.tokyo.diplo.de/Vertretung/tokyo/de/Startseite.html; 4-5-10 Minami Azabu, Minato-ku, Tokyo)

Ireland (☎03-3263-0695; www.irishembassy.jp; Ireland House, 2-10-7 Kōji-machi, Chiyoda-ku, Tokyo)

Netherlands (☎03-5776-5400; www.mfa.nl/tok-en; 3-6-3 Shiba-kōen, Minato-ku, Tokyo)

New Zealand (☎03-3467-2271; www.nzembassy.com/home.cfm?c=17; 20-40 Kamiyama-chō, Shibuya-ku, Tokyo)

South Korea (☎03-3452-7611; http://jpn-tokyo.mofat.go.kr/jpn/index.jsp, in Japanese; 4-4-10 Yotsuya, Shinjuku-ku, Tokyo)

UK (☎03-5211-1100; www.uknow.or.jp/index_e.htm; 1 Ichiban-chō, Chiyoda-ku, Tokyo)

USA (☎03-3224-5000; http://japan.usembassy.gov/t-main.html; 1-10-5 Akasaka, Minato-ku, Tokyo)

Emergency

Although most emergency operators in Kyoto don't speak English, they will refer you to someone who does. Have your address at hand when calling for assistance.

Ambulance (☎119)

Fire (☎119)

Police (☎110)

Kōban (police boxes) are small police stations typically found at city intersections. Most can be recognised by the small, round red lamp outside. They are a logical place to head in an emergency, but remember that the police may not always speak English.

Gay & Lesbian Travellers

With the possible exception of Thailand, Japan is Asia's most enlightened nation with regard to the sexual preferences of foreigners. Some travellers have reported problems when checking into love hotels with a partner of the same sex, and it does pay to be discreet in rural areas. Apart from this, however, same-sex couples are unlikely to encounter too many problems.

While there is a sizable gay community in Kyoto, and a number of establishments where gay men do congregate, they will take a fair amount of digging to discover. There's a more active scene in Osaka and many of Kyoto's gay residents make the trip there. Lesbian women are poorly served in Kyoto and Osaka and it's difficult to find specifically lesbian-friendly venues.

Utopia (www.utopia-asia.com) is the site most commonly frequented by English-speaking gay and lesbian people.

PRACTICALITIES

➡ **Newspapers & Magazines** There are three main English-language newspapers in Japan: the *Japan Times, Daily Yomiuri* and *Asahi Shimbun/International Herald Tribune*. A good source of information on Kyoto, and the rest of the Kansai area, is *Kansai Scene* (www.kansaiscene.com). The *Kyoto Visitor's Guide* is another good source of information on cultural and tourist events. You'll find these in large bookshops and international hotels. Some convenience stores carry English-language newspapers.

➡ **Weights & Measures** Japan uses the international metric system.

Health

Japan is an advanced country with high standards of hygiene and few endemic diseases. There are no special immunisations needed to visit Japan and, other than bringing prescription medications from home, no special preparations need to be to make. For information on hospitals in Kyoto, see p193.

Internet Access

In this book, an internet symbol (@) indicates that the accommodation option has at least one computer with internet access for guests' use.

ADDRESSES IN KYOTO

In Japan, finding a place from its address can be difficult, even for locals. The problem is twofold: first, the address is given by an area rather than a street; and second, the numbers are not necessarily consecutive. To find an address, the usual process is to ask directions. The numerous local police boxes are there largely for this purpose.

In this guide, we use a simplified system for addresses. We either give the area (eg Higashiyama-ku, Nanzen-ji) or we give the street on which the place is located, followed by the nearest cross street (eg Karasuma-dōri-Imadegawa). In some cases, we also give additional information to show where the place lies in relation to the intersection of the two streets mentioned. In Kyoto, the land usually slopes gently to the south; thus, an address might indicate whether a place lies above or north of *(agaru)* or below or south of *(sagaru* or *kudaru)* a particular east–west road. An address might also indicate whether a place lies east *(higashi)* or west *(nishi)* of the north–south road. Thus, Karasuma-dōri-Imadegawa simply means the place is near the intersection of Karasuma-dōri and Imadegawa-dōri; Karasuma-dōri-Imadegawa-sagaru indicates that it's south of that intersection.

ETTING ONLINE IN KYOTO

Japan is one of the world's most technologically advanced countries, but if you're expecting to find free internet hot spots wherever you go, you're in for a surprise. Sure, wi-fi or mobile internet is everywhere, but most of it is available only to subscribers of various Japanese services, many of which are not easy for travellers to join (especially those who don't speak and read Japanese). **Freespot Map** (www.freespot.com/users/map_e.html) has a list of internet hotspots in Japan; it's not exhaustive and the maps are in Japanese, but it's quite useful. Failing that, here are some ways to get online:

FON Network Virtually all Starbucks in Japan have FON wi-fi. Foneros (FON members) can connect for free; non-members can use Google services like Gmail for free. Other services are charged (credit-card payment is possible).

SIM cards If you bring an internet device that takes a SIM card, you can buy B-Mobile data SIM cards from major electronics shops in Japan. These will usually allow unlimited internet use for a specific length of time (a month is common).

Boingo Subscribers to the **Boingo** (www.boingo.com) global plan can use BB Mobilepoint wi-fi at McDonald's restaurants in Japan.

Portable internet connections You can rent data cards, USB dongles or pocket wi-fi devices from various phone rental companies in Japan. The most user-friendly option with English-language service is provided by **Rentafone Japan** (www.rentafonejapan.com), which offers two types of pocket wi-fi from ¥3900 per week with unlimited usage.

We also note where wi-fi (wi-fi icon) is available. Note that wi-fi is far less common in Japanese hotels than in their Western counterparts. About one-third of hotels in Japan have free wi-fi, another third charge for wi-fi, and the remainder have no wi-fi at all.

It is much more common to find LAN cable internet access points in hotel rooms (the hotels can usually provide LAN cables, but it's much more convenient to bring your own to avoid having to get hold of one in each place you stay).

These LAN connections usually work fine, but you may occasionally find it hard to log on due to software or hardware compatibility issues or configuration problems – in these cases the front desk staff *may* be able to help.

You'll find internet cafes and other access points in most major Japanese cities. As a rule, internet connections are both fast (using DSL or ADSL) and reliable in Japan.

Internet in a Nutshell

Current	60Hz in west Japan including Kyoto, 100V AC; 50Hz in east Japan
Plugs	flat two-pin type
Connections	Cable access more common than wi-fi
Internet cafe rates	¥200 to ¥700 per hour

Internet Terminals

The following are some places where you can log on in Kyoto.

Kyoto International Community House (KICH; Map p224; ☎752-3512; Sakyō-ku, Awataguchi, Torii-chō 2-1; per 30min ¥200; Ⓜ5min walk from Keage Station, Tōzai subway line) The machines here have Japanese keyboards and you are limited in the sites you can visit, but it's a fairly cheap place to log on.

Kyoto Prefectural International Center (Map p220; ☎342-5000; 9th fl, Kyoto Station Bldg; per 15min ¥100; ⏲10am-6pm; ⓂKyoto Station) In addition to using the machines provided, you can also log on with your own laptop here. It's closed on the 2nd and 4th Tuesday of each month.

Kinko's (Map p216; ☎213-6802; Nakagyō-ku, Tearaimizu-chō 651-1, Takoyakushi sagaru, Karasuma dōri; per 10min ¥210 (first 10min ¥262); ⏲24hr; Ⓜ5min walk from Karasuma Station, Hankyū line) This copy shop has several terminals where you can log on. It's expensive but conveniently located.

Tops Café (Map p220; ☎681-9270; www.topsnet.co.jp/5/index.html; Kyoto-eki, Hachijō-guchi; per 15min ¥120, plus registration fee ¥200; ⏲24hr; ⓂKyoto Station) This is an all-night manga/internet cafe where you can actually spend the night in the booths if you want. It's just outside the south (Hachijō) exit of Kyoto Station.

Maps

Available free at the TIC (see p196), the *Kyoto City Map* is a decent map of the city with several detailed insets of the major sightseeing districts. Also available is the *Bus Navi: Kyoto City Bus Sightseeing Map*, which has detailed information on bus routes in the city and some of the major stops written in both English and Japanese.

There are many other useful maps for sale at local English-language bookshops, some of which are practical for excursions outside Kyoto. Shōbunsha's *Tourist Map of Kyoto, Nara, Osaka and Kōbe* is the best privately produced map of these cities.

Medical Services

Medical care in Japan is reasonably priced, particularly in comparison to costs in the United States. The quality of care varies enormously, from completely competent to dangerously incompetent. You'll usually find the best doctors in large teaching hospitals, like Kyoto University Hospital. Small local clinics should be avoided unless there are no other choices.

Many hospitals and clinics will be wary of treating foreigners because they don't know how payment will be made (most Japanese belong to the national health system). Where necessary, show proof of your travel insurance or cash. If treatment is absolutely necessary, demanding firmly but politely to be treated is the best approach.

Kyoto University Hospital (Map p224; ☎751-3111; 54 Shōgoinkawara-chō, Sakyō-ku; ⏰8.30am-11am; 🚌5min walk from Konoe-dōri bus stop, bus 206 from Kyoto Station) is the best hospital in Kyoto. There is an information counter near the entrance that can point you in the right direction. Patients without appointments are seen in the morning. Go at 8.30am to reduce your wait (they start seeing patients at 9am).

Money

The currency in Japan is the yen (¥). The Japanese pronounce yen as 'en', with no 'y' sound. The kanji for yen is: 円. Yen coins come in the following denominations:

- ¥1 lightweight, silver colour
- ¥5 bronze colour, hole in the middle, value in Chinese character
- ¥10 copper colour
- ¥50 silver colour, hole in the middle
- ¥100 silver colour
- ¥500 large with silver colour

Yen banknotes come in the following denominations:

- ¥1000
- ¥2000 (rare)
- ¥5000
- ¥10,000

ATMs

Automated teller machines are almost as common as vending machines in Japan. Unfortunately, most of these do not accept foreign-issued cards. Even if they display Visa and MasterCard logos, most accept only Japan-issued versions of these cards.

Fortunately, Japanese postal ATMs accept cards that belong to the following international networks: Visa, Plus, MasterCard, Maestro, Cirrus American Express and Diners Club. Check the sticker(s) on the back of your card to see which network(s) your card belongs to. You'll find postal ATMs in almost all post offices, and you'll find post offices in even the smallest Japanese village.

Note that postal ATMs work with bank or cash cards – you cannot use credit cards, even with a PIN number, in postal ATMs. That is to say, you cannot use postal ATMs to perform a cash advance.

Most postal ATMs are open 9am to 5pm on weekdays, 9am to noon on Saturday, and are closed on Sunday and holidays. Some postal ATMs in very large central post offices are open longer hours. If you need cash outside these hours, try the **Kyoto central post office** (Map p220; ⏰ATM 12.05am-11.55pm Mon-Sat, 12.05am-9pm Sun & holidays), next to Kyoto Station.

Citibank (Map p216) has a 24-hour ATM in its lobby that accepts most foreign-issued cards. Note that only holders of Japan-issued Citibank cards can access the ATM after hours. To get there, start at the Shijō-Karasumaa intersection and walk

WARNING: JAPAN IS A CASH SOCIETY!

Be warned that cold hard yen (¥) is the way to pay in Japan. While credit cards are becoming more common, cash is still much more widely used, and travellers cheques are rarely accepted. Do not assume that you can pay for things with a credit card; always carry sufficient cash. The only places where you can count on paying with plastic are department stores and large hotels.

For those without credit cards, it would be a good idea to bring some travellers cheques as a back-up. As in most other countries, the US dollar is still the currency of choice in terms of exchanging cash and cashing travellers cheques.

... south side of ...ōri. You'll see it ...ter about 100m. ...Eleven conven... ...cross Japan ...their ATMs to international cash networks, and these often seem to accept cards that for one reason or other will not work with postal ATMs. They are also open 24 hours. So, if you can't find an open post office or your card won't work with postal ATMs, don't give up: ask around for a 7-Eleven (pronounced like 'sebun erebun' in Japanese).

Changing Money

You can change cash or travellers cheques at most banks, major post offices, discount ticket shops, some travel agents, some large hotels and most big department stores. Note that discount ticket shops (known as *kakuyasu kippu uriba* in Japanese) often have the best rates. These can be found around Kyoto Station. However, only the US dollar and euro fetch decent exchange rates (see p194).

Most major banks are located near the Shijō-Karasuma intersection, two stops north of Kyoto Station on the Karasuma subway line. Of these, **UFJ Bank** (Map p216; ☎211 4583) is the most convenient for changing money and buying travellers cheques.

USING A JAPANESE POSTAL ATM

Postal ATMs are relatively easy to use. Here's the drill:

- ➡ 1. Press 'English Guide'
- ➡ 2. Select 'Withdrawal'
- ➡ 3. Insert card
- ➡ 4. Select desired transaction
- ➡ 5. Confirm
- ➡ 6. Input PIN number
- ➡ 7. Input amount
- ➡ 8. Confirm

CURRENCY WARNING

Exchange rates for the US dollar and the euro are reasonable in Japan. All other currencies, including the Australian dollar and the currencies of nearby countries, fetch very poor exchange rates. If you want to bring cash to Japan, we suggest US dollars or euros. Or, if you must change other currencies into yen, we suggest doing so in your home country.

Credit Cards

You can get cash advances on Visa cards at the 1st-floor Kyoto Marui Department Store branch of **Mitsui Sumitomo Bank** (Map p216; ☎223-2821).

Currently there is no representation for international cardholders in Kyoto. For inquiries it is often best to try the offices in Tokyo or call the number in your home country on the back of your card:

Amex (☎0120-020-120)

MasterCard (☎03-5728-5200)

Visa (☎03-5275-7604)

Post

Opening Hours

Local post offices 9am to 5pm Monday to Friday

Central post offices 9am to 7pm Monday to Friday, 9am to 3pm Saturday, closed Sunday

Branches

The **Kyoto central post office** (Map p220; ☎365-2467; ⏰9am-9pm Mon-Fri, to 7pm Sat, Sun & holidays) is on the north side of Kyoto Station. Poste restante mail can be collected here. There's a service counter on the south side of the building open 24 hours per day for airmail, small packages and special express mail services.

Nakagyō post office (Map p216; ☎255-1112) at the Nishinotōin-Sanjō crossing is open until 7pm on weekdays, 3pm on Saturdays but is closed on Sundays and holidays. There is a 24-hour service window on the west side of the building.

Postal Rates

The airmail rate for postcards is ¥70 to any overseas destination; aerograms cost ¥90. Letters weighing less than 25g are ¥90 to other countries within Asia, ¥110 to North America, Europe or Oceania (including Australia and New Zealand), and ¥130 to Africa and South America. One peculiarity of the Japanese postal system is that you will be charged extra if your writing runs over onto the address side (the right side) of a postcard. All post offices provide a reliable international Express Mail Service (EMS), which is as good or better than private express shipping services.

Sending & Receiving Mail

The symbol for post offices is a red T with a bar across the top on a white background (〒). Mail can be sent to, from or within Japan when addressed in English (Roman script).

Public Holidays

Japan has 15 national holidays. When a public holiday falls on a Sunday, the following Monday is taken as a holiday. If that Monday is already a holiday, the following day becomes a holiday as well. And, if two weekdays (say, Tuesday and Thursday) are holidays, the day in between (Wednesday) will also become a holiday.

Ganjitsu (New Year's Day) 1 January

Seijin-no-hi (Coming-of-Age Day) Second Monday in January

Kenkoku Kinem-bi (National Foundation Day) 11 February

Shumbun-no-hi (Spring Equinox) 20 or 21 March

Shōwa-no-hi (Shōwa Emperor's Day) 29 April

Kempō Kinem-bi (Constitution Day) 3 May

Midori-no-hi (Green Day) 4 May

Kodomo-no-hi (Children's Day) 5 May

Umi-no-hi (Marine Day) Third Monday in July

Keirō-no-hi (Respect-for-the-Aged Day) Second Monday in September

Shūbun-no-hi (Autumn Equinox) 22 or 23 September

Taiiku-no-hi (Health-Sports Day) Second Monday in October

Bunka-no-hi (Culture Day) 3 November

Kinrō Kansha-no-hi (Labour Thanksgiving Day) 23 November

Tennō Tanjōbi (Emperor's Birthday) 23 December

Taxes & Refunds

There is a 5% consumption tax on retail purchases in Japan. Visitors on a short-stay visa can, however, avoid this tax on purchases made at major department stores and duty-free stores such as the Kyoto Handicraft Center (p###). For a refund on purchases, check first that the department store has a service desk for tax refunds. When you make a purchase the tax will be included; take the purchase, receipt and your passport to the service desk for an immediate refund.

If you eat at expensive restaurants and stay at first-class accommodation, you will encounter a service charge, which varies from 10% to 15%. A tax of 5% is added to restaurant bills exceeding ¥5000 or for hotel bills exceeding ¥10,000.

Telephone

The area code for greater Kyoto is ☎075; unless otherwise indicated, all numbers in this book fall into this area. Japanese telephone codes consist of an area code plus a local code and number. You do not dial the area code when making a call in that area. When dialling Japan from abroad, the country code is ☎81, followed by the area code (drop the 0) and the number.

Directory Assistance

Local directory assistance ☎104 (¥60-150 per call)

Local directory assistance in English ☎0120-36-4463 (9am to 5pm Monday to Friday)

International directory assistance ☎0057

International Calls

The best way to make an international phone call from Japan is to use a prepaid international phone card (see p195).

Paid overseas calls can be made from grey international ISDN phones. These are usually found in phone booths marked 'International & Domestic Card/Coin Phone'. Unfortunately, these are very rare; try looking in the lobbies of top-end hotels and at airports. Some new green phones found in phone booths also allow international calls. Calls are charged by the unit, each of which is six seconds, so if you don't have much to say you could phone home for just ¥100. Reverse-charge (collect) overseas calls can be made from any pay phone.

You can save money by calling late at night. Economy rates are available from 11pm to 8am. Note that it is also cheaper to make domestic calls by dialling outside the standard hours.

Useful International Numbers

Direct-dial international numbers include the following. There's very little difference in their rates. Dial one of the numbers, then the international country code, the local code and the number.

- ☎001 010 (KDDI)
- ☎0033 010 (NTT)
- ☎0041 010 (SoftBank Telecom)

For international operator-assisted calls dial ☎0051 (KDDI; operators speak English).

Prepaid International Phone Cards

Because of the lack of pay phones from which you can make international phone calls in Japan, the easiest way to make an international call is to buy a prepaid international phone card. Most convenience stores carry at least one of the following types of phone cards. These cards can be used with any regular pay phone in Japan.

- KDDI Superworld Card
- NTT Communications World Card
- SoftBank Telecom Comica Card

Local Calls

The Japanese public telephone system is extremely reliable and efficient.

Unfortunately, the number of pay phones is decreasing fast as more and more Japanese buy mobile phones. Local calls from pay phones cost ¥10 per minute; unused ¥10 coins are returned after the call is completed but no change is given on ¥100 coins.

In general it's much easier to buy a telephone card *(terefon kādo)* when you arrive rather than worry about always having coins on hand. Phone cards are sold in ¥500 and ¥1000 denominations (the latter earns you an extra ¥50 in calls) and can be used in most green or grey pay phones. They are available from vending machines (some of which can be found in public phone booths) and convenience stores. They come in a myriad of designs and are also a collectable item.

Mobile Phones

Japan's mobile-phone networks use 3G (3rd generation) technology on a variety of frequencies. Thus, non-3G mobile phones cannot be used in Japan. This means that most foreign mobile phones *will not work* in Japan. Furthermore, SIM cards are not commonly available in Japan. Thus, for most people who want to use a mobile phone while in Japan, the only solution is to rent a mobile phone.

Several telecommunications companies in Japan specialise in short-term mobile-phone rentals, which is a good option for travellers whose own phones won't work in Japan, or whose own phones would be prohibitively expensive to use here.

The following companies provide this service:

Mobile Phone Japan (☎090-6660-7645; www.mobilephonejp.com) This company offers basic mobile-phone rental for as low as ¥2900 per week. Incoming calls (whether international or domestic) are free, and outgoing domestic calls are ¥90 per minute (outgoing international calls vary according to country and time of day). Free delivery anywhere in Japan is included and a free prepaid return envelope is also included.

Rentafone Japan (☎0120-74-6487; www.rentafonejapan.com) This company rents out mobile phones for ¥3900 per week and offers free delivery of the phone to your accommodation. Domestic rates are ¥35 per minute and overseas calls are ¥45 per minute.

Time

Kyoto local time is nine hours ahead of GMT/UTC. There is no daylight-savings time. When it's noon in Kyoto, it's 7pm (the day before) in Los Angeles, 10pm (the day before) in Montreal and New York, 3am (the same day) in London, 4am in Frankfurt, Paris and Rome, 11am in Hong Kong, 1pm in Melbourne, and 3pm in Wellington.

Tourist Information

The following local tourist offices are good sources for maps and information:

Kyoto Tourist Information Center (TIC; Map p220; ☎343-0548; 2F Kyoto Station Bldg; ⏲8:30am-7pm) Located in the main concourse on the 2nd floor of the Kyoto Station building that runs between the *shinkansen* station and the front of the station (near Isetan department store), this is the main tourist information centre in Kyoto. English speakers are always on hand and, occasionally, speakers of other European and Asian languages are available. They stock useful maps of the city, as well as bus maps, and can answer most of your questions. Note that it's called 'Kyo Navi' in Japanese (in case you have to ask someone).

Kyoto City Tourist Information (Map p220; ☎343-6655; ⏲8.30am-7pm) Inside the new Kyoto Station building, on the 2nd floor, it's geared towards Japanese visitors, though an English-speaking staff member is usually on hand and it's easier to find than the following places listed here.

Tourist Information at Kyoto City Center (Map p216; ⏲10am-6pm, closed Tue) This new tourist information centre is right downtown (just north of the Shijō-Kawaramachi intersection). They stock a variety of maps and there's usually an English-speaker on hand.

Kansai International Airport tourist information counter (☎0724-56-6025; ⏲8.30am-8.30pm) This counter is on the 1st floor of the international arrivals hall. Staff here can provide information on Kyoto, Kansai and Japan.

Kyoto International Community House (KICH; Map p224; ☎752-3010; Sakyō-ku, Awataguchi, Torii-chō 2-1; ⏲9am-9pm Tue-Sun; Ⓜ5min walk from Keage Station, Tōzai subway line) An essential stop for those planning a long-term stay in Kyoto, the KICH can also be quite useful for short-term visitors. It has a library with maps, books, newspapers and magazines from around the world, and a board displaying messages regarding work, accommodation, rummage sales etc. You can send and receive faxes, and use the internet (¥200 per 30 minutes). You can also pick up a copy of its excellent *Guide to Kyoto* map and its *Easy Living in Kyoto* book (note that both of these are intended for residents). You can also chill out in the lobby and watch CNN news.

Travel Agencies

Kyoto has several good central travel agencies that can arrange discount air tickets, car rental and accommodation, as well as other services. These agencies include **IACE Travel** (Map p216; ☎212-8944; Nakagyō-ku, Karasuma dōri, Shijō agaru, Takanna-chō 688, Dai15Hase Bldg, 4F; ⊙10am-7pm Mon-Fri, 11am-6pm Sat; Ⓜ1min walk from Shijō Station, Subway Karasuma line), which offers phone consultations from 10am to 5pm Sundays and holidays on ☎06-6265-3337.

Travellers With Disabilities

Although Kyoto has made some attempts at making public facilities more accessible, its narrow streets and the terrain of sights such as temples and shrines make it a challenging city for people with disabilities, especially for those in wheelchairs.

If you are going to travel by train and need assistance, ask one of the station workers as you enter the station.

There are carriages on most lines that have areas set aside for those in wheelchairs. Those with other physical disabilities can use one of the seats set aside near the train exits; these are called *yūsen-zaseki* and are usually a different colour from the other seats in the carriage, making them easy to spot. You'll also find these seats near the front of buses; usually they're a different colour from the regular seats.

MK Taxi (☎721-2237) can accommodate wheelchairs in many of its cars and is an attractive possibility for anyone interested in touring the city by cab.

Facilities for the visually impaired include musical pedestrian lights at many city intersections and raised bumps on railway platforms for guidance.

AD-Brain (the same outfit that publishes the monthly *Kyoto Visitor's Guide*) has produced a basic city map for people with disabilities and senior citizens. It shows wheelchair-access points in town and gives information on public transport access etc. The map is available at the TIC (see p196).

The most useful information for disabled visitors to Japan is provided by the **Japanese Red Cross Language Service Volunteers** (housi@tok-lanserv.jp; www.tok-lanserv.jp/index.html, in Japanese; c/o Volunteers Division, Japanese Red Cross Society, 1-1-3 Shiba Daimon, Minato-ku, Tokyo 105-8521, Japan).

Visas

Generally, visitors who are not planning to engage in income-producing activities while in Japan are exempt from obtaining visas and will be issued a *tanki-taizai* (temporary visitor) visa on arrival.

The following nationalities are eligible for a 90-day temporary visitor visa on arrival:

- Australia
- Canada
- France
- Germany
- Ireland
- Italy
- Netherlands
- New Zealand
- Spain
- UK
- USA

Stays of up to six months are permitted for citizens of Austria, Germany, Ireland, Mexico, Switzerland and the UK. Citizens of these countries will almost always be given a 90-day temporary visitor visa upon arrival, which can usually be extended for another 90 days at immigration bureaux inside Japan.

Japanese law requires that visitors to the country entering on a temporary visitor visa possess an ongoing air or sea ticket or evidence thereof. In practice, few travellers are asked to produce such documents, but to avoid surprises it pays to be on the safe side.

Note that on entering Japan, all short-term foreign visitors are required to be photographed and fingerprinted. This happens when you show your passport on arrival.

Women Travellers

Japan is a relatively safe country for women travellers, though perhaps not as safe as some might think. Women travellers are occasionally subjected to some form of verbal harassment or prying questions. Physical attacks are very rare, but have occurred.

The best advice is to avoid being lulled into a false sense of security by Japan's image as one of the world's safest countries and to take the normal precautions you would in your home country. If a neighbourhood or establishment looks unsafe, then treat it that way. As long as you use your common sense, you will most likely find that Japan is a pleasant and rewarding place to travel.

Several train companies in Japan have recently introduced women-only cars to protect female passengers from *chikan* (men who feel up women and girls on packed trains). These cars are usually available during rush-hour periods on weekdays on busy urban lines. There are signs (usually pink in colour) on the platform indicating where to board these cars, and the cars themselves are usually labelled in both Japanese and English (again, these are often marked in pink).

Language

Japanese is spoken by more than 125 million people. While it bears some resemblance to Altaic languages such as Mongolian and Turkish and has grammatical similarities to Korean, its origins are unclear. Chinese is responsible for the existence of many Sino-Japanese words in Japanese, and for the originally Chinese kanji characters which the Japanese use in combination with the homegrown hiragana and katakana scripts.

Japanese pronunciation is easy to master for English speakers, as most of its sounds are also found in English. If you read our coloured pronunciation guides as if they were English, you'll be understood. In Japanese, it's important to make the distinction between short and long vowels, as vowel length can change the meaning of a word. The long vowels, shown in our pronunciation guides with a horizontal line on top of them (ā, ē, ī, ō, ū), should be held twice as long as the short ones. It's also important to make the distinction between single and double consonants, as this can produce a difference in meaning. Pronounce the double consonants with a slight pause between them, eg sak·ka (writer).

Note also that the vowel sound ai is pronounced as in 'aisle', air as in 'pair' and ow as in 'how'. As for the consonants, ts is pronounced as in 'hats', f sounds almost like 'fw' (with rounded lips), and r is halfway between 'r' and 'l'. All syllables in a word are pronounced fairly evenly in Japanese.

WANT MORE?

For in-depth language information and handy phrases, check out Lonely Planet's *Japanese phrasebook*. You'll find it at **shop.lonelyplanet.com**, or you can buy Lonely Planet's iPhone phrasebooks at the Apple App Store.

BASICS

Japanese uses an array of registers of speech to reflect social and contextual hierarchy, but these can be simplified to the form most appropriate for the situation, which is what we've done in this language guide too.

Hello.	こんにちは。	kon·ni·chi·wa
Goodbye.	さようなら。	sa·yō·na·ra
Yes.	はい。	hai
No.	いいえ。	ī·e
Please. (when asking)	ください。	ku·da·sai
Please. (when offering)	どうぞ。	dō·zo
Thank you.	ありがとう。	a·ri·ga·tō
Excuse me. (to get attention)	すみません。	su·mi·ma·sen
Sorry.	ごめんなさい。	go·men·na·sai

You're welcome.
どういたしまして。 dō i·ta·shi·mash·te

How are you?
お元気ですか? o·gen·ki des ka

Fine. And you?
はい、元気です。 hai, gen·ki des
あなたは? a·na·ta wa

What's your name?
お名前は何ですか? o·na·ma·e wa nan des ka

My name is ...
私の名前は …です。 wa·ta·shi no na·ma·e wa ... des

Do you speak English?
英語が話せますか? ē·go ga ha·na·se·mas ka

I don't understand.
わかりません。 wa·ka·ri·ma·sen

Does anyone speak English?
どなたか英語を話せますか? do·na·ta ka ē·go o ha·na·se·mas ka

ACCOMMODATION

Where's a ...?	…が ありますか?	... ga a·ri·mas ka
campsite	キャンプ場	kyam·pu·jō
guesthouse	民宿	min·shu·ku
hotel	ホテル	ho·te·ru
inn	旅館	ryo·kan
youth hostel	ユース ホステル	yū·su· ho·su·te·ru

Do you have a ... room?	…ルームは ありますか?	...·rū·mu wa a·ri·mas ka
single	シングル	shin·gu·ru
double	ダブル	da·bu·ru

How much is it per ...?	…いくら ですか?	... i·ku·ra des ka
night	1泊	ip·pa·ku
person	1人	hi·to·ri

air-con	エアコン	air·kon
bathroom	風呂場	fu·ro·ba
window	窓	ma·do

DIRECTIONS

Where's the ...?
…はどこですか? ... wa do·ko des ka

Can you show me (on the map)?
(地図で)教えて くれませんか? (chi·zu de) o·shi·e·te ku·re·ma·sen ka

What's the address?
住所は何ですか? jū·sho wa nan des ka

Could you please write it down?
書いてくれませんか? kai·te ku·re·ma·sen ka

behind ...	…の後ろ	... no u·shi·ro
in front of ...	…の前	... no ma·e
near ...	…の近く	... no chi·ka·ku
next to ...	…のとなり	... no to·na·ri
opposite ...	…の 向かい側	... no mu·kai·ga·wa
straight ahead	この先	ko·no sa·ki

Turn ...	…まがって ください。	... ma·gat·te ku·da·sai
at the corner	その角を	so·no ka·do o
at the traffic lights	その信号を	so·no shin·gō o
left	左へ	hi·da·ri e
right	右へ	mi·gi e

KEY PATTERNS

To get by in Japanese, mix and match these simple patterns with words of your choice:

When's (the next bus)?
(次のバスは) 何時ですか? (tsu·gi no bas wa) nan·ji des ka

Where's (the station)?
(駅は)どこですか? (e·ki wa) do·ko des ka

Do you have (a map)?
(地図) がありますか? (chi·zu) ga a·ri·mas ka

Is there (a toilet)?
(トイレ) がありますか? (toy·re) ga a·ri·mas ka

I'd like (the menu).
(メニュー) をお願いします。 (me·nyū) o o·ne·gal shi·mas

Can I (sit here)?
(ここに座って) もいいですか? (ko·ko ni su·wat·te) mo ī des ka

I need (a can opener).
(缶切り) が必要です。 (kan·ki·ri) ga hi·tsu·yō des

Do I need (a visa)?
(ビザ) が必要ですか? (bi·za) ga hi·tsu·yō des ka

I have (a reservation).
(予約)があります。 (yo·ya·ku) ga a·ri·mas

I'm (a teacher).
私は(教師) です。 wa·ta·shi wa (kyō·shi) des

EATING & DRINKING

I'd like to reserve a table for (two people).
(2人)の予約を お願いします。 (fu·ta·ri) no yo·ya·ku o o·ne·gai shi·mas

What would you recommend?
なにが おすすめですか? na·ni ga o·su·su·me des ka

What's in that dish?
あの料理に何 が入っていますか? a·no ryō·ri ni na·ni ga hait·te i·mas ka

Do you have any vegetarian dishes?
ベジタリアン料理 がありますか? be·ji·ta·ri·an ryō·ri ga a·ri·mas ka

I'm a vegetarian.
私は ベジタリアンです。 wa·ta·shi wa be·ji·ta·ri·an des

I'm a vegan.
私は厳格な 菜食主義者 です。 wa·ta·shi wa gen·ka·ku na sai·sho·ku·shu·gi·sha des

Signs

入口	**Entrance**
出口	**Exit**
営業中/開館	**Open**
閉店/閉館	**Closed**
インフォメーション	**Information**
危険	**Danger**
トイレ	**Toilets**
男	**Men**
女	**Women**

I don't eat ...	…は 食べません。	... wa ta·be·ma·sen
dairy products	乳製品	nyū·sē·hin
(red) meat	(赤身の) 肉	(a·ka·mi no) ni·ku
meat or dairy products	肉や 乳製品は	ni·ku ya nyū·sē·hin
pork	豚肉	bu·ta·ni·ku
seafood	シーフード 海産物	shī·fū·do/ kai·sam·bu·tsu

Is it cooked with pork lard or chicken stock?
これはラードか鶏の だしを使って いますか?
ko·re wa rā·do ka to·ri no da·shi o tsu·kat·te i·mas ka

I'm allergic to (peanuts).
私は (ピーナッツ)に アレルギーが あります。
wa·ta·shi wa (pī·nat·tsu) ni a·re·ru·gī ga a·ri·mas

That was delicious!
おいしかった。
oy·shi·kat·ta

Cheers!
乾杯!
kam·pai

Please bring the bill.
お勘定をください。
o·kan·jō o ku·da·sai

Key Words

appetisers	前菜	zen·sai
bottle	ビン	bin
bowl	ボール	bō·ru
breakfast	朝食	chō·sho·ku
cold	冷たい	tsu·me·ta·i
dinner	夕食	yū·sho·ku
fork	フォーク	fō·ku
glass	グラス	gu·ra·su
grocery	食料品	sho·ku·ryō·hin
hot (warm)	熱い	a·tsu·i
knife	ナイフ	nai·fu
lunch	昼食	chū·sho·ku
market	市場	i·chi·ba
menu	メニュー	me·nyū
plate	皿	sa·ra
spicy	スパイシー	spai·shī
spoon	スプーン	spūn
vegetarian	ベジタリアン	be·ji·ta·ri·an
with	いっしょに	is·sho ni
without	なしで	na·shi de

Meat & Fish

beef	牛肉	gyū·ni·ku
chicken	鶏肉	to·ri·ni·ku
duck	アヒル	a·hi·ru
eel	うなぎ	u·na·gi
fish	魚	sa·ka·na
lamb	子羊	ko·hi·tsu·ji
lobster	ロブスター	ro·bus·tā
meat	肉	ni·ku
pork	豚肉	bu·ta·ni·ku
prawn	エビ	e·bi
salmon	サケ	sa·ke
seafood	シーフード 海産物	shī·fū·do/ kai·sam·bu·tsu
shrimp	小エビ	ko·e·bi
tuna	マグロ	ma·gu·ro
turkey	七面鳥	shi·chi·men·chō
veal	子牛	ko·u·shi

Fruit & Vegetables

apple	りんご	rin·go
banana	バナナ	ba·na·na
beans	豆	ma·me
capsicum	ピーマン	pī·man
carrot	ニンジン	nin·jin
cherry	さくらんぼ	sa·ku·ram·bo
cucumber	キュウリ	kyū·ri
fruit	果物	ku·da·mo·no
grapes	ブドウ	bu·dō
lettuce	レタス	re·tas
nut	ナッツ	nat·tsu
orange	オレンジ	o·ren·ji
peach	桃	mo·mo

peas	豆	ma·me
pineapple	パイナップル	pai·nap·pu·ru
potato	ジャガイモ	ja·ga·i·mo
pumpkin	カボチャ	ka·bo·cha
spinach	ホウレンソウ	hō·ren·sō
strawberry	イチゴ	i·chi·go
tomato	トマト	to·ma·to
vegetables	野菜	ya·sai
watermelon	スイカ	su·i·ka

Other

bread	パン	pan
butter	バター	ba·tā
cheese	チーズ	chī·zu
chilli	唐辛子	tō·ga·ra·shi
egg	卵	ta·ma·go
honey	蜂蜜	ha·chi·mi·tsu
horseradish	わさび	wa·sa·bi
jam	ジャム	ja·mu
noodles	麺	men
pepper	コショウ	koshō
rice (cooked)	ごはん	go·han
salt	塩	shi·o
seaweed	のり	no·ri
soy sauce	しょう油	shō·yu
sugar	砂糖	sa·tō

Drinks

beer	ビール	bī·ru
coffee	コーヒー	kō·hī
(orange) juice	(オレンジ) ジュース	(o·ren·ji·) jū·su
lemonade	レモネード	re·mo·nē·do
milk	ミルク	mi·ru·ku
mineral water	ミネラル ウォーター	mi·ne·ra·ru· wō·tā
red wine	赤ワイン	a·ka wain
sake	酒	sa·ke
tea	紅茶	kō·cha
water	水	mi·zu
white wine	白ワイン	shi·ro wain
yogurt	ヨーグルト	yō·gu·ru·to

Question Words

How?	どのように?	do·no yō ni
What?	なに?	na·ni
When?	いつ?	i·tsu
Where?	どこ?	do·ko
Which?	どちら?	do·chi·ra
Who?	だれ?	da·re
Why?	なぜ?	na·ze

EMERGENCIES

Help!
たすけて! tas·ke·te

Go away!
離れろ! ha·na·re·ro

I'm lost.
迷いました。 ma·yoy·mash·ta

Call the police.
警察を呼んで。 kē·sa·tsu o yon·de

Call a doctor.
医者を呼んで。 i·sha o yon·de

Where are the toilets?
トイレはどこですか? toy·re wa do·ko des ka

I'm ill.
私は病気です。 wa·ta·shi wa byō·ki des

It hurts here.
ここが痛いです。 ko·ko ga i·tai des

I'm allergic to ...
私は… アレルギーです。 wa·ta·shi wa ... a·re·ru·gī des

SHOPPING & SERVICES

I'd like to buy ...
…をください。 ... o ku·da·sai

I'm just looking.
見ているだけです。 mi·te i·ru da·ke des

Can I look at it?
それを見ても いいですか? so·re o mi·te mo ī des ka

How much is it?
いくらですか? i·ku·ra des ka

That's too expensive.
高すぎます。 ta·ka·su·gi·mas

Can you give me a discount?
ディスカウント できますか? dis·kown·to de·ki·mas ka

There's a mistake in the bill.
請求書に間違いが あります。 sē·kyū·sho ni ma·chi·gai ga a·ri·mas

ATM	ATM	ē·tī·e·mu
credit card	クレジット カード	ku·re·jit·to· kā·do
post office	郵便局	yū·bin·kyo·ku
public phone	公衆電話	kō·shū·den·wa
tourist office	観光案内所	kan·kō·an·nai·jo

Numbers

1	一	i·chi
2	二	ni
3	三	san
4	四	shi/yon
5	五	go
6	六	ro·ku
7	七	shi·chi/na·na
8	八	ha·chi
9	九	ku/kyū
10	十	jū
20	二十	ni·jū
30	三十	san·jū
40	四十	yon·jū
50	五十	go·jū
60	六十	ro·ku·jū
70	七十	na·na·jū
80	八十	ha·chi·jū
90	九十	kyū·jū
100	百	hya·ku
1000	千	sen

TIME & DATES

What time is it?
何時ですか？ nan·ji des ka

It's (10) o'clock.
(10)時です。 (jū)·ji des

Half past (10).
(10)時半です。 (jū)·ji han des

am	午前	go·zen
pm	午後	go·go

Monday	月曜日	ge·tsu·yō·bi
Tuesday	火曜日	ka·yō·bi
Wednesday	水曜日	su·i·yō·bi
Thursday	木曜日	mo·ku·yō·bi
Friday	金曜日	kin·yō·bi
Saturday	土曜日	do·yō·bi
Sunday	日曜日	ni·chi·yō·bi

January	1月	i·chi·ga·tsu
February	2月	ni·ga·tsu
March	3月	san·ga·tsu
April	4月	shi·ga·tsu
May	5月	go·ga·tsu
June	6月	ro·ku·ga·tsu
July	7月	shi·chi·ga·tsu
August	8月	ha·chi·ga·tsu
September	9月	ku·ga·tsu
October	10月	jū·ga·tsu
November	11月	jū·i·chi·ga·tsu
December	12月	jū·ni·ga·tsu

TRANSPORT

boat	船	fu·ne
bus	バス	bas
metro	地下鉄	chi·ka·te·tsu
plane	飛行機	hi·kō·ki
train	電車	den·sha
tram	市電	shi·den

What time does it leave?
これは何時に
出ますか？ ko·re wa nan·ji ni
de·mas ka

Does it stop at (...)?
(…)に
停まりますか？ (...) ni
to·ma·ri·mas ka

Please tell me when we get to (...).
(…)に着いたら
教えてください。 (...) ni tsu·i·ta·ra
o·shi·e·te ku·da·sai

A one-way/return ticket (to Tokyo).
(東京行きの)
片道/往復
切符。 (tō·kyō·yu·ki no)
ka·ta·mi·chi/ō·fu·ku
kip·pu

first	始発の	shi·ha·tsu no
last	最終の	sai·shū no
next	次の	tsu·gi no

aisle	通路側	tsū·ro·ga·wa
bus stop	バス停	bas·tē
cancelled	キャンセル	kyan·se·ru
delayed	遅れ	o·ku·re
ticket window	窓口	ma·do·gu·chi
timetable	時刻表	ji·ko·ku·hyō
train station	駅	e·ki
window	窓側	ma·do·ga·wa

I'd like to hire a ...	…を借りたいのですが。	... o ka·ri·tai no des ga
bicycle	自転車	ji·ten·sha
car	自動車	ji·dō·sha
motorbike	オートバイ	ō·to·bai

For additional Transport words and phrases, see p188.

GLOSSARY

agaru – north of

ageya – traditional banquet hall used for entertainment

bashi – bridge (also *hashi*)

bentō – boxed lunch or dinner, usually containing rice, vegetables and fish or meat

bosatsu – a Bodhisattva, or Buddha attendant, who helpss others to attain enlightenment

bugaku – dance pieces played by court orchestras in ancient Japan

bunraku – classical puppet theatre that uses life-size puppets to enact dramas similar to those of *kabuki*

chadō – tea ceremony, or 'The Way of Tea'

chanoyu – tea ceremony; see also *chadō*

chō – city area sized between a *ku* and a *chōme*

dai – great; large

daimyō – domain lords under the *shōgun*

dera – temple (also *ji* or *tera*)

dōri – street

futon – cushion-like mattress that is rolled up and stored away during the day

gagaku – music of the imperial court

gaijin – foreigner; the contracted form of *gaikokujin*

gawa – river (also *kawa*)

geiko – Kyoto dialect for *geisha*

geisha – a woman versed in the arts and other cultivated pursuits who entertains guests

gū – shrine

haiden – hall of worship in a shrine

haiku – 17-syllable poem

hanami – cherry-blossom viewing

hashi – bridge (also *bashi*); chopsticks

higashi – east

hiragana – phonetic syllabary used to write Japanese words

honden – main building of a shrine

hondō – main building of a temple (also *kondō*)

ikebana – art of flower arrangement

izakaya – Japanese pub/eatery

ji – temple (also *tera* or *dera*)

jingū – shrine (also *jinja* or *gū*)

Jizō – bodhisattva who watches over children

jō – castle (also *shiro*)

JR – Japan Railways

kabuki – form of Japanese theatre that draws on popular tales and is characterised by elaborate costumes, stylised acting and an all-male cast

kaiseki – Buddhist-inspired, Japanese *haute cuisine*; called *cha-kaiseki* when served as part of a tea ceremony

kaisoku – rapid train

kaiten-zushi – automatic, conveyor-belt sushi

kampai – cheers, as in a drinking toast

kanji – literally, 'Chinese writing'; Chinese ideographic script used for writing Japanese

Kannon – Buddhist goddess of mercy

karesansui – dry-landscaped rock garden

kawa – river

kayabuki-yane – traditional Japanese thatched-roof farmhouse

ken – prefecture, eg Shiga-ken

kimono – traditional outer garment similar to a robe

kita – north

KIX – Kansai International Airport

Kiyomizu-yaki – a distinctive type of local pottery

ko – lake

kōen – park

koma-inu – dog-like guardian stone statues found in pairs at the entrance to *Shintō* shrines

kondō – main building of a temple

ku – ward

kudaru – south of (also *sagaru*)

kyōgen – drama performed as comic relief between *nō* plays, or as separate events

kyō-machiya – see *machiya*

kyō-ningyō – Kyoto dolls

kyō-ryōri – Kyoto cuisine

Kyoto-ben – distinctive Japanese dialect spoken in Kyoto

live house – a small concert hall where music is performed

machi – city area (for large cities) sized between a *ku* and a *chōme*

machiya – traditional wooden town house, called *kyō-machiya* in Kyoto

maiko – apprentice geisha

maki-e – decorative lacquer technique using silver and gold powders

mama-san – older women who run drinking, dining and entertainment venues

matcha – powdered green tea served in tea ceremonies

matsuri – festival

mikoshi – portable shrine carried during festivals

minami – south

minshuku – Japanese equivalent of a B&B

mizu shōbai – the world of bars, entertainment and prostitution

mon – temple gate

mura – village

ningyō – doll (see also *kyō-ningyō*)

niō – temple guardians

nishi – west

nō – classical Japanese mask drama

noren – door curtain for restaurants, usually labelled with the name of the establishment

obanzai – Japanese home-style cooking (the Kyoto variant of this is sometimes called *kyō-obanzai*)

obi – sash or belt worn with *kimono*

Obon – mid-August festivals and ceremonies for deceased ancestors

okiya – old-style *geisha* living quarters

okonomiyaki – Japanese cabbage and batter dish cooked on an iron griddle with a variety of fillings

onsen – mineral hot spring with bathing areas and accommodation

pachinko – vertical pinball game that is a Japanese craze

ryokan – traditional inn

ryōri – cooking; cuisine (see also *kyō-ryōri*)

ryōtei – traditional-style, high-class restaurant; *kaiseki* is typical fare

sabi – a poetic ideal of finding beauty and pleasure in imperfection; often used in conjunction with *wabi*

sagaru – south of (also *kudaru*)

sakura – cherry trees

sama – a suffix even more respectful than *san*

samurai – Japan's traditional warrior class

san – a respectful suffix applied to personal names, similar to Mr, Mrs or Ms

sen – line, usually railway line

sencha – medium-grade green tea

sensu – folding paper fan

sentō – public bath

setto – set meal; see also *teishoku*

shakkei – borrowed scenery; technique where features outside a garden are incorporated into its design

shamisen – three-stringed, banjo-like instrument

shi – city (to distinguish cities with prefectures of the same name)

shidare-zakura – weeping cherry tree

shinkaisoku – special rapid train

shinkansen – bullet train

Shintō – indigenous Japanese religion

shōgun – military ruler of pre-Meiji Japan

shōjin-ryōri – Buddhist vegetarian cuisine

shokudō – Japanese-style cafeteria/cheap restaurant

soba – thin brown buckwheat noodles

tatami – tightly woven floor matting on which shoes should not be worn

teishoku – set meal in a restaurant

tera – temple (also *dera* or *ji*)

tokkyū – limited express train

torii – entrance gate to a *Shintō* shrine

tsukemono – Japanese pickles

udon – thick, white wheat noodles

wabi – a Zen-inspired aesthetic of rustic simplicity

wagashi – traditional Japanese sweets served with tea

wasabi – spicy Japanese horseradish

washi – Japanese paper

yudōfu – bean curd cooked in an iron pot; common temple fare

Zen – a form of Buddhism

MENU DECODER

Rice Dishes

katsu-don (かつ丼) – rice topped with a fried pork cutlet

niku-don (牛丼) – rice topped with thin slices of cooked beef

oyako-don (親子丼) – rice topped with egg and chicken

ten-don (天丼) – rice topped with tempura shrimp and vegetables

Izakaya Fare

agedashi-dōfu (揚げだし豆腐) – deep-fried tofu in a dashi broth

jaga-batā (ジャガバター) – baked potatoes with butter

niku-jaga (肉ジャガ) – beef and potato stew

shio-yaki-zakana (塩焼魚) – a whole fish grilled with salt

poteto furai (ポテトフライ) – French fries

chiizu-age (チーズ揚げ) – deep-fried cheese

hiya-yakko (冷奴) – a cold block of tofu with soy sauce and spring onions

tsuna sarada (ツナサラダ) – tuna salad over cabbage

Sushi & Sashimi

ama-ebi (甘海老) – shrimp

awabi (あわび) – abalone

hamachi (はまち) – yellowtail

ika (いか) – squid

ikura (イクラ) – salmon roe

kai-bashira (貝柱) – scallop

kani (かに) – crab

katsuo (かつお) – bonito

sashimi mori-awase (刺身盛り合わせ) – a selection of sliced sashimi

tai (鯛) – sea bream

toro (とろ) – the choicest cut of fatty tuna belly

uni (うに) – sea urchin roe

Yakitori

yakitori (焼き鳥) – plain, grilled white meat

hasami/negima (はさみ/ねぎま) – pieces of white meat alternating with leek

sasami (ささみ) – skinless chicken-breast pieces

kawa (皮) – chicken skin

tsukune (つくね) – chicken meat balls

gyū-niku (牛肉) – pieces of beef

tebasaki (手羽先) – chicken wings

shiitake (しいたけ) – Japanese mushrooms

piiman (ピーマン) – small green peppers

tama-negi (玉ねぎ) – round white onions

yaki-onigiri (焼きおにぎり) – a triangle of rice grilled with *yakitori* sauce

Tempura

tempura moriawase (天ぷら盛り合わせ) – a selection of tempura

shōjin age (精進揚げ) – vegetarian tempura

kaki age (かき揚げ) – tempura with shredded vegetables or fish

Rāmen

rāmen (ラーメン) – soup and noodles with a sprinkling of meat and vegetables

chāshū-men (チャーシュー麺) – *rāmen* topped with slices of roasted pork

wantan-men (ワンタン麺) – *rāmen* with meat dumplings

miso-rāmen (みそラーメン) – *rāmen* with miso-flavoured broth

chānpon-men (ちゃんぽん麺) – Nagasaki-style *rāmen*

Soba & Udon

soba (そば) – thin brown buckwheat noodles

udon (うどん) – thick white wheat noodles

kake soba/udon (かけそば/うどん) – *soba/udon* noodles in broth

kata yaki-soba (固焼きそば) – crispy noodles with meat and vegetables

kitsune soba/udon (きつねそば/うどん) – *soba/udon* noodles with fried tofu

tempura soba/udon (天ぷらそば/うどん) – *soba/udon* noodles with tempura shrimp

tsukimi soba/udon (月見そば/うどん) – *soba/udon* noodles with raw egg on top

yaki-soba (焼きそば) – fried noodles with meat and vegetables

zaru soba (ざるそば) – cold noodles with seaweed strips served on a bamboo tray

Unagi

kabayaki (蒲焼き) – skewers of grilled eel without rice

unagi teishoku (うなぎ定食) – full-set *unagi* meal with rice, grilled eel, eel-liver soup and pickles

una-don (うな丼) – grilled eel over a bowl of rice

unajū (うな重) – grilled eel over a flat tray of rice

Kushiage & Kushikatsu

ika (いか) – squid

renkon (れんこん) – lotus root

tama-negi (玉ねぎ) – white onion

gyū-niku (牛肉) – beef pieces

shiitake (しいたけ) – Japanese mushrooms

ginnan (銀杏) – ginkgo nuts

imo (いも) – potato

konomiyaki

mikkusu (ミックスお好み焼き) – mixed fillings of seafood, meat and vegetables

modan-yaki (モダン焼き) – *okonomiyaki* with *yaki-soba* and a fried egg

ika okonomiyaki (いかお好み焼き) – squid *okonomiyaki*

gyū okonomiyaki (牛お好み焼き) – beef *okonomiyaki*

negi okonomiyaki (ネギお好み焼き) – thin *okonomiyaki* with spring onions

Kaiseki

bentō (弁当) – boxed lunch

ume (梅) – regular course

take (竹) – special course

matsu (松) – extra-special course

Alcoholic Drinks

nama biiru (生ビール) – draught beer

shōchū (焼酎) – distilled grain liquor

oyu-wari (お湯割り) – *shōchū* with hot water

chūhai (チューハイ) – *shōchū* with soda and lemon

whiskey (ウィスキー) – whiskey

mizu-wari (水割り) – whiskey, ice and water

Coffee & Tea

kōhii (コーヒー) – regular coffee

burendo kōhii (ブレンドコーヒー) – blended coffee, fairly strong

american kōhii (アメリカンコーヒー) – weak coffee

kōcha (紅茶) – black, British-style tea

kafe ōre (カフェオレ) – *café au lait*, hot or cold

Japanese Tea

o-cha (お茶) – green tea

sencha (煎茶) – medium-grade green tea

matcha (抹茶) – powdered green tea used in the tea ceremony

bancha (番茶) – ordinary-grade green tea, brownish in colour

mugicha (麦茶) – roasted barley tea

Behind the Scenes

SEND US YOUR FEEDBACK

We love to hear from travellers – your comments keep us on our toes and help make our books better. Our well-travelled team reads every word on what you loved or loathed about this book. Although we cannot reply individually to postal submissions, we always guarantee that your feedback goes straight to the appropriate authors, in time for the next edition. Each person who sends us information is thanked in the next edition – and the most useful submissions are rewarded with a free book.

Visit **lonelyplanet.com/contact** to submit your updates and suggestions or to ask for help. Our award-winning website also features inspirational travel stories, news and discussions.

Note: We may edit, reproduce and incorporate your comments in Lonely Planet products such as guidebooks, websites and digital products, so let us know if you don't want your comments reproduced or your name acknowledged. For a copy of our privacy policy visit lonelyplanet.com/privacy.

OUR READERS

Many thanks to the travellers who used the last edition and wrote to us with helpful hints, useful advice and interesting anecdotes:

Richard Allen, Seraphim Alvanides, Yoshihiko Baba, Erika Bridges, Diego Coruña, Matthias Durand, Andrew Dye, Sallyanne English, Monica Fernandez, Peter Hagander, Karel Kovanda, Elizabeth McCallum, Brandon McKinley, Petra Meier, Robert Morton, Jane Offerman, Suzanne Rex, Sally Rughani, Trevor Skingle, Carl-axel Stael von Holstein.

AUTHOR THANKS

Chris Rowthorn

Thanks to Hiroe, SK, Ijuin Koko, Hagiwara Keiko, Daniel Milne, Wes Lang, Justin Giffin, Michael Lambe and Paul Carty. Thanks to Emily K Wolman and David Connolly. I would also like to thank all the readers of Lonely Planet's Japan books who emailed us with great tips! Finally, a huge thanks to the people of Kyoto: *Osewa ni narimashita!*

ACKNOWLEDGMENTS

Climate map data adapted from Peel MC, Finlayson BL & McMahon TA (2007) 'Updated World Map of the Köppen-Geiger Climate Classification', *Hydrology and Earth System Sciences*, 11, 163344.

Cover photograph: Bentendo Hall, Daigo-ji temple, Frank Carter, Lonely Planet Images.

Many of the images in this guide are available for licensing from Lonely Planet Images: www.lonelyplanetimages.com.

THIS BOOK

This 5th edition of *Kyoto* was written by Chris Rowthorn. He also wrote the 2nd, 3rd and 4th editions. This guidebook was commissioned in Lonely Planet's Oakland office, and produced by the following:

Commissioning Editor Emily K Wolman

Coordinating Editors Monique Perrin, Pete Cruttenden

Coordinating Cartographer Andy Rojas

Coordinating Layout Designer Frank Deim

Managing Editor Kirsten Rawlings

Senior Editor Angela Tinson

Managing Cartographers David Connolly, Alison Lyall

Managing Layout Designer Chris Girdler

Assisting Editors Paul Harding, Lauren Hunt

Assisting Cartographers Alex Leung, Corey Hutchison, Csanad Csutoros

Cover Research Naomi Parker

Internal Image Research Sabrina Dalbesio

Language Content Annelies Mertens

Thanks to Naoko Akamatsu, Ryan Evans, Jane Hart, Liz Heynes, Laura Jane, Chris Love, Vivienne New, Trent Paton, Julie Sheridan, Rebecca Skinner, Raphael Richards, Gerard Walker

See also separate subindexes for:
EATING P212
DRINKING & NIGHTLIFE P212
ENTERTAINMENT P213
SHOPPING P213
SLEEPING P213

Index

Sights p000
Map Pages **p000**
Photo Pages **p000**

Sights p000
Map Pages **p000**
Photo Pages **p000**

Sights p000
Map Pages **p000**
Photo Pages **p000**

ENTERTAINMENT

SHOPPING

SLEEPING

Kyoto Maps

Map Legend

Sights
- Beach
- Buddhist
- Castle
- Christian
- Hindu
- Islamic
- Jewish
- Monument
- Museum/Gallery
- Ruin
- Winery/Vineyard
- Zoo
- Other Sight

Eating
- Eating

Drinking & Nightlife
- Drinking & Nightlife
- Cafe

Entertainment
- Entertainment

Shopping
- Shopping

Sports & Activities
- Diving/Snorkelling
- Canoeing/Kayaking
- Skiing
- Surfing
- Swimming/Pool
- Walking
- Windsurfing
- Other Sports & Activities

Sleeping
- Sleeping
- Camping

Information
- Bank
- Embassy/Consulate
- Hospital/Medical
- Internet
- Police
- Post Office
- Telephone
- Toilet
- Tourist Information
- Other Information

Transport
- Airport
- Border Crossing
- Bus
- Cable Car/Funicular
- Cycling
- Ferry
- Metro
- Monorail
- Parking
- S-Bahn
- Taxi
- Train/Railway
- Tram
- Tube Station
- U-Bahn
- Other Transport

Routes
- Tollway
- Freeway
- Primary
- Secondary
- Tertiary
- Lane
- Unsealed Road
- Plaza/Mall
- Steps
- Tunnel
- Pedestrian Overpass
- Walking Tour
- Walking Tour Detour
- Path

Boundaries
- International
- State/Province
- Disputed
- Regional/Suburb
- Marine Park
- Cliff
- Wall

Geographic
- Hut/Shelter
- Lighthouse
- Lookout
- Mountain/Volcano
- Oasis
- Park
- Pass
- Picnic Area
- Waterfall

Hydrography
- River/Creek
- Intermittent River
- Swamp/Mangrove
- Reef
- Canal
- Water
- Dry/Salt/Intermittent Lake
- Glacier

Areas
- Beach/Desert
- Cemetery (Christian)
- Cemetery (Other)
- Park/Forest
- Sportsground
- Sight (Building)
- Top Sight (Building)

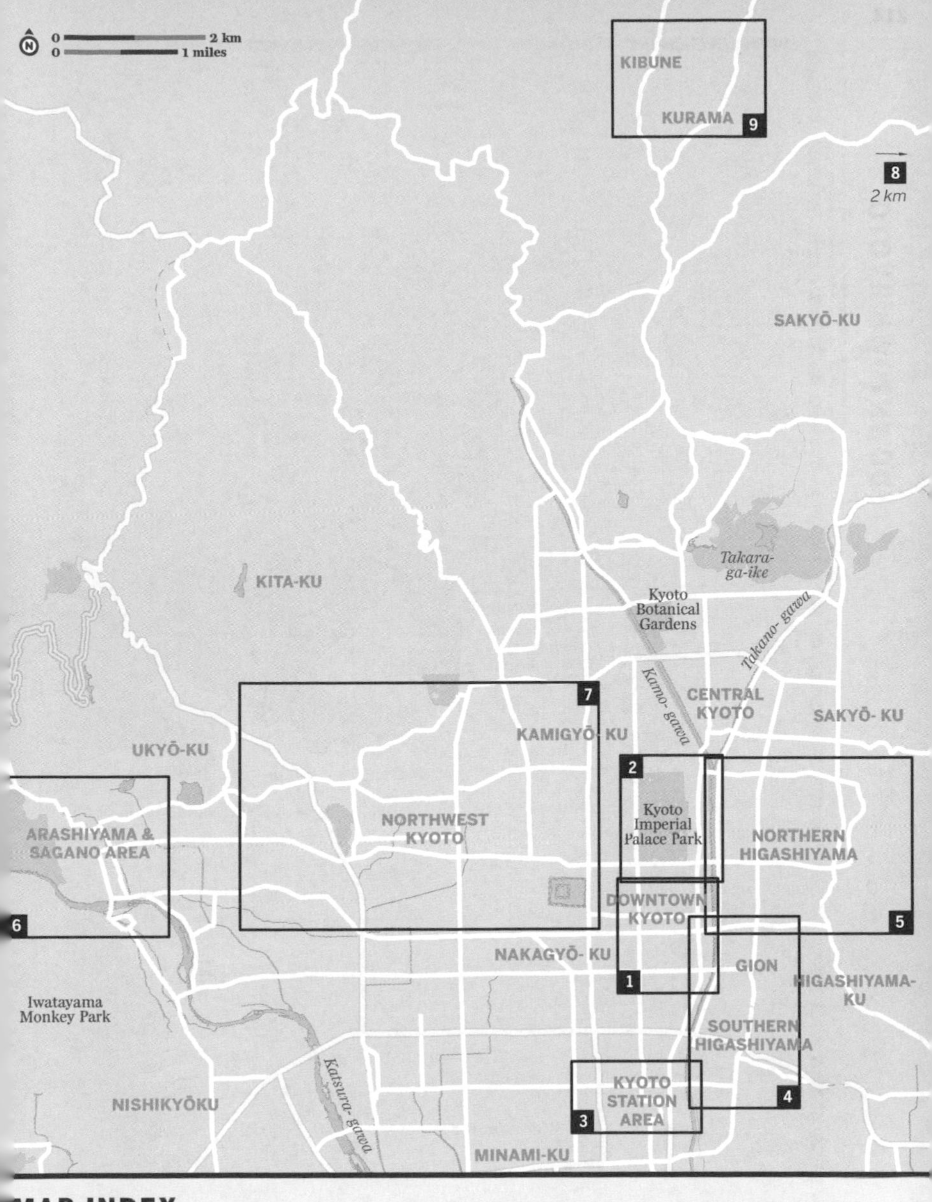
0 2 km
0 1 miles
KIBUNE
KURAMA
9
8
2 km
SAKYŌ-KU
Takara-ga-ike
KITA-KU
Kyoto Botanical Gardens
Takano-gawa
Kamo-gawa
CENTRAL KYOTO
SAKYŌ- KU
7
KAMIGYŌ- KU
UKYŌ-KU
2
Kyoto Imperial Palace Park
NORTHWEST KYOTO
NORTHERN HIGASHIYAMA
ARASHIYAMA & SAGANO AREA
DOWNTOWN KYOTO
6
5
NAKAGYŌ- KU
1
GION
HIGASHIYAMA-KU
Iwatayama Monkey Park
SOUTHERN HIGASHIYAMA
Katsura-gawa
KYOTO STATION AREA
4
3
NISHIKYŌKU
MINAMI-KU

MAP INDEX

DOWNTOWN KYOTO

Key on p218

DOWNTOWN KYOTO

DOWNTOWN KYOTO *Map on p216*

Top Sights (p56)
Nishiki Market ... D6

Sights (p57)
1 Kaleidoscope Museum of Kyoto ... C4
2 Kyoto International Manga Museum ... B3
3 Museum of Kyoto ... C4
4 Pontochō ... G6
5 Shiori-an ... A5

Eating (p58)
6 Biotei ... B4
7 Café Bibliotec Hello! ... D1
8 Café Independants ... E4
9 Capricciosa ... F4
10 Din Tai Fung ... F7
11 Fujino-ya ... G6
12 Ganko Nijō-en ... G2
13 Ganko Zushi ... G4
14 Hati Hati ... G5
15 Hinaka ... G5
16 Honke Tagoto ... E4
17 Ike Tsuru ... D6
18 Inoda Coffee ... D5
19 Ippūdō ... C6
20 Kane-yo ... F5
21 Karafuneya Coffee Honten ... F4
22 Katsu Kura ... F4
23 Kerala ... F4
24 Kiyamachi Sakuragawa ... G2
25 Kōsendō-sumi ... D4
26 Kyō-hayashiya ... G4
27 Liberte ... E2
28 Lugol ... A3
29 Merry Island Café ... G3
30 Mew'z Café ... E1
31 Mishima-tei ... E4
32 Mukade-ya ... A6
33 Musashi Sushi ... F4
34 Omen Nippon ... G7
35 Ootoya ... G4
36 Park Café ... E4
37 Ramen Kairikiya ... F4
38 Shi-Shin Samurai Cafe and Bar ... A2
39 Shizenha Restaurant Obanzai ... A3
40 Somushi Kochaya ... B4
41 Tagoto Honten ... F7
42 Tomizushi ... F7
43 Tōsuirō ... G3
44 Tsukiji Sushisei ... C7
45 Tsukimochiya Naomasa ... G4
46 Uosue ... C7
47 Warai ... C6
48 Yak & Yeti ... E6
49 Yoshikawa ... D3
50 Zu Zu ... G5

Drinking & Nightlife (p64)
51 A-Bar ... G6
52 Atlantis ... G6
53 Ing ... G5
54 McLoughlin's Irish Bar & Restaurant ... G4
Orizzonte ... (see 90)
55 Rub-a-Dub ... G4
56 Sama Sama ... G4
57 World ... G7
58 Yoramu ... C2

Entertainment (p65)
59 Kamogawa Odori ... G5
60 Kyoto Cinema ... B7

Shopping (p65)
61 Aritsugu ... E6
62 Art Factory ... E5
63 Cocon Karasuma ... B7
64 Daimaru ... C7
65 Erizen ... F7
66 Fujii Daimaru ... E7
67 Ippo-dō ... E1
68 Junkudō ... F5
69 Kamiji Kakimoto ... E1
70 Kyoto Antique Center ... E1
71 Kyoto Marui ... F7
72 Kyūkyo-dō ... E4
73 Meidi-ya ... F4
74 Mimuro ... B8
75 Mina ... F5
76 Minakuchi-ya ... C6
77 Morita Washi ... C8
78 Nijūsan-ya ... G7
79 Nishiharu ... E4
80 OPA ... F6
Rakushi-kan ... (see 3)
81 Shin-Puh-Kan ... B4
82 Takashimaya ... F7
83 Tanakaya ... D7
84 Taniyama Musen ... E8
85 Tsujikura ... F7

Sleeping (p143)
86 Best Western Hotel Kyoto ... F5
87 Hiiragiya ... E3
88 Hotel Monterey Kyoto ... B5
89 Hotel Unizo ... F5
90 Kyoto Hotel Ōkura ... F3
91 Mitsui Garden Hotel Kyoto Sanjō ... B4
92 Super Hotel Kyoto Sijjō-Kawaramachi ... F6
93 Tawaraya ... E3
94 Yoshikawa ... D3

Information (p197)
95 IACE Travel ... F4
96 Tourist Information at Kyoto City Center ... F7

Transport (p187)
97 Bicycle Parking Lot ... F6

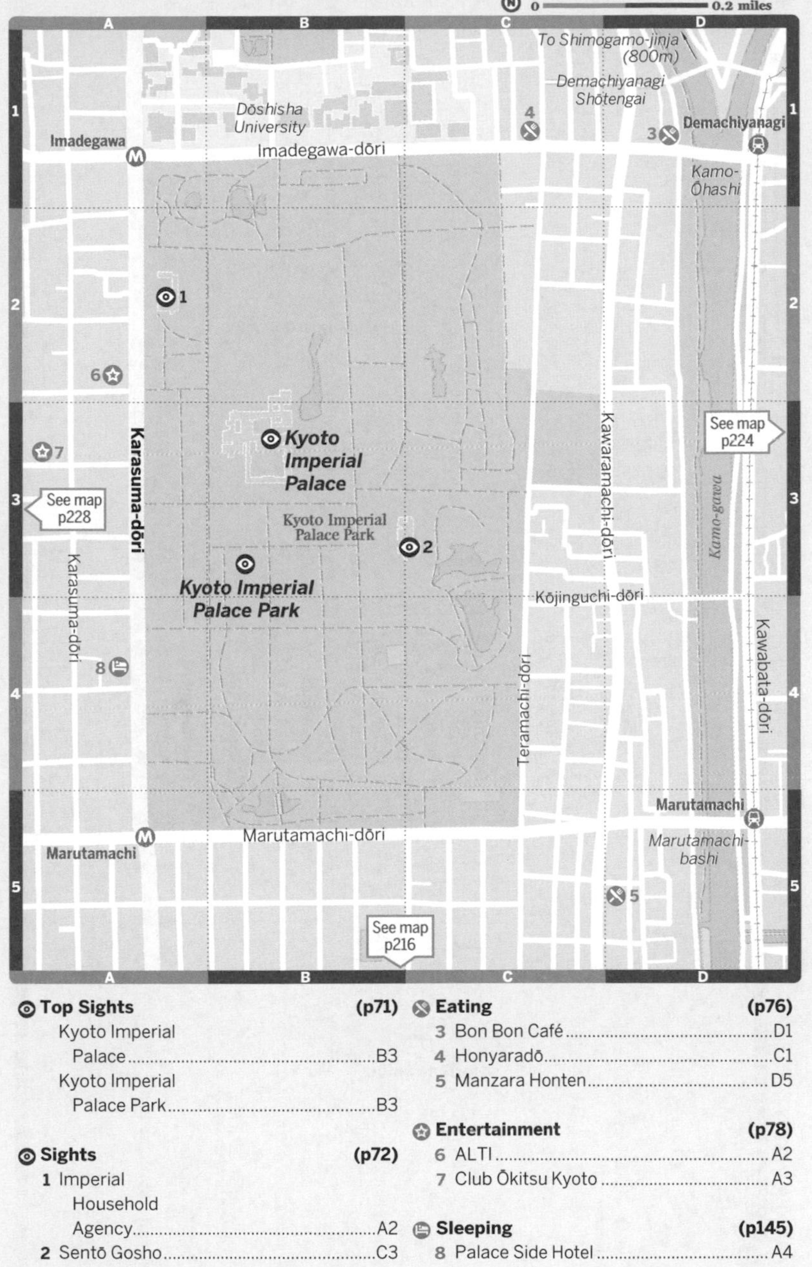

Top Sights (p71)
- Kyoto Imperial Palace B3
- Kyoto Imperial Palace Park B3

Sights (p72)
1. Imperial Household Agency A2
2. Sentō Gosho C3

Eating (p76)
3. Bon Bon Café D1
4. Honyaradō C1
5. Manzara Honten D5

Entertainment (p78)
6. ALTI A2
7. Club Ōkitsu Kyoto A3

Sleeping (p145)
8. Palace Side Hotel A4

KYOTO STATION AREA

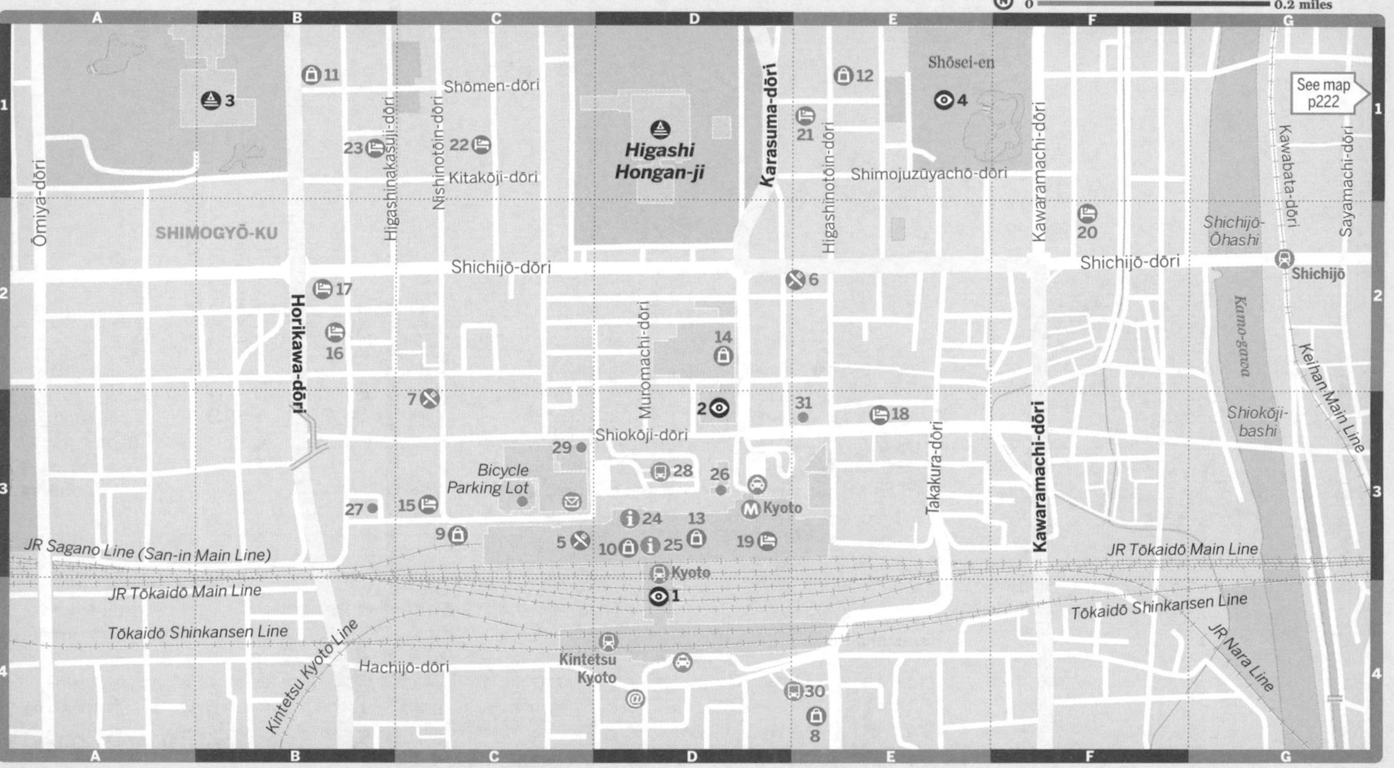

KYOTO STATION AREA

Top Sights **(p50)**
Higashi Hongan-ji ... D1

Sights **(p51)**
1 Kyoto Station ... D4
2 Kyoto Tower ... D3
3 Nishi Hongan-ji ... B1
4 Shōsei-en ... E1

Eating **(p52)**
5 Cube ... C3
Eat Paradise ... (see 5)
6 Iimura ... E2
7 Jōjō ... C3
Kyoto Rāmen Kōji ... (see 5)

Shopping **(p52)**
8 Avanti ... E4
9 Bic Camera ... C3
10 Isetan Department Store ... D3
Kōjitsu Sansō ... (see 14)
11 Kungyoku-dō ... B1
12 Kyōsen-dō ... E1
13 Porta Shopping Mall ... D3
14 Yodobashi Camera ... D2

Sleeping **(p142)**
15 APA Hotel Kyoto Ekimae ... C3
16 Budget Inn ... B2
17 Capsule Ryokan Kyoto ... B2
18 Dormy Inn Premium Kyoto Ekimae ... E3
19 Hotel Granvia Kyoto ... D3
20 K's House Kyoto ... F2
21 Matsubaya Ryokan ... E1
22 Ryokan Shimizu ... C1
23 Tour Club ... B1

Information **(p196)**
24 Kyoto City Tourist Information Center ... D3
25 Kyoto Tourist Information Center ... D3

Transport **(p184)**
26 Bus Information Centre ... D3
27 Kyoto Cycling Tour Project ... B3
28 Kyoto Station Bus Terminal ... D3
29 Nissan Rent-a-Car ... C3
30 Osaka Airport Transport Bus Stop ... E4
31 Tōkai Discount Ticket Shop ... E3

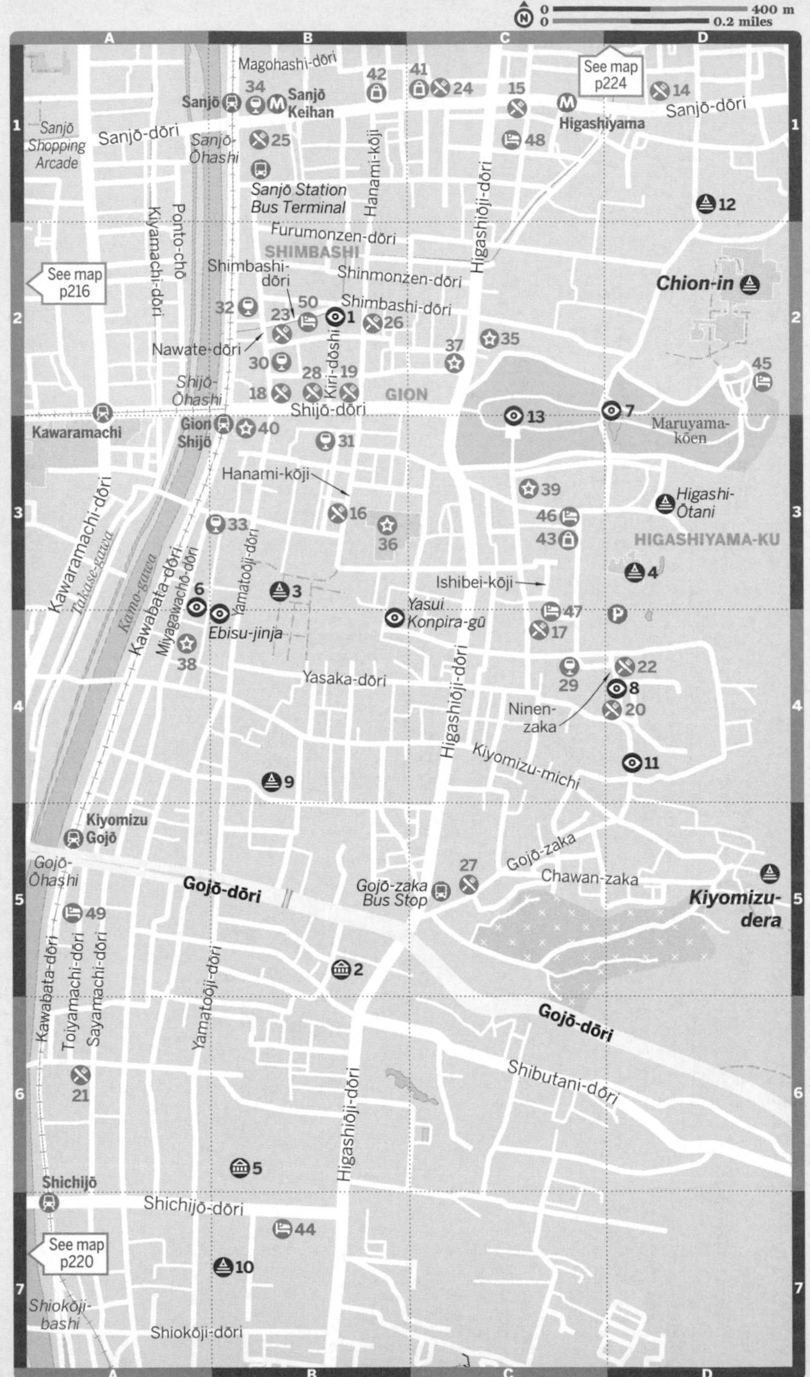

0 400 m
0 0.2 miles
See map p224
See map p216
See map p220
Magohashi-dōri
Sanjō
Sanjō Keihan
Higashiyama
Sanjō-dōri
Sanjō Shopping Arcade
Sanjō-Ōhashi
Sanjō Station Bus Terminal
Hanami-kōji
Higashiōji-dōri
Furumonzen-dōri
SHIMBASHI
Shimbashi-dōri
Shinmonzen-dōri
Kiyamachi-dōri
Ponto-chō
Nawate-dōri
Kiri-dōshi
GION
Shijō-Ōhashi
Shijō-dōri
Kawaramachi
Gion Shijō
Chion-in
Maruyama-kōen
Higashi-Ōtani
HIGASHIYAMA-KU
Kawaramachi-dōri
Takase-gawa
Kamo-gawa
Kawabata-dōri
Miyagawachō-dōri
Yamatoōji-dōri
Ebisu-jinja
Yasui Konpira-gū
Ishibei-kōji
Yasaka-dōri
Ninen-zaka
Kiyomizu-michi
Kiyomizu Gojō
Gojō-Ōhashi
Gojō-dōri
Gojō-zaka
Chawan-zaka
Gojō-zaka Bus Stop
Kiyomizu-dera
Toiyamachi-dōri
Sayamachi-dōri
Shibutani-dōri
Shichijō
Shichijō-dōri
Shiokōji-bashi
Shiokōji-dōri

SOUTHERN HIGASHIYAMA

Top Sights **(p81)**
Chion-in D2
Kiyomizu-dera D5

Sights **(p83)**
Gion Corner .... (see 36)
1 Gion District B2
2 Kawai Kanjirō Memorial Hall B5
3 Kennin-ji B3
4 Kōdai-ji D3
5 Kyoto National Museum B6
6 Maika A3
7 Maruyama-kōen D2
8 Ninen-zaka D4
9 Rokuharamitsu-ji B4
10 Sanjūsangen-dō B7
11 Sannen-zaka D4
12 Shōren-in D1
13 Yasaka-jinja C3

Eating **(p87)**
14 Asuka D1
15 Bamboo C1
16 Gion Karyō B3
17 Hisago C4
18 Issen Yōshoku B2
19 Kagizen Yoshifusa B2
20 Kasagi-ya D4
21 Machapuchare A6
22 Omen Kodai-ji D4
23 Ōzawa B2
24 Ryūmon C1
25 Santōka B1
26 Senmonten B2
27 Shibazaki C5
28 Yagura B2

Drinking & Nightlife **(p89)**
29 Bar Main Higashiyama C4
30 Gael Irish Pub B2
31 Gion Finlandia Bar B3
32 Gion S B2
33 Kisui B3
34 Pig & Whistle B1

Entertainment **(p90)**
35 En C2
36 Gion Corner B3
37 Gion Odori C2
38 Kyō Odori A4
39 Kyoto Cuisine & Maiko Evening C3
40 Minami-za B3
Miyako Odori .... (see 36)
Tōzan-Bar .... (see 44)

Shopping **(p91)**
41 Kagoshin C1
42 Takematsu B1
43 Tessai-dō C3

Sleeping **(p145)**
Gion Hatanaka .... (see 39)
44 Hyatt Regency Kyoto B7
45 Kyoto Yoshimizu D2
46 Ryokan Motonago C3
47 Ryokan Uemura C4
48 Sakara Kyoto C1
49 Seikōrō A5
50 Shiraume B2

Key on p226

NORTHERN HIGASHIYAMA
A
B
C
D
1
2
3
4
5
6
7
Demachiyanagi Shōtengai
Demachiyanagi
51
23
40
20
34
Demachiyanagi
Kamo-Ōhashi
Hyakumamben Crossing
18
Imadegawa-dōri
Kyoto University
See map p219
Yoshida-jinja
Takenaka Inari-sha
SAKYŌ-KU
Munetada-jinja
Higashiōji-dōri
Konoe-dōri
Kamo-gawa
50
47
35
22
36
29
41
Marutamachi
Marutamachi-dōri
Marutamachi-bashi
38
42
Budō Centre
46
Higashitakeyachō-dōri
3
24
Reisen-dōri
43
Okazaki-kōen
13
Kawabata-dōri
30
Nijō-dōri
7
2
6
11
19
Nijō-Ōhashi
See map p216
Niōmon-dōri
17
39
Oike-Ōhashi
44
Higashiyama
Sanjō
Sanjō Keihan
Sanjō-dōri
See map p222
Sanjō-Ōhashi

NORTHERN HIGASHIYAMA
0 500 m
0 0.25 miles
E
F
G
H
1
2
3
4
5
6
7
Imadegawa-dōri
Ginkaku-ji-Michi
Kaguraoka-dōri
Shira-kawa
Ginkaku-ji
To Daimonji-yama (1.5km)
Path of Philosophy (Tetsugaku-no-Michi)
Shirakawa-dōri
Shinnyo-dō
Kurodani Temple
Kurodani Pagoda
Okazaki-jinja
Nijō-dōri
Biwa-ko Sosui Canal
Nanzen-ji
HIGASHIYAMA-KU
To Keage Station (20m)
1
4
5
8
9
10
12
14
15
16
21
25
26
27
28
31
32
33
37
45
48
49

NORTHERN HIGASHIYAMA *Map on p224*

Top Sights (p94)
Ginkaku-ji G2
Nanzen-ji F6

Sights (p96)
1 Eikan-dō G6
2 Fureai-kan Kyoto Museum of Traditional Crafts C6
3 Heian-jingū C5
4 Hōnen-in G3
5 Konchi-in E7
6 Kyoto Municipal Museum of Art D6
7 Kyoto Municipal Zoo D6
8 Murin-an Villa E6
9 Nanzen-in F7
10 Nanzen-ji Oku-no-in G7
11 National Museum of Modern Art C6
12 Nomura Museum F6
13 Okazaki-kōen D6
14 Path of Philosophy (Tetsugaku-no-Michi) G2
15 Reikan-ji G4
16 Tenju-an F7

Eating (p100)
17 Au Temps Perdu C6
18 Ayatori C1
19 Café de 505 C6
20 Cafe Proverbs 15:17 C1
21 Cafe Terrazza G3
22 Earth Kitchen Company A5
23 Falafel Garden B1
24 Gallery Coeur D5
25 Goya E1
26 Grotto E1
27 Hinode Udon F5
28 Hyōtei E6
29 Kailash C5
30 Karako B6
31 Okariba E5
32 Okutan F6
33 Omen F2
34 Shinshindō Notre Pain Quotidien C1
35 Torito A5
36 Zac Baran C5

Drinking & Nightlife (p102)
37 Kick Up E7
38 Metro A5

Entertainment (p102)
39 Kanze Kaikan Nō Theatre C7

Shopping (p102)
40 Chion-ji Tezukuri-ichi C1
41 Kyoto Handicraft Center C5
42 Tōzandō C5
43 Zōhiko C5

Sleeping (p147)
44 Koto Inn C7
45 Kyoto Garden Ryokan Yachiyo E7
46 Three Sisters Inn Annex D5
47 Three Sisters Inn Main Building D4
48 Westin Miyako Hotel E7

Information (p190)
49 Kyoto International Community House E7
50 Kyoto University Hospital B4

Transport (p187)
51 Demachiyanagi Bicycle Parking Lot A1

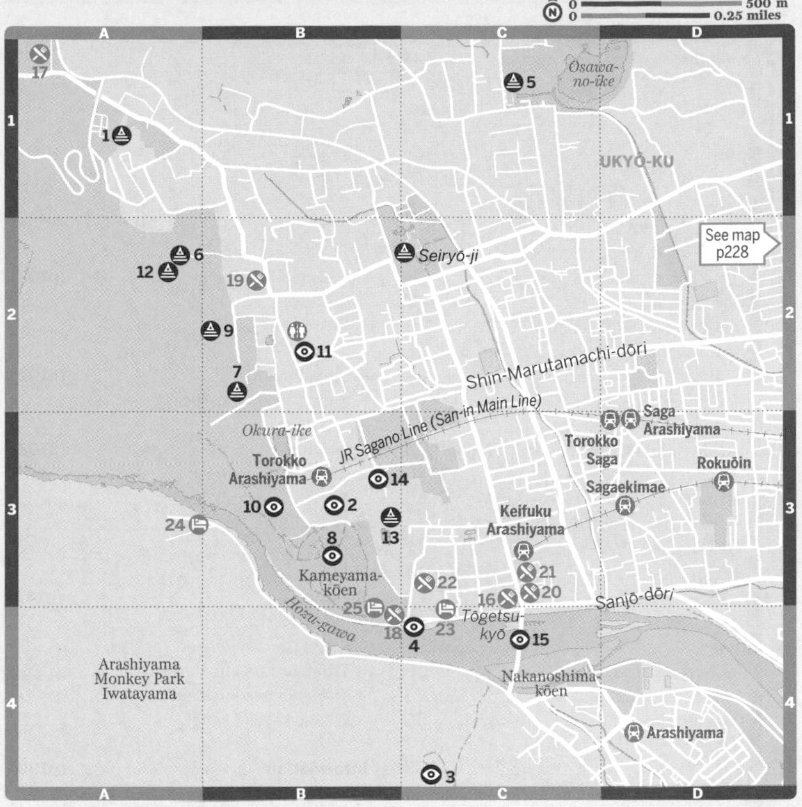

Sights (p114)

1 Adashino Nembutsu-ji A1
2 Arashiyama Bamboo Grove B3
3 Arashiyama Monkey Park Iwatayama C4
4 Boat Rental Stall C4
5 Daikaku-ji C1
6 Giō-ji A2
7 Jōjakkō-ji B2
8 Kameyama-kōen B3
9 Nison-in B2
10 Ōkōchi-sansō Villa B3
11 Rakushisha B2
12 Takiguchi-dera A2
13 Tenryū-ji B3
14 Tenryū-ji North Gate B3
15 Togetsu-kyō C4

Eating (p117)

16 Arashiyama Yoshimura C3
17 Hiranoya A1
18 Kameyama-ya B4
19 Komichi B2
20 Mikatzuki C3
Shigetsu .... (see 13)
21 Yoshida-ya C3
22 Yudōfu Sagano C3

Sleeping (p147)

23 Arashiyama Benkei C4
24 Hoshinoya Kyoto A3
25 Hotel Ran-tei B4

NORTHWEST KYOTO

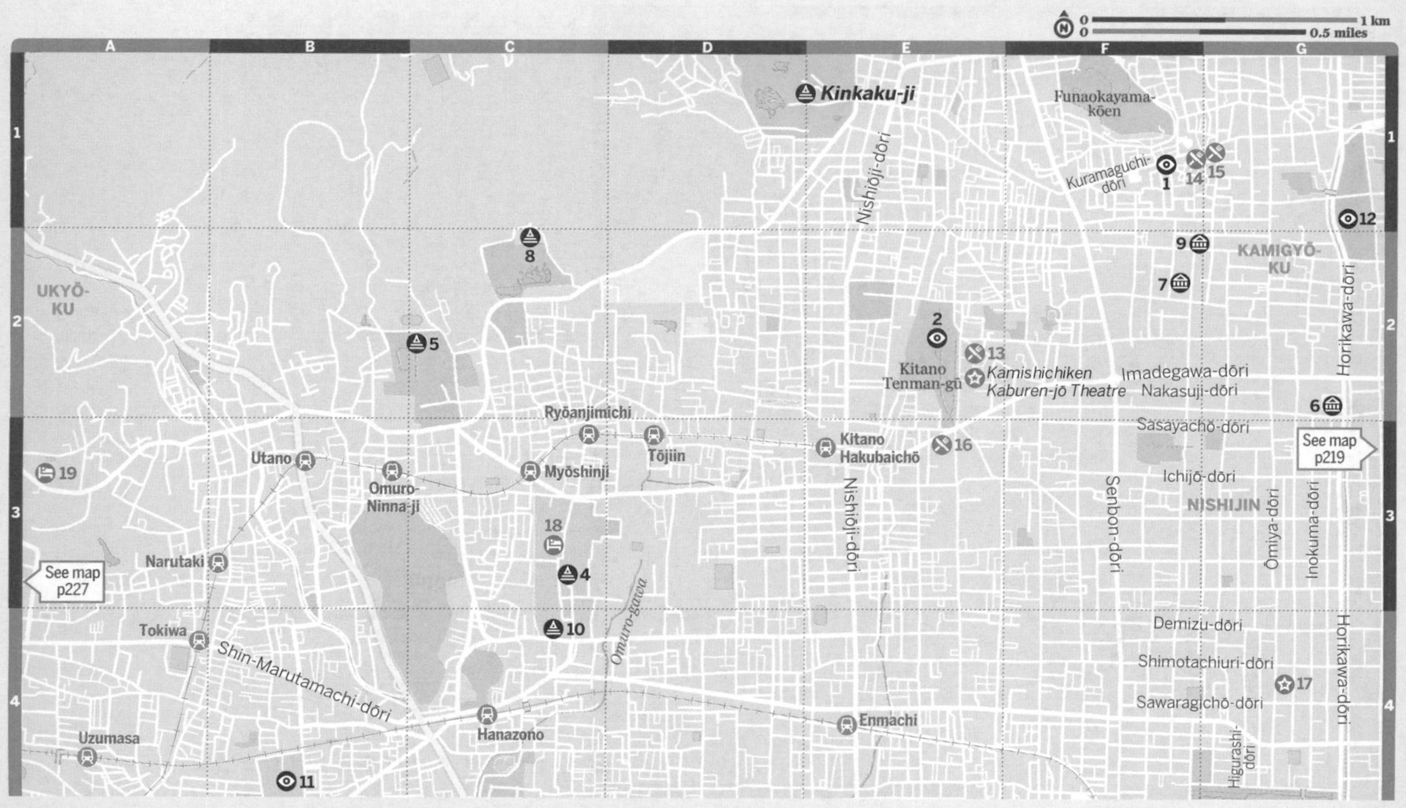

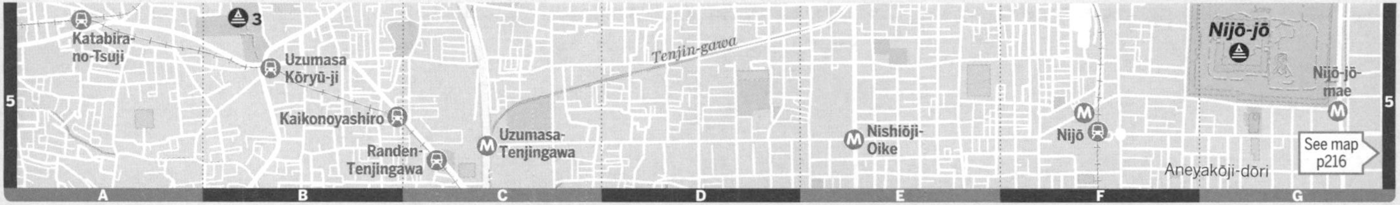
Katabira-no-Tsuji
3
Uzumasa Kōryū-ji
Kaikonoyashiro
Randen-Tenjingawa
Uzumasa-Tenjingawa
Tenjin-gawa
Nishiōji-Oike
Nijō
Nijō-jō
Nijō-jō-mae
Aneyakōji-dōri
See map p216
5
A
B
C
D
E
F
G

Top Sights (p106)
Kinkaku-ji ... E1
Nijō-jō ... G5

Sights (p108)
1 Funaoka Onsen ... F1
2 Kitano Tenman-gū ... E2
3 Kōryū-ji ... B5
4 Myōshin-ji ... C3
5 Ninna-ji ... C2
6 Nishijin Textile Center ... G2
7 Orinasu-kan ... F2
8 Ryōan-ji ... C2
9 Shōsuikaku ... F2
10 Taizō-in ... C4
11 Tōei Uzumasa Movie Village ... B4
12 Urasenke Chadō Research Center ... G1

Eating (p110)
13 Café Bebe ... E2
14 Kanei ... F1
15 Saraca Nishijin ... G1
16 Toyouke-jaya ... E3

Entertainment (p111)
17 Juttoku ... G4

Shopping (p111)
Nishijin Textile Center ... (see 6)
Tenjin-san Market ... (see 2)

Sleeping (p148)
18 Shunkōin ... C3
19 Utano Youth Hostel ... A3

ŌHARA

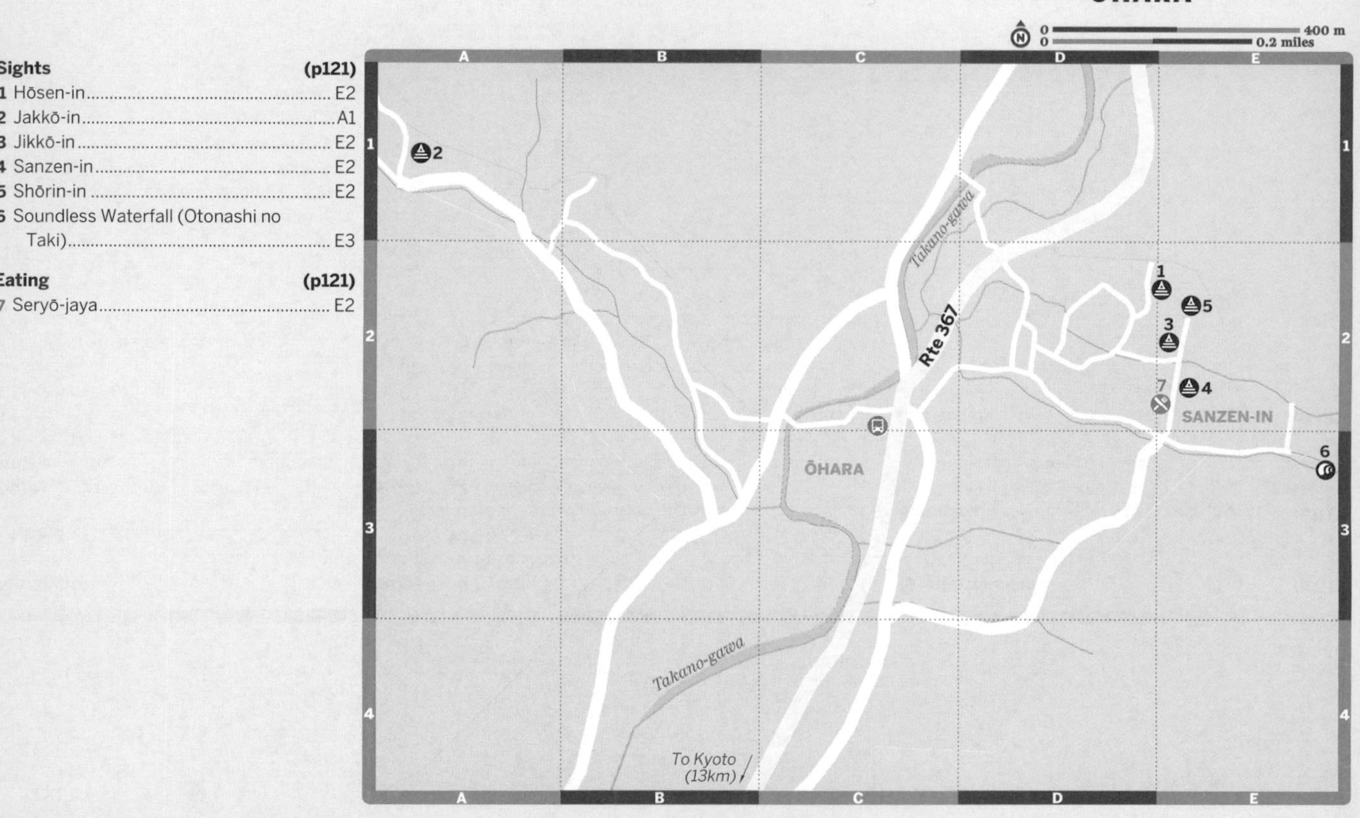

Sights (p121)

1 Hōsen-in E2
2 Jakkō-in A1
3 Jikkō-in E2
4 Sanzen-in E2
5 Shōrin-in E2
6 Soundless Waterfall (Otonashi no Taki) E3

Eating (p121)

7 Seryō-jaya E2

KURAMA & KIBUNE

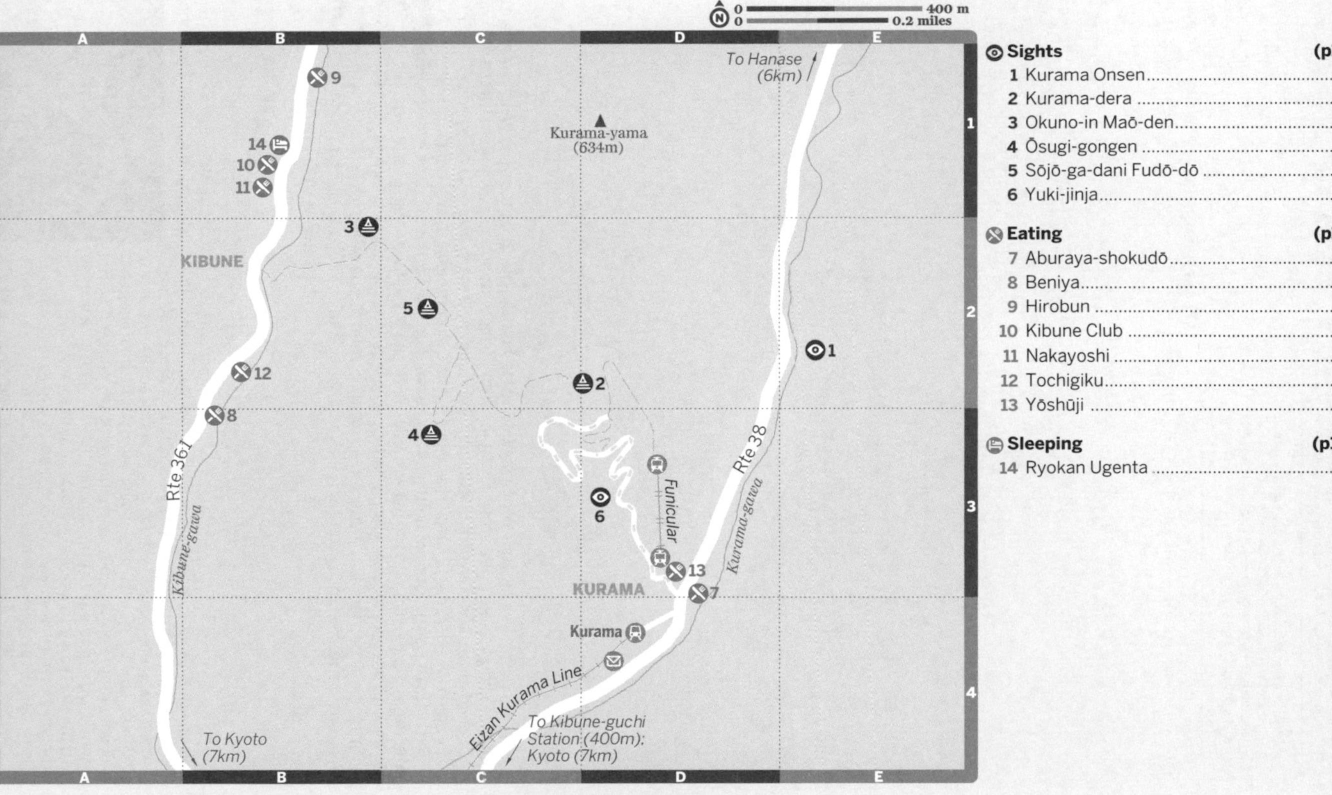

Our Story

A beat-up old car, a few dollars in the pocket and a sense of adventure. In 1972 that's all Tony and Maureen Wheeler needed for the trip of a lifetime – across Europe and Asia overland to Australia. It took several months, and at the end – broke but inspired – they sat at their kitchen table writing and stapling together their first travel guide, *Across Asia on the Cheap*. Within a week they'd sold 1500 copies. Lonely Planet was born.

Today, Lonely Planet has offices in Melbourne, London and Oakland, with more than 600 staff and writers. We share Tony's belief that 'a great guidebook should do three things: inform, educate and amuse'.

Our Writer

Chris Rowthorn

Chris has lived in Kyoto since 1992. Soon after his arrival, Chris started studying Japanese language and culture. In 1995 he became a regional correspondent for the *Japan Times*. He joined Lonely Planet in 1996 and has worked on guides to Kyoto, Tokyo, Japan and hiking in Japan. When not on the road, he seeks out Kyoto's best restaurants, temples, hiking trails and gardens. Chris wrote a book in Japanese with professional guide Koko Ijuin, called *Pro ga Oshieru: Genba no Eigo Tsuyaku Gaido Skiru (Pro English Guide Skills)*, for Japanese guides who want to explain the country to Western tourists. He conducts walking tours of Kyoto, Nara and Tokyo. Check out his website at www.chrisrowthorn.com and his blog at www.insidekyoto.com.

Published by Lonely Planet Publications Pty Ltd
ABN 36 005 607 983
5th edition – Feb 2012
ISBN 978 1 74179 401 4

10 9 8 7 6 5 4 3
Printed in China

Best-selling guide to Kyoto, Source: Nielsen Bookscan, Australia, UK and USA, June 2012 to May 2013.